Creative Nonfiction

The Final Issue: The Best of Thirty Years of *Creative Nonfiction*

Creative Nonfiction

The Final Issue: The Best of Thirty Years of *Creative Nonfiction*

Edited by Lee Gutkind and Leslie Rubinkowski

FIRST EDITION, 2024
ISBN: 978-1-953368-81-2

Belt Publishing
6101 Penn Avenue, Suite 201, Pittsburgh PA 15206
www.beltpublishing.com

Design by Angela Larkin
Cover by David Wilson

This "Final Issue" of *Creative Nonfiction* was made possible by the Juliet Lea Hillman Simonds Foundation. With our deepest appreciation to Lea Simonds, who recognized and supported our mission from the very beginning—thirty years ago.

CONTENTS

The Best of Thirty Years of Creative Nonfiction

How a little magazine defied resistance and ridicule and helped launch the true-story revolution

LEE GUTKIND

Longtime readers may recognize the paper-tear design of this final issue. It's how *Creative Nonfiction* first appeared in 1994—a plain, traditional perfect-bound literary journal. No photographs or illustrations. Just essays.

Well, they really weren't *just* essays. Essays at the time, most people believed, were scholarly, esoteric, often tedious and boring. Publishers shuddered at the "E" word. Who, they wondered, would ever read collections of essays, except for friends and colleagues of the writers—if even that? But the essays published in this first issue were very different than the traditional essay: they were dramatic, exciting, and surprising, not at all scholarly. Lots of scenes, dialogue, and characters confronting adversity and trauma and achieving clarity and resolve. They were journalistic in that they provided interesting and accurate information, but they read like short stories—almost—narratives that were rarely permitted in newspapers, magazines, and literary journals at that time. Yes, *The New Yorker* and *Esquire* were exceptions, but an unlikely destination for writers with limited experience.

Creative writing programs in English departments paid little attention to nonfiction at the time, whether or not it was deemed "creative." Even the essay was not considered an endeavor equal to poetry and fiction. Or, with few exceptions, worthy enough to deserve degree status. This was ironic considering the literary legacy of the essay—beginning with Michel de Montaigne, father of the modern essay, and later, in the eighteenth century, Daniel Defoe's historical narratives, Benjamin Franklin's autobiography, Thomas Paine's pamphlets, and, later still, Charles Dickens, Henry David Thoreau, Mark Twain, and Virginia Woolf.

Throughout the next decade, from 1994 when our first issue was published, many people in the academy and the journalistic community made light of this new or unorthodox way of writing, this nonfiction that was true and accurate and creative at the same time. Some of the pushback was quite mean-spirited. Michael Anderson, an editor for *The New York Times Book Review,* characterized the idea of creative nonfiction as "bullshit… . If it is creative, then it's not nonfiction and if it is nonfiction, it is not creative." James Wolcott, writing in *Vanity Fair*, railed against this magazine—and me: he dubbed me the "Godfather behind creative nonfiction" and "a human octopus" for all of my efforts to spread the word. He derided the intimacy and honesty revealed by memoirists like Kathryn Harrison (*The Kiss)*, Mary Karr (*The Liar's Club*), Carolyn Knapp (*Drinking: A Love Story*), and Frank McCourt (*Angela's Ashes).* He called their work "navel-gazing," nothing more than "civic journalism for the soul." He complained that "Never have so many shared so much of so little." Ten years after this rant, Wolcott published his own navel-gazing memoir.

For a long time, both journalists and academics harped on the lack of a definition of creative nonfiction. Interviewing me for a feature article in *Poets & Writers* magazine ten years after the magazine was launched, Carolyn Hughes insisted that I define creative nonfiction. "What is it?" she asked, "journalism lite? … (I)s the category," she added, "necessary at all?"

I had been asked this definition question frequently over the years, even before the magazine began, and I invariably declined to answer.

Creative nonfiction should be regarded as an art, I insisted, as open to interpretation and experimentation as poetry and fiction. I admit I was more than a little defensive when asked this question. This was the kind of writing I had been doing for many years. I had published books and essays and devoted a great deal of my professional efforts to the journal and teaching creative nonfiction. I felt that what I and many others were writing was as challenging—and in certain circumstances even more so—as fiction or poetry. Hughes was annoyed by my refusal to provide a definition. Or maybe she was delighted, so that she could write the following observation: "Alas, therein lies the rub. If one of the leading lights of a genre will not define it, the door is open for people to conclude, to echo Gertrude Stein's assessment of her home, California, 'there is no there there.'"

But there *was* something there, a hell of a lot in fact, even though quite rightly it could not and should not be defined. For despite the resistance and criticism, the idea of writing nonfiction that was personal, intimate, and cinematic, with writers opening up and exploring all possibilities, employing the tools of storytelling—first gradually and then rapidly—caught on.

Writers who had struggled with what to call their work that was neither poetry or fiction were emboldened, and they embraced the phrase and the freedom and flexibility it provided. Creative nonfiction was, in many ways, a release. It allowed and encouraged writers of poetry and fiction to cross genres, reach for new ideas, and find fresh ways of expression. I will never forget how delighted and, I admit, astonished I was to discover Charles Simic's essay "The Necessity of Poetry" in our slush pile. Here was a Pulitzer Prize-winning poet recreating a series of memory fragments that brought to life his boyhood during the bombing of Belgrade—and revealing intimate details, like why he was wearing a Nazi helmet)—and his life as a poet in Chicago and New York. It captured in less than five thousand words the essence of his life. In that same issue, Adrienne Rich discussed the challenges of living as a poet; a few issues later Louis Simpson, another Pulitzer Prize-winning poet, offered us his lovely encounter on a beach with a stranger who collected stones. Just as many fiction writers reached out to us or responded when we reached out to them. Gordon Lish turned the traditional interview form backward, to dazzling effect, and in "Looking at Emmett Till" John Edgar Wideman captured the power and meaning of the moment when he, as a fourteen-year-old thumbing through an old *Jet* magazine, first saw a photo of that murdered boy his same age and was forever haunted by the image.

Many of the essays we published prove the flexibility and potential of the genre; we were open to anything that pushed literary boundaries to their nonfiction limits. As time passed, writers were using the storytelling techniques of the genre to confront important issues that face us personally and as a nation. In "Notes on My Dying," Ruthann Robson contemplates, in a series of compelling vignettes, where and how she might want to die and the loss of the "outrageous visions" of her future. Has the ending of the story of her life already been written, she wonders, no matter how she weighs her theoretical options, what alternate story she might tell herself, or how much she resists? In "Seep," Mieke Eerken vividly recreates the devastation of marine life caused by a massive oil spill—53,569 gallons—after the drug-impaired pilot of a container ship crashed the vessel into the Golden Gate Bridge. And in "My Night with Ellen Hutchinson," Bud Shaw, a young surgeon in the mid-1980s, tells an unforgettable and dramatic story about the sadness, futility, and emptiness he felt after losing a patient during the early days of liver transplant surgery.

This is exactly what I had hoped for when I started the journal: that creative nonfiction would not just be an accepted genre in the literary world, but that it also would allow writers to confront the most serious and personal issues, reach readers who may have no interest in a subject or even fear its reality, but cannot resist the richness, honesty, and beauty of a true story.

It took a while, but the academy eventually embraced creative nonfiction and its virtues. I helped start the first MFA programs in the genre, both at the University of Pittsburgh and, in 1997, the first low-residency program at Goucher College. As I write this, there are more than 200 MFA creative nonfiction programs and three dozen PhD programs—not just in the US but in Asia, New Zealand, Australia, Ireland, the UK, and other countries. Nearly every week, creative nonfiction books appear on the bestseller lists of *The New York Times* and *The Washington Post*; they are featured and reviewed and excerpted in major magazines and on literary websites. Many newspapers today, once critical of creative nonfiction (and the New Journalism in the 1960s and 1970s) regularly solicit and publish personal essays for opinion and feature pages. News stories, once limited by the five W's—who, what, when, where, why—are often written as dramatic narratives.

I like to think, and perhaps many would agree, that the establishment of this journal, the first to publish creative nonfiction exclusively, and to campaign for its legitimacy, had a lot to do with the transition and acceptance of this outlier genre in a variety of important ways.

In every issue we introduced new writers along with well-known writers experimenting with the form. You will see many familiar names in this anthology, in addition to those I have already mentioned: recipients of the National Book Award and the Pulitzer Prize in nonfiction and poetry, along with accomplished best-selling novelists and short-story writers. Some of the writers appearing in all seventy-eight issues were just emerging or published for the first time. (You might not have recognized their names then, but you will today as you scan the table of contents.) We established a platform that allowed writers and readers to discuss, dialogue, and explore the essence of the genre. We debated and clarified many of the ethical issues of the genre—inevitable when writers are encouraged to experiment with style and structure and reveal precious secrets that they never before dared to share. We worked very hard to defend the genre against criticism and ridicule by publishing special issues and, when necessary, ambitious advocacy. We were from the beginning considered "the voice of the genre."

Perhaps more than anything else, *Creative Nonfiction* provided a rare publishing destination. It opened the doors to all writers of all genres—and not just professional writers but also people outside the literary mainstream: doctors, engineers, police officers, scientists, and anyone else with a factual, dramatic story to tell. We made a special and ongoing effort to feature the work of women writers who, perhaps because of the more personal content of their work, often found acceptance of their essays more challenging. In the beginning, in 1994 and for years after, very few literary journals were interested or open to this work. *Creative Nonfiction* came to life at exactly the right time, and before long, what seemed like a blink of the eye, we were deep into the true-story era.

The paper tear disappeared for our thirty-eighth issue and we became a quarterly magazine—with provocative illustrations, essays on craft, and interviews of the most innovative writers practicing creative nonfiction. We sponsored conferences, established a popular education program, launched a book imprint. We even created and published a pocket-sized monthly magazine, aptly named *True Story*. Amazing, I thought, considering our very humble beginnings with that tiny journal in 1994. That first issue had 173 subscribers.

Today, creative nonfiction is not just an idea or a reason to debate. It is a legitimate and accepted genre worldwide. It is remarkable, as I look back thirty years, surveying our archives, and the many hundreds of stories, craft pieces, and interviews we published, how far we have traveled. We have a legacy represented in this anthology that will live for many years after us.

Some of you longtime readers may think we have missed some great essays, and you'd be right, but the essays collected here are those that we felt most reflected the style and substance of the genre and its evolution from the paper-tear days, as the genre grew and changed over seventy-eight issues. I hope that you will enjoy reading or rereading the pieces in this collection. I also hope you'll continue to watch as the genre keeps evolving—and follow *Creative Nonfiction* as it moves into an exciting iteration with our new partner, the storytelling platform *Narratively.com*. It will carry forward our publishing mission, scouring our archives, and giving new life to the remarkable work we have published over the years.

As for me, it's been a wild and surprising journey. I never expected that *Creative Nonfiction* would have existed for so long and made such a long-lasting impact. I move on with hopes that we will always write our true stories with passion and daring, never abandon our ideas and dreams, believe in ourselves despite criticism and resistance. That is the true story of creative nonfiction: an idea and a genre no one wanted or believed in that eventually earned its place in the literary world, and the little paper-tear magazine with only 173 subscribers that helped make it happen.

Meander

MARY PAUMIER JONES

A *Nova* show about the forms of nature prompts me to look up *meander.* Having always used the word to refer to walking, I am surprised to learn that it comes from water. Rivers and streams meander, verb, have meanders, noun. *Meander,* in fact, comes from the name of a river, one in ancient Phrygia, now part of Turkey—the Maeander, now the Menderes.

Change of name notwithstanding, the waters still flow from the Anatolian plateau to the Aegean Sea. A namesake, a Meander River, meanders in northern Alberta.

In what we do on foot, *meandering* implies an aimless wandering, with the pleasant connotation that the very aimlessness of the wander is something freely, even happily, chosen.

The meanders of water seem equally aimless, but are, it turns out, very regular in their irregularity—although if you were walking along the bank of a meandering river, you might find that hard to believe. You would head in one direction, and then curve around until you are going the opposite way, and then around again, following a path which turns upon itself and makes no sense. Could a helicopter or fairy godmother, though, raise you high enough, you would see that what seems like chaos below actually forms a regular repeating pattern of serpentine flexuosity.

The shortest distance between two points may be a straight line, but a river neither knows nor cares. It seldom flows straight for a distance of more than about ten times its width. A river erodes its banks, and the way of the world is such that one side invariably erodes faster than the other. It eventually collapses and its sediment is carried along and deposited downstream. Two curves are thus begun: the erosion point becomes the outside of one; the sediment pile, the inside of the next.

The water on the outside has to flow faster to keep up, causing more erosion, more sediment movement. The outsides get deeper, the insides shallower. At any point, the shape of the river shows its history. If other forces do not prevent, the bends over time work toward becoming perfectly elliptical. *Ellipse* comes from the Greek for "to fall short," an ellipse falling as it does short of a perfect circle.

This has all been observed in nature and shown experimentally in laboratories, and is thought by many to be sufficient explanation for meanders.

Others disagree, especially now that infrared images from satellites show that ocean currents—which have no erodable banks—also meander. The jet stream appears to meander as well. Mathematicians have calculated that the most probable path between two points on a surface is in fact a meander. Meanders then may be the norm, not the exception. The question may be not why some rivers meander, but why every river we see does not.

A particular essay's shape may be more akin to one of the other basic natural forms—a sphere or hexagon, a spiral, say, or helix, or branch—but on the whole, I think, what essays do best is meander. They fall short of the kind of circular perfection we expect of fiction or poetry. They proceed in elliptical curves, diverging, digressing.

We can float or row or swim or speed or sail along the meandering course of an essay. We can meander on foot on the riverbank with the essayist. We expect only to go somewhere in the presence of someone.

Perhaps we will end up close to where we started, perhaps far away. We will not see the shape of our journey until we are done, and can look back on it whole, as it were, from the air. But we will, and very quickly, come to know the shape of our company—the mind, the sensibility, the person, with whom we are traveling. That much seems necessary to essay structure—one individual human speaking to another who wants to listen.

Flattened out, the thin human cortex, the gray matter of the brain, is much too large for the skull within which it must fit. The problem has been elegantly solved by intricate pleating and folding, as if the cortex were a piece of thick fabric gathered in tightly to fit. In anatomy books, we can see pictures of cross-section slices of the gathers. The shape is unmistakable, like a close-packed river shot from above, meandering within.

The Necessity of Poetry

CHARLES SIMIC

Late night on MacDougal Street. An old fellow comes up to me and says: "Sir, I'm writing the book of my life, and I need a dime to complete it." I give him a dollar.

Another night in Washington Square Park, a fat woman with a fright wig says to me: "I'm Esther, the goddess of Love. If you don't give me a dollar, I'll put a curse on you." I give her a nickel.

One of those postwar memories: a baby carriage pushed by a humpbacked old woman, her son sitting in it, both legs amputated.

She was haggling with the greengrocer when the carriage got away from her. The street was steep, so it rolled downhill with the cripple waving his crutch, his mother screaming for help, and everybody else laughing as if they were in the movies. Buster Keaton or somebody like that about to go over a cliff.

One laughed because one knew it would end well. One was surprised when it didn't.

I didn't tell you how I got lice wearing a German helmet. This used to be a famous story in our family. I remember those winter evenings just after the war with everybody huddled around the stove, talking and worrying late into the night. Sooner or later, somebody would bring up my German helmet full of lice. They thought it was the funniest thing they ever heard. Old people had tears of laughter in their eyes. A kid dumb enough to walk around with a German helmet full of lice. They were crawling all over it. Any fool could see them!

I sat there saying nothing, pretending to be equally amused, nodding my head while thinking to myself, what a bunch of idiots! All of them! They had no idea how I got the helmet, and I wasn't about to tell them.

It was in those first days just after the liberation of Belgrade, I was up in the old cemetery with a few friends, kind of snooping around. Then, all of a sudden, we saw them! A couple of German soldiers, obviously dead, stretched out on the ground. We drew closer to take a better look. They had no weapons. Their boots were gone, but there was a helmet that had fallen to the side of one of them. I don't remember what the others got, but I went for the helmet. I tiptoed so as not to wake the dead man. I also kept my eyes averted. I never saw his face, even if sometimes I think I did. Everything else about that moment is still intensely clear to me.

That's the story of the helmet full of lice.

Beneath the swarm of high-flying planes, we were eating watermelon. While we ate, the bombs fell on Belgrade. We watched the smoke rise in the distance. We were hot in the garden and asked to take our shirts off. The watermelon made a ripe, cracking noise as my mother cut it with a big knife. We also heard what we thought was thunder, but when we looked up, the sky was cloudless and blue.

My mother heard a man plead for his life once. She remembers the stars, the dark shapes of trees along the road on which they were fleeing the Austrian army in a slow-moving oxcart. "That man sounded terribly frightened out there in the woods," she says. The cart went on. No one said anything. Soon they could hear the river they were supposed to cross.

In my childhood, women mended stockings in the evening. To have a "run" in one's stocking was catastrophic. Stockings were expensive, and so was electricity. We would all sit around the table with a single lamp, my grandmother reading the papers, we children pretending to do our homework, while watching my mother spreading her red-painted fingernails inside the transparent stocking.

There was a maid in our house who let me put my hand under her skirt. I was five or six years old. I can still remember the dampness of her crotch and my surprise that there was all that hair there. I couldn't get enough of it. She would crawl under the table where I had my military fort and my toy soldiers. I don't remember what was said, if anything. Just her hand, firmly guiding mine to that spot.

They sit on the table, the tailors do. At least, they used to. A street of dim shops in Belgrade where we went to have my father's coat narrowed and shortened so it would fit me. The tailor got off the table and stuck pins in my shoulder. "Don't squirm," my mother said. Outside, it was getting dark. Large snowflakes fell.

Years later in New York, on the same kind of afternoon, a dry-cleaning store window with an ugly, thick-legged woman on the chair in a white dress. She's having the hem raised by a gray-headed Jewish tailor, who kneels before her as if he is proposing marriage.

There was an expensive-looking suitcase on the railroad tracks, and they were afraid to come near it. Far from any station, it was on a stretch of track bordered by orchards where they had been stealing plums that afternoon. The suitcase, she remembers, had colorful labels, of what were probably world-famous hotels and ocean liners. During the war, of course, one heard of bombs, special ones, in the shape of toys, pens, soccer balls, exotic birds—so why not suitcases? For that reason, they left it where it was.

"I always wondered what was in it," my wife says. We were talking about the summer of 1944, of which we both had only a few clear recollections.

The world was going up in flames, and I was studying violin. The baby Nero sawing away.

My teacher's apartment was always cold. A large, almost empty room with a high ceiling already in shadow. I remember the first few screechy notes my violin would make and my teacher's stern words of reprimand. I was terrified of that old woman. I also loved her because after the scolding, she would give me something to eat. Something rare and exotic, like chocolate filled with sweet liqueur. We'd sit in that big empty room, almost dark now. I'd be eating, and she'd be watching me eat. "Poor child," she'd say, and I thought it had to do with my not practicing enough, my being dim-witted when she tried to explain something to me, but today I'm not sure that's what she meant. In fact, I suspect she had something else entirely in mind. That's why I'm writing this, to find out what it was.

When my grandfather was dying from diabetes, when he had already had one leg cut off at the knee and they were threatening to do the same to the other, his old buddy Savo Lozanic used to visit him every morning to keep him company. They would reminisce about this and that, and even have a few laughs.

One morning, my grandmother had to leave him alone in the house, as she had to attend the funeral of a distant relative. That's what gave him the idea. He hopped out of bed and into the kitchen, where he found candles and matches. He got back into his bed, somehow placed one candle above his head and the other at his feet, and lit them. Finally, he pulled the sheet over his face and began to wait.

When his friend knocked, there was no answer. The door being unlocked, Savo went in, calling from time to time. The kitchen was empty. A fat gray cat slept on the dining room table. When Savo entered the bedroom and saw the bed with the sheet and lit candles, he let out a wail and then broke into sobs as he groped for a chair to sit down.

"Shut up, Savo," my grandfather said sternly from under his sheet. "Can't you see I'm only practicing?"

Another story about time. This one about the time it took the people to quit their cells after beginning to suspect that the Germans were gone. In that huge prison in Milan, all of a sudden you could hear a pin drop. Eventually they thought it best to remove their shoes before walking out.

My father was still tiptoeing hours later, crossing a large, empty piazza. There was a full moon above the dark palaces. His heart was in his mouth.

"It was just like an opera stage," he says. "All lit up, nobody in the audience, and nobody in the orchestra pit. Nevertheless, I felt like singing. Or perhaps screaming?"

He did neither. The year was 1944.

The streets are empty, it's raining, and we are sitting in the Hotel Sherman bar, listening to the bluesy piano. I'm not yet old enough to order a drink, but my father's presence is so authoritative and intimidating that when he orders for me, the waiters never dare to ask about my age.

We talk. My father remembers a fly that wouldn't let him sleep one summer afternoon fifty years ago. I tell him about an old gray overcoat twice my size, which my mother made me wear after the war. It was wintertime. People on the street would sometimes stop and watch me. The overcoat trailed the ground and made walking difficult. One day, I was standing on the corner, waiting to cross, when a young woman gave me a small coin and walked away. I was so embarrassed.

"Was she pretty?" my father asks.

"Not at all," I tell him. She looked like a hick, maybe a nun.

"A Serbian Ophelia," my father thinks.

It's possible. Anything is possible.

The huge crowd cheering the dictator; the smiling faces of children offering flowers in welcome. How many times have I seen that? And always the same blond little girl curtsying! Here she is, surrounded by the high boots of the dignitaries and a couple of tightly leashed police dogs. The monster himself is patting her on the head and whispering in her ear.

I look in vain for someone with a troubled face.

The exiled general's grandson was playing war with his cheeks puffed to imitate bombs exploding. The grim daughter wrote down the old man's reminiscences. The whole apartment smelled of bad cooking.

The general was in a wheelchair. He wore a bib and smoked a cigar. The daughter smiled for me and my mother in a way that made her sharp little teeth show.

I liked the general better. He remembered some prime minister pretending to wipe his ass with a treaty he had just signed, the captured enemy officers drinking heavily and toasting some cabaret singer from their youth.

It's your birthday. The child you were appears on the street, wearing a stupid grin. He wants to take you by the hand, but you won't let him.

"You've forgotten something," he whispers. And you, quiet as a mutt around an undertaker, since, of course, he (the child) doesn't exist.

There was an old fellow at the *Sun-Times* who was boss when I first came and worked as a mail clerk, who claimed to have read everything. His father was a janitor at the university library in Urbana, and Stanley, for that was his name, started as a kid. At first, I didn't believe any of it; then I asked him about Gide, whom I was then reading. He recited for me the names of the major novels and their plots. What about Isaac Babel, Alain-Fournier,

Aldous Huxley, Ford Madox Ford? The same thing. It was amazing! Everything I had read or heard of, he had already read. You should be on a quiz show, Stanley, people who overheard us said. Stanley had never been to college and had worked for the newspaper most of his life. He had a stutter, so I guess that explains why he never married or got ahead. So all he did was read books. I had the impression that he loved every book he read. Only superlatives for Stanley, one book better than the other. If I started to criticize, he'd get pissed off. Who did I think I was? Smartass, he called me, and wouldn't talk to me about books for a few days. Stanley was pure enthusiasm. I was giddy myself at the thought of another book waiting for me to read at home.

The night of my farewell dinner in Chicago, I got very drunk. At some point, I went to the bathroom and could not find my way back. The restaurant was large and full of mirrors. I would see my friends seated in the distance, but when I hurried toward them, I would come face to face with myself in a mirror. With my new beard, I did not recognize myself immediately and almost apologized. In the end, I gave up and sat at an old man's table. He ate in silence, and I lit a cigarette. Time passed. The place was emptying. The old man finally wiped his mouth and pushed his full, untouched wine glass toward me. I would have stayed with him indefinitely if one of the women from our party hadn't found me and led me outside.

Did I lie a little? Of course. I gave the impression that I had lived for years on the Left Bank and often sat at the tables of the famous cafés, watching the existentialists in their passionate arguments. What justified these exaggerations in my eyes was the real possibility that I could have done something like that. Everything about my life already seemed a fluke, a series of improbable turns of events, so in my case fiction was no stranger than truth. Like when I told the woman on the train from Chicago that I was a Russian. I described our apartment in Leningrad, the terrors of the long siege during the war, the deaths of my parents before a German firing squad, which we children had to witness, the DP camps in Europe. At some point during the long night, I had to go to the bathroom and simply laugh.

How much of it did she believe? Who knows? In the morning, she gave me a long kiss in parting, which could have meant anything.

My father and his best friend talking about how some people resemble animals. The birdlike wife of so-and-so, for example. The many breeds of dogs and their human look-alikes. The lady who is a cow. The widow next door who is a tigress, etc.

"And what about me?" says my father's friend.

"You look like a rat, Tony," he replies without a moment's hesitation, after which they just sit drinking without saying another word.

"You look like a young Franz Schubert," the intense-looking woman told me as we were introduced.

At that same party, I spoke to a lawyer who insisted we had met in London two years before. I explained my accent to a doctor by telling him that I was raised by a family of deaf mutes.

There was a girl there, too, who kept smiling sweetly at me without saying anything. Her mother told me that I reminded her of her brother, who was executed by the Germans in Norway. She was going to give me more details, but I excused myself, telling everyone that I had a sudden and terrible toothache that required immediate attention.

I got the idea of sleeping on the roof in Manhattan on hot nights from my mother and father. That's what they did during the war, except it wasn't a roof but a large terrace on the top floor of a building in downtown Belgrade. There was a blackout, of course. I remember immense starry skies and how silent the city was. I would begin to speak, but someone—I could not tell for a moment who it was—would put a hand over my mouth.

Like a ship at sea, we were with stars and clouds up above. We were sailing full speed ahead. "That's where the infinite begins," I remember my father saying, pointing with his long, dark hand.

If my father has a ghost, he's standing outside some elegant men's store on Madison Avenue on a late summer evening. A tall man studying a pair of brown suede Italian shoes. He himself is impeccably dressed in a tan suit, a blue shirt of an almost purple hue, with a silk tie the color of rusty rose. He seems in no hurry. At the age of fifty-three, with his hair thinning and slicked back, he could be an Italian or a South American. Belle Giorgio, one waitress in Chicago used to call him. No one would guess by his appearance that he is almost always broke.

I'm packing parcels in the Lord & Taylor basement during the Christmas rush with a bunch of losers. One fellow is an inventor. He has a new kind of aquarium with piped music, which makes it look as if the fish are doing water ballet, but the world is not interested. Another man supports three ex-wives, so he has a night job in addition to this one. His eyes close all the time. He's so pale, he could pass for a stiff in an open coffin.

Then there's Felix, a mousy fellow a bit older than I, who claims to be a distant relative of the English royal family. One time, he brought the chart of his family tree to make us stop laughing and explained the connection. What does not make sense is his poverty. He said he was a writer but wouldn't tell us what kind. "Are you writing porno?" one Puerto Rican girl asked him.

Her name was Rosie. She liked boxing. One time, she and I went on a date to watch the fights at the Garden. We sat in the Spanish section. "Kill him! Kill him!" she screamed all evening without interruption. At the end, she was so tired she wouldn't even have a drink with me and had to rush home.

At a poetry reading given by Allen Tate, I met a young poet who was attending a workshop given by Louise Bogan at NYU. I sat in a few times and accompanied my new friends for beers after class. One day, I even showed two of my poems to Bogan. One was called "Red Armchair," and it had to do with an old chair thrown out on the sidewalk for the trashmen to pick up. The other poem I don't remember. Bogan was very kind. She fixed a few things but was generally encouraging, which surprised me, since I didn't think much of the poems myself.

The other critique of my poetry came later that fall, and it was devastating. I had met a painter in a bar, an older fellow living in poverty with a wife and two small kids in a cold-water flat in the Village, where he painted huge, realistic canvases of derelicts in the manner of 1930s socialist realism. A skyscraper and underneath a poor man begging. The message was obvious, but the colors were nice.

Despite the difference in our ages, we saw each other quite a bit, talking art and literature, until one day I showed him my poems. We were sitting in his kitchen with a bottle of whiskey between us. He leaned back in the chair and read the poems slowly, slowly, while I watched him closely. At some point, I began to detect annoyance in him and then anger. Finally, he looked at me as if seeing me for the first time and said something like: "Simic, I thought you were a smart kid. This is pure shit you're writing!"

I was prepared for gentle criticism in the manner of Louise Bogan, even welcomed it, but his bluntness stunned me. I left in a daze. I was convinced he was right. If I'd had a pistol, I would have shot myself on the spot. Then, little by little, mulling over what he had said, I got pissed off. There were some good things in my poems, I thought. "Fuck him," I shouted to some guy who came my way in the street. Of course, he was right, too, and it hurt me that he was, but all the same.

I came out of my daze just as I was entering Central Park on Fifty-Ninth Street. I had walked more than sixty blocks, totally oblivious of my surroundings. I sat on a bench and reread my poems, crossing out most of the lines, attempting to rewrite them then and there, still angry, still miserable, and at the same time grimly determined.

There was this old guy in Washington Square Park who used to lecture me about Sacco and Vanzetti and the great injustice done to them. We'd share a bench from time to time, and I'd hear him say again and again how if shit was worth money, the poor would be born without assholes. He wore gray gloves, walked with a cane, tipped his hat to ladies, and worried about me. "A kid just off the boat," he'd say to someone passing by. "Sure to get screwed if he doesn't watch out."

I went to see Ionesco's *Bald Soprano* with Boris. It was being presented at the small theater in the Village. There were only six people in the audience, and that included the two of us. They gave the performance anyway. When it came to the love scene with the woman who has three noses, the actors got carried away on the couch. Their voices went down to a whisper as they started undressing each other. Boris and I just looked at each other. The other four people had suddenly become invisible. I have no recollection of the rest of the play except that at the exit, the streets were covered with newly fallen snow.

I was five minutes late from lunch at the insurance company where I was working, and my boss chewed me out for being irresponsible in front of twenty or thirty other drudges. I sat fuming at my desk for a while, then I rose slowly, wrapped my scarf around my neck, put my gloves on in plain view of everybody, and walked out without looking back. I didn't have an overcoat, and on the street it was snowing, but I felt giddy, deliriously happy at being free.

We were on our third bottle of wine when he showed me the pictures of his girlfriend. To my surprise, the photographs spread out on the table were of a naked woman shamelessly displaying herself. Leaning over my shoulder, he wanted me to note each detail, her crotch, her ass, her breasts, until I felt aroused. It was an odd situation. My host's pregnant wife was asleep in the next room. The photographs were spread all over the dining room table. There must've been close to a hundred of them. I looked and I listened. From time to time, I could hear the wife snore.

Approaching Manhattan on the train at night, I remember the old Polish and Ukrainian women wielding their mops in the brightly lit towers. I'd be working on some ledger that wouldn't balance, and they'd be scrubbing floors on their knees. They were fat, and they all wore flowered dresses. The youngest would stand on a chair and dust off the portrait of the grim founder of the company. The old Black man who ran the elevator would bow to them like a headwaiter in a fancy restaurant as he took them from one floor to the next. That would make them laugh. You'd see they had teeth missing. More than a few teeth missing.

It was a window with a view of a large office with many identical desks at which men and women sat working. A woman got up with papers in hand and walked the length of the floor to where a man rose to meet her at the other end.

He waved his arms as he talked while she stood before him with her head lowered, and I went on tying my necktie in the hotel room across the street. I was about to turn away from the window when I realized that the man was yelling at the woman, and that she was sobbing.

Here's a scene for you. My father and I are walking down Madison when I spot a blue overcoat in a store called the British American House. We study it, comment on the cut, and my father suggests I try it on. I know he has no money, but he insists since it's beginning to snow a little and I'm only wearing a tweed jacket. We go in, I put it on, and it fits perfectly. Immediately, I'm in love with it. We ask the price and it's $200—which was a lot of money in 1959. Too bad, I think, but then my father asks me if I want it. I think maybe he's showing off in front of the salesman or he's come into some money he hasn't told me about. Do you want it? he asks again while the salesman goes to attend to another customer. You've no money, George, I remind him, expecting him to contradict me or come to his senses. "Don't worry," is his reply.

I've seen him do this before, and it embarrasses me. He asks for the boss and the two of them sequester themselves for a while. I stand around waiting for us to be kicked out.

Instead, he emerges triumphant, and I wear the overcoat into the street. A born con man. His manner and appearance inspired such confidence that with a small down payment and promise to pay the rest in a week or two, he'd get what he wanted. This was in the days before credit cards and credit bureaus, when store owners had to make such decisions on the spot. They trusted him, and he eventually did pay whatever he owed. The crazy thing was that he pulled this stunt only in the best stores. It would never occur to him to ask for credit from a grocer, and yet he often went hungry despite his huge salary.

My father had phenomenal debts. He borrowed money any chance he had and paid his bills only when absolutely necessary. It was nothing for him to spend the rent money the night before it was due. I lived in terror of my landlords and landladies while he seemingly never worried. We'd meet after work, and he'd suggest dinner in a French restaurant, and I'd resist, knowing it was his rent money he was proposing to spend. He'd describe the dishes and wines we could have in tantalizing detail, and I'd keep reminding him of the rent. He'd explain to me slowly, painstakingly, as if I were feeble-minded, that one should never worry about the future. We'll never be so young as we are tonight, he'd say. If we are smart, and we are, tomorrow we'll figure out how to pay the rent. In the end, who could say no? I never did.

On the street corner, the card trickster was shuffling his three cards, using a large cardboard box as a table. The cards, the quick hands fluttered. It looked like a cockfight. Five of us watching without expression, our heads, in the meantime, buzzing with calculations and visions of riches. The day was cold, so we all had to squint.

Tough guys, he said, time to place your bets.

I became more and more lucid the later it got. This was always my curse. Everybody was already asleep. I tried to wake my dearest, but she drew me down on her breasts sleepily. We loved, slowly, languidly, and then I talked to her for hours about the necessity of poetry while she slept soundly.

How Does a Poet Put Bread on the Table?

ADRIENNE RICH

But how does a poet put bread on the table? Rarely, if ever, by poetry alone. Of the four lesbian poets at the Nuyorican Poets Café about whose lives I know something, one directs an under-funded community arts project, two are untenured college teachers, one an assistant dean of students at a state university. Of other poets I know, most teach, often part time, without security but year-round; two are on disability; one does clerical work; one cleans houses; one is a paid organizer; one has a paid editing job. Whatever odd money comes in erratically from readings and workshops, grants, permissions fees, royalties, prizes can be very odd money indeed, never to be counted on and almost always small: checks have to be chased down, grants become fewer and more competitive in a worsening political and economic climate. Most poets who teach at universities are untenured, without pension plans or group health insurance, or are employed at public and community colleges with heavy teaching loads and low salaries. Many give unpaid readings and workshops as part of their political "tithe."

Inherited wealth accounts for the careers of some poets: to inherit wealth is to inherit time. Most of the poets I know, hearing of a sum of money, translate it not into possessions, but into time—that precious immaterial necessity of our lives. It's true that a poem can be attempted in brief interstitial moments, pulled out of the pocket and worked on while waiting for a bus or riding a train or while children nap or while waiting for a new batch of clerical work or blood samples to come in. But only certain kinds of poems are amenable to these conditions. Sometimes the very knowledge of coming interruption dampens the flicker. And there is a difference between the ordinary "free" moments stolen from exhausting family strains, from alienating labor, from thought chained by material anxiety, and those other moments that sometimes arrive in a life being lived at its height though under extreme tension: Perhaps we are waiting to initiate some act we believe will catalyze change but whose outcome is uncertain; perhaps we are facing personal or communal crisis in which everything unimportant seems to fall away and we are left with our naked lives, the brevity of life itself, and words. At such times we may experience a speeding-up of our imaginative powers, images and voices rush together in a kind of inevitability, what was externally fragmented is internally reorganized, and the hand can barely keep pace.

But such moments presuppose other times: when we could simply stare into the wood grain of a door, or the trace of bubbles in a glass of water as long as we wanted to, almost secure in the knowledge that there would be no interruption—times of slowness, of purposelessness.

Often such time feels like a luxury, guiltily seized when it can be had, fearfully taken because it does not seem like work, this abeyance, but like "wasting time" in a society where personal importance—even job security—can hinge on acting busy, where the phrase "keeping busy" is a common idiom, where there is, for activists, so much to be done.

Most, if not all, of the names we know in North American poetry are the names of people who have had some access to freedom in time—the privilege of some that is actually a necessity for all. The struggle to limit the working day is a sacred struggle for the worker's freedom in time. To feel herself or himself, for a few hours or a weekend, as a free being with choices—to plant vegetables and later sit on the porch with a cold beer, to write poetry or build a fence or fish or play cards, to walk without a purpose, to make love in the daytime, to sleep late. Ordinary human pleasures, the self's re-creation. Yet every working generation has to reclaim that freedom in time, and many are brutally thwarted in the effort. Capitalism is based on the abridgment of that freedom.

Poets in the United States have either had some kind of private means, or help from people with private means, have held full-time, consuming jobs, or have chosen to work in low-paying, part-time sectors of the economy, saving their creative energies for poetry, keeping their material wants simple. Interstitial living, where the art itself is not expected to bring in much money, where the artist may move from a clerical job to part-time, temporary teaching to subsistence living on the land to waitressing or doing construction or translating, typesetting, or ghostwriting. In the 1990s this kind of interstitial living is more difficult, risky and wearing than it has ever been, and this is a loss to all the arts—as much as the shrinkage of arts funding, the censorship-by-clique, the censorship by the Right, the censorship by distribution.

Taking Care

JANE BERNSTEIN

My Uncle Ben is ninety years old—maybe. He isn't exactly sure anymore, and no one is left to argue that his real age is eighty-nine or ninety-one, or tell those in the next generation the actual date of his birthday. Both Ben and his brother took the Fourth of July as their birth dates when they came here from Russia or Romania—there's even disagreement about the name of the country they emigrated from, since the borders in that region have changed so often.

Forgetting his age is the least of Ben's problems. He remembers his two daughters, but not necessarily his sister or brother, or his first wife, though they had been married for forty-three years when she died. On a more practical level, he cannot remember where he put his toothpaste, or his shirts. He cannot remember why he has been separated from his second wife, Rose. Every day, dozens of times a day he asks, "Where's Rose?"

His daughter says, "Rose is in Florida, Dad."

Why can't he see her?

Ben's younger daughter, a patient, soft-spoken woman, says, "Rose is sick, Dad," and once again explains why Rose is in Florida and he is thousands of miles away. Ben nods in understanding, and minutes later asks, "Where's Rose?"

Rose is the one person Ben never forgets—not for a moment it seems. Wife and companion for the last sixteen years, it's as if her presence, her importance, has expanded to fill the void. The world of both the past and present has become treacherous and unfamiliar, and the image of Rose has become gigantic. He is obsessed.

Why isn't he in Florida with Rose? Because Ben drove her crazy. Literally, says the daughter who lives in Chicago. The daughter in a suburb of New York is dubious, or perhaps too enraged to care about the breakdown of this wife of sixteen years, no mother to her. Rose had been complaining a lot about Ben over the last few years, the way he hounded her with the same questions, over and over; how, whatever she told him, he forgot. In the summer of 1993, the calls started: Rose yelling over the line at Ben's daughters, increasingly agitated; the calls becoming more frequent. They better get their father. She couldn't live with him anymore. In October the big call came. She was kicking him out. They had to get him immediately or they'd find him on the street. This was absolutely it.

Remember the story that was picked up by every wire service and all the network news: old-timer abandoned at an airport in his wheelchair, gaunt and unshaven. And to further tug on us and confuse us, the lap blanket tucked carefully over his knees, the adult diapers and teddy bear alongside him. My Uncle Ben strolled off the plane, a fit, bantam-sized gent, with a smile that crinkles up his eyes. Arms around his daughter, happy to see her; getting his luggage, belting himself in the car. Hello, hello.

"Where's Rose?"

"Rose is in Florida."

Without time to plan for Ben's future, the sisters, made hasty, temporary arrangements: the New York son-in-law, who ran a business from his home, would look after Ben until they could think clearly about what was best for their father.

Imagine hearing this for a first time: a ninety-year-old man, thrown out of his house by his wife of sixteen years. Wandering in his daughter's house, a place that has become as unfamiliar as the rest of his landscape. Following whomever he sees. Down in the basement; barging into his granddaughter's room. Why were they keeping him here? Why wouldn't they let him go home and be with Rose?

I'm listening to this story from my kitchen in Pittsburgh. The image I have of Ben is from childhood, when he was one of two little look-alike uncles, Ben Tsion, who took the name Sidney, and Dov Baer, who became Ben, both busy taking pictures at family gatherings. One dour as he arranges people: Sit here, move left, bend your head closer, where's the smile, say cheese; the other edging through the crowd, big smile crinkling up his face, quietly snapping photos. The second one is Ben.

I am no stranger to taking care of people. In the foreground there's my ten-year-old daughter with intellectual disabilities, language described in a report as "abundant and disordered," and so many other diagnoses. In the background: a husband with chronic liver disease, and aging parents who left their home of forty years and moved to the city where I now live. Like Ben, they are in good physical shape, though my father complains with good reason that the marbles are rattling around in his head.

Even so, I am disgusted by Rose, utterly without sympathy. There are social services in Florida, local programs. Rose is no dummy; she is a woman of experience and education. All right, it's hard, but to kick him out? Why couldn't she have asked for help?

My Chicago cousin has no answers, but while scrambling for solutions, she has learned a number of things: In places like Florida, where there are so many elderly people, there's an abrupt loss of status when one's mate has dementia. Instead of getting help or sympathy from friends, people are often dropped, left behind. Perhaps it's because old age, with all its attendant ailments, looms over everyone like a plague, and as in plague days, the healthy lock their doors to ward off contagion. Or maybe, instead of seeing their health as the luck of the genetic draw, people consider it a kind of superiority, albeit a fragile one that must be closely protected.

But to kick out her husband! What about commitment?

My cousin in Chicago tells me that her father's story isn't so uncommon. "Apparently the commitment isn't always as great in second marriages."

It's six thirty on a December evening, and I'm on the phone to my Chicago cousin, getting an update on Uncle Ben. This is the only time I can make calls because I'm getting dinner ready and, therefore, not fully engaged.

Ben is miserable. They had tried letting him call Rose, but she screamed at him on the phone. So now he is writing her instead, long letters that are eloquent and clear. Love letters, filled with grief.

How could you do this to me? We were in love. My cousin has been looking for day programs for her father, but all he wants is to be with Rose.

Same as every night, my daughter Rachel trails beside me as I roam from counter to sink to stove. She is so close that often I bump or elbow her accidentally. Sometimes she is stunned, but neither words nor the memory of her bruises are strong enough to convince her to back up.

My cousin tells me: "When I explain that Rose is sick, he understands completely, but then ten minutes later he asks me why he can't be with her." Rachel murmurs when I murmur, speaks loudly when I raise my voice. My husband thinks she stands on top of us because she's visually impaired; in my opinion it's because, among other things, she lacks a sense of personal space.

Where's Rose?

My daughter says, "I'm hungry, can I have an apple?"

She's just finished an apple.

We were good together, I loved her. Where's Rose?

Can I have an apple? I'm hungry, can we have tortellini?

I clutch my daughter by the shoulders to steer her away from me, and, thinking of my own beloved father, say, "It must be awful. I don't know how you can take it."

I'm hungry, can I have an apple? Are we having tortellini?

The day programs were for people with Alzheimer's. When Uncle Ben saw all the people slumped in wheelchairs, or pacing across the room, vacant looks on their faces, he said, "They're old!" Why did his daughter take him there?

He turned away, puzzled and alarmed. These people suffered from the plague of physical disabilities, while Ben was a tough old bird, only, as my father says about himself, his marbles were rattling around.

How could Rose get rid of him, as if he were a vicious dog? How could she be so despicable?

For a long time, whenever I was asked to describe my daughter Rachel, I stressed her sweetness. How different she was from the boy who bit her twice at school, or the girl who pulled a hank of hair out of her head and had to wear a restraining device on the bus because she was, in the jargon of special education, physically disinhibited. No, I would say; my daughter is good-natured. Good-natured, and completely dependent upon us, from the moment she wakes—and she wakes early—until she is tucked in bed.

Total dependency means not merely that I must help her dress and get her meals, but that she is right beside one of us, most often me, whenever she is home. During the school week, this isn't so bad. In the morning, she is at her most alert and able, cheerful with the routine: same cereal, medication, seat at the table; same toothbrush, jacket, backpack on the hook, yellow school bus outside at 8:00 a.m., Flo in the driver's seat, tooting the horn. She is gone until six o'clock, when one of us picks her up at a childcare center, notable for its inclusion of children like Rachel, and takes her home, where she chants about apples and tortellini, or whatever food she's locked into that week.

It's the weekends that are tough. If I am home, wherever I am, third floor to basement, she is an inch away from me, talking, talking, her language perseverative, painfully limited, reminding me of my silent entreaties when she was a baby—Please, oh, please, let her talk. Who knew my most fervent wish would be granted in such an exaggerated way—a daughter who talks ceaselessly, except when she's asleep? If I want to take a walk with my older daughter, go shopping with her, sit and have a cookie without Rachel's continual birdlike, in-your-face chatter, I have three choices: pay for it; bargain with my husband; not do it. I don't know what other people's weekends are like, but ours most often begin with negotiating for time and freedom. If you take Rachel Saturday morning, I'll take her Sunday afternoon. ... Like that.

And yet, when people, knowing my situation, regard me with mournful eyes, I think: Hey, it's my life, I'm used to it. I think: Good days and bad days, same as for you. And: There are worse kids, worse situations. The fatigue I sometimes feel is natural and cyclic. True, weekends are tough and school vacations tougher. True, she seems overwhelming at times.

But so does the awesome responsibility of watching over my teenage daughter, and the pile of manuscripts on my desk.

Around the time when Rose evicted Ben, the voice that said, "Hey, it's my life," began to be replaced by a whisper that said, "How much longer can I ... " It's not just the number of years I have already taken care of her—eleven—or the number of years before she becomes an adult—ten. It's that I've gotten tired; I have more people to take care of, and Rachel has become more difficult. My once pleasant daughter has begun to shriek at me, apropos of nothing as far as I can tell. Sometimes she simply says, "I hate you!" and other times, "You have no right to talk to students that way!" I might be examining apples in a supermarket when she yells, "DON'T YOU DARE YELL AT ME." Or helping her down a flight of stairs, when suddenly, "You're not the boss!"

It took me a while to understand that the origin of the expressions is unimportant, as are the words themselves. The emotion underlying her yelling is what's real, an emotion caused by fatigue or frustration. I understand this and try not to take it personally, but try listening to someone—to a recording, a disembodied voice—say, "I hate you!" several hundred times, and the diminishing effect of these words will become clearer.

As I trudge onward with my furious child, I am reminded that I cannot use hugs or sweet talk to jolly her out of her mood. Nor can I fall back on the usual (if regrettable) "If ... then" statements that parents use as a last resort. In a world of things with the capacity to delight, nothing much delights her—not dolls or stuffed toys or the pictures I hang on the wall of a room decorated to please some child, but not her; not undershirts with hearts on them or trips to the zoo; not me. I cannot tempt her, threaten her, get her to remember simple things. Once I saw myself as the one who knew her best: protector, teacher, expert, but, because my efforts have not come to much, there are times when it feels ridiculous to keep struggling to fit her into our household. Her chatter is so incessant, my own marbles have begun to rattle, too. May I have an apple? Didn't you just have an apple? Yes. May I have an apple?

Where's Rose?

How do we placate ourselves during hard times? Things will change. Isn't that what we say? I imagine my cousins thinking: We will help him. He will get used to it here. Things will get smoother.

As the weeks pass, Ben becomes more miserable at his daughter's house. More confused, more disoriented. The only program even vaguely appropriate for him meets two days a week until three o'clock. The rest of the time, he wanders through the house, barging into rooms, demanding to know why the hell he is there and Rose is not. He has become increasingly hostile. The house is a prison. They are feeding him shit. Where the hell is Rose?

I imagine my cousin switching off the bedside lights, wondering how much longer she can hold out. She loves her father. (I love my daughter.) I can imagine Ben's son-in-law, Richard, prime caregiver of Ben, afraid to even form that question. Richard, born and raised in Argentina, his own parents dead, burst into our extended family with a passionate need to be one of us, not just a relative by marriage. He is an emotional man, the staunchest defender of Ben, the one who is angriest at Rose. His sister-in-law has begun to say that Rose had a mental breakdown, and her anger has lessened, but to Richard, family and responsibility are holy words, and Rose cannot be excused for her actions.

I can imagine my cousin, awake at night, thinking: He is my father.

She is my daughter.

If she really hates me? If my parenting is irrelevant, my place in her life unimportant?

This is what you do: You take care of your children and your parents.

At the expense of our emotional needs and our professional goals?

Some would say: Yes, this is what you do.

At the expense of the others in the family? Some, fewer perhaps, would say: Caring for those who cannot care for themselves comes first.

At the expense of our physical and mental health?

Richard had a heart attack in January. In between trips to the hospital, his wife drove Ben to LaGuardia Airport, where he got on a flight to Chicago. He stepped off the plane at O'Hare, fit and grinning, and asking about Rose, his problems now in the hands of his older daughter.

For most caregivers, there is heartache, but no cardiac arrest, no clear physical manifestation that allows us to say "enough" and feel certain about our decisions. This is not to say that Richard staged his heart attack as a metaphor for the occasion. No, it was real, and it was clearly stress-related.

And now Richard must struggle to prevent further damage to his weakened heart. But there was no question that his heart attack ended his three-month stint as caregiver.

My Chicago cousin found an apartment for her father in a development, where, for a fee, aides help him with whatever he cannot do, or, more often, what he cannot remember to do. Ben's room is spacious and cheerful, and he has a private bath. For a fee, he is escorted to his meals; for a fee, someone takes him for a walk. To save money, my cousin keeps a list of his activities on her desk at work. Although he is not interested in attending any of them, several times each day she stops work and calls her father to remind him to go downstairs. When I ask if he might make friends she laughs ruefully: He cannot remember on Tuesday the person he met on Monday. It's a hard condition for friendship.

When my cousin started Ben's phone service, she got him speed-dialing to her home, fifteen minutes away. He calls her twenty times, day and night, frustrated because he can't find his toothpaste, or toothbrush, or shirts. There is no phone service to Rose, which is a good thing. He is still enraged, still beginning every conversation with questions about Rose.

I am very far from making a decision about Rachel. The only change is that once I assumed that she would live with us until she was a young adult, and now the word "enough" slips into my head with alarming frequency.

Not long ago, a woman who chose to send her profoundly disabled son to an institution castigated me for short-changing my older daughter and my husband by keeping Rachel at home. As she spoke, I felt my heart seize with alarm and heard myself defend my lovely, defenseless daughter. Not yet! We can still handle things. But two days into a holiday, when she has been stuck to me like Velcro, chanting, chattering, so that I am reminded that I cannot hear my own voice—death to a writer!—I wonder how much longer I can hold out. (It is no accident that this essay took hold as I was driving to the airport to catch a plane to New York, and that at the gate, while all around me babies yowled and adults cursed and rumbled about the delays, I wrote in a frenzy, my head unusually clear.)

Of course, this is the issue that most polarizes parents of kids with serious disabilities.

On one side are people like the woman who accused me of expending my energy in the wrong place, and on the other side the ones who say: Tough luck if your career suffers. This is a living, breathing child, your daughter, your responsibility. I ricochet between these sides, bounce off these walls so regularly that when students—young women struggling with relationships and careers, say in breathless awe-stricken tones: You teach! You write! You have a family! How do you do it? I hear myself answer: Badly. This is perceived as a joke, when in fact it's how I feel much of the time.

My mother says, "You moved us here!" because she has not seen me in a week.

Rachel hates me.

My husband says, "You're always running around."

My older daughter feels that because I worry more about Rachel, I love her more, a formula that is utterly untrue. Just when I feel as if I can explain this to her, and have her believe it, a friend who grew up with a sister "like Rachel" and moved oceans and continents away from her family, tells me that Charlotte will grow up and never come home. It will be too painful for her to confront what she left behind.

That makes me cry. Even so, I'm not sure what will shake the bonds enough for me to say "enough." Sometimes I think it will be hearing Rachel say "I hate you" for the millionth time. Sometimes the knowledge that, if I fell through a gaping hole, she wouldn't miss me much. Or perhaps circumstance will change things for me, the way it changed things in Ben's family. My husband is ill; my daughter is spreading her wings.

When Richard looks back to the time he took care of Ben, he says, "I don't know how Rose could stand it for so many years." A far cry from his rage at her abandonment. "In just three months, he gave me a heart attack!"

On that trip to New York, I tried to imagine a time when Rachel would be living away from home, tried to drum up a feeling of relief or pleasure, to shape a memory of reading a newspaper in peace. But I find myself imagining my years without her as a little fable:

Once upon a time there was a woman named Jane who took care of a lot of people. Many years passed, and soon, one by one, everyone was gone. So Jane lived all alone for the rest of her life. The end.

The Conching Rooms

JOHN MCPHEE

Pools and pools and pools of chocolate—fifty-thousand-pound, ninety-thousand-pound, Olympic-length pools of chocolate—in the conching rooms in the chocolate factory in Hershey, Pennsylvania. Big, aromatic rooms. Chocolate, as far as the eye can see. Viscous, undulating, lukewarm chocolate, viscidized, undulated by the slurping friction of granite rollers rolling through the chocolate over crenelated granite beds at the bottoms of the pools. The chocolate moves. It stands up in brown creamy dunes. Chocolate eddies. Chocolate currents. Gulfs of chocolate. Chocolate deeps. Mares' tails on the deeps. The world record for the 50-yard freestyle would be two hours and ten minutes.

Slip a little spatula in there and see how it tastes. Waxy? Claggy? Gritty? Mild? Taste it soft. That is the way to get the flavor. Conching— granite on granite, deep in the chocolate—ordinarily continues for seventy-two hours, but if Bill Wagner thinks the flavor is not right he will conch for hours extra, or even an extra day. Milky? Coarse? Astringent? Caramelly? For forty-five years, Mr. Wagner has been tasting the chocolate. His taste buds magnified a hundred times would probably look like Hershey's kisses. He is aging now, and is bent slightly forward—a slender man, with gray hair and some white hair. His eyeglasses have metal rims and dark plastic brows. He wears thin white socks and brown shoes, black trousers, a white shirt with the company's name on it in modest letters. Everyone wears a hat near the chocolate. Most are white paper caps. Wagner's hat is dapper, white, visored: a chocolate-making supervisor's linen hat.

A man in a paper cap conies up and asks Wagner, "Are we still running tests on that kiss paste?"

"Yes. You keep testing."

Wagner began in cocoa in 1924. The dust was too much for him. After a few weeks, he transferred to conching. He has been conching ever since, working out the taste and texture. Conching is the alchemy of the art, the transmutation of brown paste into liquid Hershey bars. Harsh? Smooth? Fine? Bland? There are viscometers and other scientific instruments to aid the pursuit of uniformity, but the ultimate instrument is Wagner. "You do it by feel, and by taste," he says. "You taste for flavor and for fineness—whether it's gritty. There's one area of your tongue you're more confident in than others. I use the front end of my tongue and the roof of my mouth." He once ate some Nestlé's; he can't remember when. He lays some chocolate on the tip of his tongue and presses it upward. The statement that sends ninety thousand pounds on its way to be eaten is always the same. Wagner's buds blossom, and he says, "That's Hershey's."

Milton Hershey's native town originally was called Derry Church, and it was surrounded, as it still is, by rolling milkland. Hershey could not have been born in a better place, for milk is 20 percent of milk chocolate. Bill Wagner grew up on a farm just south of Derry Church, "it was a rented farm. We didn't own a farm until 1915. I lived on the farm through the Second World War. I now live in town." Wagner's father, just after 1900, had helped Milton Hershey excavate the limestone bedrock under Derry Church to establish the foundations of the chocolate plant. Derry Church is Hershey now, and its main street, Chocolate Avenue, has streetlamps shaped like Hershey's kisses—tinfoil, tassel and all. The heart of the town is the corner of Chocolate and Cocoa. Other streets (Lagos, Accra, Para) are named for the places the beans come from: quotidian freight trains full of beans that are roasted and, in studied ratios, mixed together—base beans, flavor beans, African beans, American beans—and crushed by granite millstones arranged in cascading tiers, from which flow the falls of dark cordovan liquor. This thick chocolate liquor is squeezed mechanically in huge cylindrical accordion compressors. Clear cocoa butter rains down out of the compressors. When the butter has drained off, the compressors open, and out fall dry brown discs the size of manhole covers. These discs are broken into powder. The powder is put into cans and sold. It is Hershey's cocoa— straight out of the jungle and off to the A&P, pure as a driven freak, pure as the purest sunflower seed in a whole-earth boutique.

Concentrate fresh milk and make a paste with sugar. To two parts natural chocolate liquor add one part milk-and-sugar paste and one part pure cocoa butter. Conch for three days and three nights. That—more or less—is the recipe for a Hershey bar. (Baking chocolate consists of nothing but pure chocolate liquor allowed to stand and harden in molds. White chocolate is not really chocolate, it is made from milk, sugar, and cocoa butter, but without cocoa.) In the conching rooms, big American flags hang from beams above the chocolate. "Touch this," Mr. Wagner says. The cast iron walls that hold in the chocolate are 130 degrees Fahrenheit. "We have no heat under this. It's only created heat—created by the friction that the granite rollers produce."

"What if the rollers stop?"

"The chocolate will freeze."

When that happens, the result is a brown icecap, a chocolate-coated Nome. Sometimes fittings break or a worker forgets to shut off a valve and thousands of pounds of chocolate spill over, spread out and solidify on the floor. Workers have to dig their way out, with adzes, crowbars, shovels, picks—chocolate Byrds, chocolate Amundsens.

"The trend today is people want to push buttons," Wagner says. "They'll try to find ways to shortcut. It's a continual struggle to get people to do their share. There's no shortcut to making Hershey's. There have been times when I wished I'd stayed on the farm." Every day, he works from six in the morning until four thirty in the afternoon, so he can cover parts of all shifts. He walks (twelve minutes) from his home on Para Avenue. "Para is a bean, I think. It's a bean or a country, I'm not sure which. We have another street called Ceylon. That's not a bean. It's a country." In the conching rooms, Wagner can see the subtleties of hue that escape the untrained eye;

he can tell where the kiss paste is, and the semisweet, and the chocolate chips, and the bar milk chocolate. Kiss paste has to be a little more dense, so the kisses will sit up. Wagner has grandchildren in Hershey, Colebrook, and Mechanicsburg. When he goes to visit them, he slips them kisses.

Within the connoisseurship, there are acknowledged superior chocolates and, God knows, inferior ones, but undeniably there is no chocolate flavor quite like that of a Hershey bar. No one in Hershey can, or will, say exactly why. There is a voodoo in the blending of beans, and even more voodoo in the making of the milk-and-sugar paste. There is magic in Bill Wagner when he decides that a batch is done. All this, however, does not seem to add up to a satisfactory explanation of the uniqueness of the product. Mystery lingers on. Notice, though, in the conching rooms, what is happening to the granite rollers rolling under the chocolate on the granite beds. Slowly, geologically, the granite is eroding. The granite beds last about thirty years. The granite rollers go somewhat sooner than that. Rolling back and forth, back and forth, they become flat on one side. Over the days, months, years, this wearing down of the granite is uniform, steady, consistent, a little at a time. There seems to be an ingredient that is not listed on the label, infinitesimal granitic particles have nowhere to go but into the chocolate. A Hershey bar is part granite.

Ask management where the granite comes from. The official answer is "New England."

"Where in New England?"

"New England. That's all we are saying. Nestlé's won't say anything about anything. Mars is the same way. So we don't say anything, either."

The Stone Collector

LOUIS SIMPSON

A month ago my wife and I were walking our dogs on the beach. A stiff breeze was raising whitecaps and Connecticut was plainly visible. There are days when you can hardly see the coast and days when it seems to loom. This was one of the clear days.

A man was walking ahead of us, a tall man wearing a cap and black leather jacket. He was walking slowly. From time to time he would stop and pick something up. Then he would stand still and look at what he had found.

We caught up with him. He had a thin face and high-bridged nose, the kind that is called Roman. His hair was gray … I would say he was between forty and fifty. I am inclined not to speak until I am spoken to, so I try to make a point of speaking first and have the reputation of being a sociable, friendly fellow. I said, "Hi." He turned his head and looked at me as though he had to think about it. He said hello and went back to looking at whatever he had in his hand.

I walked over and said, "What did you find?" He didn't look up but continued looking into his palm. Then he held it out … a round stone about an inch in diameter, flannel-gray in color. He said, "It's almost perfect." He put the stone in a pocket of his jacket and took out another. This was oval-shaped, reddish-brown. He said, "Look at it."

I asked if it was his hobby, collecting stones. "No," he said, "I just collect them." But he was particular. They had to be a certain size, not too big or too small. They had to go through the mouth of a bottle—a wide mouth, of course. And have a good shape and color. There was a variety of shapes and colors on this beach. You wouldn't find stones like these in other places.

No, he wasn't a geologist; finding them just gave him pleasure. He was the manager of a furniture store.

I've been reading a story by Chekhov. He says, "All sorts of things are done in the provinces through boredom." Why the country? Would he have said that people who live in the city aren't bored? City people do all sorts of things to relieve their boredom. They create new fashions in clothing, interior decoration, diet, art, you name it. They shoot one another. The newspapers and television are full of the things they do.

Chekhov knew about boredom—he wrote stories and plays about it. In our village we have a way of dealing with this feeling. We just continue doing whatever it is that bores us. After a while the feeling that we ought to do something to relieve it goes away.

Many of the residents have a hobby: gardening, tennis, golf, boating, fishing, cabinetmaking. But collecting stones can hardly be called a hobby. It's not something you do with others. There's probably not a club you could join, or a magazine with articles on the subject and ads in the back by people who want to exchange information. Bending over from time to time to pick up a stone doesn't give you enough exercise to keep you healthy, and it's not something you can talk about afterwards ... a silver cup, a stuffed fish, a cabinet you made with your own hands.

Filling a bottle with stones isn't art. If you put it on display people will think you naive, to say the least. It looks childish. You can imagine them on the way home telling each other that you're "losing it," and they've seen this coming for some time.

You may even find yourself agreeing with them. When other people have reasons for what they do, it's not easy to say that you don't. You may try to explain that your bottle can be used as a bookend or a doorstop.

There he is again on the beach in front of me. He stoops, picks up a stone, looks at it, and lets it fall. I've tried talking to him, but the only interesting thing about him is what he does, and he seems to have no ideas about it. The last time we talked I said that since he spoke of stones as being "almost perfect," he must have an idea of the perfect stone. What would it be like? He stared at me as if the idea hadn't occurred to him. Then he said, "I'd know it if I saw it."

I could talk to him about the furniture business, but I have no wish to. He seems to have no other interests. All he cares about are his stones.

Self-Interview

GORDON LISH

Auditor's note: According to the author, a reporter from Interview *magazine initially interviewed Gordon Lish for an article. Evidently,* Interview *was unsatisfied; it subsequently sent Lish a list of questions, asking him to make the interview "more accessible"; this "Self-Interview" was the result.*

This a setup, right? It's all a setup, right? I mean, I am not sitting somewhere shooting my mouth off to somebody sitting the same somewhere with me. There is no tape-recording going on. There is no note-taking going on. What the deal is instead is that I, Lish, am sitting by my lonesome with a list, which list is the product not of my contrivance but of *Interview*'s. (How else have the composure to manage the acoustical divertissement of *list* and *Lish* whilst evincing seeming indifference to an exhibition of an absence of humility?) I mean, the entries that constitute it, this list, *Interview* entered them. Fine. I'm ready. Got pencil and paper. Actually, it's a lie—got felt-tip and paper. Anyway, here is the list as *Interview* made it—Death and Immortality, the Most Overrated Writers in America, Harold Brodkey, Harold Bloom, My Being Called the Antichrist, Knopf, What Writing Means to Me, What My Enemies Mean to Me, and, finally, Me, Gordon Lish. Hey, that's me again—Lish again! Swell. Here goes. *Death?* Scared shitless of it. Not of dying—which I elect to accuse of being sexy and dramatic and an occasion for rapturous opportunism and for a certain ultimacy in narcissism—but of being dead. Which state of non-being, reported allure of consciouslessness notwithstanding, I would do anything to get out of. Even art. Like remarking, for example, the hallucination written into the gerund just used: because you're not going to, I'm not going to, no one's going to, be anything. So to say *being dead* is to get it wrong because you are saying it wrong. And ditto, less tellingly but tellingly enough, goes for saying *non-being*, fair enough? So by my *saying* speech says it wrong, I can believe myself to be in charge of the conditions, which is indeed an illusion, but, I claim, a not unprofitable one. Skip it, it goes without saying I am not in charge of anything by saying. But I give myself to believe that I sort of maybe tragically magically pretty pathetically pitiably a little am—by placing into motion a spoken token of myself, a meagerness, yes, but one whose dialectical action I can pretend transmutes me, its origin, into a muchness by reason (irrational reason) of my being the father of it, *OK?* Doing art is not a way of saying it right but of saying it as wrong you can say it—namely, an act of saying under the sign of your hallucination, not under anyone else's. Which is why the other famous faith system we devised for ourselves doesn't do a job for me. Likelier for me to get myself to think I can overcome, or can march myself to a distance from, Beckett's sign than God's. God's sign—the event of my end, that unimpeachable dissolution—is very dense and specific. Whereas Beckett's transgression against me, his text, is nowhere near as material and aggressive. I wake up innocent but hours nearer my undoing. This is an offense God delivers to me—Jesus, Jesus!—in irrepressibly vivacious and precise detail. Everything else in experience (we can take Beckett again, or take *pease porridge hot, pease porridge cold*, or take the mortification of the flesh) is comparatively soft and insubstantial and thus more or less resistible, yes? God—God's agent nature—is the one object whose incommensurate power nothing I can do can subdue. Oh, fiddlesticks. Give me Beckett—and the other mighty dead— that I may vie to be among them or even to trick myself to believe that I am over them. Give me—guess I am quoting Frost—any chance bit that I might manipulate it—am done with the quoting—that I might make of the labor a deformation in my name—the controlled conjunctions, continuities, turbulences, morbid deviations, and so forth. False, false, false, to be sure, but here's a deception I can let myself succumb to because my name is Gordon, is Lish, is language, is not God, is not the clock, is not the rock. Vanity, vanity, vanity—you bet. So, therefore, why not—next-entry-wise—notions of *immortality*? Which all it is is vanity imagining for itself a future, no? Well, immortality, yes, such a notion is right up there with the other enabling fictions— those of no fear, no severance, unbreachable sovereignty, anxiety-free freedom, perfection, completion. It couldn't hurt. It could only help. Glad to go along with it for the time being. *Most Overrated Writers in America*? You mean writers of fiction of my generation in the context of their fictions? Okay, how about this— how about every writer of fiction but Lish? That's one answer to your question—probably the only unquestionably durable answer the person named Lish could contribute. But here's another—every writer of fiction but the Don DeLillo who wrote any novel Don DeLillo wrote, every writer of fiction but the foregoing and the Cynthia Ozick who wrote "Bloodshed" and "Usurpation: Other People's Stories," every writer of fiction but the foregoing and the Cormac McCarthy who wrote *Outer Dark* and *Blood Meridian*, every writer of fiction but the foregoing and the Harold Brodkey—of course, of course!—who wrote "His Son, in His Arms, in Light, Aloft," who wrote "Verona: A Young Woman Speaks," who wrote "Ceil," who wrote "S. L.," who wrote "Largely an Oral History of My Mother," who wrote "The Boys on Their Bikes." Please, you want for me to badmouth? I am happy to badmouth—both the living and the dead. I could give you names and addresses till the cows come home. But so go pick for yourself. Because whatever proposition you come back to me with, chances are it wouldn't be in me to rumpus around with you on account of it. Neither, it seems reliable to assert, will it be in history for it to do so. On the other hand, I beg you not ever to come back to me with any of the dozens of, with any of the scores of, with any of the hundreds of grandeurs America underpraises, dispraises, or—the fuckers!—appraises neither one way nor the other. I mean, ignores, is ignorant of, proclaims its smug ignoramusness because of. As witness your *New York Times*, your *Village Voice*, your *New York Review of Books*, to cite certain more notable igginesses in sight. Having not one word to say, the lot of them, either for or against, for instance, Dawn Raffel's *In the Year of Long Division*—or either for or against Sam Michel's *Under the Light*, for instance. Ditto Brian Evenson's *Altmann's Tongue*, ditto Victoria Redel's *Where the Road Bottoms Out*, which for-instancing I guess I could also get myself to keep up until kingdom come. *Harold Brodkey*? We used to be friends. Or we used to appear to be friends. Now we are no longer friends—neither actually nor apparently. *Harold Bloom*? We used to be friends. We used to appear to be friends. Now we are no longer friends—neither actually nor apparently. Ah, but these states of affairs hardly rule out my reading Brodkey and Bloom. You would have to watch me pack up and take myself off to jail if there were a law made that tried to make me quit reading Brodkey and Bloom. Which would just this minute go double for Donoghue and Kristeva and Deleuze and Guatarri and Levinas and Lentricchia and Langer and Nelson Goodman and Adorno and—who have I just now got laid out on the tiny table next to my toilet?—Hegel. Hey, hey—how about, what about "Gordo, why come is it that you are no longer friends with Brodkey, for one, and with Bloom, for another?" Answer? Because he's a shit, for one, and a shit, for another! Answer? Because he's a stinking rotten shit, for one, and a stinking rotten shit, for another! But who's calling names? Am I calling names? These men will be among the mighty dead one day—gods, be gods, such as anyone might come gloriously to install either or both for himself. But better revered as ghosts changelessly vaporous in the firmament than spotted as all too fleshly moral dishevelments for the children to see panhandling on the Rialto. *My Being Called the Antichrist?* No kidding. Somebody did that? Who did that? Maybe in Los Angeles maybe. Maybe in Portland. Maybe in Chicago. Here in NYC all I am trying to do is betray, betray—but on the page, baby, on the page!—such that the ties that bind me will be let loose from me for long enough for me to get a toe or two into a hitherto untrampled domain. This means being against everything—against it!—but that means, first and foremost, being against myself. So, check, if there is good in me, then I am against it—but let us seek to keep the categories discrete. I'm all for anything, all for being Yertle the Turtle, plus also all for opposing what I say I'm all for—but on the page, baby, on the page! Which happens to be the elsewhere I chose and still choose. Well, OK, I admit it—maybe also, you know, forgive me, don't get excited, but, right, right, no argument, it's true, put the cuffs on me, you got me, I give up—it all goes ditto for in the class, where I am the demons consort, its thing, its conduit. *Knopf*? We used to be friends. We appeared to be friends. (Come on, you know the rest of the dirge by now.) But so what's the deal here, so friendless at sixty-one? Am I, at long last, wising up? Which, however, is not to say you will catch me looking one inch inattentive to the careers of any of the following Knopf undertakings—Gary Lutz's *Stories in the Worst Way*, Jason Schwartz's *A German Picturesque*, Diane Williams's *The Stupefaction*, Christine Schutt's "Nightwork," Ben Marcus's *The Age of Wire and String*, Ken Sparling's *Dad Says He Saw You at the Mall*, Anne Carson's *Plainwater*—since it was I who, before my being Knopfed off, took them all on— not to mention, proud to mention, Denis Donoghue's *Walter Pater*. Oh, and another thing— Wayne Hogan's *Book of Life*—no, correct that, *Book of Tubes*—be smart and get in touch with me at the Q, at 212-888-4769, if you are a publisher who is not too chickenshit to stand strong for a corker. Now then, *What Writing Means to Me*? Meaning itself. Despite the meaninglessness of it. An answer to the insult. Despite the exorbitance of it. The works, or Works, which was my dead wife's name before it was Lish. But best to say time. Because time beats meaning. Best to say writing means life lived in Lish-made time, not life spent in given time, not life suffered in death-row time, which is nature's time, dig? *What My Enemies Mean to Me*? Everything—the works (oh, don't worry, I know all too well, I know exactly what I am saying) again—the inertia-taunting otherness in me—starting with God and with time and with Mommy and Daddy and ending with the vicious incurable ironizing instability of the sentence. Oh, heck—of the comma, of the period. On the other hand, who, what, is there anything exterior or, for that matter, interior, that is not the enemy? That is not an impediment to your existence, to your freedom? *Gordon Lish*? Hey, that's me, that's me!—my name, not the first governance but the most agreeable governance. Well, isn't it, wasn't it, a naming, the whole damned deal, an onomatologically determined act of being? Which, when you get right down to it—which is where we're all going to one day have to get to—namely, right down on your back on your deathbed to it—which would you sooner say? Give you two choices: "Oh, well, that's life." Or: "Yeah, that was me." It of course being conceded there is any say left in you.

The Story of My Father

PHILLIP LOPATE

IS IT NOT CLEARER THAN DAY, THAT WE FEEL WITHIN OURSELVES THE INDELIBLE MARKS OF EXCELLENCE, AND IS IT NOT EQUALLY TRUE THAT WE CONSTANTLY EXPERIENCE THE EFFECTS OF OUR DEPLORABLE CONDITION?

–*Pascal*

Old age is a great leveler: the frailer elderly all come to resemble turtles trapped in curved shells, shrinking, wrinkled and immobile, so that, in a roomful, a terrarium of the old, it is hard to disentangle one solitary individual's karma from the mass fate of aging. Take my father. Vegetating in a nursing home, his character seems both universalized and purified, worn to its bony essence. But, as LSD is said to intensify more than alter one's personality, so old age: my father is what he always was, only more so. People meeting him for the first time ascribe his oddities (the withdrawn silences, sloppy eating habits, boasts, and pedantic non sequiturs) to the infirmities of time, little realizing he was like that at thirty.

A man in his thirties who acts the octogenarian is asking for it. But old age has set his insularities in a kinder light—meanwhile drawing to the surface that underlying sweetness that I always suspected was there. Dispassionate to the point where the stoical and stony meet, a hater of sentimentality, he had always been embarrassed by his affections; but now he lacks the strength even to suppress these leakages. I have also changed and am more ready to receive them. These last ten years—ever since he was put away in old-age homes—have witnessed more expressions of fondness than passed between us in all the years before. Now when I visit him, he kisses me on sight and, during the whole time we are together, stares at me greedily, as though with wonder that such a graying cub came from his loins. For my part, I have no choice but to love him. I feel a tenderness welling up, if only at the sight of the wreck he has become. What we were never able to exhibit when he had all his wits about him—that animal bond between father and son—is now the main exchange.

Yet I also suspect sentimentality; and so I ask myself, how valid is this cozy resolution? Am I letting both of us off the hook too quickly? Or trying to corner the market on filial piety, while the rest of my family continues mostly to ignore him? Who is, who was, this loner, Albert Lopate, neglected in a back ward? I look at the pattern of his eighty-five years and wonder what it all adds up to: failure, as he himself claims, or a respectable worker s life for which he has little to be ashamed, as I want to believe? We spend most of our adulthoods trying to grasp the meanings of our parents' lives; and how we shape and answer these questions largely turns us into who we are.

My father's latest idea is that I am a lawyer. The last two times I've visited him in the nursing home, he's expressed variations on this theme. The first time he looked up at me from his wheelchair and said, "So, you're successful—as a lawyer?" By my family's scraping-by standards, I'm a worldly success; and worldly success, to the mistrustful urban-peasant mind of my father, befogged by geriatric confusion, can only mean a lawyer.

Lawyers, I should add, are not held in the highest regard in my family. They are considered shysters: smooth, glib, ready to sell you out. You could say the same about writers. In hindsight, one reason I became a writer is that my father wanted to be one. An autodidact who started out in the newspaper trade, then became a factory worker and, finally, a shipping clerk, he wrote poetry in his spare time, and worshipped Faulkner and Kafka. I enacted his dream, like the good son (or usurped it, like the bad son), which seems not to have made him entirely happy. So he turns me into a lawyer.

Not that my father's substitution is all that far-fetched. I had entered college a pre-law major, planning to specialize in publishing law. Secretly I yearned to be a writer, though I did not think I was smart enough. I was right—who is?—but bluff got the better of modesty.

The last time I visited my father, he said, "I know what you want to be. *Abogado.*" He smiled at his ability to call up the Spanish word you see on storefronts in barrios, alongside *notario.* So this time I was not yet the successful attorney, but the teenage son choosing his vocation. Sometimes old people get stuck on a certain moment in the past. Could it be that his mental clock had stopped around 1961, right about the time of his first stroke, when he'd just passed fifty (my present age) and I was seventeen? *Abogado.* It's so characteristic of my father's attachment to language that a single word will swim up from the dark waters of dotage. Even before he became addled, he would peacock his vocabulary, going out of his way to construct sentences with polysyllabic words such as "concomitant" or "prevaricate." My father fingers words like mah-jongg tiles, waiting to play a good one.

Lately he has been reverting to Yiddish phrases, which he assumes I understand, though I don't. This return to the mother tongue is not accompanied by any revived interest in Judaism—he still refuses to attend the home's religious services—but is all part of his stirring the pot of language and memories one last time.

I arrive around noon, determined to bring him outside for a meal. My father, as usual, sits in the dining room, a distance apart from everyone else, staring down at his chin. There are a group of old ladies whom he manages to tantalize by neither removing himself entirely from their company, nor giving them the benefit of his full attention. Though he has deteriorated badly in recent years, he still remains in better shape than some, hence a "catch." One Irish lady in particular, Sheila, with a twinkle in her cataracted eye, is always telling me what a lovely man my father is. He pays her no attention whatsoever.

It was not always thus. A letter he dictated for my sister Leah in California, when he first came to this home, contained the passage: "There's a woman by the name of Sheila who seems to be attracted to me. She's a heavyset woman, not too bad-looking, she likes me a lot, and is fairly even-tempered. I'm not sure of my feelings toward her. I'm ambivalent." (*Ambivalent* is a favorite Albert Lopate word. Purity of heart is for simpletons.) "Should I pursue this more aggressively, or should I let things go along at a normal pace?" The last line strikes me as particularly funny, given my father's inveterate passivity (what would aggressive pursuit entail for him?) and the shortage of time left to these ancients.

It took me a while to give up the hope that my father would find companionship, or at least casual friendship, in a nursing home. But the chances were slim: this is a man who never had nor made a friend for as long as I can remember. Secondly, "friendship" is a cuddly term that ill describes the Hobbesian enmity and self-centeredness among this tribe of old people.

"Don't push anything out of the window!" yells one old woman to another. "If anything's pushed out the window, it's going to be you!"

"I want to get out of here, I want to forget you, and I won't forget you unless I get out of this room!" yells the second.

"You dirty pig."

"You're one, too."

So speak the relatively sane ones. The ward is divided between two factions: those who, like my father, can still occasionally articulate an intelligent thought, and those with dementia, who scream the same incoherent syllables over and over, kicking their feet and rending the air with clawed hands. The first group cordially detests the second. *Meshugana,* crazy, my father dismisses them with a word. Which is why, desperately trying to stay on the right side of Alzheimer's, he has become panicked by forgetfulness.

Asked how he is, he responds with something like: "It worries me I'm losing my memory. We were discussing the All-Star pitcher the Dodgers used to have. Koufax. I couldn't remember Koufax's first name. Ridiculous!" For a man who once had quiz-show recall, such lapses are especially humiliating. He has been making alphabetical lists of big words to retain them. But the mind keeps slipping, bit by bit. I had no idea there could be so many levels of disorientation before coming to rest at senility.

This time, he has forgotten we've made a lunch date and sits ready to eat the institutional tray offered him. In a way, I prefer his forgetting our date to his response a few years ago, when he would wait outside three hours before my arrival, checking his watch every ten minutes. As usual, he is dressed too warmly, in a mud-colored, torn sweater, for the broiling summer day. (These shabby clothes seem to materialize from nowhere: Where does his wardrobe come from, and whatever happened to the better clothes we bought him? Theft is common in these establishments.)

I am in a hurry to wheel him outside today, before he becomes too attached to his meal—and before the atmosphere of the nursing home gets to me.

I kiss him on top of his pink head, naked but for a few white hairs, and he looks at me with delight. He is proud of me. I am the lawyer, or the writer—in any case, a man of accomplishment. In another minute, he will start introducing me to the women at the next table, "This is my son," as he has already done a hundred times before, and they will pour on the syrup about what a nice father I have, how nice I am to visit him (which I don't do often enough), and how alike we look. This time I start to wheel him out immediately, hoping to skip the routine, when Sheila croaks in her Irish accent, "Dontcha say hello to me anymore?" Caught in the act of denying my father the social capital a visitor might bring him, I go over and schmooze a bit.

Meanwhile, the muskrat-faced Miss Mojabi (in the caste division of this institution, the nursing staff is predominantly Pakistani, the attendants mainly Black, and the upper management Orthodox Jewish) reminds me that I must "sign the form" to take legal responsibility for our outing. Were Armaggedon to arrive, these nurses would be waiting pen in hand for a release signature. Their harsh, officious manner makes me want to punch them. I temper my rage with the thought that they are adequate if not loving—that it was we, the really unloving, who abandoned him to their boughten care.

My father's nursing home, located in Washington Heights, is perched on the steepest hill in Manhattan. After straining to navigate the wheelchair downhill, fantasizing what would happen if I let the handlebars slip (careening Papa smashing into tree), I bring us to a Chinese-Cuban takeout place on Broadway, a hole in the wall with three Formica tables. It's Sunday, everything else is closed, and there are limits to how far north I am willing to push him in the August heat. My father seems glad to have made it to the outside; he wouldn't mind, I'm sure, being wheeled to Riverdale. Still, he has never cared much about food, and I doubt if the fare's quality will register on him one way or the other.

After asking him what he would like, and getting an inconclusive answer, I order sesame chicken and a beef dish at the counter. He is very clear on one thing: ginger ale. Since they have none, I substitute Mountain Dew. Loud salsa music on the radio makes it hard to hear him; moreover, something is wrong with his false teeth, or he's forgotten to put in the bridge, and he speaks so faintly I have to ask him to repeat each sentence several times. Often I simply nod, pretending to have heard. But it's annoying not to understand, so as soon as he clears his throat—signaling intent to speak—I put my ear against his mouth, receiving communiques from him in this misted, intimate manner.

From time to time, he will end his silence with an observation, such as, "The men here are better-looking than the women." I inspect the middle-aged Dominican patrons, indoor picnickers in their Sunday best—the men gray-templed and stout, wearing dark suits or brocaded shirts; the women in skirts, voluptuously rounded, made-up, pretty— and do not share his opinion, but nod agreement anyway. I sense he offers these impressions less to express his notion of reality than to show he can still make comments.

Ten minutes later, another mysterious remark arrives, from left field, like the one about "abogado." I prefer this system of waiting for my father to say something, between long silences, rather than prying conversation out of him. If my wife Cheryl were here, she would be drawing him out, asking him about the latest at the nursing home, whether he had seen any movies on television, what he thought of the food, if he needed anything. And later, she would consider the effort a success: "Did you see how much better he got, the longer we spoke? He's just rusty because nobody talks to him. But he's still sharp mentally...." I'm glad she's not here to see me failing to keep the conversational shuttlecock aloft.

You must have heard that corny idea: A true test of love is when you can sit silently next to the beloved, without feeling any pressure to talk. I have never been able to accomplish this feat with any woman, howsoever beloved, but I can finally do it with one human being: my father. After fifty years of frustration as this lockjawed man's son, I no longer look on his uncommunicativeness as problematic or wounding. Quite the contrary: In my book, he has at last earned the right to be as closemouthed as he wants, just as I have earned the right to stare into space around him, indulging my own fly-on-the-wall proclivities.

He eats, engrossed, engaged in the uneven battle between morsel and fork. With the plastic utensils they have given us, it is not easy for a man possessing so little remaining hand strength to spear chicken chunks. So he wields the fork like a spoon to capture a piece, transport it to his mouth, and crunch down, one half dropping into his lap. Those dark polyester pants, already seasoned, absorb the additional flavor of sesame sauce. He returns to the plate with that morose, myopic glare which is his trademark. My wife, I know, would have helpfully cut up the pieces into smaller bits. Me, I prefer to watch him struggle. I could say in my defense that I am respecting his autonomy more by letting him work out the problem on his own. Or I could acknowledge some streak of cruelty for allowing him this fiasco. The larger truth is that I have become a fly on the wall, and flies don't use utensils.

Eventually, I too cut up everything on my father's plate. So we both arrive at the same point, my wife and I, but at differing rates. Cheryl sizes up a new situation instantly and sets about eliminating potential problems for others—a draft, a tipsy chair—as though all the world were a baby she needed to protect. My tendency is to adjust to an environment passively, like my father, until such time as it occurs to me to do what a considerate Normal Person (which I am decidedly not, I am a Martian) would do in these same circumstances: shut the window, cut up the old man's meat. My father is also from Mars. We understand each other in this way. He too approaches all matter as obdurate and mystifying.

My father drops some broccoli onto his lap. "Oh, Al, how could you?" my mother would have cried out. "You're such a slob!" We can both "hear" her, though she is some eight miles downtown. As ever, he looks up sheepish and abashed, with a strangely innocent expression, like a chimp who knows it is displeasing its master but not why.

It gives me pleasure to spare him the expected familial reproach. "Eat it with your hands, Pop. It's OK," I tell him. Who can object to an old man picking up his food? Certainly not the Dominicans enjoying themselves at the next table. Many African tribes eat with their fingers. The fork is a comparatively recent innovation, from the late Middle Ages; Ethiopians still think that the fork not only harms the food's taste, imposing a metallic distance, but also spoils the sociability of each eater scooping up lentils and meat with soft porridgy bread from the common pot. Mayhap my father is a noble Ethiopian prince, mistransmigrated into the body of an elderly Jew? Too late: the tyranny of the fork has marked him, and he must steal "inadvertent" bits for his fingers' guilty pleasures.

I empathize with that desire to live in one's head, performing an animal's functions with animal absent-mindedness. Sometimes I too eat that way when I'm alone, mingling culinary herbs with the brackish taste of my fingers, in rebellious solidarity with his lack of manners. Socially, my older brother Hal and I have striven hard to project ourselves as the opposite of my father—to seem forceful, attentive, active and seductive. But I feel my father's vagueness, shlumpiness and mania for withdrawal inhabit me like a flu when no one is looking.

Across the street from the cafe, a drunken bum about sixty is dancing by himself on a park bench to Latin jazz. He has no shirt on, revealing an alkie's skinny frame, and he seems happy, moving to the beat with that uncanny, delayed rhythm of the stoned. I point him out as a potentially diverting spectacle to my father, who shows no interest. The drunk, in a curious way, reminds me of my dad: they're both functioning in a solipsistic cone.

Surrounded by "that thick wall of personality through which no real voice has ever pierced on its way to us," as Pater phrased it, each of us is, I suppose, to some degree a solipsist. But my father has managed to exist in as complete a state of solipsism as any person I have ever known. When he gets into an elevator, he never moves to the back, although by now he must anticipate that others will soon be joining him. Inconsiderateness? The word implies the willful hurting of others whose existence one is at least aware of.

I once saw an old woman in the nursing home elevator telling him to move back, which he did very reluctantly, and only a step at a time for each repeated command. (Perhaps, I rationalized for him, he has a faulty perception of the amount of space his body takes up.) The old woman turned to her orderly and said: "When you get on in years you have to live with old people. Some of them are nice and some are—peculiar." Meaning my father. When we got off the elevator he said, loudly: "She's such a pain in the ass, that one. Always complaining. I'll give her such a *luk im kopf*" (a smack in the head). His statement showed that he had been aware of her, but not enough to oblige her.

My father has always given the impression of someone who could sustain very little intensity of contact before his receptive apparatus shut down. Once, after I hadn't seen him in a year, I hugged him and told him how much I loved him. "OK, OK. Cut the bullshit," he said. This armor of impatience may have been his defense against what he actually wanted so much that it hurt.

"OK" is also his transitional marker, indicating he has spent long enough on one item and is ready for new data. If you haven't finished, so much the worse for you.

My sister Molly is the only one who can challenge his solipsism. She pays him the enormous compliment of turning a deaf ear to his self-pity and assuming that, even in old age, there is still potential for moral growth. Years ago, hospitalized with pneumonia, he was complaining to her that nobody cared enough to visit him, and she shot back: "Do you care about anyone? Are you curious about anyone besides yourself?" She then tried to teach him, as one would a child, how to ask after others' well-being. "When you see them, say: 'How are you? What have you been up to lately? How are you feeling?'" And for a while, it took. My father probably said, "How are you?" more times between the ages of seventy-five and seventy-nine than in all the years preceding. If the question had a mechanical ring, if he speedily lost interest in the person's answer, that ought not to detract from the worthiness of my sister's pedagogy.

My father's solipsism is a matter of both style and substance. When I was writing an essay on the Holocaust, I asked him if he had any memories of refugees returning from the camps. He seemed affronted, as though to say: Why are you bothering me with that crazy business after all these years? "Ask your mother. She remembers it."

"But I'm asking you," I said. "When did you find out about the concentration camps? What was your reaction?"

"I didn't think about it. That was them and this was me," he said with a shrug.

Here was solipsism indeed: to ignore the greatest tragedy of modern times—of his own people!—because he wasn't personally involved. On the other hand, my father in his eighties is a hardly credible witness for the young man he was. What his reaction does underline is the pride he takes in being taciturn, and in refusing to cough up the conventionally pious response.

As I ask the Chinese waiter for the check, my father starts to fiddle with several napkins in his breast pocket. He has developed a curious relationship to these grubby paper napkins, which he keeps taking out of his pocket and checking. I've never seen him blow his nose with them. I wonder if old people have the equivalent of what clinical psychologists call "transitional objects"—like those pacifiers or teddy bears that children imbue with magical powers—and if these napkins are my father's talismen.

Just to show the internalized superego (God or my wife) that I have made an effort to *communicate,* I volunteer some news about myself. I tell my father that Cheryl and I are soon to have a baby. His response is: "C'est la vie!" This is carrying philosophic resignation too far—even good news is greeted stoically. I tell him we have bought a house, and my teaching post is secure. None of these items seems to register, much less impress. Either he doesn't get what I'm saying, or knows it already and is indifferent.

My older brother Hal called him recently with the news that he had had his first baby. On being told he was a grandfather, my father's answer was, "Federico Fellini just died." This became an instant family joke, along with his other memorable non sequiturs. (If indeed it was a non sequitur. The translation might be: "What do I care about your new baby when death is staring me in the face?") Though I could sympathize with Hal's viewing it as yet another dig to add to his copious brief against our father, who has always tended to compete with his sons rather than rejoice in our good fortune, this Fellini response seemed to me more an expression of incapacity than insult. The frown on his face nowadays when you tell him something important, the *c'est la vie,* is a confession that he knows he can't focus enough to hold on to what you are saying; he lacks the adhesive cement of affect.

Even sports no longer matter to him. It used to be one of our few common topics: I was guaranteed a half-hour's worth of conversation with my father, working my way through the Knicks, Mets, Rangers, Giants, Jets.... His replies were curt, yet apt: "They stink. They got no hitting." He it was who taught me that passionate fandom that merges with disenchantment: loyalty to the local team, regardless of the stupid decisions the front office made; never cross a picket line, just stick with the union, for all their corruption; vote Democratic no matter how mediocre this year's slate. I would have thought being a sports fan was part of his invincible core, as much as his addiction to newspapers. He continues to have *The Times* ordered for him, but now it sits on his lap, unopened, like a ship passenger's blanket.

Sea Changes

Traveling the Staten Island Ferry

A.D. COLEMAN

We're all drawn by nature to the source. *Rock me on the water,* sings one of our voices, *got to get back to the sea somehow.* No cause for surprise, then, in the discovery by a photographer and a writer that they had in common not only residence in New York City but the sharing of a particular Atlantic voyage.

Not that they'd traveled together; far from it. In fact, they'd only met on shipboard once, late at night, and then by accident. (The photographer had refused to be pulled out of his solitary orbit into conversation, moving on with only a curt nod of recognition.) Nor, as the evidence indicates, could it even be said that they'd taken the same trip. There's no remarkable confluence of events here, only the coincidence that something in the shape of their quite separate lives had led them repeatedly to crossing this small stretch of the great water aboard the Staten Island Ferry and, characteristically, to making something of it.

But what sort of a something? For the photographer, a series of fractioned seconds totalling five minutes, surely no more. Judiciously parceled into precise epiphanies, they're meant only to reveal what one might truly see if one could deglaze one's eyes for such a short while and to imply what else might be perceived if one could keep them open. For the writer, a jumble of scraps—fragments overheard, experienced, intuited, felt, read, witnessed, remembered—that washed ashore in the wake. Loosely stitched together where the junctures of their edges permit, they form a patchwork that might serve to warm the images. But nowhere would it be so snugly fitted that it could not be easily removed.

Daytimes, at rush hour, the fantasy is that this ship full of dancing celebrants will emerge from the morning mists and pull into a city pulsing with rhythm. Minstrels are drawn to it, so often there's music, sometimes even a steel-pan band.

But hardly anybody dances, not even the tipsy prom couples who parade the decks from midnight till dawn in the warmth of June, strolling unrealities of tulle, giggles, tuxedos, adolescence, wilted corsages. Only the children, sometimes on the sunny days, stop for a moment long enough to realize that with only wood below their feet they're walking on water.

There are half a dozen of these boats. Let's assume we're all in the same one, named after someone no longer alive—a local politico, an explorer, an assassinated president, perhaps a war hero. Four kinds of people ride it. Three of those are the tourists, the commuters, and the hands.

For the sightseers (and for their professional paradigms, the fashion photographers with their models), it's a set, a backdrop. For them the voyage ends at its beginning, when it starts to become an experience acquired instead of one anticipated, suddenly memorable only for having been intercepted on film.

For the mass of riders it's a function, a commonplace, assumed and ignored—a punctuation mark in their sentences. Newspapers serve to block it out. From the smoking cabin on the lower deck you can see the water up close, watch the whitecaps snap in the wind or the swells roll calmly on balmier days. But decades of stale nicotine hang in the air, the windows are coated with salt crystals and grime. Almost no one looks out.

They could never really figure out how or why it happened. So they assumed it was an accident–that, parked there at the front of the boat, she had inadvertently hit the gas instead of the brake, broken through the flimsy gates, and plunged herself and her boy into the harbor. It took hours to hoist the car out. All the other passengers had to change to another boat.

Hard to say what this vessel and its shuttling mean for the crew and the ferry workers. They know it best; no one else stays on any one boat more than twenty-five consecutive minutes under normal circumstances. Cured in sauerkraut steam, the angry ladies behind the coffee counter snarl among themselves and avoid the eyes of customers. The shoeshine men announce only the name of their trade; when one of them who'd worked the boat for twenty years came in drunk, fell off and drowned, none of the passengers noticed his absence. The crew does not mingle any more than is absolutely necessary. Occasionally a pretty girl is invited up to enjoy the view from the captain's cabin.

The fourth kind of people who sail these ships: call them voyagers, those who reach awareness—if only for a moment—of what they're really doing, of where they really are. More often than you might expect, they're children, inquiring into the possibility of catching a ray of sunlight in the hand, dreaming past the confines of a mother's devoted attention, allowing the world to be in all its incomprehensible fullness because they are too small to conceive of reducing it down.

One weekday afternoon at five the ferry terminal was packed with three thousand people in office uniforms. A legless man on a dolly wheeled himself through this crowd, which displayed not even a faint awareness of his distinctive presence. Then a boychild walked straight up to him and announced in loud surprise, "You've got no legs!" All the adults within earshot gasped, or winced, or looked away, discomfited. Everyone except the man on the dolly. He knew he had no legs. He talked amiably with the one person who had been unafraid to look him in the eye and acknowledge that he'd seen him.

The older voyagers take what they can find, depending on their inclination. For some it's a time warp, in whose quieter spaces they can coast past Ellis Island wearing their grandparents' immigrant eyes, or bid adieu to their bon voyage party and embark for the continent on their own grand tour. Others meditate as they're cradled on the bosom of the world. Still others take it for what it is—an interlude, a transition, a few minutes' peace in which to pull oneself together or (like that mellow, dapper, dark-skinned gentleman) to relax in one's hard-earned coherence.

At night this scenario can evoke the sea-set dramas of Conrad, O'Neill, Melville—all recurrent there in miniature. No matter where one is in the cycle of the hours, there's room and time enough here for love, hate, romance, adventure, mystery—a floating metaphor. Small wonder that one evening you could walk into the upper cabin and find a famous Russian poet's shadow thrown violently onto the wall by a television station's lights as he chanted his hymn to the bells of Moscow with the twilight deepening and the glittering skyline falling behind. He was there like all the others, writers, musicians, photographers, seduced into this microcosm and then flung out again like so much flotsam, clinging to their bits of wreckage, their endless unanswerable questions. How did that old man feel, what did he think, eyeball to eyeball with his own ghost in the glass? Could that napping fat man have known that he looked like Lou Costello? Are these truly the first moon pix? Are we significantly different from acres of rocks in a vacuum?

Late summer afternoon, alone together outside on the upper deck, leaning on the rail, looking back at the shrinking city. His fingers brushed again and again her hardened nipple through her thin gauze shirt, her hand squeezed his swelling cock, slid the zipper slowly down. The sun hot on his heated flesh …

Day into night, this voyage is as short as you make it, or as long. Because it is a space apart, afloat, unmoored, you can take it as permission to shift position, to unlock the door and leave it slightly ajar, to glimpse the possibilities of rage, passion, sweetness, numbness in others, in yourself. Will you read the short story about that young couple with their motorcycle? Have you time enough to open the unwritten novel in the sad eyes of that blond woman who looks at you and past you from her seat? Are you still on speaking terms with the mother of liberty astride the harbor, patiently waiting for those who yearn to breathe free? Will you play the game of life wherever you find it, whether it's right in front of you or off to one side and moving fast, something terribly important caught with the corner of your eye?

Once, on a winter's morning, the boat he took got lost in a driving snow. There was no visibility past the edge of the deck; when they pulled away from the dock the world disappeared. Tasting eternity, those on board fell silent, all listening to the spectral foghorns converse in the white darkness. It took an hour and a half to inch back into reality.

Two on Two

BRIAN DOYLE

Once upon a time, a long time ago, I rambled through thickets of brawny power forwards and quicksilver cocksure guards and rooted ancient centers, trying to slide smoothly to the hoop, trying to find space in the crowd to get off my shot, trying to maneuver at high speed with the ball around corners and hips and sudden angry elbows, the elbows of twenty years of men in grade school high school college the park the playground the men's league the noon league the summer league, men as high as the seven-foot center I met violently during a summer league game, men as able as the college and professional players I was hammered by in playgrounds, men as fierce as the fellow who once took off his sweats and laid his shotgun down by his cap before he trotted onto the court.

I got hurt, everyone does eventually; I got hurt enough to quit; back pains then back surgery then more surgeries; it was quit or walk, now I walk.

The game receded, fell away, a part of me sliding into the dark like a rocket stage no longer part of the mission. Now I am married and here come my children: my lovely dark thoughtful daughter and then three years later suddenly my squirming twin electric sons and now my daughter is four and my sons are one each and yesterday my daughter and I played two on two against my sons on the lovely burnished oak floor of our dining room, the boys who just learned to walk staggering across the floor like drunken sailors and falling at the slightest touch, my daughter loud lanky in her orange socks sliding from place to place without benefit of a dribble but there is no referee only me on my knees, dribbling behind my back and trick-dribbling through the plump legs of the boys, their diapers sagging, my daughter shrieking with glee, the boys confused and excited, and I am weeping weeping weeping, in love with my perfect magic children, with the feel of the bright-red plastic tiny ball spinning in my hands, my arms at home in the old motions, my head and shoulders snapping fakes on the boys, who laugh; I pick up a loose ball near the dining room table and shuffle so slowly so slowly on my knees toward the toy basket eight feet away, a mile, one hundred miles, my children brushing against my thighs and shoulders like dreams like birds; Joe staggers toward me, reaches for the ball, I wrap it around my back to my left hand, which picks up rapid dribble, Joe loses balance and grabs my hair, Lily slides by suddenly and cuts Joe cleanly away, he takes a couple of hairs with him as he and Lily disappear in a tangle of limbs and laughs, a terrific moving pick, I would stop to admire it but here comes big Liam, lumbering along toward the ball as alluring and bright as the sun; crossover dribble back to my right hand, Liam drops like a stone, he spins on his bottom to stay with the play, I palm ball, show-fake and lean into short fallaway from four feet away, ball hits rim of basket and bounces straight up in the air, Lily slides back into picture and grabs my right hand but I lean east and with the left hand catch and slam the ball into the basket all in one motion; and it bounces off a purple plastic duck and rolls away again under the table, and I lie there on the floor as Joe pulls on my sock and Lily sits on my chest and Liam ever so gently so meticulously so daintily takes off my glasses, and I am happier than I have ever been, ever and ever, amen.

Memories Like Splintered Glass

SUSAN FROMBERG SCHAEFFER

I am in a small black carriage, moving fast. The roof is in place. The gray sidewalk is running away beneath the wheels, as it always runs when you bend over to see it. Ahead of us on a bench is a man in a black coat and black hat. As we come along, moving fast, the sidewalk running and bumping, he slowly raises his hand and waves. Everything about him is slow. He is sitting in front of a gate. It is the gate to the Prospect Park Zoo. He is my great grandfather. Later my mother says I am too young to remember him sitting there.

I am sitting on the dark green linoleum of the kitchen floor, under the sink. Our kitchen window is open and directly across the alley, our neighbor's kitchen window is open. In my kitchen, my mother and grandmother are cooking. Long orange curls of carrot skin drop from their hands into the garbage pail. Across the alley, our neighbor and her mother are also cooking. Their radio is playing, tuned in to the station that plays *Stella Dallas.* When my grandmother notices this, she turns our radio off. Why waste electricity playing ours when we can hear theirs perfectly well? A new and unfamiliar voice comes over the radio. Everyone stops what they are doing. My grandmother's arm is arrested in midair, a wooden spoon almost to her mouth. My mother has turned her head slightly and is staring across the alley at the other kitchen. In that kitchen, too, the women have stopped moving and are staring at us. Someone says, "He's dead." Everyone begins to cry. Much later, when they notice me again, I ask them who is dead. They say Roosevelt is dead. Then they begin crying again. I try to see what difference this makes to me but fail.

Was it summer or winter? I don't remember. The windows were open. But during the day, there was so much cooking on the four burners that the kitchen was perpetually hot and so the windows were open in winter and summer.

If you stand on the corner of our block on Bedford Avenue where it meets Avenue U, and look down, then all the identical houses form a wall of houses that stretch from one end to the other, but the houses are only connected two by two. A narrow alley separates each pair of houses from the next. The houses are identical but they do not look the same. Some have painted their steps and front doors bright red, others blue. The second stories of all the houses have porches, divided from one another by a low brick wall. Some porches are green with potted trees. Others are bright with porch swings, some of which sport brightly striped awnings. Small children hang over the edges of these porches and are pulled back by white-haired women. In many houses, the apartments are divided this way: the grandparents on the first floor, the child and its family on the second floor. These are called mother-daughter houses. Families have not yet heard of separating.

There is a long narrow hall leading down from the second-floor apartment to the narrow front door. No one uses these steps. People come and go on the back steps. They stop on the landing and listen to conversations taking place inside the apartment below them. When the mail comes, someone goes down the long front steps and picks up the mail, the long envelopes that lie in the pool of darkness like a dead bird. This is my job. I ask my mother why I don't get more mail. She says that to get letters you have to write them. It occurs to me that writing is something worth doing. I write letters to my grandmother, who lives in our front room, get stamps from my grandfather, and carefully write our address on the envelopes.

When I can find someone to cross me to the other side of the street, I mail them in the shiny blue box.

I often catch my grandmother putting her letters to me on the floor at the bottom of the steps. She doesn't want to waste money on stamps. After a while I write to my grandfather. Then I begin to get letters of my own.

Everyone comes to our house for Thanksgiving. The big, shiny mahogany table is opened for the adults, the card tables for the children. When anyone is late, his itinerary becomes the subject of discussion. He is taking the IRT or the BMT and walking the rest of the way to the house. He is taking a bus or a trolley and walking the rest of the way. The entire geography of Manhattan and the suburbs spreads out in the air, everyone converging on our house. Of course everyone gets there. No one thinks of crossing a state boundary, of spending more than a few days upstate. Except, perhaps, my uncle, who will one day end up in Sing Sing, at which point he vanishes from conversation we can hear, and is discussed by adults, and then only in whispers.

One Thanksgiving, a strange woman appears with my uncle. She wears bright red lipstick and has black, black hair. She does not send me back to the children's table when I sit in a temporarily empty chair next to her. Later on, I forget her name. Everyone swears there was no such person.

When I am nineteen, again at the table, I look up and say, "Her name was Stella." My mother, grandmother, and aunts look at one another but avoid looking at me. "I remember now," I say.

My aunt says they didn't mention Stella because she wasn't Jewish. My cousin says they didn't mention Stella because she was part of the scheme to sell fraudulent bonds that landed my uncle in Sing Sing. My father says he once went to visit my uncle there and it was a terrible thing. My grandmother says the last time she saw her brother, my uncle, he began singing, "I'm forever blowing bubbles, pretty bubbles in the air, they rise so high, almost touch the sky, then with a quiver, they shiver and die," and he put his head down on his desk and began to cry. A few days later the cleaning woman found him dead in his chair. Of course by now she is crying, too. I understand that I am not always beloved for my memory.

The alleys are wonderful. They quickly fill with snow. In the winter of 1947 there was a blizzard. The drifts came up to the top of the first-floor windows. We burrowed under the drifts knowing we were invisible. I heard my mother's voice shouting for us, quivering with terror. My mother thought we were kidnapped or dead. I liked that. I thought it was very sophisticated.

In the small backyard grows a pussy willow tree. It takes up most of the window, but in winter you can see through it to the houses behind us. In spring it changes its nature. It flowers and the pussy willows appear. Then the branches change one last time and are covered with fuzzy green things. I am sure they are green bees. No one can persuade me to open my window. At night I hear them buzzing. When the moon catches itself in the tree's branches, I become frantic and hide under the blanket. Hot weather and insects: I begin to dislike them both.

I am calling for my friend Tina exactly as she calls for me. None of us ever ring the doorbells. Someone might have a cold. Someone might be working at night. If we wake someone who is sleeping, then our friend's mother will shout at us. Instead we stand in the alley and shout our friend's name. The mother opens the window and asks, You want Tina? and when I say yes, Tina comes to the window and leans out. I ask if she can come out to play. She says yes or no, usually yes. At times she tells me to come in. In our neighborhood, this is an eternal sound: children in alleys, looking up at blank windows, shouting for their friends. No one is yet used to telephones. Everyone views the telephone receiver as a machine capable of sucking the family income into it. I learn to dial my grandparents' early: their number is Dewey 2-0123. The address of my father's loft is 123 Fifth Avenue. I assume we have such low numbers, the first ones I learn, because we got to the city so early. I never tell anyone this theory and so no one contradicts me.

My mother sits in the kitchen with her friend Hilda, who is Puerto Rican. They speak Spanish or what they call Spanish. From my room down the hall, I imitate them. All night long I make noises that sound, to me, exactly like the noises they make.

Finally my mother receives her master's degree. Much later, in a new house, I find her master's thesis in a white cardboard box, at the bottom of a closet in the attic. Hanging above it is her wedding dress, its hem barely brushing the lid of the box. I am older now and when I see the dress brushing the sealed box, I shake my head and say, This will never happen to me.

When my father is a child, he helps my grandfather. Once there is a strike of finishers. My grandfather hires many Italian women to finish his suits. In the morning, he and my father carry the garments up five flights of tenement buildings and in the evening, they climb back up and carry them down again. That night, he and my grandfather walk from the cottage my grandfather rents in Rockaway to take a swim. "I'm tired," says my father.

"You're tired?" says my grandfather. "What did you do?" "What did I do?" says my father, who turns on his heel and walks away. He never works for his father again.

I arrive, followed by my brother, both of us followed by the Depression. My father, who has his law degree, not from Harvard, to which he was accepted, but from CCNY, decides to give up his practice and go into the clothing business. His father pleads with him: he will break his mother's heart. His mother pleads with him: he will break his father's heart. He says he will break his own heart if he cannot support his wife and children. He buys a loft, a cutting table, and begins making suits. When I complain about my maps or reports, he says, Inability is no excuse. He made up his entire law school thesis, he tells me. He sat around and listened to the men talk in his father's place and he wrote down what he heard there. For this thesis—on the unions and the men's clothing business—he graduates with honors. A few months later, he sneaks into the school library and steals the only copies of his thesis. He doesn't want to be found out. It occurs to me that his sayings have become mine, that his methods are also mine.

After my grandfather is shot, my grandmother comes to live with us. According to her, nothing my father does is good enough for us. For instance we have a very shabby car with at least three rust spots. Every day she stops and points out a car to us: This is the kind of car my daughter should have, she tells my father. Naturally we do not see what is wrong with our car, which always starts and always keeps going until we arrive, usually at my father's mother's house.

One morning we are about to leave for the bungalow colony and our annual summer vacation. When we come downstairs, my grandmother points to a shiny red Hudson and says, This is the kind of car my daughter should have.

Then get in, my father says.

I wish I could get in, says my grandmother.

Here, says my father. I'll open the door for you.

Irving! says my mother. Don't touch that car!

My father opens the door. Get in, he tells my grandmother.

Well, he says, if you won't get in, I'll try it out. He opens the door and sits down in the front seat, behind the wheel.

The idiot wants to get himself arrested for nothing, my grandmother says.

Edith, says my father. Get in.

My mother looks up and down the street, opens the back door and gets in. That's enough, Irving, she says.

Tell the children to get in, my father says. Get in! he shouts at us. We climb in over my mother.

My father has his hand over the car horn. Don't touch that! says my grandmother. You'll bring a policeman running!

My father honks the horn. In the back seat, we are terrified.

My father takes out a key and starts the car. What are you doing? my grandmother and mother scream at once.

My father pulls away from the curb. You said this is the kind of car your daughter should have, he says. Now she has it.

A stolen car, says my grandmother.

It's not stolen, says my mother. Is it, Irving?

No, it's not stolen, he says. What's left to complain about now? he asks my grandmother.

That a daughter of mine should have to live in a rented house! she says.

My grandmother lives with us until, according to my father, she comes after him with a knife. And why does she come after him with a knife? Naturally because of me. I misbehave all day long and then when he comes home my mother reports on my doings and he is expected to spank me. One evening, advancing upon me, my grandmother—armed with a kitchen knife—advanced upon him. Don't touch the child, she says.

I won't live with a woman who comes after me with a knife, my father says. After that, my grandmother lives in a small apartment on Cortelyou Road. I become a constant visitor. I am everyone's audience, if not confidante. No one seems to think I understand what I'm told.

My grandmother left my grandfather because he was jealous and threatened her with a knife to get the truth out of her. Also he followed her everywhere. She would turn around on the street and find him trying to hide himself behind a lamppost. I thought: How exciting life is! The adults who appear so dull do all these things! When my grandmother and I took the train to the movies, I would stare up and down the long gray platform, looking for my grandfather, hiding behind one of the posts. I never see him. I am insulted: Am I not worth following? Don't tell your grandfather what I said, my grandmother tells me.

Don't tell your grandmother I let you eat a bacon sandwich, says my grandfather. I am stuffed with things I can't tell anyone else. But when we come home, my grandmother inhales my coat collar and says, I know what you've been eating. Then shouts come from the living room. But the next week, we do the same thing.

At least twice a year we are taken into Manhattan to shop: winter coats, spring coats. Then we go to Macy's and walk through the bridge connecting the two sections of the store. We come back on the train. The train seats are covered in woven, lacquered rattan and leave their criss-crossed pattern on our knees. When we are back in Brooklyn, I sit up, looking for the fountain that plays all year long in back of one of the tall apartment buildings. It is the most glamorous thing I have ever seen. Except, perhaps, for my aunt's elevator, whose floor numbers turn bright red when the elevator reaches them. I walk to her house, ride up and down in her elevator, and eat junket, a slippery pudding that appears to me an elegant food. Then I walk home. I walk to the library for my books and when I come home the marshy, empty fields are to my left. Occasionally a duck rises up out of them and flies in front of the setting sun in front of the cattails.

There is nothing to fear from the city. But my grandmother says: Never go into a public bathroom. There is a bad man with scissors who hides in there and cuts off the braids of little girls.

Every day my father goes to The Place. The Place is a clothing loft on Fifth Avenue. One-Two-Three Fifth Avenue. At home, my favorite story is "Bluebeard." I learn to read it when no one else will read it to me: they say they are sick of it. The loft reminds me of Bluebeard's house: thousands and thousands of suits, black, gray, brown, blue, bodies without heads or hands or feet hanging in the air, terribly sad places, these lofts, the same thing again and again, so that even a minute seems like a month, a year, a lifetime. Lofts are places to get out of.

But in the back is the scrap barrel, filled with scraps of suit-lining, silk, brilliant colors, red, orange, patterned blues, all shining, odd-shaped, some suited to dolls' clothes. I find a bag and pack it up with scraps.

We are familiar with many lofts, not just this one. If we need skirts, we are taken to my uncle's Place, and fitted out with whatever he has available.

Then a tailor stands us on a chair and marks the clothing with waxy soap. This is how we get our jackets, many of our coats, our hats, even our party dresses. For some time it seems that no one's Place makes shoes, but one winter, my father comes home with four pairs of boots and four pairs of galoshes. They fit us perfectly and he is well pleased with himself.

When I am older, and once more in The Place, I notice rows and rows of navy blue suit jackets, their bright gold buttons marked with large, noticeable R's. My father's store is named Remley Clothes. I think the buttons are advertising the store. What are all these R's doing here? I ask my father. Oscar de la Renta wants it that way, he says.

Because of my father's Place and the many other Places we visit, I begin to acquire a peculiar view of Manhattan. While we press our heads to the cold plate glass windows, watching the snow or the rain fall upon the hurrying black and gray people on the sidewalk below, the people we know manufacture beautiful clothing for the exquisite people we see when we go to look at the Christmas windows. Every now and then, I see a man dressed in a suit whose jacket buttons are conspicuously marked with R's. I know where the jacket comes from. I know who makes it.

My father, dressed in his baggy clothes, gives the order to the cutter: how many suits, how many jackets. The tailor, who is five feet, one inch tall, finishes the garments. This is where glamour comes from: from my father's Place. He is entirely unimpressed with it. So am I. Anything a family member can create is homely, not glamorous. From all this, a vision of the city grows up: all over, in lofts, unglamorous creatures create costumes for people who would look glamorous. What is the difference between them? I am too young to understand money. The difference must be in what role someone wants to play. At any moment someone can change his mind. The underside of glamour is forever the man in the baggy suit, the tailor, or finisher, who is almost a dwarf. Sometimes the glamorous people come to the Place and leave with a suit in a garment bag. It is as if they have lost their way. It is as if they are giving away a secret by coming to this world, the wrong side of the fabric, where all the threads show, the tangly, chaotic wrong side of the tapestry.

You have to get dressed up, my mother says.

What is she saying, really? Tomorrow you will be a changeling. When the sun goes down, you can change back. Why are these metamorphoses necessary? In the city they are.

My grandfather owns a pharmacy, which means that he has a telephone before anyone else, and people who come into his store call him Doctor Levine. He also has a soda fountain so that when I come to the store in my snowsuit, I am set on a stool and given an ice cream soda. I prefer eggnogs with coffee ice cream although I am tempted by the pink concoctions in tall cups ordered by the girls from the high school. The bottles behind the counter are lined with jars and inside are pills and liquids of all colors. Behind the counter, my grandfather is grinding something with his brass mortar and pestle. A woman farther down the counter asks for a cup of coffee and gives it to her daughter to drink: to warm her up after the ice cream soda. My grandfather frowns.

I regard my grandfather as mine, the way a child regards his dog as his personal possession. He is only five feet, two inches tall.

Some time before I was born, a man came into his store. He had a gun and asked my grandfather for opium. My grandfather saw the man intended to shoot him and took his own gun from the cash register and shot the man instead. In due course, the man died. My mother kept the newspaper accounts of this accident and one day I found them. The assailant was a tall man, over six feet tall.

One day the man's sister came to my grandfather's pharmacy and asked if Mr. Levine was there. He said he was. She said she was the dead man's sister and that he should not feel bad because sooner or later someone was going to shoot her brother and she was glad it was sooner. But my grandfather never got over having shot a man. My mother said he was such a good shot because in Russia he was expected to shoot the foxes who raided the chicken coop.

Later, my grandmother and grandfather separated, and my grandfather, who had retired, went back to work. A man came in, took out a gun, and asked my grandfather for the money. My grandfather had his gun in his cash register but he did not want to shoot another man. The man took the money and shot him. My grandfather died that night in the hospital. I found this out when I went into my mother's room and asked her if she knew where my book was and she said, "Don't bother me! Didn't I have enough for one night? They killed my father!"

Thus we learn blame. If the first man had not come, if my grandfather had not killed him, he would have shot he second man. He would not have died as he did. If my grandmother had not separated from him he would not have gone back to work and would not have been in the store when the second armed man came in. If things could be undone, if time could be wound back, like a film, if the past could be kept alive to compensate for the deficiencies of the present: these are the wishes that form character, that grow out of events that form character. It does not take much. The tree bends once, twice, then does not bend again. It grows now as it always will.

My grandmother, like my mother, is a great lover of movies and decides she is going to see *Gone with the Wind* the day it opens. She takes her lunch with her, two egg salad sandwiches and a slice of banana cake in a brown bag, but when she gets to Radio City Music Hall, the line is already halfway around the block. When an usher comes by, she collapses at his feet and when he helps her up, she tells him she has a terrible heart. He scolds her and takes her inside.

The first person seated, she opens up her bag, eats her egg salad sandwiches and looks around at the canopies and velvet curtains. Well satisfied, she watches *Gone with the Wind.* My mother asks her, "Aren't you ashamed?" but of course she is not.

My great-grandmother saved her son's life when his diphtheria closed his throat and he began to strangle. She poured boiling hot buttermilk down his throat. It opened and somehow he survived. Later, other women brought their choking children to her and she applied the same remedy and most of them survived.

We take a train to the orthodontist's office, and as I sit in the dentist's chair I stare out at the Statue of Liberty and here, I think, a sense of irony begins to stir. On the way back, when we walk down the steps from the train station, if I have behaved, my mother buys each of us either a frankfurter or a charlotte russe. We both have to buy the same thing. A charlotte russe is a little slice of sponge cake set in a round cardboard cylinder whose upper border is serrated so that it looks like a crown. A whirl of sweetened whipped cream rests upon and rises above the sponge cake and the pure white cardboard of the cylinder. I am always very careful when I am ready to eat the last bite: If I drop it, it will seem as if I have missed the best part. The charlotte russes, that look like mysterious, foreign buildings built of snow. The dollhouses in the toy store windows that I stop and stare at on the way home. To see these things, it is worth opening one's mouth to the drill.

I am in the school play at PS 206. It is my job to hold up a sign that says, I AM WHEAT. I am terrified for days in advance, and when it is my turn, I say "I AM WHEAT" as quickly as possible. It occurs to me I would rather write the plays than act in them.

My father's "Place" is not just one place. While we are at his Place, everyone else talks about his Place. Some of my uncles work for my grandfather, in his Place, and they tell endless stories about one of the uncles who is very lazy but is also married to my grandfather's youngest daughter, the baby of the family. One day my uncle followed my grandfather around the shop, talking, and finally sat down on a chair. My grandfather, who was a very short man but very strong, became so enraged that he picked my uncle up, chair and all, and threw him over the cutting table.

When we go to my grandfather's Place, he is cutting peacoats because he has a contract with the Navy. During the Second World War, he cut uniforms for the Army. He is a very wealthy man now, as he was once before when he had a limousine, a chauffeur and little crystal vases filled with fresh flowers fastened to the side of the car. During the Depression he lost everything and wanted to give up and open a dry cleaning store. My grandmother refused to hear of such a thing. "So you'll sit all day while the machines go around and we'll starve," she said. My father always said she forced him to go back into the business. He bought a truck and a sewing machine and began selling suits from the back of it. Eventually he had more sewing machines and enough money to rent a loft. Then the war came and he became a millionaire.

Whenever I am in his Place, there are whispered discussions about how to handle the government inspectors when they come around. His Place is more crowded than my father's and noisier. He is always shouting.

One night my father comes home late. It seems he was robbed. The burglars tied him, his tailor, and his cutter to their chairs and stole two hundred pairs of pants. My father says, It wouldn't have bothered me so much if they'd taken the whole suit.

What am I going to do with two hundred pairs of suits and no pants? Later he says, We should get out of the city. Everyone looks blank. There is no world beyond the city. At the edge of the knowable universe is Monticello and Rhinebeck where wives and children are sent for the cooler summers. Leave the city?

Every now and then, someone calls and says, "You have to come and see my loft." My new agent has a loft whose address is 105 Fifth Avenue. One-Two-Three Fifth Avenue is not far away.

I cannot go into these lofts without seeing the almost-invisible blue and black and gray racks of suits stretching into the distance. The shadows of my family walk among the brightly colored modern furniture. The ebony bathrooms remind me of the old toilet in the Place. It flushed when you pulled a wooden handle attached to a long chain that descended from a white box just beneath the bathroom ceiling. As you come up to these lofts, I am run down by the same mobile clothing racks that were pushed through the same streets when I was a child. But there are less and less lofts used for clothing manufacturing. Publishers have taken them over, agents, artists who want "great spaces." I remember when a loft was a great space if it was large enough to hold the order that had to be filled.

I look at streets on the Lower East Side that have been restored in the interest of preserving the city's cultural heritage and remember stories I was told about children who came home and shouted up for the key and their mothers leaned out the fifth-floor window and threw the key, wrapped in a rag, down to them.

It seems clear to me now that in the fate of the individuals the fate of the city was already written and was probably already readable: the separation of my grandmother and grandfather, my grandfather's death in his drugstore, the closing down of one Place after another. Fewer and fewer things come from the ubiquitous Place. Things come from Burma and Thailand and Ecuador. It is as if some magical walls surrounding the city have fallen.

Everything repeats itself, but unnaturally. The women in the kitchen cried for a president dead of natural causes.

You eat the city's food, you sense the mood of the city, like cold air, like the touch of a wild animal's cold fur, on your skin, and all of this forms you. Because I was told so often of what the city was like for my great-grandparents and grandparents, I saw how the city was already changing. I was formed not only by my own experiences of the city, but also theirs. I became reclusive, as if I had already lived many lives in the city. There was always someone to tell me what had happened before my birth or what was happening ten miles from where I lived. Everything was equally alive, equally present, as if I had no sense of past time. It never seemed that my own life was bounded by the years in which I myself had lived. Everyone else's story—everyone else's city—flowed in and out of me. I am still not sure there is such a thing as past time. Writing as preserving, writing as memory, writing as elegy: This was what I wanted to do. With few exceptions, my books are inhabited by the characters, by themes, the city thrusts upon me: Vietnam veterans, movie stars first glimpsed in the great movie palaces, in Radio City Music Hall, women from the Caribbean, one of whom worked for us for over twenty years.

The city is a kind of parent. You may not like it. You may flee from it. But, one way or another, against your will or with your cooperation, it forms you. I tell the stories of the past in the present tense, because, when I heard these stories, they were not over. They were happening before my eyes and they continue to happen, bits of time refugee from another present, stuck in my own. In the end, we are not cut whole from one bolt of cloth. In the end, we are all parti-colored quilts stitched up in the one "Place" that still remains: the city, the world.

In Search of Alice Walker, or Alice Doesn't Live Here Anymore

VALERIE BOYD

Alice Walker hasn't arrived yet.

On this warm, wet October evening, a patchwork quilt of people is gathering at the Crowne Plaza Hotel in Macon, Georgia. The mayor is here, along with several members of the City Council. The movers and shakers mingle uneasily with the town's backbone—the working-class Black folks who are here, too, at twenty-five dollars a head, to have dinner with Alice Walker, to hug her neck, as we say here in the South, and to watch her receive the 1997 Shelia Award from the Tubman African-American Museum—the town's vanguard cultural institution.

This event promises to be a homecoming of sorts for Alice Walker. Many of her relatives—the Grants, from her mother's side of the family—live in Macon. And, at about 7:00 p.m., as these close and distant kinfolk make their way to the tables reserved for them, they are all aglow in sequins, polyester, and family pride.

Alice's older sister, Ruth Walker-Hood, is here with her fourteen-year-old grandson. One of Alice's big brothers has driven from Eatonton—the town about forty miles down the road, where Alice grew up—to bring her some homemade fruit preserves. Someone else has brought her an old black-and-white photograph of herself, taken at least thirty years ago. Two young women from Atlanta—an hour and a half away—have brought her flowers.

I also have come from Atlanta, along with a couple of other members of the Alice Walker Literary Society, an international organization founded at Spelman College and Emory University last year to urge readers, both scholarly and casual, to become immersed in Walker's works.

I was baptized in Alice Walker's words more than fifteen years ago by the late great Chicago novelist Leon Forrest, in an African-American literature class at Northwestern University. I had read Walker before, in high school, but what Professor Forrest encouraged was beyond reading—it was reveling.

One of the first books I remember diving into, heart-first, was *Meridian,* Walker's 1976 tale of a young civil rights activist whose caring for her people sometimes outweighed her need to take care of herself. When I first read *Meridian,* I was a seventeen-year-old whose political and literary sensibilities were just awakening. And, because I recognized something of myself in Meridian Hill, the tenderness and tautness of that novel gripped me like nothing else I'd ever read.

I felt a similar burst of recognition a year or so later when I read Walker's 1983 essay collection, *In Search of Our Mothers' Gardens.* I read the book the same summer that I came home from college to help care for my sick grandmother.

An Alabama sharecropper, my grandmother was a loud, boisterous woman who liked to laugh, liked to eat and, most of all, liked to talk.

This summer, though, my grandmother couldn't talk. She'd had a stroke a few months earlier, and she could only communicate with her eyes, her sounds, her tears.

As I dressed her for bed each night, and dressed her for the day each morning, I realized how much talking we hadn't done. I realized that I had so many questions for her—about my father's childhood memory of her holding a Ku Klux Klansman at bay with a shotgun; about her forty-seven-year marriage to my grandfather, whose death a few years earlier had drawn a permanent veil across her face; about the "hoodoo sack" she always wore close to heart—even now, as she knocked on heaven's door.

My grandmother never answered these questions; she died a few months after our summer of silence.

I did, however, find answers to the mysteries of my Grandma Ura in reading Alice Walker's *In Search of Our Mothers' Gardens.* In the title essay, she talks about her own mother, a Georgia sharecropper who "adorned with flowers whatever shabby house" the Walkers lived in.

"Because of her creativity with flowers," Walker writes, "even my memories of poverty are seen through a screen of blooms."

Her mother, Walker explains in this essay, was an artist whose canvas was her garden.

That summer of 1984, reading this essay at my grandmother's bedside, I realized that she, too, was an artist—and her artistry was right before my eyes. It was in her quilts, which adorned every bed in the house.

Made of bits and pieces of worthless rags, the quilts were priceless displays of creativity and imagination. And my grandmother had made dozens of them.

After she died, my parents and I discovered in her house a closet full of quilts—stacked, literally, from floor to ceiling. There was "the double wedding ring quilt," "the wind mill," "the drunken path"—patterns whose names my parents recalled easily. My favorite was the one whose name made my parents blush: "the pussy quilt"—a sort of prefeminist, unabashed paean to the flowery beauty of the vulva. This quilt hangs in my home today.

Alice Walker—whose 1992 novel, *Possessing the Secret of Joy,* is dedicated "to the blameless vulva"—would like this quilt, I'm sure. When I asked my parents why I'd never seen the quilt, or the countless others crowded in my grandmother's closet, they explained that these were just old quilts "for everyday use"; there was no need to display them.

Soon after, I read a short story by Alice Walker, called "Everyday Use," about a quiltmaker whose artistry wasn't always recognized. When I read that story, which could have been about my grandmother, I knew, in a profound and enduring way, that Alice Walker and I were kindred spirits.

Since that summer, I've consumed each of Walker's books—her five novels, two collections of short stories, four collections of essays and five volumes of poetry—with a kind of hunger.

A more common hunger is creeping upon me now, though, as I warily eye the wilting lettuce that constitutes the pitiful first course of this banquet. As I look around, I realize that for most people here, as for me, the food isn't the main attraction. While a few folks are gamely chomping on their nutrient-free iceberg, most people are watching the door, looking for Alice.

This is not the first time I've been in a small Georgia town looking for Alice Walker. A few weeks earlier, on a radiant, no-humidity day, I'd taken a drive to Eatonton, about seventy-five miles east of Atlanta.

I'm not sure what I was looking for there, but I do know that as I've become more and more of a writer, my sense of connection to Alice Walker has continued to grow.

Like Walker, I was born and raised in Georgia, though I know, even before I visit Eatonton, that it is a far cry from Atlanta, my hometown. And, like Walker, I count Zora Neale Hurston, another Black Southern-born writer, as my literary foremother. Recently, though, it occurred to me that if Zora is my spiritual and artistic grandmother, a literary counterpart to my quilt-making Grandma Ura, then Alice Walker—who put a marker on Hurston's weed-choked grave in 1973—is my mother.

So I suppose I took my drive to Eatonton, to borrow Alice's phrase, in search of my mother's garden.

Heading into town on Highway 441, I am greeted by a flurry of signs: "Welcome to Putnam County, Dairy Capital of the US." I make a note of this and remember it later when the sight of cows grazing along the countryside has become commonplace.

Then I see a more revealing sign: A huge billboard urges passers-by to "Join the Sons of Confederate Veterans." I don't write down the 800-number, but I do notice the Confederate flags adorning either side of the billboard.

"You're not in Atlanta anymore," I tell myself. "You're in Georgia."

More signs follow: "Lawrence's BBQ"; "General Putnam's Motel and Restaurant"; "Country Buffet, All You Can Eat, $6." Then I see the one I've been looking for: "Welcome to Historic Eatonton, Home of Joel Chandler Harris and Alice Walker." Walker's name is below Harris's and at least a point size smaller. On the same sign, Eatonton brags that it is "Close to Everything … Next to Perfect."

Within the next three miles, I see three signs inviting me to visit the Uncle Remus Museum and reminding me that Eatonton is the birthplace of Joel Chandler Harris, author of the infamous Uncle Remus tales. I don't see any more Alice Walker signs.

When I walk into the little yellow house that is home to the Eatonton-Putnam Chamber of Commerce and the Tourist Information Center, I am greeted by a woman with platinum blond hair, wide blue eyes, and a Band-Aid struggling to hold down a wad of cotton in the crook of her right elbow. She seems surprised to see me. As her eyes do a quick sweep, checking out my purple batik pants and down-the-back dreadlocks, I tell her that I am visiting Eatonton for the first time and would like to explore the area attractions.

She recommends, with a straight face, the Uncle Remus Museum, the Tour of Homes, and the nearby Lake Oconee and Lake Sinclair Recreation areas, pulling down brochures from a bookshelf.

"What about Alice Walker?" I ask. "I'm interested in Alice Walker."

"Of course," the woman says perkily. She pulls a lilac-colored brochure off the shelf and hands it to me. On the front, there's a fifteen-year-old black-and-white photograph of Alice Walker, back when she was still wearing an Afro—the same photo that was on the cover of *In Search of Our Mothers' Gardens.*

Inside the trifold brochure, the literary chronology only goes up to 1992's publication of *Possessing the Secret of Joy.* The brochure doesn't mention Walker's more recent books—*The Same River Twice* and *Anything We Love Can Be Saved.* Still, I'm heartened by the fact that the brochure even exists and that it promises an Alice Walker Driving Tour.

Yet the Chamber employee seems a bit apologetic, warning me that the driving tour is strictly for driving. "You can't get out and walk around on the property," she says, "because Alice Walker still has family who live in the area."

"Really?" I ask. "What family?"

"Sisters and cousins, I believe," the woman replies. Actually, the brochure—which the Chamber employee obviously hasn't read in a while—says Alice's brother, Fred, now lives in the house where their mother was born. The brochure doesn't mention that two more of Alice's brothers—Jimmy and Bobby—are also among the town's 4,737 residents.

"So has the chamber asked Alice Walker about doing more to mark her origins in Eatonton?" I ask.

"Yes, we have," the woman replies, bright-eyed as ever.

"And she's said no?" I prompt, sounding more suspicious than I mean to.

"Yes. I mean, since she's still alive and all, she just doesn't want us to do a lot. And I can't blame her. I'd probably be the same way if I was her," she adds. "I mean, the Uncle Remus stuff is dead. But she's still alive, and she's still got family here. So we try real hard to protect her privacy."

Privacy is important to Alice, her sister Ruth Walker-Hood acknowledges. But there's more to it than that. The truth, according to Ruth, is that any efforts Eatonton wants to make now to honor Alice Walker may be too little, too late.

For instance, Ruth says, the local newspaper, The Eatonton Messenger, never reported Alice's successes—despite Ruth's constant calls—until the day she won the Pulitzer Prize in 1983. "That day, the paper called me," Ruth says.

"Alice has reached the very top of her field. And she's done it without the support of her hometown, and I'm quite sure she doesn't need it now," Ruth says.

So if Alice doesn't care about being properly honored in her hometown, why should I? Why should you?

We should care because Alice Walker is a leading light in the literary world and should be properly recognized as such, not just in cosmopolitan places like New York or San Francisco—where she currently lives, and where her book signings often attract block-long lines of readers—but everywhere, particularly in her hometown.

We should care because Eatonton's refusal to honor her—its insistence, in fact, on making her subservient to a lesser writer, Joel Chandler Harris—is historically and politically incorrect, an insult to anyone who believes in literature as a tool for revelation and revolution.

We should care for the same reason that Ruth cares: "It's important to give these kids today someone to look up to. You can see her, you can touch her, you can ask her questions. We need to let these kids know that a little Black girl from Eatonton has reached this level."

Guided by the map inside the brochure, the first place I find is the church. As I get out of my citified green sports car to walk around—in defiance of the Chamber of Commerce's recommendation—a warm breeze rustles through the congregation of trees on the side of the tiny white church, and I notice that the yard seems to attract more than its share of butterflies.

In case you've forgotten that you're on the Alice Walker Driving Tour, there is a small purple sign—maroon, really— to remind you. Anchored in the church yard by a wooden stake, the metal sign has an icon of a woman sitting in a rocking chair—recognizable as Celie from Walker's Pulitzer Prize-winning novel, *The Color Purple.* This church, the sign says, is where "Alice Malsenior Walker was baptized and faithfully attended services."

Near the front door of the church, a hand-drawn sign is decorated with an old rugged cross, colored a fading gray. The sign says: "Ward Chapel AME Church. Service every 2nd. and 4th. Sunday." Later, Ruth tells me that because the old church's descendants "are scattered to the four corners," services are no longer held here—not even on the second and fourth Sundays. These days, the church is only used for an occasional funeral.

Still, despite the too-high grass around the steps, the broken windowpanes and the nineteen crushed Budweiser cans strewn in the back yard, there is something about this church that remains alive.

Perhaps it's the butterflies and the birds, which seem to guard the church from malevolent spirits. I wonder if cardinals and robins ever fly through the broken glass and into the sanctuary during the eulogies or, better yet, while the choir is sending some soul home with "Amazing Grace."

Alice Walker likes birds. I recently heard her talk about this in an audiotaped interview, called "My Life as My Self." She specifically talks about vultures, considered sacred in many African countries—particularly in Egypt—because they can eat death and not die. I wonder if vultures ever come to the funerals at Wards Chapel AME I wonder if the people know that the big dark birds are holy—or if they are frightened when the vultures appear.

The church is, as Alice Walker has written, "simple, serene, sweet." In a 1986 article in *The Eatonton Messenger,* Fannie L. Simpkins put it even better: "The big church is still moving. One of my reasons for saying it's big is because Jesus is there, second is because Alice Walker came out of it.'"

Across the street from the church is the Wards Chapel Cemetery, where Alice's parents—Willie Lee Walker and Minnie Tallulah Grant Walker—are buried, along with other family members. Another *Color Purple* sign marks the spot. Surely, Alice Walker had something to do with the stone on her mother's tomb. It says simply: "Loving Soul, Great Spirit."

My map leads me three-tenths of a mile up Wards Chapel Road to another *Color Purple* sign, this one marking the site of the home where Alice Walker grew up. The house that sits on the huge expanse of farmland is a small wooden cabin that looks too new to be the actual home where Alice was raised. It sits far back from the road, and a long gravelly trail leads to it. Several slender black-and-white cows lounge contentedly on nature's green carpet.

Less than two miles up the road is the site of Walker's birth home. A foreboding fence protects the land from trespassers. Just outside the fence, though, is another purple sign, and behind the sign is a stubby, stocky wild tree. A funeral flower is laid lovingly at the foot of the tree, next to a white cross with a name that at first glance appears to be "Janie" stenciled across it. This makes me think of Janie from Zora Neale Hurston's novel *Their Eyes Were Watching God*—about which Walker has said: "There is no book more important to me than this one." On closer inspection, I see that the name of the person being remembered here is Jamie. As I wonder who this Jamie was, and if she died in that spot, the intoxicating smell of pine trees wafts through the air.

I drive on, looking for the fifth and final stop of the Alice Walker Driving Tour—the Grant Plantation, the birthplace of Alice's mother. I can't find it, despite three attempts. No *Color Purple* sign marks the spot. There is, however, a sign for Uncle Remus Realty, whose mascot is a nattily attired, dancing white rabbit. Br'er Rabbit, I suppose.

At the Uncle Remus Museum—situated in the center of town—the rabbit hailing passersby is a dirty gray, but he's still nattily dressed. The museum is catty-corner to the Putnam Middle School. The kids, Black and white together, have a good view of the former slave cabin that became the Uncle Remus Museum in 1963—the same year another famous Georgian, Martin Luther King Jr., gave his "I Have a Dream" speech.

Joel Chandler Harris is heralded—in this town, damn near worshipped—as the creator of Uncle Remus. But even Harris admitted his creativity was questionable: "[Uncle Remus] was not an invention of my own," Harris said in an interview once, "but a human syndicate, I might say, of three or four old darkies whom I knew. I just walloped them together into one person and called him 'Uncle Remus.'"

Alice Walker wrote eloquently about her hometown's strange exaltation of Harris in a 1981 essay called "The Dummy in the Window: Joel Chandler Harris and the Invention of Uncle Remus," which is collected in her book *Living by the Word.*

"Joel Chandler Harris is billed as the creator of Uncle Remus. Uncle Remus told the stories of Br'er Rabbit and Br'er Fox, all the classic folk tales that came from Africa and that, even now in Africa, are still being told. We, too, my brothers and sisters and I, listened to them," Walker writes.

"But after we saw *Song of the South* [the 1946 film of Uncle Remus and the little white children to whom he told his tales], we no longer listened to them. They were killed for us. In fact, I do not remember any of my relatives ever telling any of those tales after they saw what had been done with them."

A generation younger than Alice Walker, I never saw *Song of the South,* and my parents never told me Uncle Remus tales. But, even in relatively progressive Atlanta, I've had my own encounters with Joel Chandler Harris.

For years, I lived around the corner from the Wren's Nest, the huge Victorian home where Harris resided for many years, and where he died in 1908. Though it is described as "a shrine to Harris's memory," the Wren's Nest never had the impact on my psyche that the Uncle Remus Museum apparently had on Walker's.

Here's why: the historic home is in the middle of what is now an all-Black neighborhood, and it is surrounded by what Eatonton lacks—images that tell a different story about Black people.

Two blocks down the street from the Wren's Nest, for instance, is the Shrine of the Black Madonna bookstore, where Walker and countless other African American authors read and sign their books. Also nearby is an African American fine arts museum called the Hammonds House; a massive church that, in my childhood, was pastored by civil rights leader Ralph David Abernathy; a Black-owned photography studio; and the Atlanta University Center, an educational complex that includes the well-regarded Morehouse College (Dr. King's alma mater) and Spelman College (where the Alice Walker Literary Society was chartered).

At the Wren's Nest itself, the storyteller-in-residence is an African-American poet who renders the tales of Br'er Rabbit and Br'er Fox in their original African context. Wearing a traditional dashiki and long beard, the storyteller, Akbar Imhotep, resembles a West African griot—not an Uncle Remus.

Eatonton doesn't have these kinds of balancing images. In addition to the Uncle Remus Museum, Alice Walker writes, "there was also, until a few years ago, an Uncle Remus restaurant. There used to be a dummy of a Black man, an elderly, kindly, cottony-haired darkie, seated in a rocking chair in the restaurant window. In fantasy, I frequently liberated him, using Army tanks and guns. Blacks, of course, were not allowed in this restaurant."

Almost to my surprise, I am allowed in Eatonton's Uncle Remus Museum. The museum volunteer, a gracious Southern belle named Kathryn Walden, greets me warmly and invites me to sign the guest book. I am the thirty-fifth adult visitor of the day, she proudly announces. As I sign in, I notice that earlier visitors had come from as far away as Pennsylvania and Massachusetts.

"Oh, yes," Mrs. Walden assures me. "We get about a thousand visitors a month. And we've had visitors from all fifty states and thirty-right foreign countries."

I had heard that the museum's docent keeps a folder of information on Alice Walker here at Uncle Remus headquarters. I guess the logic would be to put both of the town's famous African Americans under one roof.

But when I ask Mrs. Walden about it, she says, "No, we don't have anything on her here," emphasizing the last word. "I hope they're going to do something for her—like start a museum for her—but we don't have anything about her here."

As I cautiously make my way around the museum, I am captivated by newspaper clippings of stories covering the Harris Centennial Celebration on December 9, 1948—the day that would have been Joel Chandler Harris' one hundredth birthday. Alice Walker had been born a few years before the Centennial Celebration, on February 9, 1944.

Reading the newspaper reports, I wonder if Alice's parents knew Sam Cole, the local actor who portrayed Uncle Remus during the celebration. I wonder if her parents read *The Atlanta Constitution*'s coverage of the event, which reportedly included "a parade that circled the Confederate monument on Eatonton's main street, passing storefronts decorated in antebellum fashion."

I wonder if Alice and her siblings were among the children the reporter referred to when he wrote this: "And the descendants of Uncle Remus' darky friends took part, too, with Negro school children marching along."

A couple of white kids come into the museum with their grandmother. They are fascinated by the bolls of cotton placed in a basket in a brightly lit corner of the slave cabin. They want to buy some to take home.

Near the bale of cotton, an old tin poster advertises Uncle Remus brand syrup. It features a picture of a smiling, bearded Black man—the typical portrait of Uncle Remus—along with what are presumably his words: "Dis sho' am good."

I am surprised as a rush of shame heats up my face. I am embarrassed that these white children see this poster and accept it as a true representation of a Black man, past or present. They don't blink at the exaggerated mockery of his words—words that a white advertising copywriter imagined an uneducated Black man would say; words that are alien to me and every Black person I've ever known, including poorly educated folks from Uncle Remus' generation—people like my Grandma Ura.

"Joel Chandler Harris and I lived in the same town, although nearly one hundred years apart," Alice Walker has said. "As far as I'm concerned, he stole a good part of my heritage. How did he steal it? By making me feel ashamed of it."

At the Eatonton-Putnam County Library, things are a little more egalitarian. The library carries most of Alice Walker's books and, in the library computer, her name appears forty times. To be fair, there are also forty occurrences of Br'er Rabbit, and—edging out the competition—forty-two of Joel Chandler Harris.

I ask one of the librarians if there is a special Alice Walker collection.

She wants to educate me on Walker's versatility as a writer: "No, we don't have a special collection separate from everything else because she writes all kinds of books. Some are fiction, some are poetry, some are essays—"

"Yes, I'm familiar with her work," I interrupt.

"Now, I do have a vertical file of clippings I've kept over the years in my office," she offers.

"So are the materials in the vertical file accessible to the public?"

"Yes. Well, it's in my office. But I can bring the materials out to you." Somewhat reluctantly, the woman steps through a glass door.

I am excited. This is what I want to see. Not just a little folder on Alice in the Uncle Remus Museum, but a vertical file. A whole file.

The librarian brings out a thin manila folder. "Here it is," she announces.

Trying to suspend my disbelief, I phrase my question delicately: "This is everything you have, right?"

"Uh-hunh. You can sit right there and go through it," she says, pointing to a table within her eyeshot, so she can make sure I don't try to sneak off with this treasure chest of information.

"Thanks," I say dryly.

The most recent clipping in the folder is from 1994—and it's not even about Alice, but about her daughter, feminist writer/activist Rebecca Leventhal Walker, named by *Time* magazine in this December 5, 1994, article as one of the fifty "most promising leaders age forty and under." The most recent clippings about Alice herself are undated stories from *The Eatonton Messenger* concerning her 1992 visit to Eatonton with television newswoman Diane Sawyer, who did a segment about Walker for *Primetime Live.*

Among the other gems in the folder: an undated review of Alice Walker's first published book of poetry, 1968's *Once;* an undated clipping of a 1975 *Ms.* magazine article by Walker called "Beyond the Peacock: The Reconstruction of Flannery O'Connor"; a January 8, 1984, cover story on Walker in *The New York Times Magazine*; and *The Eatonton Messenger*'s extensive January 23, 1986, coverage (including a full page of photos) of Alice's visit to Eatonton for the premiere of the film version of *The Color Purple* at the now-closed Pex Theatre.

Alice's sister, Ruth, who organized the premiere at the Pex, is surprised when I tell her the library has copies of Walker's books. "Once upon a time," she says, "the library had two *Color Purple*s and that's it."

Still, there's no place in Eatonton to buy *The Color Purple* or any other book by Alice Walker—though you can buy many of Joel Chandler Harris' books at the museum.

The only bookstore in town is a Christian bookstore, Ruth explains, and the people there don't sell Alice's books. If Ruth supplies them, though, the folks at Yarbrough's Jewelry Store will sell Walker's titles.

A vocal champion of Alice and her writing, Ruth used to be better about keeping the jewelry store stocked. Before 1993, when their mother was living and Ruth made the drive from Atlanta to Eatonton every weekend, she'd sell Alice's books out of the trunk of her car, she says. "People from Ireland and England have come to my mama's house looking for traces of Alice."

Alice Walker strides into the hotel ballroom in Macon at about 7:40 p.m. She looks smart in a black tuxedo-style pantsuit, an open-collar silky gray shirt and black lace-up ankle boots.

Before heading for the dais, she stops at a table near the door where many of her relatives have already begun their meals. She embraces everyone at the round table and introduces them to her traveling companion, a tall Hawaiian woman with long hair the color of the perfectly sweetened iced tea that folks here are swilling like water.

Shortly after Alice and her guest are seated, an elderly Black man wanders up to the dais. Wearing a fading olive-green hat over his long white hair, he could have been the model for the Uncle Remus poster, but there is something about him that's too strong, too proud, to ever let white people call him "uncle."

Alice can call him uncle, though. She stands up to greet him.

He envelops her hands in his. "To all these people, you're Alice Walker," he says. "But to me, you'll always be Baby Alice."

It will be this way all night—warm hugs, warm smiles, warm words. A letter is read from Georgia first lady Shirley Miller, wife of Governor Zell Miller. Alice Walker, Mrs. Miller writes, has been "a jewel in the state of Georgia's crown for many years."

When Macon Mayor Jim Marshall stands up to present Walker with a key to the city, he is plain-spoken about the fact that this is a homecoming: "Any child coming home deserves a key to the house," he says, "and I've got a key to the city for Alice Walker."

Alice goes to the microphone and says a simple thank you. She repeats this humble thank you several times through the night as various guests continue to shower her with praises. She enthusiastically starts standing ovations for each of the three young women who serenade her with songs, and for the four-woman African dance group that performs for her.

Finally, after receiving the Shelia Award—an award given to Black women of high achievement—Walker hugs the crowd with soft, loving eyes. "I haven't been in Macon in a long time," Walker begins. "I used to come as a little girl to see my family ... I see relatives here I haven't seen in ten years."

Earlier in the day, Walker says, she had gone to Eatonton to visit her parents' graves. She draped a lei—made by her friend's mother— around her mother's tombstone. She then went to visit her first-grade teacher, who still lives in Eatonton. "Even though the weather has been wet," Walker says, "I was met by warm and wonderful people."

Noting the legacy of Harriet Tubman, the museum's namesake, Walker says, "It's not necessary any longer to be a slave." Then she addresses the gathering—her family, in one way or another—directly: "In our daily us-ness—with our nappy hair, our brown skin, our Black skin, our natural fingernails—we are art," she says quietly. "Everything that nature creates is art, and so are we.

"If there is a sin," she adds, "it's to be in all this glory and not enjoy it, because you're not fully yourself or you're not paying attention."

Alice Walker is attentive to each well-wisher, careful to spell the names correctly as she signs books for about two hours after the program. She hugs children, laughs with the elders, and agrees to have her photograph taken again and again.

As the crowd thins, Alice spots those of us who've come from the Alice Walker Literary Society in Atlanta. She's met us before—most recently, at the society's chartering a few months back—so she greets us with gracious hugs and then invites us to a gathering at the home of the museum's director.

We watch as she and her companion, Zelie, get into the backseat of a white Lincoln Continental that still has price stickers on its side window. Perhaps the museum borrowed it from a local car dealership for tonight's occasion, we muse.

We follow the car to the downtown home of museum director Carey Pickard. Alice and Zelie retreat, momentarily, into the lovely country inn next door to Carey's building. They want to drop off some of Alice's gifts, they say, promising to join us in the apartment in a few minutes.

It is perhaps ten thirty when we enter Carey's apartment, which is full of carefully selected antiques, folk art, and shelves of books and magazines. Even though Carey is white, he obviously has a great and sincere interest in

African American culture, and his home reflects that—as well as an interest in Elvis and other Southern cultural icons.

Anita Ponder, the director of communications at the museum, had been the emcee for the evening's program. A local judge, she wore a suit (blue with white pinstripes) and tie (yellow with blue diamonds) for the occasion. At Carey's she loosens her tie a little and kicks off her high-heeled shoes as someone brings her a glass of ginger ale. With various drinks in hand, we all wander around Carey's place making small talk until Alice arrives.

She comes in smiling. The black hair bungee that had held a handful of her dreadlocks back during dinner is now a bracelet on her right wrist. Her hair hangs free as she sips a glass of white wine.

With the ten or so guests, Walker converses easily on a range of subjects—the political situation in Cuba, her recent guest appearance on *Sesame Street,* and her upcoming novel, *By the Light of My Father's Smile* (published by Random House in 1998), which she declines to detail, except to say that it is going to be "scandalous."

When the conversation starts to get depressing—including a brief foray into talk about female genital mutilation, a topic she has written about extensively—Alice smoothly changes the subject.

"It's important for good people to be happy," she says firmly. "Are you happy?" she asks one guest. He says he is. She says she is, too.

And it's easy to believe her. She is kind, relaxed, magnanimous. She is among friends. She is comfortable in her body, in her skin, in her life. She is at home.

This celebration in Macon may be as close to a hometown embrace as Alice Walker is going to get, despite the claim Eatonton makes on its website—that it is "a town known for proudly honoring its heroes."

On the same website, a three-page article on the history of Eatonton predictably includes a couple of lengthy paragraphs on Joel Chandler Harris, along with a photo of Br'er Rabbit and a link to the Uncle Remus Museum web page.

A short paragraph on Alice Walker follows. It starts out talking about two other Black women—perhaps more acceptable than Walker to Eatonton's ruling class—Oprah Winfrey and Whoopi Goldberg.

The website informs us: "Oprah Winfrey and Whoopi Goldberg made their own contribution to Eatonton when they starred in the film version of *The Color Purple.* The renowned author and poet Alice Walker was born in Eatonton in 1944 and is famed for writing the novel, *The Color Purple,* winner of a Pulitzer Prize and the American Book Award in 1983. Whoopi Goldberg's 'big screen' debut in the film gained an Academy Award nomination in 1985."

Hmmmm. Two mentions of Whoopi, and only one of Alice. What is this telling us?

How is it that, in her hometown, a woman whom *The Washington Post* has called "one of the best American writers of today" is considered less important than Joel Chandler Harris (surely a less accomplished writer and, arguably, a plagiarizer, if you count the Black folk tales as stolen texts)?

How is it that a writer who makes a guest appearance on a TV show as ubiquitous and American as *Sesame Street* doesn't get any R-E-S-P-E-C-T from the powers that be in her hometown?

I put some of these questions to the president of the Eatonton Historical Society, Jimmy Marshall.

He tells me that the Chamber of Commerce and the Historical Society "have been trying for several years to raise enough money for an Alice Walker marker" to go in a small garden in the side yard of the chamber's office. The garden is full of purple flowers, he says, and "they want to call it The Color Purple Garden or the Alice Walker Garden." He doesn't remember which.

I don't remember seeing the garden when I was in Eatonton, and neither the woman at the Chamber nor the one at the museum mentioned this garden to me or the fund-raising efforts for the marker. But I listen on.

"Right after the premiere of the movie," he says, "they started trying to raise about six thousand dollars for a large granite or marble monument."

That was more than ten years ago, I remind him.

"That kind of money is hard to raise in a small community," he explains. "Maybe in your article you could make an appeal to Alice Walker devotees to contribute money for the marker—maybe that's one good thing that could come out of your story," Marshall adds, apparently unaware that he may be saying something offensive.

He recommends I talk with one of the Black elected officials in Eatonton, a town that is 30 percent African American. At Marshall's suggestion, I call County Commissioner Jimmy Davis. A member of the Chamber of Commerce, Davis says he knows nothing about the Chamber's efforts to raise money for an Alice Walker marker. There's never been anything in *The Eatonton Messenger* about it, he says. "I would be glad to give a donation, and I know of several organizations that would be happy to give a donation, too."

When I ask Davis, who grew up with Walker's older siblings, if he thinks racism may be a factor in the town's failure to properly honor Alice, he is quick to answer: "No, I don't think nothing like that. It's just that nobody's ever brought it up."

Marshall, the historical society president, takes a pragmatic approach: "People in the community have supported The Color Purple Foundation," he says, a "what-more-do-you-people-want?" tone creeping into his voice.

The Color Purple Foundation is an educational fund that Ruth Walker-Hood started eleven years ago to provide scholarships for rural youngsters—of any race—who might not otherwise be able to afford to attend college.

"That may be the best payoff in the long run," Marshall reasons.

He adds that Ruth "deserves a great deal of credit" for pushing The Color Purple Foundation. "I really admire her spunk," he says. I agree with him.

Perhaps disarmed that he and I have found common ground, he then makes a telling statement: "If Alice made more of an effort like that toward the community, people might respond more positively toward her."

An effort like that. The words ring in my ears as I thank Marshall for his comments and hang up the phone. Alice Walker, Ruth says, has been The Color Purple Foundation's biggest financial supporter.

But this doesn't seem to be the kind of effort Marshall is talking about. Perhaps he means if Alice were chattier with the locals—the local white folks, that is—they might give her the recognition she deserves.

Being an internationally acclaimed, Pulitzer Prize-winning author, Marshall's statement implies, just isn't enough.

Before our conversation ended, Marshall told me that Ruth is "a good friend" of his. I wonder if he'd be surprised at her blunt assessment of the situation: "If Alice were white, her books would be all over Eatonton, just like that Uncle Remus crap they've forced down our throats all our lives."

The Uncle Remus Museum may be the best a town like Eatonton can do.

I find it interesting that the museum is called the Uncle Remus Museum—rather than, say, the Joel Chandler Harris Museum or the Br'er Rabbit Museum. Perhaps this is Eatonton's attempt at honoring African Americans, as represented by Uncle Remus—a certain kind of mythic Black figure looming large and languid in the ancestral memories of many white Southerners.

Uncle Remus is a fiction, sprung from the fantasies of a white writer who lifted his stories from Black folk culture. He is a servile, gentle, happy cartoon character of a Black man with no sense of history, no awareness of injustice, no anger—and no weapons.

Unlike Uncle Remus, Alice Walker is real. She is outspoken, sexual, political, intrepid, inspired, and occasionally angry. And her mind and her pen are her weapons.

In short, for a town like Eatonton, Alice Walker is dangerous.

For this reason, at least for now, a woman like Alice Walker can't be truly honored in Eatonton. Uncle Remus will have to represent us all.

Fruitland

STEVEN KURUTZ

Some years back, an unusual and astonishing album began circulating among record collectors and fans of lo-fi music. Will Louviere was one of the first to hear it. A Bay Area vinyl dealer, Louviere is an authority on private-press LPs from the 1960s and 1970s—records self-produced and released by amateur musicians and destined, in most cases, for the bins of thrift stores and flea markets. In a year, Louviere and his fellow collectors between them might buy one thousand of these obscure albums. Of those, maybe ten would be artistically interesting. Maybe one would astonish.

This record had been sent to Louviere by a collector, but still, his expectations weren't high. The group was a duo, Donnie and Joe Emerson. The cover featured a studio portrait of them: teenagers with feathered brown hair, faces dappled with acne, sincere eyes meeting the camera. They were posed against the swirly blue backdrop you'd see in a school photo, with the album's title—*Dreamin' Wild*—written above them in red bubble script. Both boys were dressed flamboyantly in matching spread-collared white jumpsuits, like the outfit Evel Knievel wore vaulting over the Snake River Canyon, though the jumpsuits had name patches on the chest, like a mechanic's work shirt, an odd counter to the attempt at showbiz slickness. Donnie, posed in the front, held a Les Paul and looked a little stoned.

Given the packaging and the era—late seventies, Louviere was certain—he expected teen-idol cheese, a third-rate Osmonds knockoff. What he heard was something else entirely.

The opening track, "Good Time," was a burst of power pop, with a catchy fuzz-guitar riff over crashing drums and a jittery vocal mocking a selfish lover. "Give Me the Chance" followed it—a funk jam, this time with soulful singing interrupted by wavy blasts of echo distortion coming out of nowhere like acid flashbacks. The other songs included an orchestral-disco instrumental; an R&B groove that recalled the Temptations in their Psychedelic Shack period; an earnest, David Gatesian piano ballad. Layered throughout were assured musical nods to Fleetwood Mac, Hall & Oates, and The Brothers Johnson.

Louviere checked the back credits. Of the eight tracks on *Dreamin' Wild,* young Donnie wrote or cowrote all of them. He also played lead and rhythm guitars, bass, piano, and synthesizer and handled all the lead and harmony vocals. Joe drummed, and he often fell behind the beat or flubbed his fills. But instead of detracting from the music, Joe's drumming added to its appeal. It gave the songs an amateur charm, and created thrilling near-chaos as if the music might collapse on itself.

It was clear to Louviere that Donnie and Joe hadn't worked with a professional studio engineer or producer. Songs went on too long, had unorthodox structures, faded out rather than ended. But he loved the muffled, homemade sound and heard serious ambition and talent. Teenage Donnie's voice was especially compelling—"so stony and hazy," Louviere told me, as if he sang from some private interior room.

Donnie's voice reached new levels of stoniness on "Baby," the standout track. Simply defined, it's blue-eyed soul. But its effect on listeners isn't simple. The first time I heard "Baby" I broke out in goose bumps and felt a ghost had come in the room. The music is gestural and fades in: soft, pulsing piano, one guitar playing a simple repeated pattern, rim hits on the snare. Sung in a reverb-soaked near-falsetto, the lyrics are mostly indecipherable—the chorus sounds like "Baby, you're so baby." It hardly matters. The song's power is 90 percent atmosphere. You hear this magic quality in old country-blues recordings or some of the early rock 'n' roll stuff—say, "I Only Have Eyes for You" by The Flamingos. Beyond the instruments, what really got put on tape was a vibe, some molecular thing in the room that got baked into the recording. With "Baby," as with much of *Dreamin' Wild,* that subatomic thing, incredibly, is the emotional intensity—all the yearning and heartache—of being a teenager.

As Louviere told me, "It was hard to believe what I was hearing."

Intrigued, he contacted the collector who had sent him the album, Jack Fleischer. Where had *Dreamin' Wild* come from? Who were the Emersons? It turned out Fleischer had chanced upon the album in 2008 as a twenty-two-year-old anthropology student at the University of Montana, who had advanced in his listening from mainstream art rock to rarer psychedelic stuff to what he called "the big ocean" of private-press music underneath. "Once you find the passageway down there," he warned me when we first spoke, "you can really lose your mind."

Fleischer admired the way Louviere and others were unearthing records only a handful of people had heard before, and distributing them through small labels they ran. Wild music like Crystal, which Louviere released through his Companion Records—an album of sludgy stoner rock that a middle-aged keyboardist and poet named Stan Hubbs recorded in his hand-built cabin in Northern California in 1982, years before (it was rumored) he died from a weed overdose.

Fleischer saw what the collectors were doing as a form of anthropology. He was determined to find his own precious lost thing, and on a record-hunting trip to Spokane, Washington, he did: in a junk shop he spotted a sealed copy of *Dreamin' Wild* behind the counter, priced at five bucks. Fleischer was won over by the cover photo's comic bizarreness—the way Joe is posed so his body is hidden behind Donnie's and his head grows out of Donnie's left shoulder, suggesting rock's first conjoined twins. Fleischer recalled, "The look in those kids' eyes—there was no way I wasn't going to give it a shot."

Private-press collectors often track down the artists, to see if additional copies are available and to hear the creation story. Fleischer was so floored by *Dreamin' Wild* that he went to the Missoula Public Library and searched the Spokane phone book. He found a listing for Don Emerson Sr.—Donnie and Joe's father.

Don Sr. still had stacks of LPs gathering dust in his house, in an outlying community called Fruitland. He wanted fifteen dollars per "vinyl." Fleischer bought ten copies and sent them to Louviere and other collectors. They made copies. Word spread. The lo-fi kids down in Los Angeles got hipped, including Ariel Pink, the indie singer-songwriter. Fleischer celebrated the album on his music blog, *Out of the Bubbling Dusk.* In 2010, the website Soul Sides wrote about the record, bringing it to the wider attention of DJs, who loved the break on "Give Me the Chance." Soon Louviere was calling Don Sr. directly to get more copies. "I don't know that I've had as strong a response to any record. I don't know that I've sold more of a record," Louviere said. The albums arrived from Fruitland packed in egg cartons as if from a farm.

Finally, at a listening party at a music producer's house in Los Angeles, *Dreamin' Wild* reached the person who would give Donnie and Joe a second shot. Matt Sullivan is a co-owner of Light in the Attic, a reissue label that's had success putting out records overlooked in their time—in the parlance, "buried treasures." The label reissued *Cold Fact,* the 1970 debut by the singer-songwriter Rodriguez, whose life story was the focus of the Oscar-winning documentary *Searching for Sugar Man.* When the music producer dropped the needle on his copy of *Dreamin' Wild,* Sullivan was floored. "I was expecting The Partridge Family, that vibe," he recalled. "Nothing that would have the depth and sincerity and beauty this album possesses." He wanted to reissue *Dreamin' Wild* on his label.

He began tracking the album back to its source, eventually speaking to Don Sr., then Joe, and finally the elusive Donnie. The album's creation story, he discovered, was as remarkable as the music.

The Emersons were loggers and farmers in rural eastern Washington. During the sixties and seventies, Don Sr. grew hay, wheat, and alfalfa and cut a good bit of timber. Donnie and Joe, the oldest sons among the five Emerson children, were farm boys. Before school, after school, during summer breaks, they worked like grown men. They fixed fences. Changed irrigation pipes. Operated heavy equipment at fourteen years old.

From an early age, Donnie showed an interest in music. He took flutophone and clarinet lessons in school and taught himself piano and guitar in his teens. He played with a facility that amazed and startled. His was the freaky raw talent that befuddles family members. Don Sr., a third-generation logger, could only shake his head at his son writing a song, or two songs, a day. Still, he knew the grinding hard work of the farm, and wanted to save his sons from it. And he believed in supporting his children's interests, though "support" seems an insubstantial word for what he did.

In 1977, when Donnie was fifteen and Joe was seventeen, Don Sr. built them a log cabin studio on the farm. The boys named it the Practice Place. Then he went to a bank, borrowed against his land, and, with guidance from the school music teacher, stocked the cabin with pro audio gear: Gibson guitars, Fender amps, an eight-piece Rogers drum kit, a Fender Rhodes stage piano. He bought the boys a Polymoog synthesizer that alone cost $12,000. To record their tunes, Donnie and Joe had a TEAC 80-8, the same reel-to-reel tape machine with which the Eagles recorded basic tracks.

To self-record and release an album today requires only making the effort to download GarageBand to your MacBook Pro and post some tunes to Facebook. To do it in the late seventies, before digital technology, demanded tremendous commitment. You had to rent a studio or build your own. You had to hire people to master the tapes, press the vinyl, print the sleeves, distribute the product. It's why collectors love private-press records—the artists invested their money and hopes into moonshots. Don Sr. wasn't on a Joseph Jackson trip. He had no ambitions for himself in the music business. But he believed in his sons' talent and applied practical farmer logic to an impractical endeavor: Donnie and Joe would be successful not by covering other people's material but by making an album of their own songs. They still had to do their chores. But essentially, Don Sr. was saying to his sons: "Here are all the tools. Go be artists."

Between buying the gear and recording and pressing *Dreamin' Wild* in 1979, the Emersons spent close to $100,000.

What happened next? Nothing. The Emersons had an album of songs, but no contacts in the music industry, no manager or booking agent, no clue how to get their music heard. Donnie and Joe played a handful of gigs at fairs in nearby farm towns, but even locally, *Dreamin' Wild* was met with indifference. Probably only a few dozen copies of the album ever made it off the farm, one of them, miraculously, the copy that Fleischer found in the junk shop in Spokane.

In 2012, Sullivan drove to the farm with a filmmaker to make a short documentary. On camera, Donnie reflected on the music's initial failure to find an audience. "When you do an album like that—'Oh, wow, I just did an album, and everyone is going to be amazed with this album,'" he said, laughing at his naivete. "You see? And they weren't.... We just thought, 'I suppose they're going to call us.' And it never happened."

In the short film, which is available on YouTube, Donnie and Joe are sitting inside the Practice Place, in the "control room"—a wood-paneled time capsule of analog equipment the size of a walk-in closet. They both look amused and slightly puzzled to be talking about music they recorded half a lifetime ago. Donnie, especially, has a dazed expression, as if a chance encounter has brought the past rushing back.

Joe still has the matching jumpsuits at his house, he shows the camera. The white fabric is virginal. "The good old days," he says, wistfully.

Sullivan stayed on the Emersons' farm, with Don Sr. and his wife, Salina, while shooting the film. To hear him describe it, he'd entered a place untouched by the shallow, hurried quality of modern life and met the last sincere people in a cynical land. "It was one of the most moving and emotional experiences I've ever had," he told me.

Place mattered deeply to the music, the brothers make clear repeatedly. Whatever was special about *Dreamin' Wild* had to do with where it was created. As Donnie tells Sullivan in the film, the farm and the Practice Place were a creative Eden. He lost himself writing and recording. "I was so engulfed in what I was doing—the tones, setting the equalizers and everything. I could just do anything I wanted to do. Without anybody bothering me."

His eyes are closed and his head sways as he speaks. He's traveling back there.

To get out to Fruitland from Spokane, you drive west on US Route 2, past the city airport and Fairchild Air Force Base and the suburb with its Walmart-anchored shopping center called Airway Heights. Very quickly you're in farmland. This part of Washington is nothing like the Pacific Northwest—it's not rainforest green but heartland brown, with rolling wheat fields stretching to the horizon. I'm tempted to say it feels like a John Mellencamp song, but actually it feels pre-Reagan, before the VCR-digital-electronics age. A better reference would be Steve Miller, how hearing one of his radio songs can put you in a tank-solid Chevelle somewhere out in flyover country, in the last days of cheap gas and good-paying factory jobs.

After a turn north, the two-lane gets windier, the hills bigger, and the land emptier. The scenic highlight is crossing the Spokane River at Fort Spokane, the old US Army fortification built to protect settlers against Native tribes. Now it's a recreation area in a beautiful river valley. A sad little casino and gas station on the other side mark Spokane Indian Reservation land, which borders this whole area. From here you crest a hill and drive a few miles before dropping into a wide, harvest-gold valley like something out of a Technicolor Western.

Joe had told me on the phone to watch for a sign advertising firewood for sale, and to turn in there. I followed a dirt driveway past a workshop and some logging trucks and a field of ancient cars, trucks, and farm machinery rotting in high grass under the sun. At the end of the road sat a house made of Doug fir, with a white stone facade and a broad low metal roof that gave it a winged aspect. It was Joe's house; he'd never left the family farm.

He and Don Sr. were standing outside, waiting for my arrival. Joe was bald on top, with cropped light-brown sides and a moustache. He wore a blue T-shirt tucked into blue jeans and sneakers. Don Sr. had washed up after working all morning and was dressed in a short-sleeved sport shirt. Even at eighty-one, with glasses, he looked big and hale. What hair was left was white, including his sideburns, which he wore in the boxy, short-trimmed style of sixties NFL players.

Joe invited me inside, into a large kitchen/living room dominated by a pinewood breakfast bar and a pool table. He lived alone—you knew that from the cavernous stillness. He spoke in a gentle, friendly voice with a slight twang. He laid out rolls and individual Tupperware containers with ham, turkey, lettuce, tomatoes, cheese. He got us cold beers to wash down the sandwiches.

"So you live in New York City?" he said, and his eyes genuinely twinkled, like someone coming from New York to Fruitland was incredible.

It was August 2012, a few months after Sullivan's visit. Light in the Attic had reissued *Dreamin' Wild* in June, and so many incredible things had happened since then, you would have thought Joe might have grown used to surprises. Pitchfork awarded the album an eight out of ten, with the reviewer calling it "a godlike symphony to teenhood." The extensive press coverage that followed was equally gushing. Ariel Pink was quoted as saying he put "Baby" on every mixtape he gave to friends, and he recorded a new version with DâM-FunK that became a minor sensation, creating an unlikely Donnie and Joe fan base among hipster millennials. One music writer put "Baby" in company with "Stand by Me" as a soul classic. It was used in the film *Celeste and Jesse Forever* and would soon appear in another, *The Spectacular Now*, as audiovisual code for aching young love. To illustrate just how weird things were getting, Jimmy Fallon would soon appear on Bravo's *Watch What Happens Live* and discuss with host Andy Cohen their shared love of "the baby song."

Joe seemed happy with the attention; it brought excitement to his life and rare visitors to Fruitland. "It's pretty neat," was how he put it. But the deeper weirdness of what was happening hadn't upended his brain or affected his day-to-day at fifty-three, which so far as I could tell pretty much resembled his life at nineteen. At one point as we talked, I noticed a little cabin set off in a grove of ponderosa pines. I knew instantly it was the Practice Place. It wasn't fifty yards from Joe's house.

I visited Fruitland twice over three years, spending several days on the farm. That first time, I was sent by *The New York Times* to write about the hoopla surrounding the reissue. Like any good celebrity, Donnie would be arriving last—he lived with his wife and two kids in Spokane, and was driving up the next day—so Don Sr. offered to show me around in his blue Taurus.

On the way out, we passed the field of dead machines and Joe said, "One of these cars he drove from New York, a '49 Oldsmobile, didn't you, Dad?"

"Yep," Don Sr. said. "When I got out of the military, I bought it in New Jersey, in Perth Amboy. Actually, I wanted a Packard. They had the best motors, a big V-8. See, I'm a mechanic, and if you know anything about cars, it had enormous bearings. Great balance and power in the motor. Packard, back then, was above a Cadillac."

At the highway, Joe pointed across to the small white farmhouse where his parents lived, the same house he and Donnie were raised in. Just down the road was the community Grange Hall, where they'd held their first rehearsals. Joe and his younger brother Dave currently worked with Don Sr. in the logging yard behind us. Joe's house and the Practice Place were beyond it. All the compass points, right there, within safe distance.

Down the highway a few miles, a sign announced FRUITLAND and we passed a gas station that doubled as a grocery store and post office. I searched for more buildings, streets. Joe laughed. "That's the town."

I asked Joe, "What did you do on Saturday nights as a teenager?"

"I think I can remember going to a fair dance in Davenport"—a town forty miles south. "They had fairs in these small towns like Colville or Davenport," he went on. "I ended up going to the evening dance. Shoot, I might've only gone two or three times in my whole lifetime."

I was curious about the boys' exposure to live music. Had they driven down to Spokane to see rock concerts? "I didn't go to concerts," Joe said.

"Maybe because I hadn't been exposed to it, I didn't miss it. I didn't know the excitement of it." If he and Donnie heard live music, he explained, it would've been at a farm over in Fruitland Valley. "The neighbors up there"—the McLeans—"were friends of ours. They would get together and have little beer parties." Jim McLean played drums, his brother Lawton guitar. Someone nicknamed the place the Hilton.

They wanted to show me Hunters, a town ten miles north, where Donnie and Joe, and before them Don Sr., had attended school. On the way, Don Sr. kept pointing off to all the woodland spots he'd logged and showed me Emerson Road, the dirt lane he'd been raised down. Hunters had a theater, a bank, two creameries, a barbershop, a doctor's office, and a Catholic church, but they existed only in memory. What was there now was a café, a bar, and a little grocery, buildings and houses spread across a gulley and up a hillside. Compared to Fruitland, a metropolis.

The school—one long, low building, K through twelve—rested on a scenic plateau above town. The hallways had that unnatural drowsy quality schools get in summertime. Framed class portraits going back to the 1920s ringed the walls in the half-size gym. Joe pointed to his class of '77. Sixteen kids. The class of '79, Donnie's class, had fourteen graduates. I wondered about the current students, what their lives were like out here so far from the shopping centers and reliable 4G. Were these the last kids in America spared the Internet?

By now, I'd been in Fruitland for an hour or so, but I'd understood in the first ten minutes what Matt Sullivan was talking about. Living in early twenty-first-century America, let's say there's a cynicism that sets in. Also an incessant, self-alienating noise. If you live in a major coastal media city, as Sullivan and I both do, it's only noisier. You talk enough about the latest celebrity Twitter feud or the newest bougie food trend and you start thinking that stuff actually matters. Fruitland was a return to the real. I know, I know, but this wasn't rural romanticizing, not without merit, anyway. Being there, I found myself thinking about my grandparents on my father's side, and the community where they'd lived. It was one of these places in America that's no more than a scattering of houses and families along a rural highway, a zip code. Whatever was happening out in the rest of the country or the world barely touched down there. My grandparents used to sit out on the porch swing after supper, and the air was so heavy and still, you could hear a car coming half a mile off. Fruitland had that same elemental, out-of-time quality. I hadn't thought about that part of my life in years. Fruitland made me realize how much I missed it.

Something about the place—and, really, I mean the Emersons—rewired your jaded heart, put you back in touch with basic goodness. You shook hands with Joe and Don Sr. and instantly felt you'd known them forever; they were that kind of welcoming, unaffected people. The sincerity that you heard in the music was manifest in them. They radiated it.

Don Sr. had a remarkable even-keeled mellowness. A reporter had flown in from New York and was sitting shotgun in his car asking him questions, and he didn't bat an eye. Neither had he shown any surprise when Jack Fleischer called out of the blue, or at any point after. He took it as it came. If a UFO crash-landed on the farm, you could imagine him looking up and observing, "There are little green men in the lower field," then going back to work.

Driving back, we got to talking about the unlikely second life of *Dreamin' Wild.* Had the Emersons thought about it in the years before Jack Fleischer called?

"It was almost forgotten," Joe said.

"It was in our basement all right," said Don Sr. "Donnie was still writing songs, collaborating with artists," Joe said. "We just didn't think of it." The liner notes of the reissue mentioned that Donnie's music career had continued after *Dreamin' Wild.* He'd lived in LA and recorded an album down there. Was another lost masterpiece gathering dust in Don Sr.'s basement?

Back in downtown Fruitland, Joe instructed Don Sr. to turn onto a side road. We headed deeper into the grassy, heat-singed countryside. After two miles or so, Joe said, "Now, Dad, if we come up to this hill, can we stop at the top?" We idled on the empty, silent road. Far off stood an abandoned farmhouse and beside it a few leaning outbuildings, weathered and sunbaked. This had been the Hilton.

"Still the same as it was back then, no one around," Joe said. "There was beer drinking and pot smoking going on. We didn't do none of the pot smoking."

Joe mentioned one of the Hilton regulars, Bill Alex. Dead now from brain cancer, but once so strong he could pick up the back end of a Chrysler. Joe said, "Bill used to ride his horse from over here in Fruitland Valley to our farm, to visit my younger sister Rose. That's a four-, five-mile ride."

Donnie and Joe made *Dreamin' Wild* as teens in the seventies, but they didn't really live through what we collectively think of as that decade—Watergate and disco and punk rock. The world they experienced in the seventies had been more like the forties, in the way rural communities can feel decades behind. Moreover, I had the sense that the Fruitland I was seeing now was essentially unchanged from Joe and Donnie's childhood. That the distance between 1979 and the present was mere months.

I looked up at the Hilton. You could almost see the blond farm kids laughing with their beers and hear Bachman-Turner Overdrive echo across the valley.

Later, after Don Sr. dropped us off and drove home, Joe showed me around his house. There was a lot of Western-style furniture and dark wood throughout and, to a degree I hadn't noticed earlier, Catholic imagery. Everywhere I looked a Blessed Virgin refrigerator magnet or votive candle bearing a portrait of Christ on the cross stared back. Each time I visited I was put in mind of the silent, solitary quarters of a priest.

Upstairs, however, was an unfinished open room with a bar and amplifiers and a drum kit on a plywood riser. Joe had since switched to guitar and led an instrumental power trio, Emerson, Smith, and Bischoff, which rehearsed here on Monday nights and performed sporadically. Joe plugged his Joe Satriani-model Ibanez into an amp and turned on the overdrive. He wailed in my direction for twenty minutes, wildly jerking the whammy bar. Watching the soft-spoken, devoutly religious man shredding made me smile.

There was a deck off the jam room. Sitting out there, Joe told me the story of his house. He'd designed and built it himself, he said. He'd planned to live there with a woman he fell in love with from the reservation. He broke ground in 1993, so he would've been thirty-four. Lonna was twenty-two. She was a single mom with two young kids. "She was real bad into drugs," Joe said. "I tried to help her. She got tied up with some bad people."

It was unclear from Joe's description how serious the relationship had been, or if she'd shared his plans for their future. Lonna was arrested on drug charges at one point, Joe said, and imprisoned near Seattle. "Never thought I'd be doing something like that," Joe said about visiting her in jail. Whatever their relationship had been, it had ended long ago, and Joe had never married. Lonna had died the year before, at forty. Joe had written a song for her called "Freesia," after the flower.

As I was leaving to drive back to Spokane for the night, Joe showed me a spare room downstairs, empty except for a standing metal cabinet. Boxes of recording tape from the *Dreamin' Wild* sessions were stacked inside, along with rehearsal footage shot on an early camcorder. In a separate box were copies of a 45 the teens recorded at a Spokane studio before the Practice Place. A Donnie and Joe archive, which Joe had catalogued and maintained for years, and which had suddenly, with the success of the reissue, acquired value.

"It's quite amazing, Donnie's ability back then, for such a young artist and such a secluded area," Joe said. "It's a sense of genius, truthfully."

I asked Joe how much credit he gave himself for their sound.

"I was just doing the drums. Just doing the drums. Donnie would really give me freedom. Basically, he wanted me to keep the tempo and not slack." He chuckled. "Well, there was slack in there."

In a way, Joe had reversed the big brother role: he supported his gifted younger sibling, becoming half of Donnie and Joe, but more crucially, he looked up to Donnie as his No. 1 fan.

"I had this thought," Joe said, closing the cabinet. "I'd like to get together with Don and do some new recordings. Kind of a new *Dreamin'*

Wild. An album with what's going on in my head and what's going on in his head."

Which made you wonder: What was going on in Donnie's head?

The next morning, Donnie picked me up outside my hotel in downtown Spokane in his white Chevrolet Starcraft van, a massive, plush-carpeted road machine you could pretty much move into if you suddenly became homeless. We'd barely gassed up the beast when he started telling me about being raised Catholic and hearing the priest sing at a church on the reservation.

"Really sing," Donnie stressed. "Half of these guys can't sing. You go to all kinds of churches, and they suck." He stopped and took my measure. "Am I being too crude? I'm a little different than my brother, bro." He laughed. "I love him. But just so you can handle me."

Indeed, Donnie showed none of the cicada-hum slowness of the farm. His mind was amped, naturally. Conversation topics ping-ponged. Scattered thoughts were relayed in the bro-and man-inflected speech of a veteran gigging musician. The stillness you felt about Joe's life wasn't there with Donnie. It seemed the opposite, like a lot had gone down since 1979. As Donnie explained rapid-fire while we drove, he'd played all over—Nashville, Denver, Detroit Lakes, Minnesota. For a few years in the eighties he'd lived in Las Vegas, where he and his wife, Nancy, a city girl, a California girl, an aspiring dancer he'd met on a blind date, performed as a duo at the Rio. They'd moved back to the Spokane area and formed a local band. Donnie had done—still did—all the things you have to as a full-time musician scratching a living in a small market. He'd played weddings, written radio jingles for car dealerships, sung cover tunes at the casino over in Coeur d'Alene. He'd met and befriended incredible players. He mentioned Stanley Clarke, the jazz bass virtuoso.

Donnie was clearly tripped out by the album's rediscovery, by all the attention his early music had received and the portal to the lost past it'd opened up. He'd yearned for fame and artistic recognition, and now it had come in this strange way, thirty years late. He had trouble articulating his feelings. "It's weird … it's kind of surreal," he stumbled. "It's hard for me to talk about. I feel like my life is all upside down."

When fans like Louviere and Sullivan had called up asking about the vocal sound on "Baby," he was dumbfounded. "At first I didn't know what to say. Until the person on the other end of the line said, 'How did you make that?' It opened me up." He added, emoting, "All my life I've been struggling to find out who I really am. I got out of there and I went into the world and I got convoluted. Am I making sense? So when I talked to them on the phone, it was almost like I was talking to a therapist. Isn't that strange?"

One of the difficult things for him to reconcile, Donnie said, was being thrown back together with Joe. They hadn't made music together in decades. They were different people, with very different lives. They didn't even look like brothers. Donnie's olive skin and hair color—coal black—gave him a Mediterranean appearance. But fans of *Dreamin' Wild* saw them as a duo, a brother act. Donnie was torn. He wanted to be loyal to Joe, but he found it hard to play with him. Musically, there were rooms he couldn't enter with Joe on drums. "It doesn't mean it's his fault or my fault," Donnie said with the resignation of age. "It's just circumstance, it's what it is."

We turned north toward Fruitland. I asked about his influences, the music he'd loved as a kid. I expected the usual tales of playing a record until the grooves were worn. But Donnie said he didn't have a stereo growing up, much less records.

"Not even a little Fisher-Price hi-fi and a couple of Beatles 45s?"

Donnie shook his head. "I had none of that." Astonishingly, *Dreamin' Wild* was created in a near-total pop-culture vacuum.

"You're going to laugh at me—it's kind of corny," Donnie said. "But as a kid I watched *The Lawrence Welk Show.*"

I myself grew up in the East, in a remote rural community. In such places, I said, seeing a musician on TV, whoever it is, takes on greater meaning.

"It does!" Donnie exclaimed.

What changed Donnie's life was a tractor—a Case Agri King that Don Sr. bought around 1977. The tractor had an enclosed cab, with a radio. "KJRB, out of Spokane," Donnie remembered. "Back then they had all genres of music out of one station. I could listen to Smokey Robinson. I could listen to Hall & Oates. I could listen to Brothers Johnson. In fact, sometimes I could even hear some country music on there." He'd spend eight, ten hours in the tractor, tilling the earth, soaking up sounds. "I felt everything I did was from that dial. Like hearing Smokey on the radio—I could see him in my mind. I could connect to him."

He absorbed what he heard on the radio and spent hours in the Practice Place—and in his head. "I would daydream and transpose things on my mind down on the piano," Donnie said. "I would daydream all the time."

I asked Donnie the question I'd asked Joe: Had he thought about *Dreamin' Wild* in the years before Jack Fleischer called?

"Oh, I often did," he said. "I play the 'Baby' tune live. That comes from a real innocent time in my life. I was really connected to my first girlfriend. I knew her since second grade. It was a way of expressing myself."

I mentioned my favorite song on the album, "Don't Go Lovin' Nobody Else." Even more than "Baby," the vocals destroy. Teenage Donnie repeats the title phrase over and over, his adolescent voice cracking in the most heartbreaking way. Hearing it, I think of myself at sixteen, alone in my room, obsessing over a girl who broke up with me before senior year, wanting so badly for it not to be over, the pain of that.

Donnie didn't respond for a long time. When he did, his voice was thick with emotion. He said some of the songs he'd written not about himself but about Joe, from his viewpoint.

My brother had really bad acne," Donnie said. "It was so bad that at an early age I swore to myself I would never, ever let a child go through that when I had kids. My brother had it all over his face. Everywhere, man. It bothered me so much—" Donnie began to cry. "I'm sorry," he said. "That's weird."

There were times when I couldn't listen to *Dreamin' Wild.* The music was too emotional. Its power lay in its pure expression of teenage naiveté and yearning, but it's not always easy to go back there. And it wasn't even my adolescence we were revisiting.

We crossed the wide river at Fort Spokane, the home stretch. Donnie collected himself. "This has brought back many feelings I suppressed that I didn't realize," he said. "But the world will do that to you."

Contact with a private-press artist can be unpredictable, even confrontational. Fleischer told me about another musician whom collectors consider a lost genius, a Minnesota native named Tom Nehls. In 1973, he self-recorded an acid-folk album titled, wonderfully, *I Always Catch the Third Second of a Yellow Light.* When collectors contacted Nehls, Fleischer said, he didn't want to discuss the brilliant music he'd made for an uncaring world. "He could not even begin to talk about that record. Its lack of success and the amount of energy he put into it was so painful to him."

He added: "You just never know until someone picks up the other end of the phone. It could be anything from somebody who's too excited and you go, 'Look, I'm happy that we connected, but you're not the next Tom Petty.' Or it can be people who are openly hostile. I had one guy where I had to talk to a couple of his family members to get his number. He was so hostile that I'd bothered his family. This was in the context of me telling him how much I loved his record and wanted to get it out to people."

Sullivan, who has had similar run-ins, told me, "You're bringing ghosts out of the closet. Sometimes they're just like, 'Sorry, I don't want to go there.'"

But for many private-press collectors, possessing the music isn't enough. There's a strong desire to speak with or meet the unrecognized artists who created it. Recently, Sullivan and Fleischer teamed up to locate a handsome blond playboy who, while living in LA in the early eighties, recorded an album of delicate acoustic music titled *L'Amour* under the name Lewis. (Light in the Attic reissued the record to acclaim.) After months of searching, on a tip, they flew to Vancouver, British Columbia. They canvassed the city for two days, and found Lewis, now going by Randy, dressed entirely in white and sunning himself outside a Starbucks.

"We pulled out the rereleased album," Fleischer recalled. "We said, 'We want you to sign these royalty contracts.' You could almost see a chill go through him to look at the old album. He didn't want to touch the contracts. He said, 'Those were different times, man. I'm not into coin now. I'm not into coin.'"

For Donnie, and for the Emerson family, there were in fact ghosts. For starters, the recording sessions in LA, in 1981, had been a catastrophe. By then Donnie was a solo act. As sometimes happens, the family had made a decision to focus on the more talented brother. Dutifully, Joe stepped aside. To fund Donnie's solo album, Don Sr. further mortgaged the family's land. The studio, in North Hollywood, ran through the money like water. The loan interest rate was punishing. Of the farm's 1,700 acres, the bank repossessed more than 1,500. Whole pastures and hillsides—gone. Don Sr.'s back seized up from the stress. As Donnie recalled on the drive up, "a void of hopelessness" descended on the farm.

Maria Emerson, the oldest daughter, who was sixteen at the time, said losing most of the farm was traumatic and confusing for the whole family. "You don't completely understand how much money is being put out," she told me. She and her siblings didn't blame Donnie, she stressed, but added, "That was our life, living on the farm. To see pieces of it sold and gone because of that decision was sad."

When I asked Don Sr., he said, "We wanted Donnie to go forward," and expressed no regret. But he was quick to add, "I wouldn't mind having a little of the money back."

Despite the near bankruptcy and now a second self-produced album that didn't advance Donnie's career, the family continued to promote his music, often at their expense. There was a shift into country, a video for a twangy single called "Rocky Start," a European radio promotional tour.

But the pure creative dream state—and that singular raw soul sound—proved elusive for Donnie in the years after he left the farm. He chased musical trends and listened to other voices instead of his own. At Joe's house the day before, Joe had played me a couple of tracks off Donnie's LA album, *Can I See You.* The production was ghastly eighties AOR: bright keyboards, canned metronomic drumming, big, hollow choruses. You heard the strained effort to sound like Christopher Cross. The Donnie of "Baby" was buried under there.

Even now, Donnie is still trying to find his artistic groove, still hoping the world will recognize his multifaceted talent. He's always loved classical music, and he recently spent two years writing a "wind-chime score," he said, which he hopes to sell to spa chains. He acknowledged some wrong turns taken.

"The only time I didn't make those mistakes is when I was on the farm," Donnie said. "When I was isolated and my parents gave me this time to find myself. And when you get away from that, and start getting into the world, especially the music business …"

When we got to the farm, Donnie's mood changed. In the van he'd been a little scattered, but funny and talkative. Now he became increasingly quiet, withdrawn. I didn't notice at first.

We gathered at Joe's house with their younger brother Dave, a handsome, easygoing guy who lived in a room over the workshop in the lumberyard. We were kidding around in the driveway and drinking beer on a summer afternoon. (The Emersons, by the way, are the platonic ideal of beer drinkers, believing a hot day calls for a cold beer.) The photographer from the newspaper was there, too. He'd spent the morning touring Fruitland with Joe. The idea was to get portraits of Donnie and Joe on the farm, a then-and-now thing. The Case tractor with the radio was still around, in the field of dead machines. Donnie climbed up for a photo. Dave went back to work. Someone—Joe, I think—suggested we drive over to the Hilton, maybe also check out the Catholic church on the reservation where Donnie heard the priest sing.

As the journey through the past continued, Donnie grew morose. At the little stone church, he darkly hinted that something had happened to him there. He was bodily agitated and wanted to leave. Joe had a fine barometer for his brother's moods, and he tried to fill the strained silence, keep things light and friendly. But by the time we returned to the farm to shoot inside the Practice Place, Donnie looked like someone in the midst of a crisis.

Eventually, when I came to know him better, I understood that in some ways it was Donnie being Donnie. He's an intense guy; the swirling emotions didn't end with his teens. He once told me, "Life is complicated for me, man."

But he really was struggling—and for good reason. Jack Fleischer's record-hunting trip to Spokane had set off a personal earthquake. It had dredged up an intense time in Donnie's life and literally returned him to the farm. It was clear that he didn't drive out here very often, or easily. The distance between Spokane and Fruitland seemed greater, somehow, than seventy miles.

I thought about what Fleischer and Sullivan had said about ghosts resurfacing. For Donnie, it was that, but also something else. Record collectors were calling; talk show hosts were gushing about "Baby"; record label owners and reporters were showing up to Fruitland. As the creative mastermind, Donnie, more than Joe or Don Sr., was the focus of their attention. The success must have seemed, on some level, like a cosmic slipup. Here he was, at fifty, witnessing the overnight fame of his seventeen-year-old self. What was he supposed to do with it?

Rodriguez, the subject of the Oscar-winning documentary *Searching for Sugar Man,* also experienced this dissonance. He'd released two albums on a small label in the early seventies; both were totally ignored in America. For years, he worked construction jobs in Detroit and led a hand-to-mouth existence. Meanwhile, his music found its way to South Africa, where his songs were adopted as anti-apartheid albums and the elusive artist (much to his surprise, when he finally found out) was embraced as a rock poet on the level of Bob Dylan. But there was one big difference: Rodriguez was already a mature artist when he made that music. So when Light in the Attic reissued it to wide acclaim, he could—and did—strap on a guitar and perform his sly protest song "Crucify Your Mind" on Letterman that same summer at age seventy. What people loved about *Dreamin' Wild,* by contrast, was its innocence, its "accidental greatness," as Pitchfork put it. Matt Sullivan had invited Donnie and Joe to perform at his label's tenth-anniversary party in Seattle later that year. But the brothers couldn't reproduce themselves as sheltered farm boys jamming together. Even if they could, somehow, Donnie didn't want to; he'd honed his chops. And his wife, Nancy, was his musical partner now. The stony, hazy sound he and Joe created, like the years the brothers lived together on the farm, belonged to the past.

The Practice Place, however, remained. Now Donnie and Joe stood as middle-aged men outside the tiny cabin. Its heavy door was padlocked. Joe held the key.

If you loved *Dreamin' Wild* and knew its creation story, as I did, you felt the moment. Here was the very room where it had gone down. Where teenage Donnie had spent hours teaching himself to thread tape through the eight-track. Where he and Joe had recorded their beautiful and heartbreaking and soulful record. Imagine, for a moment, you're them at that age. You live on a wheat farm seventy miles northwest of Spokane and three hundred miles from the nearest metropolitan area, Seattle. Not that you ever visit those places. You're geographically and culturally isolated. The radio is practically a foreign concept. But making music is your passion, your brotherly bond, and into your world, against all odds, appears a recording studio.

On nights when they recorded, Joe had told me, he changed out of his farm clothes, got cleaned and dressed up. "It was a special thing to do," he said.

Behind that door, in a very real sense, was Donnie and Joe's boyhood, preserved. Instruments had been left for thirty years, lyric sheets in Donnie's adolescent hand, the rainbow shag carpet used on the walls as soundproofing.

The air felt late Carter Administration. They sat on a stuffed green couch, clutching pounder cans of Busch Light. Joe listened uneasily as Donnie, in an alcohol-slowed voice, spoke about recording. He used to shave down the drumsticks to get a softer hi-hat sound, he said. But there was none of the warm nostalgia and easy banter seen in Sullivan's short film. That was made before the reissue and all the attention, when it was still a lark. The brothers sat at opposite ends of the couch. Donnie wore dark sunglasses the entire time—less as eye protection, it seemed, than as a psychic shield.

I was moved by Donnie's anguish and felt complicit in it. He wanted people to hear his new songs, he'd told me in the van, the stuff he'd written as a mature musician. And here I was like everyone else, asking him to show me the spot where he'd sung the "oohs" in "Baby" at sixteen. It was like asking a practiced artist, "Hey, show me your first raw scribblings." And yet, Donnie's first raw scribblings had been brilliant. They'd drawn me and others to Fruitland. So, like it or not, there was an inevitability about the course of the day; the last station of the cross was the Emerson homestead. We drove there.

At the entrance road, a white sign with painted black letters announced Camp Jammin' The Barn. The sign had been poled into the ground to attract passing motorists. There was indeed a barn down the lane, beside the small white farmhouse, and near it, a wooden ticket booth. During the nineties, in what had been Donnie's country phase, Don Sr. converted this cow barn into a three-hundred-seat concert hall. He'd gotten banquettes from an old café and put them inside. There was an if-you-build-it-they-will-come aspect that defied all logic. When Matt Sullivan first saw Camp Jammin', he found it "mind-boggling," he said. "I asked them, 'Who in the heck did you think was going to drive out here? It's five hours from anywhere.'"

The farmhouse itself was reminiscent of shotgun cabins you see in the rural South—one story, dull white paint, green metal roof. A battered brown Chevy Nova, a farm car, was parked in the dusty driveway. Beside the fence gate hung a wooden sign, with "The Emersons" carved in cursive letters.

Donnie and Joe entered through a mud porch that led into the small yellow kitchen, where Don Sr. stood. He'd already hauled a load of logs to the sawmill in Colville that morning, waking at five to make the hundred-mile round-trip on winding roads. Now he was cleaned up, in jeans and a fresh shirt, eating a slice of cheese.

The photographer brought his gear into the other room and began setting up. The living room was a domestic scene from a bygone America. A World Book Encyclopedia set, that mainstay of self-education in rural homes before Google, occupied a bookshelf. The paneled walls were covered with family photos: school portraits of the children with their dated bowl cuts and feathered bangs, more recent shots of the younger generation. A color-tinted wedding picture of Don Sr. and Salina hung by a window. Near it, a hunky head shot of Donnie from around 1986. Even more than in Joe's place there were saintly calendars, Jesus candles, clumps of rosary beads strung on hooks, a Vatican gift shop's worth of Catholic souvenirs. There was a closed-in stuffiness to the room that was not unpleasant.

Salina had fussed over Donnie when he came in, and now she fussed over her guests. A tiny woman with glasses and blackish-gray hair pulled into a bun, she appeared the temperamental opposite of her husband, nervously expressive and eager for personal connection. She spoke in rapid, heavily-accented English, and Joe explained, "Mom is from the island of Malta."

Without prompting, Salina told the story of how she'd come to Fruitland, beginning with her childhood during the war. With its proximity to Africa in the Mediterranean, Malta had been a strategic island for both the Allies and the Axis forces. The German Luftwaffe had nearly bombed it to rubble in the Siege of Malta. Salina's family—she's one of twelve children—lived perilously close to the Allied base. One day her father had an idea, Salina said. He told his family they'd go to a cave in the cliffs above the sea and shelter there until the bombing ended.

"We took some blankets, clothes, not much, a couple of pillows, and we go there. My father says, 'Nobody will be there.' Was five hundred people!

Hole here, hole here, hole there—each hole had a family." She went on: "We just live with prayers. Three times a day we took turns saying the rosary."

Salina and her mother and siblings huddled in the cave, while her father returned to their farm. The bombing lasted more than a year.

Salina met Don Sr. after the war, when he was in the Navy and stationed on Malta. She was twenty. After he shipped out, he wrote to her. Salina couldn't read, so her sister would read his letters to her and write down her replies. They kept up a correspondence that way, and two years later he returned to marry her.

When the newlyweds came to Fruitland, as a wedding gift a friend of Don Sr.'s gave them part of a house. It was on land back in the woods down Emerson Road. Don Sr. added the front portion and moved the house to where we stood.

As Salina recounted her life story, I listened, slack-jawed. I think that's when I came to love the Emerson family. To paraphrase Whitman, they contained multitudes. Just when you thought you knew them as rural American farmers, you were hearing about Malta and German bombers and sheltering in a sea cave like Saint Paul after his shipwreck. Here, I realized, was the source of Donnie's Mediterranean complexion—and, possibly, his musical gift.

Salina picked up an acoustic guitar. She wanted to play us a folk song she'd written. She sat on a stuffed chair, facing us, and began talk-singing:

Why I should worry Why I should complain
When I have the sun in the morning and the moon at night
And the stars up above keep shining bright
And I can walk and I can talk and I can hear and I can sing

Salina was singing her words from memory; she had never learned to read or write English. She hadn't learned to drive, either. She depended on Don Sr. or Joe to take her to church and elsewhere. The farm was her world.

Donnie, still troubled, disappeared into the kitchen to call his wife. We heard him talking in a hushed voice. Salina stood and went to get something for me. She returned holding a CD. It was another album by Donnie, or Don Emerson. This one, titled *Whatever It Takes,* was recorded in '97, during the country phase. Donnie's hair has that coiffed Randy Travis look in the cover photo. As before, the family formed a private label to release the album, and the youngest sister, Rose, acted as Donnie's publicist. Salina said she carried CDs in her purse to sell to people she met, sometimes going door to door. She showed me a notebook she asked Donnie's fans to sign. I wondered how many attempts had been made, how much of the family's limited resources had been marshaled for the dream.

When Donnie rejoined his family, his dark mood suddenly lifted, though not his shades, which gave him the appearance of a blind musician. The photographer got him smiling and joking around with Joe. A truce with the past, for now.

With all of us in there, the house seemed about to burst. It was hard to believe, I remarked, that seven people once shared these two small rooms.

"It was even smaller then," Donnie said. He pointed to a room behind a door, nothing more than a makeshift nook really, where all five siblings slept when they were little. Don Sr. had built them a platform bed, and they'd shared it. Eventually the girls needed privacy and a wall was built to separate the room. But Donnie, Joe, and Dave continued to share the bed through high school.

It wasn't until that very moment that I fully grasped the miracle of *Dreamin' Wild.* A recording studio had been financed and built by a family that slept five to a bed. Richly layered music had emerged from a household with no stereo. A third-generation logger and farmer and his wife had risked their land so their sons could be musicians. And two isolated farm boys had made a classic soul record. It didn't seem possible.

The Emersons had believed the music was special. They'd been laughed at and ignored and nearly lost everything—but they'd been right. As painful as parts of their story were, there was also triumph, made possible through a second miracle: one of the few copies of *Dreamin' Wild* to get out into the world was rescued from the forgotten dustbin of time. People heard it, and they believed, too. With the royalties and film licensing deals, Don Sr. might recoup a little money. But the point was, he'd lived to see it. So had Salina. So had Joe. So had Donnie, who earlier that day had told me, with something like peace in his voice, "If I died tomorrow, hey, man, someone got it." When you strip away everything else, that's the desire of every artist, lost or found.

Almost a year after my first trip to Fruitland, Matt Sullivan emailed me. "I'm having a difficult time comprehending this, but it's true," he wrote. "Next month, I'll be flying out to New York along with Donnie and Joe for their NYC debut."

A woman in Brooklyn wanted to surprise her boyfriend on their anniversary by having Donnie sing "Baby," the couple's song, in person. She'd cover his travel. Sullivan seized on the chance to line up a gig for Donnie and Joe at the Mercury Lounge. The booker, it turned out, loved *Dreamin' Wild.*

The trip almost didn't happen. Donnie had scheduling challenges with his wife and two kids. Joe was afraid to fly and wary of the big city. You realized there would never be a Donnie and Joe tour. This might be the only chance to see them live. In the end, they came through. Sullivan arrived a day early. He met Donnie and Joe at the airport. "From the minute they got off the plane it was magical," he said. "Picking them up and seeing them come down the escalator so giddy and excited. They were like, 'I can't believe we're in New York!'"

Donnie and Joe rode the ferry to Jersey City to be interviewed live on WFMU. They were asked by a reporter from the downtown fashion magazine *Nylon* their view on gay marriage ("I have to follow what my religion teaches," Joe said). At McSorley's Old Ale House, they tried to explain to the drunk guys at the next table the improbable path that had brought them there. One night, Sullivan arranged a visit to Dunham Studios, a Brooklyn recording studio owned by Thomas Brenneck, who'd played guitar for Amy Winehouse as one of the Dap-Kings. Brenneck, a fan, manned the board while Donnie and Joe improvised songs and recorded late into the night like they were teens back on the farm. Sullivan thought it sounded so good he wanted to release the recordings as a seven-inch single. Already, his label was planning a follow-up album of songs from later sessions at the Practice Place, *Still Dreamin' Wild*. On Sunday, Joe genuflected inside Saint Patrick's Cathedral, a personal dream.

I met the Emersons one evening and took them and Sullivan to an old-school Italian restaurant. To share a meal with Donnie and Joe in the East Village was like meeting old friends in a foreign country. Walking the streets later, Joe had the skittish eyes of the first deer to dart from the herd. Donnie was in his glory, grinning ear to ear, a gigging musician in New York.

In Brooklyn, the boyfriend walked into the bar to find his girlfriend and all their friends gathered for a celebration. Watching Donnie sing "Baby," the boyfriend wept with joy. And the Mercury Lounge show the next night—absolute magic.

The place was sold out. Jack Fleischer was there. Brenneck and his eight-months-pregnant wife were there. The anniversary couple were there. Every person in the room knew the story of *Dreamin' Wild,* the time and distance Donnie and Joe had traveled to be on stage. This was a once-in-a-lifetime event. We all knew it. Sullivan and I have probably been to a thousand concerts between us, and we agreed we'd never seen anything like it. The goodwill toward Donnie and Joe from the audience was a physical force in the room. As he reflected on it more than two years later, in his label's offices in LA, Sullivan's eyes moistened. "It was hard coming back and trying to explain it," he said. "People were like, 'Oh, it sounds like an awesome show.' No, it was more than that. To see that type of connection between the audience and musicians—it was like one."

Donnie and Joe rose to the moment. Especially Donnie. The tortured guy I'd seen in Fruitland was replaced by a joyful and charismatic performer, totally at home on a stage. His voice was different, of course, but incredible and moving in new ways. It's true the music would've been tighter with a more professional drummer. But the magic of the songs—and you could tell deep down Donnie knew this—came from the brotherly union, from all that Donnie and Joe had shared together on the farm, which found its way into the notes they passed between them and directed out to the audience. They played without a set list. They opened with "Baby."

Notes on My Dying

RUTHANN ROBSON

I believe in death with dignity, don't you? At least in the abstract.

Grace. Nobility. Even beauty. As abstract as that.

As abstract as other people.

As abstract as characters in fiction.

"All anyone wants is a good death," I read. This is in a short story.

It's a prize-winning story, a story about a nurse who is dying of cancer. She is graceful, noble, and even beautiful.

I hate the story. I hate stories about people dying of cancer, no matter how graceful, noble, or beautiful.

When I read the author's note, I learn that he is an administrator in the famous cancer center where I am enduring chemotherapy and the news that I am going to die very shortly.

This is what I say to his story: I do not want your good death.

This is what I say to his biography: You make your living off other people's deaths.

This is what I insist: I am not your story.

If I were constructing this as a story, with myself as the protagonist, I would not only be dignified, I would be brave and beautiful, courageous and kind, humorous and honorable.

I would enshrine myself in narrative.

But this cannot be a success because the elements of narrative are corrupted.

There is no beginning. The beginning is not diagnosis.

The beginning is before that. Before the suspicions, before the reconstructed past when one began to feel this or that, before everything except a tiny cell that got twisted and frisky. The absence of the beginning is compounded by the middle collapsing into the past.

Everything is end.

Some endings are longer than others. I am trying to act as if I have a future.

When I'm not too weak, I go to work. I go to the library and the post office. I go for walks. And when I am too weak, I go anyway. The worst that could happen to me is already happening.

I cannot pretend I am who I was a few months before, so I pretend I am a fashion model. I am a Buddhist nun with a shaved head. I am anorexic. I have a lovely pallor. I have a noble beauty, a beautiful nobility.

I am not interested in fooling anyone except myself.

I call it survival.

I survived a dangerous adolescence.

In school, the sentiments of *Death Be Not Proud* belied its title. On the large and small screens, *Love Story* jerked tears, and the body bags and the immolated monks screamed for my attention. In the streets and bathrooms, needles in the arm and suicide sang their romantic dirges.

Not all of us made it.

When I made it to twenty-one, I assumed I would live until eighty-seven. Death was for the young. And the old.

At twenty-six, I was hospitalized intermittently for six weeks with a strange malady that spiked my temperature to 107 degrees.

"You should be dead," the doctor said, confirming my temperature.

"I'm not," I replied, thinking myself witty. The year was 1984.

I was sure I had AIDS.

Instead, I was diagnosed with pesticide poisoning, contracted from the sugarcane fields where the migrant farm workers who were my clients worked.

A nurse told me I should be grateful for the advancement of antibiotics.

No one told me I should be irate about the development of agribusiness.

I knew I had almost died.

I thought I was cured.

There are those who argue that cancer is ancient, prevalent now because other diseases have been cured and humans live longer, and unconnected to environmental degradation.

My body knows differently.

But who is there to blame? Industrialization? Capitalism? Corporate greed?

Anger is the second stage of dying in the classic work of Elisabeth Kübler-Ross. She notes that dying can cause a "usually dignified" person to act "furious," but with a bit of tolerance by the caregivers, the patient's anger can be soothed. Dying people, above all, want to be heard.

I do not want to be heard.

I do not want to talk.

I want to live.

My first decision about dying is that I will die at home. I will have the control and comfort I would not have in a hospital. The winter sun will be weak but brilliant, sifting through my window, refracting through a prism I have had since I was young. Then the light will fade, leaving only a slat of brilliant pink. Twilight was once my favorite time of day.

My second decision about dying is that I won't. Like all my most outrageous ambitions, it first appears on my horizon as a question: "What if?" What if I refused to die? I am neither stupid nor naive and know that it isn't a simple matter of choice. Nevertheless, my aspiration persists.

The first stage of dying is denial.

Ask anyone who has read Elisabeth Kübler-Ross.

Or who has not.

Still, what if I refused to cooperate?

The manifestations of my resistance are illogical and small. I refuse Ensure, Ativan, a port, a wig. I refuse to talk to my oncologist, who warns me about depression. Depression, the fourth stage of dying, is the "preparatory grief that the terminally ill patient has to undergo in order to prepare himself for his final separation from this world."

If I were talking to her, I would tell her I am not depressed, although I may seem defeated, decimated.

I am simply deep.

I am inside myself so deeply the world is an abstraction. I cannot bridge the distance between my self and everyone else, including the ones I love most. The ones I said I loved more than life itself. Now, this is no longer true.

My death is only my own. No matter the connection, no matter the love. No matter that I came from the bodies of my parents or that my child came from my body or that my lover and I have joined as if we inhabit one body without boundaries. Each body lives separately. And dies separately. Perhaps I knew this before. In the abstract.

I think about taking someone with me.

If I'm going to die anyway, shouldn't I kill someone? Shouldn't my death be useful? I scan my personal life but find no one evil enough to deserve to die. My passions are faded. I concentrate on the person I once hated most, but cannot seem to despise him enough to deprive him of his narrow miserable life.

Assassination is a possibility. I imagine buying a semi-automatic weapon. I have enough time for the license waiting period, to learn how to shoot, to do the legwork necessary to find a gap in the security. I think it would be relatively easy, since I'm not worried about getting caught. I would prefer not to die in prison, so I guess I'd kill myself as soon as my deed is done. I settle on a certain Supreme Court justice. But I find I don't care enough to kill him. Or even to think about it more than once.

Dying is lonely.

I am popular in my dying: people I have not heard from in several years call me.

"Is there anything you want to say to me?" she asks.

She is crying.

"My mother died of cancer," he says to me.

He must think this is an expression of empathy.

"You have always meant so much to me," she blurts.

She does not stumble over the past tense.

I never respond.

They must think I am being dignified.

Someone actually tells me this: "I really admire the way you are conducting yourself with such dignity," she says to me.

"I'm not."

"Well, it seems like that to us," she persists. She is a colleague and has always been comfortable speaking for everyone at work.

"That's not the way it seems to me." I prove I can still argue.

She smiles as if she thinks I am being modest.

I am not.

I am trying to be honest: I am all claws and sobs and vomit. I am small and getting smaller. I am bereft and bald. I am more tired than tired.

How could she not see that when she looks at me?

But she does see that. Despite the dignity, when she looks at me she sees I am dying.

And when I look at her, I see my dying reflected back to me, a shiny silvery object without form or function, an abyss of pity.

I am grateful for the people who do not pity me. Or at least who do not show their pity.

We have written letters for almost twenty years. When I write to tell her the news that I am dying, I ask her to try to write to me as she always has, to write to me about her life and what she is reading. She writes me every day. Every single fucking day. Beautiful exquisitely boring letters about her job or what she ate for breakfast or something she hopes will be amusing. I live for her letters.

We have written letters for eight years. I fudge the fact that I am dying, but also ask her to keep writing to me as she always has. Her letters get longer. Pages and pages that require extra postage, pages filled with assessments of novels, pages brimming with struggles about her own writing, pages of poetry. I reread every page until I believe that I am strong enough to write back.

We have never written letters. She sends me a card. "Here's a second opinion: You're the greatest." It's in a package of gourmet food that once would have been appetizing.

We have lived together for more years than I can count. She was once my lover, now she is my caretaker. She tries not to cry in my presence. I am not so considerate.

She brings me books from the library when I can't get there myself. "Novels," I tell her, "from the new-fiction section." Sometimes she brings me the same book twice. Three times. Sometimes I recognize when this has happened.

Maybe I believe I can save myself through reading. Or at least escape.

Or maybe it is that I have always read. Books were my first acquaintance with grace.

Although soon I stop reading fiction. I know she is screening the selections, but death penetrates the pages. Sometimes it is in the prize-winning story. Sometimes it is there casually and without warning. It seems there is always a convenient cancer death in the background somewhere, even if only in a character's memory.

In novels, they never recover. Loss. Grieving. But life goes on.

I close the book and reach for the next one.

Soon, I am requesting biographies. As if I have forgotten that the person in the biography is going to die. As if I didn't know somehow that Rachel Carson died, at fifty-seven, of cancer. She hid it from the world, as if her dying was a recrimination of her work linking the toxins with tumors in humans, an irrefutable rebuke that she was less than objective. Or perhaps she was trying to be dignified.

Desperation is not dignified.

Perhaps that is why Kübler-Ross does not name desperation as a stage. There is "bargaining," the third stage, but she gives it short shrift.

She theorizes it as a belief in a reward for good behavior. She doesn't seem to understand the will to live.

It allows the decision to be strapped into a chair and poison injected into my veins to seem rational.

It propels me into the alleys of alternative healing, alternative theories, alternative alternatives. I visualize and vitaminize. I spread myself on the floor of an apartment in Chinatown so that a man can bruise my flesh as a way of clearing my meridians. I ingest herbs from different continents, animal parts pressed into pill form, teas that smell like mentholated piss.

I meditate.

There are those who argue that cancer is a message: "Appreciate the beauty of each moment."

The moments most often invoked are populated with children. What could be more precious than the kiss of a toddler?

Other moments to be cherished occur in nature: oceans, sunsets, trees and their turning leaves.

Even a circumscribed life has its moments to be appreciated. The soft sheets of the bed, the taste of a strawberry, the flames in the fireplace.

Never mentioned are the moments in which I am managing to live. The moments, long and slow, during which I am dizzy and puking red on the bathroom floor, trying to appreciate the texture and temperature of the tile against my cheek. (How smooth! How cool!) The moments, as panic-filled as a fire, when I can feel the chemical burn in my veins and watch the skin on my arm lose all its color. The moments, shallow and distant, when I try to think about anything other than what is happening to me.

Acceptance is the fifth and final stage of dying, according to Kübler-Ross. She warns that the harder the struggle to avoid the inevitable death and the more denial, the more difficult it will be to reach acceptance with peace and dignity. In her examples, the patient wants to die, but the medical professionals believe it is better to prolong life.

This is not my experience.

My medical professionals are very accepting of my death. They proclaim it inevitable and do not deny or struggle. They do not seem to believe it is better to prolong my life. They are very noble.

Perhaps they read Kübler-Ross in medical school. Or perhaps they're simply burnt out. Or they know the grim statistics for my rare cancer and see no reason why I should be in the smallest of minorities who might survive.

I loot the world for survival stories. Not the narratives of Himalayan treks or being lost at sea, but illness. The bookstore has an entire section on diseases and five shelves on cancer. I inspect every title, except the "prevention" ones, looking for possibilities. I buy a book by a Christian fundamentalist woman who attributes her survival to prayer and coffee enemas. I buy a book by a scientist who attributes his survival to vitamins. I buy books on healing by popular writers who intersperse their homilies with anecdotes of people given "six months to live" but who are alive ten years later.

Possibilities.

I do not want nobility or beauty.

I do not want a good death.

I want possibility.

I am in my office, looking at the diplomas on my wall and sobbing over all that accomplishment, now utterly worthless. The skills I had mastered are the wrong skills for my situation. I know no medicine; my last biology class was in the ninth grade. I can't even cope: my degrees are not in psychology or divinity. I learned how to think, how to read, how to argue.

My faith—in hard work, in intellectual pursuits, in books—has been misplaced. Nothing I know could save me. I want to rip my diplomas from the wall.

With dignity.

But I don't have the strength to carry a single book down the hall to the classroom. I can't stand up more than three and a half minutes. I no longer have the ability to assassinate that Supreme Court justice or to recall which one I had singled out as especially dastardly.

Still, I refuse to accept I am dying. I prefer denial, anger, and even desperation.

When I can sit up, I spend hours at the computer, leaving no website unturned. I become an expert in my rare type of cancer. A medical dictionary replaces my thesaurus.

I read books, articles, pamphlets. I have begun to eschew fiction. I want true stories of survival. I relish attacks on statistics and science.

I avoid all eulogies, all obituaries. I do not update my will or think about the existence of my property without me. I don't care what happens to those hundreds of letters, the ones I have written or the ones I have read. I don't worry about my office and its diplomas. I am not interested in any legacy.

I try to think. To argue.

There are those who argue that cancer is an infectious disease, like tuberculosis, because a gene-based disease would have been eliminated through natural selection. Cancer could be cured by the correct antibiotic.

I would like this to be true.

Now.

I had thought I had looked at death before. I had seen her dance with the ones I loved who have died. I had suffered my own flirtations. This time, though, death is gazing back. Not just a glance, but a full seductive stare. As if we are in a bar and I am dressed in black leather, ready for adventure tinged with danger.

How alluring to be chosen.

This is what she whispers: I can follow her with grace and dignity. Or I can resist and it can get ugly. Either way, she will win, she promises me.

That is her story.

If she writes my story, I will be brave, beautiful, and dignified. The word *struggle* will be used, but with no incidents of sweating or cursing or thrashing. In her story, it will be as if I have fallen into a deep sleep.

As long as I am still able to write, this is my story: I resist the lure of dignity; I refuse to be graceful, beautiful, and beloved. I am not going to sleep with her. I'm going home, alone.

Back to my books, my computer, my Australian herb and shark cartilage, my visualizations, meditations, and bruised meridians. Back to my bedroom with the prism at twilight. Back to my office and its useless diplomas.

Back to my life.

The Brown Study

RICHARD RODRIGUEZ

Or, as a brown man, I think.

But do we really think that color colors thought? Sherlock Holmes occasionally retired to a "brown study"—a kind of moribund funk; I used to imagine a room with brown wallpaper. I think, too, of the process—the plunger method—by which coffee sometimes is brewed. The grounds commingle with water for a time and then are pressed to the bottom of the carafe by a disk or plunger. The liquid, cleared of sediment, is nevertheless colored, substantially coffee. (And coffee-colored has come to mean coffee-and-cream-colored; and coffee with the admixture of cream used to be called blond. And vanilla has come to mean white, bland, even though vanilla extract, to the amazement of children, is brown as iodine, and vanilla-colored, as in Edith Sitwell's "where vanilla-coloured ladies ride," refers to Manila and to brown skin.) In the case of brown thought, though, I suppose experience becomes the pigment, the grounds, the *mise-en-scène*, the medium of refraction, the speed of passage of otherwise pure thought.

In a florescent-lit jury room attached to a superior court in San Francisco, two jurors were unconvinced and unmoving. I was unconvinced because of the gold tooth two bank tellers had noticed. The other juror was a man late in his twenties—rather preppy, I thought on first meeting—who prefaced his remarks with "As a black man, I think …"

I have wondered, ever since, if that were possible. If I do have brown thoughts.

Not brown enough. I was once taken to task—rather, I was made an example of—by that woman from *The Threepenny Review* as the sort of writer, the callow, who parades his education. I use literary allusion as a way of showing off, proof that I have mastered a white idiom, whereas the true threepenny intellectual assumes everybody knows everything, or doesn't, or can't, or shouldn't, or needn't, and there you are. Which makes me a sort of monkey-do.

Well, you see, I thought I was supposed to. I wasn't decorating my remarks. Was I too eager to join the conversation? It's only now I realize there is no conversation. Allusion is bounded by spell check.

After such a long education, most perceptions authentically "remind." And I'm not the only one. The orb Victoria held in her hand has passed to her brown children who, like Christ children in old paintings, toy with the world a bit, and then, when no one is looking, pop it into their mouths. The only person I know for whom the novels of Trollope are urgent lives in India.

It is interesting, too, to wonder whether what is white about my thought is impersonation, minstrelsy. Is allusion inauthentic, Ms. Interlocutor, when it comes from a brown sensibility? My eyes are brown. *Cheeks of tan?*

Most bookstores have replaced disciplinary categories with racial identification, or sexual. In either case I must be shelved Brown. The most important theme of my writing now is impurity. My mestizo boast: As a queer, Catholic, Indian Spaniard at home in a temperate, Chinese city in a fading, blond state in a post-Protestant nation, I live up to my sixteenth-century birth.

The future is brown, is my thesis—is as brown as the tarnished past. Brown may be as refreshing as green. We shall see. LA, unreal city, is brown already, though it wasn't the other day I was there—it was rain-rinsed and as bright as a dark age. But on many days, the air turns fuscous from the scent glands of planes and from Lexus musk. The pavements, the palisades—all that jungly stuff one sees in the distance—are as brown as an oxidized print of a movie—brown as old Roman gardens or pennies in a fountain, brown as gurgled root beer, tobacco, monkey fur, catarrh.

We are accustomed, too, to thinking of antiquity as brown, browning. Darkening, as memory darkens, as the Dark Ages were dark. They weren't, of course; they were highly painted and rain-rinsed. We just don't remember clearly. I seem to remember the ceiling, how dark it was. How tall it seemed. The kitchen ceiling. And how frail we are! What used to be there? A shoe store? A newsstand? I seem to remember it, right about here … a red spine, wasn't it? Have I felt that before? Or is this cancer?

At last, the white thought, the albin pincer—pain—an incipient absence, like a puddle of milk or the Milky Way. *The glacier knocks in the cupboard.* Why is cancer the white ghost? Why are ghosts white? And what year was that? Which play? Well, obviously it's Shakespeare. "Lear"? "Cymbeline"? *Golden lads and girls all must* ... Death is black. Coffee may be black, but black is not descriptive of coffee. Coffee is not descriptive of death. Can one's life be brown? My eyes are brown, but my life? Youth is green, and optimism; Gatsby believed in the green light.

Whereas there is brown at work in all the works of man. By the eighteenth century, the majority of Mexico was mestizo, neither "pure" Indian nor "pure" Spaniard—brown. Time's passage is brown. Decomposition. Maggots. Foxing—the bookman's term—reddish-brown, reynard. Manuscripts, however jewel-like, from Dark Ages, will darken. Venice will darken. Celluloid darkens, as if the lamp of the projector were insufficient sun. College blue books. Fugitive colors. My parents!

If we wish to antique an image, to make memory of it, we print it in sepia tone—sepia, an extract from the occluding ink of the octopus, of the cuttlefish, now an agent for kitsch. Whereas the colors, the iridescent Blakes at the Tate, are housed now in perpetual gloom, lest colors be lifted from the page by the cutpurse sun. The Kodachrome prints in your closet—those high-skied and hopeful summer days—are dimming their lights, and the skies are lowering. Would we be astounded by the quality of light in 1922?

Unreal City
Under the brown fog of a winter dawn,
A crowd flowed over London Bridge, so many,
I had not thought death had undone so many.

The prince had always liked his London, when it had come to him. And it had come to him that morning with a punctual, unembarrassed rap at the door, a lamp switched on in the sitting room, a trolley forced over the threshold, chiming its cups and its spoons. The valet, second floor, in alto, Hindu Cockney—and with a startled professionalism (I am browner than he)—proposed to draw back the drapes, brown, thick as theater curtains.

Outside the hotel, several floors down, a crowd of blue- and green-haired teenagers kept a dawn vigil for a glimpse of their Faerie Queene. Indeed, as the valet fussed with the curtain, they recommenced their chant of "Mah-don-ahh. Mah-don-ahh."

Madonna was in town and staying at this hotel. All day and all night, the approach or departure of any limousine elicited the tribute.

Mah-don-ahh was in town making a film about Eva Perón (both women familiar with the uses of peroxide. Not such a bad thing to know in the great, brown world, oi, mate?).

I was in London because my book had just come out there. My book about Mexico. Not a weight on most British minds.

Did I ever tell you about my production of *The Tempest*? I had been at the theater the previous evening. Not *The Tempest* but the new Stoppard, and I watched with keener interest as the Asian in front of me leaned over to mouth little babas into the beringed ear of his Cockney hire. One such confidence actually formed a bubble. Which in turn reminded me of my production of *The Tempest*. (South Sea Bubble.) I would cast Maggie Smith as Miranda—wasted cheeks and bugging eyes—a buoyant Miss Haversham, sole valedictorian of her papa's creepy seminary. Caliban would be Johnny Depp. No fish scales, no seaweed, no webbed fingers, no claws, no vaudeville. No clothes. Does anybody know what I'm talking about? Ah, me. I am alone in my brown study. I can say anything I like. Nobody listens.

Will there be anything else, sir?

No, nothing else, thank you.

Brown people know there is nothing in the world—no recipe, no water, no city, no motive, no lace, no locution, no candle, no corpse that does not—I was going to say descend—that does not become brown. Brown might, as well, be making.

My little Caliban book, as I say, bound in iguana hide, was about Mexico. With two newspapers under my arm, and balancing a cup of coffee, I went back to my bed. I found the Book Section; I found the review. I knew it! I read first the reviewer's bio: a gay, Colombian writer living in London.

What the book editor had done—dumb London book editor of the *Observer* had done, as Kansas City does and Manhattan does—is find my double, or the closest he could find, in greater London. It's a kind of doppelgänger theory of literary criticism and it's dishearteningly fashionable among the liberal-hearted. In our age of "diversity," the good and the liberal organize diversity. Find a rhyme for *orange*. If one is singular or outlandish, by this theorem, one can't be reviewed at all. Worse than that, if one is unlike, one will not be published. Publishers look for the next, rather than the first, which was accident. But the *Observer* wasn't even within bow-range. Their gay gaucho was clueless.

The liberal-hearted who run the newspapers and the university English departments and organize the bookstores have turned literature into well-meaning sociology. Thus do I get invited by the editor at some magazine to review your gay translation of a Colombian who has written a magical-realist novel. Trust me, there has been little magical realism in my life since my first trip to Disneyland.

That warm, winter night in Tucson. My reading was scheduled for the six thirty slot by the University of Arizona. A few hundred people showed up—old more than young, mostly brown. I liked my "them," in any case, for coming to listen, postponing their dinners. In the middle of a paragraph, a young man stood to gather his papers, then retreated up the aisle, pushed open the door at the back of the auditorium. In the trapezoid of lobby light thus revealed, I could see a crowd was forming for the eight o'clock reading—a lesbian poet. Then the door closed, silently sealing the present. I continued reading but wondered to myself, Why couldn't I get the lesbians for an evening? And the lesbian poet serenade my Mexican-American audience? Wouldn't that be truer to the point of literature?

Well, what's the difference? I do not see myself as a writer in the world's eye, much less a white writer, much less a Hispanic writer, much less "a writer" in the 92nd Street Y sense. I'd rather be Madonna. Really, I would.

The Frankfurt Book Fair has recently been overrun with Koreans and Indians who write in English (the best English novelist in the world is not British at all but a Mahogany who lives in snowy Toronto and writes of Bombay). Inevitably, the pale conclusion is that brown writers move "between" cultures. I resist between, prefer *among* or *because* of. You keep the handicap. After all, it has taken several degrees of contusion to create a jaundice as pervasive as mine. It has taken a lifetime of compromises, the thinning of hair, the removal last year of a lesion from my scalp, the assurance of loneliness, the difficulty of prayer, an amused knowledge of five-star hotels—and death—and a persistence of childish embarrassments and evermore prosaic Roman Catholic hymns, to entertain a truly off-white thought. Here comes one now. *Un marron!*

No, I guess not. There's a certain amount of "So what?" that comes with middle age. But is that brown thought?

Thus did literary ambition shrivel in my heart, in a brown room in a creamy hotel in London, constructed as a nineteenth-century hospital and recently renovated to resemble a Victorian hotel that never existed except in the minds of a Hispanic author from California and a blond movie star from New Jersey.

Eve's apple, or what was left of it, quickly browned.

"Christ! A white doorway!" was Bukowski's recollection of having taken a bite on the apple. When Eve looked again, she saw a brown crust had formed over the part where she had eaten and invited Adam's lip. It was then she threw the thing away from her. Thenceforward (the first

Thenceforward), Brown informed everything she touched. Don't touch! Touch will brown the rose and the Acropolis, will spoil the butterfly's wing. (Creation mocks us with incipient brown.) The call of nature is brown, even in five-star hotels. The mud we make reminds us that we are: *In the sweat of thy face shalt thou eat bread, till thou return into the ground; for out of it wast thou taken …*

Toil is brown. Bruegel's peasants are brown, I remember noting in a Vienna museum.

In his book *Abroad*, Paul Fussell reminds us how, early in the twentieth century, the relative ease of modern travel and boredom allowed moneyed Americans and Europeans to extrude the traditional meaning of the laborer's brown and to make of it a glove of leisure. What the moon had been for early nineteenth-century romantics, the sun became for bored twentieth-century romantics. The brown desired by well-to-do Europeans was a new cure altogether: tan.

There is another fashionable brown. An untouchable brown. Certain shrewd, ancient cities have evolved an aesthetic of decay, making the best of necessity. Decrepitude can seem to ennoble whomever or whatever chic is placed in proximity—Anita Ekberg, Naomi Campbell. The tanned generation, aka the Lost Generation, gamboled through the ruins of the belle époque. The *cardinali* of postwar drug culture—Paul Bowles, William Burroughs—found heaven in North Africa, mansions white. It's a Catholic idea, actually—that the material world is redeemed; that time is continuous; that one can somehow be redeemed by the faith of an earlier age or a poorer class if one lives within its shadow or its *arrondissement*, breathes its sigh. And lately fashion photographers, bored with Rome or the Acropolis, have ventured further afield for the frisson of syncretism. Why not Calcutta? Why not the slums of Rio? Cairo? Mexico City? The attempt is for an unearned, casual brush with awe by enlisting untouchable extras. And if the model can be seen to move with idiot stridency through tragedy, then the model is invincible. Luxury is portrayed as protective. Or protected. Austere, somehow—"spiritual." Irony posing as asceticism or as worldly-wise.

One of the properties of awe is untouchability. *Silenzio*, the recorded voice booms through the Sistine Chapel at five- or ten-minute intervals. *Do not speak. Do not touch.* Even resurrected Christ—the white doorway himself—backed away from Mary Magdalene's dirty fingernails. Don't touch! I would have expected a Roman Catholic understanding of time to accommodate centuries of gaping mouths, respiration, prayer, burnt offerings—and reticence—offering the exemplum of a clouded ceiling to twentieth-century pilgrims. After all, we live in time. Our glimpse of the Eternal must be occluded by veils of time, of breath, of human understanding.

The human imagination has recently sustained a reversal.

One would have expected the pope, as the preeminent upholder of the natural order, to have expressed reservations about the cleaning of the Sistine ceiling. The pope, however, in a curiously puritanical moment, gave his blessing to a curator's blasphemy, which was underwritten by the Japanese fetish for the cleaning of history. The blasphemy was to imagine that restoring the ceiling might restore the Vatican's luster. The blasphemy was to imagine that time might be reversed. The blasphemy was to believe that time should be reversed.

The human imagination has recently sustained a reversal. We have cleaned the ceiling. Michelangelo's *Creation* and *Judgment*, the first and the last and the pride of centuries—a vault over the imagination of the world—have been cleaned, have been restored, unhallowed, changed and called "original," though no one has any idea what that might mean. (What was the light of day in 1540?) Nile greens and rose-petal pinks, tangier oranges and the martyred saints—what supernal beaver shots. Well, we want them preserved, of course we do. And we are keen to see them as *they*, the dead, saw them, as Michelangelo painted them. The very Tree of Knowledge has been restored, each leaf rinsed and all the fruit polished, the fruit and the sin repolished. Having seen, we also want them back the way they were.

We want what Eve wanted. ... *Just curious.*

We had become accustomed to an averted eye, to seeing darkly, as old men see. It required many thousands of Q-tips, many thousands of gallons of distilled water, which is to say, merely a couple of years, to wipe away the veil of tears, the glue from awakened eyes, to see born-again Adam touched by the less complicated hand of God. Now our distance from the representations, both alpha and omega, has been removed. And with it all credibility.

Blind John Milton—*brown all!*—dictating *Paradise Lost* to his aggrieved daughter in the dark, understood that what changes after Adam's sin is not creation but our human relationship to creation. (We cannot be content, even on a warm, winter day in LA, but we must always carp about a white Christmas.)

Maybe Milton, in this sense, in his preoccupation with the Fall, was more an ancient, swarthy Catholic than a true, ready Protestant. (Protestantism was also an attempt to clean the ceiling.) Those famous religious refugees from Restoration England were (like Milton) Puritans who believed they had entered a green time and were elected by God to be new Adams, new Eves (as old John Milton could not, with the scabs of Europe grown over his eyes, and painted tropes of angels plaguing his memory—*brown all, brown all*).

Let us speak of desire as green. In the Roman church, green is the color of Ordinary Time, a prosaic pathway. For American Puritans, green was extraordinary. They supposed themselves remade by their perilous journey to a new world they were determined to call green, proclaiming by that term their own refreshment. They had entered a garden ungardened and felt themselves free of history, free to re-enact the drama of creation.

Green became the founding flag of America; and so it would remain for generations of puritans to come, whatever our religion or lack. American optimism—our sense of ourselves as decent, naive, primary people (compared to those violet, cynical races); our sense of ourselves as young, our sap rising, our salad days always before us, our belief that the eastern shore the Europeans "discovered" and the fruited plain beyond were, after all, "virgin"—all this would follow from an original belief in the efficacy of green.

Thus did the Dutch sailors in F. Scott Fitzgerald's *Great Gatsby* spy the sheer cleft of an approaching "fresh green breast." That same green breast is today the jaded tip of Long Island, summer home to New Amsterdam investment bankers and other rewarded visionaries who do not resemble their portraits. And the tragic hustler's ghost:

Gatsby believed in the green light, the orgiastic future that year by year recedes before us. It eluded us then, but that's no matter–tomorrow we will run faster, stretch out our arms farther. ... And one fine morning ...

We—I write in the early months of the twenty-first century—we are now persuaded by Marxist literary critics to goddamn any green light, to hack away at any green motif. Someone offstage has suffered, and no good can come of it. We are a college of victims, we postmoderns; we are more disposed to notice Fitzgerald's Dutch sailors were not alone upon the landscape (we easily pick out chameleon Indians hidden among the green tracery) than we are to wonder at the expanding, original iris: How the Indians must have marveled at those flaxen-haired Dutchmen.

Well, most likely the Indians were too terrified to morphologize or eroticize on the spot. What happens next? Watch, as the Indians did watch—with darker dread and puzzlement—what cargo these pale sailors unloaded. From below deck emerged Africa in chains, the sun in thrall to the moon.

Thus, perceiving Europeans having only just arrived, the Indians already saw. Indians saw Original Sin. The dark ceiling. The stain spreading like oil spill. Rumor, too, must have spread like wildfire across the Americas—making green impossible from that moment except as camouflage or tea.

Forgetting for the moment the journeys of others and the lateness of the hour, considering only the founding triad of our clandestine exhibit—Indian, European, African—we see (as well as the Founding Sin) the generation of the erotic motif of America. A brown complexity—complexity of narrative and of desire—can be foretold from the moment Dutch sailors and African slaves meet within the Indian eye.

I think I probably do. (Have brown thoughts.)

Looking at Emmett Till

JOHN EDGAR WIDEMAN

For Qasima

A nightmare of being chased has plagued my sleep since I was a boy. The monster pursuing me assumes many shapes, but its face is too terrifying for the dream to reveal. Even now I sometimes startle myself awake, screaming, the dream's power undiminished by time, the changing circumstances of my waking life.

I've come to believe the face in the dream I can't bear to look upon is Emmett Till's. Emmett Till's face, crushed, chewed, mutilated, his gray face swollen, water dripping from holes punched in his skull. Warm, gray water on that August day in 1955 when they dragged his corpse from the Tallahatchie River. Emmett Till and I both fourteen the summer they murdered him. The nightmare an old acquaintance by then, as old as anything I can remember about myself.

Yet the fact that the nightmare predates by many years the afternoon in Pittsburgh I came across Emmett Till's photograph in *Jet* magazine seems to matter not at all. The chilling dream resides in a space years can't measure, the boundless sea of Great Time, nonlinear, ever abiding, enfolding past, present, and future.

I certainly hadn't been searching for Emmett Till's picture in *Jet*. It found me. A blurred, grayish something resembling an aerial snapshot of a landscape cratered by bombs or ravaged by natural disaster. As soon as I realized the thing in the photo was a dead Black boy's face, I jerked my eyes away. But not quickly enough.

I attempted to read *Jet*'s story about the murder without getting snagged again by the picture. Refusing to look, lacking the power to look at Emmett Till's face, shames me to this day. Dangerous and cowardly not to look. Turning away from his eyeless stare, I blinded myself. Denied myself denying him. He'd been fourteen, like me. How could I be alive and Emmett Till dead? Who had killed him? Why? Would I recognize him if I dared look? Could my own features be horribly altered like his? I needed answers, needed to confront what frightened me in the murdered Black boy's face. But Emmett Till just too dead, too gruesomely, absolutely dead to behold.

Years afterward during college I'd recall how it felt to discover Emmett Till's picture when one of my summer jobs involved delivering towels and sheets to the city morgue, and the booze-breathed old coroner who got his kicks freaking out rookies lifted a kettle's lid to prove, yes, indeed, there was a human skull inside from which he was attempting to boil the last shreds of meat.

Now when I freeze-frame a close-up shot of Emmett Till's shattered face on my VCR, am I looking? The image on the screen still denies its flesh-and-blood origins. It's a smashed, road-killed thing, not a boy's face. I'm reminded of the so-called "nail fetishes," West African wood sculptures, part mask, part free-standing head, that began appearing when slaving ships crisscrossed the Atlantic. Gouged, scarred, studded with nails, glass, cartridge shells, stones, drools of raffia, hunks of fur and bone, these horrific creatures police the boundary between human and spirit worlds. Designed to terrify and humble, they embody evil's power to transcend mere human conceptions of its force, reveal the chaos always lurking within the ordinary, remind us the gods amuse themselves by snatching away our certainties.

Whether you resided in an African American community like Homewood, where I spent half my early years, or in white areas like Shadyside, with a few houses on a couple of streets for Black people—my turf when we didn't live in my grandparents' house in Homewood— everybody colored knew what was in *Jet* magazine. *Jet*'s articles as much a part of our barbershop, poolroom, ball field, corner, before-and after-church talk as the *Courier,* Pittsburgh's once-a-week newspaper, aka the "Black Dispatch." Everybody aware of *Jet* and the *Courier* even though not everybody approved or identified to the same degree with these publications, whose existence was rooted in an unblinking acknowledgment of the reality of racial segregation, a reality their contents celebrated as much as protested.

Jet would arrive at our house on Copeland Street, Shadyside, in batches, irregularly, when Aunt Catherine, who lived down the block and never missed an issue, finished with them and got around to dropping some off. Aunt Catherine was my father's sister, and they were Harry Wideman's kids and inherited his deep-brown, South Carolina skin, while my mother s side of the family was light, bright and almost white, like my other grandfather, Daddyjohn French, from Culpepper, Virginia.

Skin color in my family, besides being tattletale proof segregation didn't always work, was a pretty good predictor of a person's attitude toward *Jet* magazine. My mother wouldn't or couldn't buy *Jet.* I've never asked her which. In pale Shadyside, *Jet* wasn't on sale. You'd have to go a good distance to find it, and with neither car nor driver's license and five kids to care for twenty-four seven, my mother seldom ranged very far from home. Tight as money was then, I'm sure a luxury like subscribing to *Jet* never entered her mind. If by some miracle spare change became available and Brackman's Pharmacy on Walnut Street had begun stocking *Jet*, my mother would have been too self-conscious to purchase a magazine about colored people from old, icy, freckle-fingered Brackman.

Although apartheid stipulates Black and white as absolutely separate categories, people construct day by day through the choices they make and allow to be made for them what constitutes Blackness and whiteness, what race means, and Mr. Brackman presided over one of the whitest businesses on Walnut Street. Clearly he didn't want folks like us in his drugstore. His chilliness, disdain, and begrudging service a nasty medicine you had to swallow while he doled out your prescriptions. White kids permitted to sit on the floor in a corner and browse through the comic-book bin, but he hurried me along if he thought I attempted to read before I bought. (I knew he believed I'd steal his comics if he turned his back, so in spite of his eagle eye, I did, with sweet, sweet satisfaction every chance I got, throwing them in a garbage can before I got home to avoid that other eagle eye, my mom's.)

Though copies reached us by a circuitous and untimely route, my mother counted on *Jet*. Read it and giggled over its silliness, fussed at its shamelessness, envied and scoffed at the airs of the "sididdy folks" who paraded through it weekly. In my grandparents' house in Homewood, when my mom got down with her sisters, Geraldine and Martha, I'd eavesdrop while they riffed on *Jet*'s contents, fascinated by how they mixed Homewood people and gossip into *Jet*'s features, improvising new stories, raps, and sermons I'd never imagined when I'd read it alone.

By the time an issue of *Jet* reached me, after it had passed through the hands of Aunt Catherine, Uncle Horton, my mother, my father when he was around, the pages were curled, ink-smeared, soft and comfortable as Daddyjohn French's tobacco-ripe flannel shirts. I could fan the pages, and the widest gaps opened automatically at the best stories.

With its spatters, spots, rings from the bottom of a coffee cup, smudges of chocolate candy or lipstick, pages with turned-down corners, pages ripped out, torn covers, *Jet* was an image of the Black world as I understood it then: secondhand, beat-up, second-rate. Briar patch and rebuke.

But also often truer and better than the other world around me. Much better. *Jet,* with its incriminating, renegade, embarrassing, topsy-turvy, loud, proud focus on colored doings and faces expanded my sense of possibility. Compared to other magazines of the fifties—*Life, Look, House & Garden, Redbook*—*Jet* was like WAMO, the radio station that blasted rhythm and blues and gospel, an escape from the droning mediocrity of *Your Hit Parade*, a plunge into versions of my life unavailable elsewhere on the dial, grabbing me, shaking me up, reminding me life could move to a dance beat.

In 1955, the year Emmett Till was murdered, I, like him, had just graduated from junior high. I'm trying to remember if I, like him, carried pictures of white girls in my wallet. Can't recall whether I owned a wallet in 1955. Certainly it wouldn't have been a necessity since the little bits of cash I managed to get hold of passed rapidly through my hands. "Money burns a hole in your pocket, boy," my mom said. Wanting to feel grown up, manly, I probably stuffed some sort of hand-me-down billfold in my hip pocket, and carrying around a white girl's picture in it would have been ocular proof of sexual prowess, proof the color of my skin didn't scare white chicks away or scare me away from them. A sign of power. Proof I could handle that other world, master its opportunities and dangers. Since actual romances across the color line tended to be rare and clandestine then, a photo served as evidence of things unseen. A ticket to status in my tiny clan of Shadyside brown boys, a trophy copped in another country I could flaunt in Black Homewood. So I may have owned a wallet with pictures of white girlfriends/classmates in it, and if I'd traveled to Promised Land, South Carolina, with my grandfather Harry Wideman one of those summers he offered to take me down home where he'd been born and raised, who knows? Since I was a bit of a smart aleck, like Emmett Till, I might have flashed my snapshots. I liked to brag. Take on dares like him. *OK. OK, Emmett Till. You so bad. You talking 'bout all those white gals you got up in Chicago. Bet you won't say boo to that white lady in the store.*

Two years before Emmett Till was beaten and murdered, when both Emmett Till and I were twelve, a stroke killed my mother's father, John French. I lapsed into a kind of semi-coma, feverish, silent, sleeping away whole days, a little death to cope with losing my grandfather, my family believed. Grieving for Daddyjohn was only part of the reason I retreated into myself. Yes, I missed him. Everybody was right about that, but I couldn't confide to anyone that the instant he died, there was no room for him in my heart. Once death closed his eyes, I wanted him gone, utterly, absolutely gone. I erected a shell to keep him out, to protect myself from the touch of his ghostly hands, the smells and sounds of him still lurking in the rooms of the

Homewood house where we'd lived for a year with my mother's parents and her sisters after my father left our house on Copeland Street.

Losing my grandfather stunned me. He'd been my best friend. I couldn't understand how he'd changed from Daddyjohn to some invisible, frightening presence I had no name for. He'd stopped moving, speaking, breathing. For two interminable days, his body lay inside a coffin on a spindly-legged, metal stand beside the piano in the living room, the dark, polished wood of one oblong box echoing the other. Until we had to sell the piano a few years later, I couldn't enter the room or touch the piano unless someone else was with me. Sitting on the spinning stool, banging away for hours on the keys had been one of my favorite solitary pastimes, as unthinkable suddenly as romping with my dead grandfather, chanting the nonsense rimes he'd taught me—"Froggy went a-courting, and he did ride/Uh-huh, uh-huh."

Stunned by how empty, how threatening the spaces of my grandfather's house had become, I fought during the daylight hours to keep him away, hid under the covers of my bed at night. Stunned by guilt. By my betrayal of him, my inability to remember, to honor the love that had bound us. Love suddenly changed to fear of everything about him. Fear that love might license him to trespass from the grave.

I'd never understood the dead. Shied away from talk of death, thoughts of the dead. The transformation of my grandfather the instant he became one of the dead confirmed my dread. If I couldn't trust Daddyjohn, what horrors would the rest of the dead inflict upon me? Given the nightmare's witness, am I still running, still afraid?

Emmett Till's murder was an attempt to slay an entire generation. Push us backward to the bad old days when our lives seemed not to belong to us. When white power and racism seemed unchallengeable forces of nature, when inferiority and subserviency appeared to be our birthright, when Black lives seemed cheap and expendable, when the grossest insults to pride and person, up to and including murder, had to be endured. No redress, no retaliation, no justice expected. Emmett Till's dead body, like the body of James Byrd just yesterday in Texas, reminded us that the bad old days are never farther away than the thickness of skin, skin some people still claim the prerogative to burn or cut or shoot full of holes if it's dark skin. It's no accident that Emmett Till's dead face appears inhuman. The point of inflicting the agony of his last moments, killing and mutilating him, is to prove he's not human.

And it almost works. Comes close to working every time. Demonized by hot-blooded or cold-blooded statistics of crime, addiction, disease, cartooned, minstrelized, criminalized, eroticized, commodified in stereotypical representations, the Black body kidnapped and displayed by the media loses all vestiges of humanity. We are set back on our collective heels by the overwhelming evidence, the constant warning that beneath Black skin something other, something brutal lurks. A so-called "lost generation" of young Black men dying in the streets today points backward, the way Emmett Till's rotting corpse points backward, history and prophecy at once: This is the way things have always been, will always be, the way they're supposed to be.

The circle of racism, its perverse logic, remain unbroken. Boys like Emmett Till are born violating the rules, aren't they? Therefore they forfeit any rights law-abiding citizens are bound to respect. The bad places—ghettos, prisons, morgue slabs—where most of them wind up confirm the badness of the boys. Besides, does it hurt any less if the mugger's a product of nurture, not nature? Keeping him off your streets, confining him in a world apart is what matters, isn't it?

But what if the disproportionate numbers of African American males in prison or caught in the net of economic marginality are not a consequence of inborn, Black deviancy? What if incarceration and poverty are latter-day, final solutions of the problem of slavery? What if the dismal lives of so many young Black people indicate an intentional, systematic closing off of access to the mainstream, justified by a mythology of race that the closing off simultaneously engenders and preserves?

Nearly five hundred years ago, European ships began transporting captive Africans to the New World. Economic exploitation of the recently "discovered" Americas provided impetus for this slave trade. Buying and selling African bodies, treating them as property, commodities, livestock, produced enormous profit and imprinted a model for ignoring the moral and ethical implications of financially successful global commerce we continue to apply today. The traffic in human bodies was also fueled by a dream, a Utopian dream of escape from the poverty, disease, class, and religious warfare of Europe, a dream of transforming through European enterprise and African slave labor the wilderness across the sea into a garden of wealth and prosperity, with the European colonist cast as the New Adam exercising divinely sanctioned dominion over all he surveyed.

Racism and genocide were the underside of this Edenic dream, persist today in the determined unwillingness of the heirs of the dream to surrender advantages gained when owning slaves was legal.

During its heyday slavery's enormous profit and enormous evil sparked continuous debate. Could a true Christian own slaves? Do Africans possess souls? Because it licensed and naturalized the subjugation of "inferior" Africans by "superior" Europeans, the invention of the concept of "race"—dividing humankind into a hierarchy of groups, each possessing distinct, unchangeable traits that define the groups as eternally separate and unequal—was crucial to the slaveholder's temporary victory in these debates. Over time, as slavery gradually was abolished, a systematic network of attitudes and practices based on the concept of race evolved across all fields and activities of New World societies with a uniquely pervasive, saturating force. The primary purpose of this racialized thinking was, under the guise of different vocabularies, to rationalize and maintain in public and private spheres the power European slave owners once held over their African slaves.

Emmett Till was murdered because he violated taboos governing race relations in 1955 in Money, a rural Mississippi town, but his killers were also exercising and revalidating prerogatives in place since their ancestors imported Emmett Till's ancestors to these shores. At some level everybody in Money understood this. Our horror, our refusal to look too closely at Emmett Till, reside in the same deep, incriminating knowledge.

Perhaps an apartheid mentality reigns in this country because most Americans consciously hold racist attitudes or wish ill on their neighbors of African descent. I don't think so. Emmett Till dies again and again because his murder, the conditions that ensure and perpetuate it, have not been honestly examined. Denial is more acceptable to the majority of Americans than placing themselves, their inherited dominance, at risk.

Any serious attempt to achieve economic, social, and political equal opportunity in this nation must begin not simply with opening doors to selected minorities. That impulse, that trope, that ideology has failed. The majority must decide to relinquish significant measures of power and privilege if lasting transformations of self and society are to occur. There have always been open doors of sorts for minorities (emancipation, emigration, education, economic success in sports or business, passing as white). What's missing is an unambiguous, abiding determination declared in public and private by a majority of the majority to surrender privileges that are the living legacy of slavery. Begin now. Today. Give up walls, doors, keys, the dungeons, the booty, the immunity, the false identity apartheid preserves.

A first step is acknowledging that the dangerous lies of slavery continue to be told as long as we conceive of ourselves in terms of race, as Black or white.

Emmett Till and the young victims of drug and territory wars raging in African-American neighborhoods today are signs of a deeply flawed society failing its children. Why do we perceive the bodies of dead Black boys, imprisoned Black men, homeless Black people, addicted Black people as Black problems? Why do we support cynical politicians who cite these Black problems as evidence for more brutal policing of the racial divide?

In 1955, one year after the Supreme Court's *Brown v. Board of Education* school-desegregation decision, a great struggle for civil rights commenced. The lynching of Emmett Till should have clarified exactly what was at stake: life or death. As long as racialized thinking continues to legitimize one group's life-and-death power over another, the battered face of Emmett Till will poison the middle ground of compromise between so-called "whites" and so-called "Blacks." His face unmourned, unburied, unloved, haunting the netherworld where incompatible versions of democracy clash.

It was hard to bury Emmett Till, hard, hard to bury Carole Robertson, Addie Mae Collins, Denise McNair, and Cynthia Wesley, the four girls killed by a bomb in a Birmingham, Alabama, church. So hard an entire nation began to register the convulsions of Black mourning. The deaths of our children in the civil-rights campaigns changed us. The oratory of great men like Martin Luther King Jr. pushed us to realize our grief should be collective, should stir us to unify, to clarify our thinking, roll back the rock of fear. Emmett Till's mangled face could belong to anybody's son who transgressed racial laws; anyone's little girl could be crushed in the rubble of a bombed church. We read the terrorist threat inscribed upon Emmett Till's flesh and were shaken but refused to comply with the terrorists' demands.

Martin Luther King Jr. understood the killing of our children was an effort to murder the nation's future. We mourned the young martyrs, and a dedicated few risked life and limb fighting with ferocity and dignity in the courts, churches, and streets to stop the killing. Young people served as shock troops in the movement for social justice, battling on the front lines, the hottest, most dangerous spots in Alabama and Mississippi. And though they had most to gain or lose (their precious lives, their time on this earth), they also carried on their shoulders the hopes of older generations and generations unborn.

Now there seems to be in our rituals of mourning for our dying children no sense of communal, general loss, no larger, empowering vision. We don't connect our immediate trials—drugs, gang violence, empty schools, empty minds, empty homes, empty values—to the ongoing, historical struggle to liberate ourselves from the oppressive legacies of slavery and apartheid. Funerals for our young are lonely occurrences. Daily it seems, in some ghetto or another somewhere in America, a small Black congregation will gather together to try to repair the hole in a brother's or mother's soul with the balm of gospel singing, prayer, the laying on of dark hands on darkened spirits.

How many a week, how many repetitions of the same, sad, isolated ceremony, the hush afterward when the true dimensions of loss and futility begin to set in? A sense of futility, of powerlessness dogs the survivors, who are burdened not only by the sudden death of a loved one but also by the knowledge that it's going to happen again today or tomorrow and that it's supposed to happen in a world where Black lives are expendable, can disappear, click, in a finger-pop, quick like that, without a trace, as if the son or sister was hardly here at all. Hey, maybe Black people really ain't worth shit, just like you've been hearing your whole life.

Curtis Jones, a cousin who accompanied Emmett Till on the trip from Chicago, Illinois, to Money, Mississippi, in August 1955, relates how close Emmett Till came to missing their train, reminding us how close Emmett Till's story came to not happening or being another story altogether, and that in turn should remind us how any story, sad or happy, is always precariously close to being other than it is. Doesn't take much to alter a familiar scene into chaos. Difficult as it is to remember what does occur, we must also try to keep alive what doesn't—the missed trains, squandered opportunities, warnings not heeded. We carry forward these fictions because what might have been is part of what gives shape to our stories. We depend on memory's capacity to hold many lives, not just the one we appear to be leading at the moment. Memory is space for storing lives we didn't lead, room where they remain alive, room for mourning them, forgiving them. Memory, like all stories we tell, a tissue of remembering, forgetting, of *what if* and *once upon a time,* burying our dead so the dead may rise.

Curtis Jones goes on to tell us about everybody piling into Grandpa Wright's automobile and trundling down the dusty road to church. How he and his cousin Emmett Till took the car into Money that afternoon while Moses Wright preached.

A bunch of boys loafing outside Bryant's General Store on Money's main drag. Sho'nuff country town. Wooden storefronts with wooden porches. Wooden sidewalks.

Overhanging wooden signs. With its smatter of brown boys out front, its frieze of tire-sized Coca-Cola signs running around the eaves of its porch, Bryant's the only game in town, Emmett Till guessed.

Climbing out of Moses Wright's old Dodge, he sports the broad smile I recall from another photo, the one of him leaning, elbow atop a TV set, clean as a string bean in his white dress shirt and tie, his chest thrust out mannishly, baby fat in his cheeks, a softish, still-forming boy whose energy, intelligence, and expectations of life are evident in the pose he's striking for the camera, just enough in-your-face swagger that you can't help smiling back at the wary eagerness to please of his smile.

To Emmett Till, the boys in Money's streets are a cluster of down-home country cousins. He sees a stage beckoning on which he can perform. Steps up on the sidewalk with his cousin Curtis, to whom he is Bo or Bobo, greets his audience. Like a magician pulling a rabbit from his hat, Emmett Till pulls a white girl from his wallet. Silences everybody. Mesmerizes them with tales of what they're missing, living down here in the Mississippi woods. If he'd been selling magic beans, all of them would have dug into their overalls and extracted their last, hot penny to buy some. They watch his fingers slip into his shirt pocket. Hold their breath waiting for the next trick.

Emmett Till's on a roll, can't help rubbing it in a little. What he's saying about himself sounds real good, so good he wants to hear more. All he wants really is for these brown faces to love him. As much as he's loved by the dark faces and light faces in the junior-high graduation pictures from Chicago he's showing around.

He winks at the half-dozen or so boys gathered round him. Nods. Smiles like the cat swallowed the canary. Points to the prettiest girl, the fairest, longest-haired one of all you can easily see, even though the faces in the class picture are tiny and gray. Emmett Till says she is the prettiest, anyway, so why not? Why not believe he's courted and won her, and ain't you-all lucky he come down here bringing you-all the good news?

Though Emmett Till remains the center of attention, the other kids giggle, scratch their naps, stroke their chins, turn their heads this way and that around the circle, commence little conversations of eye-cutting and teeth-sucking and slack-jawed awe. Somebody pops a finger against somebody's shaved skull. Somebody's hip bumps somebody else. A tall boy whistles a blues line, and you notice someone's been humming softly the whole time. Emmett Till's the preacher, and it's Sunday morning, and the sermon is righteous. On the other hand, everybody's ready for a hymn or a responsive reading, even a collection plate circulating, so they can participate, stretch their bones, hear their own voices.

You sure is something, boy. You say you bad, Emmett Till. Got all them white gals up North, you say. Bet you won't say boo to the white lady in the store.

Curtis Jones is playing checkers with old Uncle Edmund on a barrel set in the shade around the corner from the main drag. One of the boys who sauntered into the store with Emmett Till to buy candy comes running. *He did it. Emmett Till did it. That cousin of yours crazy, boy. Said, "Bye-bye, Baby," to Miss Bryant.*

The old man gets up so fast he knocks over the crate he's been sitting on. *Lord have mercy. I know the boy didn't do nothing like that. Huh-uh. No. No, he didn't. You-all better get out here. That lady come out that store blow you-all's brains off.*

Several months later, after an all-white jury in the town of Sumner, Mississippi, had deliberated an hour—would have been less if we hadn't took time for lunch—and found Roy Bryant and J.W. Milam not guilty of murdering Emmett Till, the two men were paid $4,000 by a journalist, William Bradford Huie, to tell the story of abducting, beating, and shooting Emmett Till.

To get rid of his body, they barb-wired a fifty-pound cotton-gin fan to Emmett Till's neck and threw him in the Tallahatchie River. The journalist, in a videotaped interview, said, "It seems to a rational mind today—it seems impossible that they could have killed him."

The reporter muses for a moment, then remembers, "But J.W. Milam looked up at me, and he says, 'Well, when he told me about this white girl he had, my friend, well, that's what this war's about down here now, that's what we got to fight to protect, and I just looked at him and say, *Boy, you ain't never gone to see the sun come up again.*'"

To the very end, Emmett Till didn't believe the crackers would kill him. He was fourteen, from Chicago. He'd hurt no one. These strange, funny-talking white men were a nightmare he'd awaken from sooner or later. Milam found the boy's lack of fear shocking. Called it "belligerence." Here was this nigger should be shitting his drawers. Instead he was making J.W. Milam uncomfortable. Brave or foolhardy or ignorant or blessed to be already in another place, a place these sick, sick men could never touch, whatever enabled Emmett Till to stand his ground, to be himself until the first deadly blow landed, be himself even after it landed, I hope Emmett Till understood that Milam or Bryant, whoever struck first with the intent to kill, was the one who flinched, not him.

When such thoughts come to me, I pile them like sandbags along the levees that protect my sleep. I should know better than to waste my time.

In another dream we emerge at dawn from the tree line. Breeze into Money. Rat-tat. Rat-tat-tat. Waste the whole motherfucking ville. Nothing to it. Little hick town 'bout same today as when they lynched poor brother Emmett Till.

Some the bitches come rubbing up against us after we lined 'em up by the ditch. Thinking maybe if they fuck us they won't die. We let 'em try. You know. Wasn't bad pussy, neither. But when the time come, you know, they got to go just like the rest. Rat-tat-tat. Uh-huh.

Money gone. Burnt a hole in its pocket.

I asked a lover, a woman whose whiteness made her a flesh-and-blood embodiment of the nightmare J.W. Milam discovered in Emmett Till's wallet, what she thinks of when she hears "Emmett Till."

"A Black kid whistling at a white woman somewhere down South and being killed for it, is what I think," she said.

"He didn't whistle," I reply. I've heard the wolf-whistle story all my life and another that has him not moving aside for a white woman walking down the sidewalk. Both are part of the myth, but neither's probably true. The story Till's cousin Curtis Jones tells is different. And for what it's worth, his cousin was there. Something Emmett Till said to a white woman inside a store is what started it.

She wants to know where I heard the cousin's version, and I launch into a riff on my sources—*Voices of Freedom,* an oral history of the civil rights movement; Henry Hampton's video documentary, *Eyes on the Prize*; a book, *Representations of Black Masculinity in Contemporary American Art,* organized around a museum exhibit of Black male images. Then I realize I'm doing all the talking, when what I'd intended to elicit was her spontaneous witness. What her memory carried forward, what it lost.

She's busy with something of her own, and we just happened to cross paths a moment in the kitchen, and she's gone before I get what I wanted. Gone before I know what I wanted. Except standing there next to the refrigerator, in the silence released by its hum, I feel utterly defeated. All the stuff spread out on my desk isn't getting me any closer to Emmett Till or a cure. Neither will man-in-the-street, woman-in-the-kitchen interviews. Other people's facts and opinions don't matter. Only one other person's voice required for this story I'm constructing to overcome a bad dream, and they shut him up a long time ago, didn't they?

Here is what happened. Four nights after the candy-buying and "Bye-bye, Baby" scene in Money, at 2:00 a.m. on August 21, 1955, Roy Bryant, with a pistol in one hand and a flashlight in the other, appears at Moses Wright's door. "This is Mr. Bryant," he calls into the darkness. Then demands to know if Moses Wright has two niggers from Chicago inside. He says he wants the nigger done all that talk.

When Emmett Till is delivered, Bryant marches him to a car and asks someone inside, "This the right nigger?" and somebody says, "Yes, he is."

Next time Moses Wright sees Emmett Till is three days later when the sheriff summons him to identify a corpse. The body's naked and too badly damaged to tell who it is until Moses Wright notices the initialed ring on his nephew's finger.

Where were you when JFK was shot? Where were you when a man landed on the moon? When Martin Luther King Jr. was shot? Malcolm shot? When the Rodney King verdict announced? Where were you when Emmett Till floated up to the surface of the Tallahatchie River for *Bye-bye Babying* a white woman?

A white man in the darkness outside a tarpaper cabin announcing the terror of his name, gripping a flashlight in his fist, a heavy-duty flashlight stuffed with thick D batteries that will become a club for bashing Emmett Till's skull.

An old Black man in the shanty crammed with bodies, instantly alert when he hears, "You got those niggers from Chicago in there with you?" An old man figuring the deadly odds, how many lives bought if one handed over. Calculating the rage of his ancient enemy, weighing the risk of saying what he wants the others in his charge to hear, Emmett Till to hear, no matter what terrible things happen next.

"Got my two grandsons and a nephew in here."

A Black boy inside the cabin, a boy my age whose name I don't know yet, who will never know mine. He rubs his eyes, not sure he's awake or dreaming a scary dream, one of the tales buried deep, deep he's been hearing since before we were born about the old days in the Deep South when they cut off niggers' nuts and lynched niggers and roasted niggers over fires like marshmallows.

A man in my own, warm bed, lying beside a beautiful woman rubbing my shoulder, a pale, blond woman whose presence sometimes is as strange and unaccountable to me as mine must be to her, as snow falling softly through the bedroom ceiling would be, accumulating in white drifts on the down comforter.

Why am I telling Emmett Till's story this way, attempting the miracle or cheap trick of being many people, many places at once? Will words change what happened, what's missing, what's lost? Will my nightmare dissolve if I cling to the woman almost asleep now next to me, end if I believe this loving moment together might last and last?

The name *Emmett* is spoiled for me. In any of its spellings. As big a kick as I get from watching Emmitt Smith rush the football for the Dallas Cowboys, there is also the moment after a bone-shattering collision and he's sprawled lifeless on the turf or the moment after he's stumbled or fumbled and slumps to the bench and lifts his helmet and I see a Black mother's son, a small, dark, round face, a boy's big, wide, scared eyes. All those yards gained, all that wealth, but like O.J. he'll never run far enough or fast enough. Inches behind him the worst thing the people who hate him can imagine hounds him like a shadow.

Sometimes I think the only way to end this would be with Andy Warhol-like strips of images, the same face, Emmett Till's face, replicated twelve, twenty-four, forty-eight, ninety-six times on a wall-sized canvas. Like giant postage stamps end to end, top to bottom, each version of the face exactly like the other but different names printed below each one. Martin Luther Till. Malcolm Till. Medgar Till. Nat Till. Gabriel Till. Michael Till. Huey Till. Bigger Till. Nelson Till. Mumia Till. Colin Till. Jesse Till. Your daddy, your mama, your sister, brother, aunt, cousin, uncle, niece, nephew Till …

Instead of the nightmare one night, this is what I dream. I'm marching with many, many men, a multitude, a million men of all colors in Washington,

D.C., marching past the bier on which the body of Emmett Till rests. The casket, as his mother demanded, is open. *I want the world to see what they did to my baby.* One by one from an endless line, the men detach themselves, pause, peer down into the satin-lined box. Pinned inside its upright lid a snapshot of Emmett Till, young, smiling, whole, a jaunty Stetson cocked high across his brow. In the casket Emmett Till is dressed in a dark suit, jacket wings spread to expose a snowy shroud pulled up to his chin. Then the awful face, patched together with string and wire, awaits each mourner.

My turn is coming soon. I'm grateful. Will not shy away this time. Will look hard this time. The line of my brothers and fathers and sons stretches ahead of me, behind me. I am drawn by them, pushed by them, steadied as we move each other along. We are a horizon girding the earth, holding the sky down. So many of us in one place at one time it scares me. More than a million of us marching through this city of monumental buildings and dark alleys. Not very long ago, we were singing, but now we march silently, more shuffle than brisk step as we approach the bier, wait our turn. Singing's over, but it holds silently in the air, tangible as weather, as the bright sun disintegrating marble buildings, emptying alleys of shadows, warming us on a perfect October day we had no right to expect but would have been profoundly disappointed had it fallen out otherwise.

What I say when I lean over and speak one last time to Emmett Till is *I love you. I'm sorry. I won't allow it to happen ever again.* And my voice will be small and quiet when I say the words, not nearly as humble as it should be, fearful almost to pledge any good after so much bad. My small voice and short turn, and then the next man and the next, close together, leading, following one another so the murmur of our voices beside the bier never stops. An immensity, a continuous, muted shout and chant and benediction, a river gliding past the stillness of Emmett Till. Past this city, this hour, this place. River sound of blood I'm almost close enough to hear coursing in the veins of the next man.

In the dream we do not say, *Forgive us.* We are taking, not asking for something today. There is no time left to ask for things, even things as precious as forgiveness, only time to take one step, then the next and the next, alone in this great body of men, each one standing on his own feet, moving, our shadows linked, a coolness, a shield stretching nearly unbroken across the last bed where Emmett Till sleeps.

Where we bow and hope and pray he frees us. Ourselves seen, sinking, then rising as in a mirror, then stepping away.

And then. And then this vision fades, too. I am there and not there. Not in Washington, DC, marching with a million other men. My son Dan, my new granddaughter Qasima's father, marched. He was a witness, and the arc of his witness includes me as mine, his. So, yes, I was there in a sense but not there to view the face of Emmett Till because Emmett Till was not there, either, not in an open casket displayed to the glory of the heavens, the glories of this republic, not there except as a shadow, a stain, a wound in the million faces of the marchers, the faces of their absent fathers, sons, and brothers.

We have yet to look upon Emmett Till's face. No apocalyptic encounter, no ritual unveiling, no epiphany has freed us. The nightmare is not cured.

I cannot wish away Emmett Till's face. The horrific death mask of his erased features marks a site I ignore at my peril. The site of a grievous wound. A wound unhealed because untended. Beneath our nation's pieties, our self-delusions, our denials and distortions of history, our professed black-and-white certainties about race, lies chaos. The whirlwind that swept Emmett Till away and brings him back.

Attention Please, This Island Earth

DIANE ACKERMAN

Excerpts from *An Alchemy of Mind*

Attention, Please

One day a Stone Age tribe in Papua, New Guinea, greeted a charter pilot with bananas for his airplane and a desire to know what sex it was. The plane's wheels were the first wheels they'd ever seen, and the huffing, twirling sky beast had their urgent attention. We humans respond to far less-startling sights. Any novelty is riveting. Heed change, life demands, especially an erratic or peculiar change, because it's elemental to survival. Notice anything new. Something will matter.

Learn something or of someone new, and you discover an avalanche of details. But soon the brain switches to a kind of shorthand. Once the brain perceives something, it's primed to recognize it faster the next time, and even faster after that, until it needn't look at it carefully again. Then, as Hegel says, "The known, just because it is known, is the unknown." Knowing people better, you notice them less. What we call boredom is a form of mental abbreviation, a kind of waking slumber. Until things change. Or unless we choose to revive some of the sharp sensations we felt earlier but lost when their startling shine began to dull. Piggybacking on a child's discoveries or being enthralled by an artist's informed innocence, we pay fresh attention to what's grown stale, scrape some of the rust and lichen off the brain, and find the world renewed.

Some years ago, I taught a class of writing students whose work was surprisingly jaded and featureless. Where was the texture of life, I wondered, the feel of being alive on this particular planet? Didn't it strike them as astonishing that they shared the planet with goldfinches and heli-arc welders and dung beetles and blood brothers and shiitake mushrooms? Where was their fascination with the world pressing indelibly on what they wrote? Most of the students weren't even twenty-five; how could life already have bored them?

One afternoon I suggested we begin class at the large, open window by enjoying the phenomena visible at that moment, which included lens-shaped clouds signaling high winds aloft; slate shingles on the library tower overlapping like pigeon feathers; magnolia buds burgeoning in fuzzy-coated hulls that looked like fledglings almost ready for flight; half a dozen dog, squirrel, and bird dramas; and many human pantomimes, as small groups of students coalesced and drifted apart. Everyone had to choose one sensory event that seemed eloquent. For a few minutes, we stood quietly and paid attention.

I wondered if I could reacquaint them with a cunning we inherited from our ancestors: we can seize a phenomenon with mental pincers and stop the world in its spin, if only briefly. Look patiently, affectionately, at anything, gather six or eight perceptions, and it will never look the same again. When we read Federico García Lorca's "A thousand glass tambourines/were wounding the dawn," we know he once sat and watched a crystal sunrise jingling with color as splinters of light reddened the horizon.

We can't enchant the world, which makes its own magic, but we can enchant ourselves by paying deep attention. My life had been changing. I'd been near death several times, and the simple details of being had become precious. But I also relished life's sensory festival and the depot where nature and human nature meet. Everything that happens to us—from choosing the day's shoes to warfare—shines at that crossroads.

In *Roderick Hudson,* Henry James wrote, "True happiness, we are told, consists in getting out of one's self; but the point is not only to get out—you must stay out; and to stay out, you must have some absorbing errand." An absorbing errand as simple as becoming aware of each breath. All forms of meditation are simply ways of paying close attention. Entice the brain to pay attention, and the newsy, noisy self drains away below the thought horizon like a molten sun at dusk. One can lose one's self while listening to a mockingbird's stolen medley or staring at a stapler's tiny fangs. Not all of the self; the unconscious goes about its chores, runs the blood factory, conducts sub-rosa board meetings of the psyche, and protects its fragile marshes, where flocks of feeling, thought, behavior, and belief all roost.

We don't regard just breaths, objects, and nature, of course. We were emotional beasts long before we were thoughtful ones. A palette of primary emotions guided our distant ancestors in most situations, and they still do. It's a productive, if sloppy, process. The brain attends to a feeling, is distracted by events, ruminates on other things, associates, follows a tangent, returns to the first with additional insight from its travels, perhaps putting it in a wider perspective, perhaps reevaluating it, then moves on, repeating the process in a slowly opening fan of thought. The brain isn't tidy or linear enough to corral all of its ideas about something. The brain notices, feels, learns, moves on, notices more, learns more, feels more, refines its picture based on what it has learned, moves on, endlessly.

What matters is change, the shifting strata of clouds or society. As Emerson says in "Self-Reliance," one of his loveliest essays, power stops in quiet moments. It thrives on the change "from a past to a new state, in the shooting of the gulf, in the darting to an aim." At great cost, we pay attention, scouting for change. Change leads to actions as bold as a dash from a burning barn, as calculated as the reappraisal of status. It always rouses the brain from rest or distracts it from other business. Everything was safe a moment ago, as proven by the fact that nothing bad happened, but if something changes, however small, my safety must be reassessed. Life becomes a lost archipelago, islands of safety, most barely conscious, all vanishing behind us as we focus on a newly seen sliver of coral sand within reach.

We share this instinct with other animals, which is why it's wise not to make eye contact with an aggressive dog you're biking past. When it notices you've noticed it, that you're paying attention, you become a greater threat, just as the dog seemed a greater threat when it noticed you and started barking. Or you could stop, leap from your bike, which you then use as a barricade, and bark at the dog in a glowering, alpha-male tirade of "No! Go home! Bad dog!" The dog wouldn't feel rebuked or ashamed, of course, but it might defer to your louder threat.

No time is more alive than the intimate now, where truths are eternal. How long is a now? Now is everything the mind and senses can cram into about one-tenth of a second. In that tiny lagoon, any news arriving from the outskirts and inskirts of the body feels like a single moment, a right now. Any novelty can distract an animal from whatever it's doing. Chewing and digesting stop. Instinctively it turns toward the culprit and becomes rigidly aware. It loses sight of everything else for about half a second, in what's known as an attention blink. Even slugs do it. After a garden talk the other evening, in which I confessed to liking many things about slugs (for example, their yen to mate at the end of slime gallows), a man shared with me a curious slug story of his own. He'd been doing construction work when a tractor overturned, trapping him under it. While he waited for help, he noticed a small movement nearby and, turning his head, saw a slug standing up like a tiny giraffe, raptly watching him.

This orienting reflex alerts an animal, cramming its senses with new information, while blocking previous plans or activities. Many things can trigger the orienting reflex— surprise, novelty, sudden change, conflict, uncertainty, increased complexity or simplicity. "Be prepared" is its Boy Scout motto. An emergency may be looming. An instance of this used to happen regularly in the Falkland Islands, home to penguins and the RAF airbase, Mount Pleasant. Crews discovered that whenever they flew over a penguin colony, the resident penguins would all look up, turning their heads to keep the plane in sight. It was irresistible: The pilots soon began flying out to sea, making a tight turn, then flying above the penguins, whose bills pointed up more steeply as the jets flew overhead, until suddenly they would topple in unison.

Novelty excites by nudging us off balance and weakening our stranglehold on habit. An urgent need arises to improvise new skills, learn new rules and customs. This is especially true of mild novelty, when things change only enough to be noticeable. Complete novelty can seem absurd, something to ignore. But partial novelty makes sense, up to a point, and yet requires a bright response, so it must be taken seriously. Our lidless curiosity, as well as our passion for mystery, exploration and adventure spring from this basic reflex, the body's instinctive call to novelty or change. Once an animal becomes curious, it grows alert, and that arousal doesn't quit until it explores the sensory puzzle and can assure itself that all is well, nothing much has changed, no fresh action is required. That repeated pattern of arousal, tension, fear and suspense, followed by a feeling of safety and calm, provides a special kind of pleasure shared by animals the world over. That we enjoy such tidy escapades enough to excite or scare ourselves on purpose hints at what connoisseurs of pleasure and pain we've become. Rapture always begins with being rapt.

A herd of primates has gathered at a watering hole to drink and socialize. One female sitting in a group of several others notices her mate flirting with a receptive female a few yards away. Dividing her attention, she switches back and forth, from her circle to her mate, able to pay attention to only one conversation at a time. His face says he's altogether too interested in the female draping herself around him in provocative ways, at which, with jealousy, she listens hard and glowers and is almost ready to bound over and stake her claim, but for the moment, she keeps an eye on the pair while half-heartedly grooming a neighbor in her own group.

This is called a cocktail party, and it's almost always a scene of divided attentions, especially among couples.

There are many towpaths of attention, along which the mules of worry plod, and they can change with age. Young children seem infinitely distractable, with attention spans short as a drawbridge, because the reticular formation, a brain part needed for paying attention (and also for filtering out lots of unnecessary data), doesn't finish developing until puberty. A lover pays attention to the beloved with shared life and limbs, soulful passion, passionate soul. That usually rallies one's full, doting, if inaccurate, attention. Inaccurate is okay among lovers, where it's sometimes best to blur the details a little. As W.H. Auden writes in "I Am Not a Camera":

lovers, approaching to kiss,
instinctively shut their eyes before their faces
can be reduced to
anatomical data.

With advancing age, splitting one's attention becomes harder, as does sifting through warring stimuli. Our filters begin to falter, and more sensory noise seeps in, which we find distracting and confusing. A prime example of this is noisy-restaurant syndrome, when ambient conversations drown out people at one's own table. But other attention skills can take over. I remember entomologist E.O. Wilson explaining that, when a fishing accident blinded him in one eye, he sadly abandoned his plans of studying big animals. But, as he began to focus differently, paying loving attention to the close and small, he developed his famous passion for ants. What we pay attention to helps define us. With what does a man choose to spend the irreplaceable hours of his life? For Wilson it's ants. For another it might be the entrails of pocket watches.

Worrisome for people who talk on cell phones in heavy traffic, an MRI study of multitasking (the polite word for attention bingeing), reveals that paying attention to two things at once doesn't double the brain's activity but lowers it, short-changing both. Try pulling an extra wagon uphill. When important things clamor for attention, the brain savors the adages "One thing at a time" and "Divide and conquer," which is probably why brains devised them in the first place. And forget about learning two things warring for attention. A focus precise as a single coffee bean works best to store memory. Or noting how coffee beans are shaped like tiny vulvas. But

I digress. Ignore that. Ignoring something doesn't mean it won't register, since subliminal images wing in silently and roost in shadows.

Somewhere I left a bowl of Reliance seedless grapes, whose taut, red skins burst open with a melon-flavored gush, and I'm hungry for them. But I was mentally composing this paragraph as I removed grapes from the refrigerator, dangled them into a bowl, washed them under the faucet, and carried them. That's the last I remember of their travels. I'm not sure where I unthinkingly left the bowl. Is it still in the kitchen? Did I set it down on a bookshelf when I paused to read a book about absent-mindedness?

This Island Earth

I was reading this morning about the discovery of a new species of gecko, no larger than a peso, the tiniest reptile on Earth. Found in a sinkhole and a cave in a balding region of the Jaragua National Park, on the remote Caribbean island of Beata, off the southwestern coast of the Dominican Republic, *Sphaerodactylus ariasae* could curl up on the head of a dime and leave room for an aspirin and a deforester's heart. At 1.6 millimeters (about three-quarters of an inch), it's not only the tiniest lizard, but, according to evolutionary biologist Blair Hedges, who discovered it, "the smallest of all twenty-three thousand species of reptiles, birds, and mammals." A female lays but one fragile egg at a time, a minute naïf easily crushed by paws and shoe heels alike, in a rainforest more endangered than the Amazon.

Hedges and his colleague Richard Thomas have found only eight of these geckos and are delighted but not shocked by their size. The men were searching for tiny, overlooked reptiles with limited ranges, because the smallest versions of life tend to inhabit islands. On an island's detached world, over a vast sprawl of time, animals may fill ecological niches snared by others on the mainland. *Sphaerodactylus ariasae* (named in honor of Yvonne Arias, an avid conservationist in the Dominican Republic) is tiny enough, for instance, to compete with spiders elsewhere. The Caribbean is home to many such endangered species and probably many undiscovered ones that will vanish before they're witnessed or named. How that saddens me, to think of an animal surviving the rip-roaring saga of life on Earth, minting unique features and gifts, only to vanish without name or record because of human folly. I'm not sure why witnessing a life form and celebrating its unique marvel matters so much to me, but it does. Let's just say it occupies an emotional niche others may fill with prayer. Absorbing Earth's phenomena with the full frenzy of human relish and insight is our destiny.

Biologists had carefully explored the island of Beata, and yet *Sphaerodactylus ariasae* lay hidden for hundreds of years. Could an even smaller reptile exist on Earth? Probably not. There are size limits imposed by gravity and basic biology. But we should always expect the unexpected on remote islands. A century ago Darwin wrote about the effects of isolation and inbreeding and how easily island populations diverge from the mainstream and evolve their own genetic dialect. Hence kangaroos only in Australia (though marsupials abound elsewhere) and hummingbirds only in North and South America (which is why American columbines, unlike their European cousins, evolved spurs).

When we become a space-faring species, leaving our home planet to voyage to other worlds, the same fate will befall us. Many people won't survive the trips, leaving open niches for stronger, more specialized or more extreme people to fill. Islands become unique gene pools where uniquely compelled creatures evolve. Multigenerational spaceships, as well as colonies on other planets, if not refreshed by outsiders' genes, will function as islands. We may become the bizarre aliens depicted in sci-fi dramas.

Then, although many of *Homo sapiens'* relatives died out in the past, more will evolve elsewhere, given time's elasticity and the exuberance of human curiosity. With our restless yen to explore, will our outposts blossom until they're common as pond scum in the cosmic night? I doubt it. But we may become strangers with different sensory talents, develop lizardy skin, evolve into that alien "Other" we fear. New habitats will produce new essentials, scarcities, politics and values. In smaller social groups, different dynamics emerge.

That's what happened in our past on this island Earth, and our brains reflect that evolution.

Over 500 million years, a span of time too vast to imagine in detail, our brains were gradually molded by environmental pressures and breeding successes while also succumbing to random genetic mutations. As brains grew, women's pelvises and leg bones widened (hence the characteristic hip-swivel). But the skull can only expand so much and still pass through the birth canal. Even after the brain folded in, under and around itself, it still needed to add important skills. The only solution was to drop some abilities to make room for more important ones. No doubt, fascinating gifts were lost. Based on what other animals evolved, we might have had sophisticated navigational systems that relied on magnetism or echolocation (like bats or whales). Or a complex sense of smell that made a simple stroll the equivalent of reading a gossip column (like dogs). We might have shared the praying mantis's skill at high-pitched ultrasonics or the elephant's at low, rumbling infrasonics. Like the duck-billed platypus, we might once have been able to detect electrical signals from the muscles of small fish. We might have enjoyed the vibratory sense that's so highly developed in spiders, fish, bees, and other animals. But of them all, the best survival trick was language, one worth sacrificing large areas of trunk space for, areas that might once have housed feats of empathy that would put ESP to shame. Indeed, it is possible that people unusually blessed with ESP are simply ones for whom those areas haven't completely atrophied. What the brain really needed was space without volume. So it took a radical leap, something unparalleled in the history of life on Earth. It began storing information and memories outside of itself on stone, papyrus, paper, computer chips, and film. This astonishing feat is such a familiar a part of our lives that we don't think much about it.

But it was an amazing and rather strange solution to what was essentially a packing problem: Store your essentials elsewhere and avoid cluttering up the cave. Equally amazing was the determination and skill to extend our senses beyond their natural limits, by devising everything from the long eyes of television to the cupped ears of radio telescopes. Forget about being too big for our boots—we became too big for our skulls. Once we imagined gods with supernatural powers; it was only a matter of time before we aped them. On fabricated wings, we learned to fly. With weapons, we hurled lightning bolts. Using medicines, we healed. Our ancient ancestors would think us gods.

"Are you out of your mind?!" we sometimes demand. The answer is yes, we are all out of our minds; we left long ago when our brain needed more room to do its dance. Or rather, out of our brain. A born remodeler, it made as many additions as building codes allowed, then designed two kinds of external storage bins. Information could be put into things like books, which felt good in the hand, and also onto invisible things, like airwaves and ethernets.

Common sense tells us that if life exists elsewhere in the universe, it will be far more technologically advanced than we. But our evolution has been deliriously quirky, resulting in beings with bizarre traits and personalities, including, for example, the idea of a personality. I wonder how many other planetarians might feel the need to share and document their personal existence in such elaborate ways. We think of a human being as a distinct, definable creature, and its life complex. But we may once have been very different animals, with different minds and concerns and mental habits. We are who and what we are only after many trade-offs. It's sobering to imagine what was traded.

Beginning Dialogues

TOI DERRICOTTE

On the way, he said, "When you visit the cemetery, you do it for yourself. They don't know you're there." But maybe some part of me believes she will know, that she's brought many good things to me after her death, that she's taking care. Maybe I visit her grave because she would have visited the grave of her mother, because she taught me to send thank-you notes and be a good girl. Maybe I'm going to find signs of whether she's still there; maybe she hasn't blown open the ground, and we'll find an angel lounging on her gravestone, saying, "She's not here. Go and find her elsewhere."

I don't seem to suffer the pains of anguish that many women whose mothers have died feel. Last night, a group about my age, all in that midlife past midlife, late fifties or early sixties, ate dinner and talked about our mothers' deaths. It's not a new conversation; women whose mothers die always talk about it. They did even when I was in my twenties. Yet, here, no one is hearing these stories with expectancy; everyone has faced that which at one time was unthinkable. It's as if we're all in the same club, as if we have all finally arrived, as if we could all look back at those women on the other side and know we are totally new.

One woman talked about that inconsolable stabbing in the heart when she realized she wouldn't buy a Christmas present for her mother again this year. I've wondered about it, about perhaps having grieved the separation between my mother and me in my early childhood for, in a way, I truly do not miss her like that, do not feel that irreversible moment of no return, as

I did when she would go into the bathroom and shut the door, the ache that breaks the heart and has no answer. I felt the goneness of her then, as if the center of me was gone, and I tried to bring it back by peering under the crack at the bottom of the door, trying to see anything, even her feet.

I said this to the women who talked last night about their mothers. One woman, who said that her mother had died a few days after she was born, had always struck me before as cold, contained, and, now, as she spoke, I noticed she was squeezing the fleshy part of her cheek near her mouth, making a little fat bubble of flesh between her ring and baby fingers. I have seen that before, a kind of clumsy, unconscious pinching of the self, and it makes me feel great pity. Her fingers seemed squat, doing an act whose purpose I couldn't imagine—perhaps a partial holding to signify that she could not hold the whole of what she needed held. Now, clumsily, here was her body (was it her clumsy body that had killed her mother, ungracefully slipping out?)—her liveliness covered by a dreary cape, her hair dreary, her face unmade, as if who would care?—speaking about her mother's death (we had never heard of this, though we had known her for years!), without tears, just those two fingers clenching and opening, pinching a clump of cheek, letting go and clenching again, moving slightly, as if she couldn't find the right spot and, since the cheek is larger than what those two fingers can grasp, and, since the two fingers form a small vise and take in only a slot of flesh, it seemed she was stopping the flesh from moving, clamping it in place. It seemed inadequate, incomplete, and ill-chosen; in literature, the small thing signifies the whole of something we can imagine from the reference to the small thing, but here, the small reference did not convey. It was a clumsy effort, as a child might pinch the breast. Or perhaps it was an effort to make another mouth, to pucker the face, as the lips of the child might pucker for its mother's breast.

At my mother's grave, I tried to imagine what I should do. My partner had taken my picture at the grave and a picture of the inscription. He was sitting in the car. How long should I stay? My mind didn't know what to settle on. No particular feeling or idea carried me. I became lost in nothing. Just me, stuttering over an immensity that I couldn't absorb, the way I used to feel guilty for not feeling enough happiness at Christmas, after my mother's great efforts. I guess I felt that I was incompetent, too broken to hold. I sang her favorite song: "This little light of mine, I'm gonna let it shine." I wanted to give her a promise; I wanted to change my life because of her, just the way I did before.

I am struck with my own inability to feel grief. It feels like a refusal to face an end. I know I have great trouble facing boundaries, my own and others. So, instead, perhaps there is this magical thinking built on my own inadequacy to face the truth: I say I get messages from my mother that she is still in my life, and, now, perhaps even more, she is reaching me, since her destruction is out of my way.

Once, when I called a friend to say I couldn't go on teaching at the prestigious workshop I was visiting because I could not stand the torturing voices in my head, twenty-four hours a day, saying I was no good, stupid, not as smart as the others, not as respected or loved, that I had no value, that I was only there because I was Black, that I had done or said the wrong thing, that I was not really a poet, my friend said, "Why not ask the torturing voices from where they get their information?" I did, and, without hesitation, they answered, "From your mother."

Things had changed by then, so I flipped back, "You haven't got the latest information!"

Just a few months before she died, my mother turned the universe of an unloved daughter around with one sentence. Instead of screaming at me when I asked her not to come to one of my readings because I might read things that would make her uncomfortable, she said, "Oh, dear, would you be uncomfortable? I don't want you to be uncomfortable, so I won't come."

I've written a lot about messages from her—I won't repeat them here—just to say my conversation with my mother isn't over, and I think it isn't over for her, either.

In the manuscript of my mother's book, I read about the women in her childhood—her mother, aunts, and grandmother—who helped each other beyond the bounds of the imaginable. Because of their hard labor, our family succeeded. I read this manuscript, which she put into my hands to publish only two days before her death, and I think that, although my mother began writing after I did, after I was published, she was a writer before she began writing. Though she is dead, our stories are in dialogue: my writing has been against her writing, as if there was a war between us. It is more than our writing that is in dialogue; it is our lives.

When I was seven, she told me how, when she left the house of the rich white people her mother worked for, the white kids were waiting to beat her up on her way to school, and, as soon as she crossed the line to the Black part of town, the Black kids were there to beat her up, too. Why would she tell me that story? Why would a mother tell a seven-year-old such a sad story, such a defeating one? I thought it was her way of saying, "Trust no one but your mother," a way of binding me to her by making me fear.

It's a question—what she said and did that I didn't understand, what she did to hurt me. It is not over; it is still a riddle being solved. I do not need to be held, and so, therefore, isn't my mother free, too? Is that why she told me those stories? Was I to be the mother who freed her?

My partner and I have just spent a delightful weekend together, a sunny, windy, fall weekend with the trees half shredded, the bright blue sky both miraculous and unavoidable through the nude branches and their silence. On the drive home, my mind comes to how my life has changed since my mother's death: slowly, I have been loosed from those heavy, nearly inconsolable fears like Houdini's chains, lock by lock, as if some magician part of me occasionally appears, from some unseen and undetectable room, with one more chain gone. Finally, I am gloriously undrowned.

Everyone says that I changed for the better, as if, when my mother's slight body, not even one hundred pounds, slipped into the earth, the whole world suddenly belonged to me. The first year I stopped jogging. People said it was grief, but whatever grief felt like—except for the first few days after her death, especially the burial day, heavy lodestar—it was too indistinct for me to grab onto. Two years later, I bought a house and found a man in my life like a spectacular hatpin in just the right hat. The simple explanation would have been my mother's narcissism—the way she pushed me toward independence, screaming, "You're weighing me down," and yet, when I was sixteen and came in late one night, slamming the door, she was behind it in the shadows, like a burglar, and her hand went around my neck while she screamed, "I'll kill you!" Who hasn't wanted to kill the one she loved?

But there was so much unaccounted for, so much in my mother's past that I couldn't fix, not ever, or make up for. Maybe my mother never had such a weekend of happiness with a man as I have just had, though a former lover of hers once told me, when I asked about the affair, how much she had loved to make love to him. Perhaps he told me because he loved me and thought I should know that aspect of my mother, because knowing might help me put a necessary piece in the puzzle. Perhaps he had sympathy for me—in spite of the fact he had loved my mother—and didn't feel the need to protect her. Perhaps he thought it was better to give a daughter that important piece than to keep still about a dead woman. And perhaps he was bragging a bit when he said it.

My mother had slept alone, in another room, in another bed, for eighteen years of her marriage, until my parents divorced. I never saw her kiss my father, and the only touch was the time I heard him smash her against the table. My mother always gave abundantly with one hand and pushed you away with the other. The mystery of a beautiful woman. Perhaps in some reciprocal way, my unhappy, angry, guilt-producing mother had also been a planter, had been planting the seeds of my happiness with an invisible hand, the hand I didn't see. She left me enough money to buy a house. She told me all my life she loved me, as if she completely forgot the hundred slights, humiliations, threats, and insinuations. Of course, she loved me; why would I think otherwise? She loved me more than anything. Sometimes she'd scream, as if my doubts were another evil, another proof of my unworthiness. How exasperating my complaints must have been when, all along, she was planting seeds with that invisible hand.

The women of that generation, my mother and aunts, counted their blessings: Chinese food and beer on Friday nights after work and fried chicken breasts, twice-baked potatoes, and broccoli for early Sunday-afternoon dinners. And there were parties with bounteous tables; polished glasses and silver, a chandelier, every bauble ammonia-shiny; and heat's seven coolnesses, the little cups of rice turned over and decorated, each small, white breast with a nipple of parsley. Polished floors, shopping trips, lunch at Hudson's—these were the good things, the punctuation marks that held back despondence, that danced away despair. No hardship was unredeemable to women who had one endless belief: Bread on the water always comes home. It wasn't until I was in my sixties that I realized it did, but not necessarily to the ones who cast it. I am eating bread from hands that are no longer there. I cannot reach back to touch their actual bodies. It is good that they are gone.

My mother helps me. She sends me signs: her African violet bloomed for the first time on my windowsill three years after her death, on the first day of her death month. She says, "Remember me. My miracles are still there for you, still becoming apparent as you have eyes to see." I love my mother now in ways I could not have loved her when she was alive, fierce, terrifying, unpredictable, mad, shame-inducing, self-involved, relentless, and determined by any means necessary. When she was a child, she would hold her breath until she was blue and pass out to get what she wanted from her mother. Even if she had to inflict the greatest pain—making me see her suffer, making me fear her death and that I had caused it—she would do it without thinking, without hesitation. That worst threat was always between us—that she could take herself away, that she could hurt herself in my eyes—and it was out of my control to stop it. She was the hostage of an insane government, her own body. And so I revoked my love: I took away, as much as I could, the only real currency between us. I would not count on her to save me from her death. And, therefore, I saved myself by cutting the part of my heart that was in her heart; I cut it off as if snipping a pigtail. It is only now, when I am at a safe distance, that my heart begins to grow again, as if a surgeon has inserted a little gray balloon to open it up to blood. There begins to be an invisible cell, a chamber, a thumping like the thump inside the embryo shell, tissues paper-thin, of hardly any substance, except that, somewhere in it, it still knows what it is, what it will grow up to be used for.

Without a Map

MEREDITH HALL

"Don't be mad," I telegram Steve, care of the American Express office in Amsterdam. Heading off alone. See you in India." The telegram takes a startling $4.50 out of the $70 I have left after paying for my hotel. Steve has the other $600. I feel some concern about this, but I stuff the $65.50 into my jeans pocket and walk out of the telegraph office into the streets of Luxembourg. It is a cold, drizzly, metallic winter day. I am scared, but I like the feeling. The city is just waking up: delivery trucks park on the sidewalks, and men in wool jackets lower boxes and crates down steep stone steps to men waiting in basements below. Bare bulbs hang in the gloom; voices come in bursts of yelling and laughter. I can't understand a thing they are saying. I shoulder my new, red backpack—fifty-six pounds, including the lumpy cotton sleeping bag I bought at the Army-Navy store—and shift its weight on my small shoulders until it feels less painful. The men on the street stop their work and turn to watch me walk by One of them smiles and tips his cap. There is a murmur among them and then laughter. I am twenty-two years old and afraid. I feel shaky and powerful, recognizing a reckless potency as it takes over decision-making. Nothing can hurt me. I smile back at the workers, lean forward against the weight of the pack and choose a direction. Luxembourg is silver in the morning mist. Men and women come out, one by one, onto the sidewalks to make their way to work. I walk among them, the human stream, but I have been outside that life for a long time and make my way alone now.

Steve and I had been playing for a few months at the edges of love. It was winter, 1972. I lived on Dartmouth Street in the Back Bay section of Boston, in a small, shabby apartment with high ceilings and stained-glass windows in the bathroom door. At night, I sat in the big bay window at the back of the house with the lights low, watching rats take over the nighttime alley. A man, across the alley and up a story, stood each night at his window, watching me through binoculars. I stared back. Sometimes I filed my toenails for him or read poetry out loud. 1 returned each night after work to the rats, my books, the man who watched me. I resisted spending time with Steve. He was a good and earnest boy who wanted me to love him, but I had little to offer. Sometimes I left a note for him on my door, saying I had taken off for a while and would call when I got back. But when he came one snowy December night and asked me if I wanted to go to India with him, I immediately said yes. Maybe, on the road to a faraway country, I would find release from the griefs of my past.

The plan was that Steve would fly ahead to Amsterdam. I would follow two weeks later, flying to Luxembourg on a cheap flight and taking a train to Amsterdam, where I would meet him. He would simply wait at the station on January 6 until I climbed off one of the trains, and we would start our four-month hitchhiking trip, joining the flow of American and European hippies, young people seeking adventure and, maybe, enlightenment in India. I was nervous as I flew to Reykjavík and on to Luxembourg, anxious about getting from the airport into the city alone and finding a place to spend the night. I decided I would just sleep in a chair at the train station, but when I got there, it was locked up. It was a very cold and damp night. I didn't have the right clothes; I had packed for India, forgetting the continents in between. As I made my way into a nearby hotel, I felt inept and alone. I went to sleep worried about the train ride to Amsterdam the next day and what would happen if Steve, for some reason, never showed up. He had almost all our money and our maps. Our only line of communication was through American Express, the hub for hitchhikers in Europe. Our plan seemed, in the damp, lonely room, flimsy and uncertain.

Before it was light, I was up, frightened. I washed in cold water at the stained sink behind the door, watching myself in the mirror. I was a girl in big trouble, and I knew this as I stared back at myself: at the guarded, haunted eyes; at the tight, closed face—a record of loss.

I had a baby when I was sixteen. My mother kicked me out. Then my father kicked me out. I gave my baby away.

My baby, five years old now, was somewhere, maybe loved, maybe not. Mourning with no end and a sense that I had lost everything—my child, my mother's love and protection, my father's love and protection, the life I had once imagined for myself—hollowed me out. Every day, I floated alone and disconnected and could not find comfort or release. I understood clearly that my history had harmed me, had cut me off from the normal connections between people. Every day for five years, I had been afraid of this disconnection, feeling the possibility of perfect detachment within my reach, like a river running alongside me, inviting me to step into its current.

Something shifted in the early morning's coming light as I looked back at the broken life reflected in the mirror. In that moment, the river swept in close beside me, the current smooth and swift. I stepped in finally, reckless and grateful, a calm giving up. I had nothing more to lose. I walked toward the telegraph office. I did not care what happened to me anymore.

The winter air is heavy with sweet coal smoke as I walk and hitchhike, following the Rhone River through eastern France. I am walking blind, with no maps, and learn the names of the cities I am passing through from small, brown signs: Nancy, Dijon, Lyon, Montélimar, Aries. Everything—buildings, fields, chugging factories, workers' faces and clothes—is gray. Snow falls and turns to slush. I am cold and wet, but I am strangely excited. My money is going fast on bread and cheese and hot soup. Each late afternoon, I have one purpose—to find a dry place to sleep where no one will find me. I am furtive as each day closes, slipping into farm sheds and factory storerooms and derelict warehouses. Sometimes I am caught, and an angry or indignant man or woman sends me back into the night. I sleep lightly, listening for footsteps. If I am near a town in the morning, I like to find a public place—a café or market—and spend a few minutes warming up, my backpack resting against my legs near the sweaty windows. Often, the owner realizes I have no money to spend and shoos me out. Sometimes a man or a young woman—a mother with a small, wide-eyed child, perhaps—smiles and motions me to sit down. My French is poor: "Yes, I am walking to India," I say. "Thank you," I say, again and again. I eat a pastry and drink a bowl of steaming coffee. Sometimes the men who pick me up in their green Deux Cheveaux or blue Fiats or black Mercedes pull over at a market and buy me bread and tins of sardines and cheese. The world feels perfectly benign, generous even, and I go on my way, following the river.

I think of Steve, hoping he did not sit long in the train station waiting for me before he realized there was trouble, before he made his way to the American Express office and ripped open my telegram. I half-expect to see him waving at me across an intersection where roads meet and part again. I have no idea where I am.

One cold, windy day, as I walk through another little town with no name, I meet a man named Alex, who is absent without leave from the British Army. He is tall and very, very thin, with hollowed-out cheeks and sunken eyes. His boots are rotting away; he has tied newspapers around the soles, in his dirty, wet canvas satchel, he carries a brown wool blanket, which is thin and filthy, and a miniature chess set. He has no passport. He has not contacted his family for over a year. He looks haunted, as if he no longer belongs to the world. He teaches me to play chess in the back stairwell of an apartment building. He is curt with me and never smiles. He smells unwashed, but, more than that, he seems to be fading from the world. I feel as if I am looking at myself a year from now.

The next morning, Alex points down the empty road and tells me, "Go that way until you reach the Mediterranean Sea. Turn left there. It will take you to a warmer place." I leave him sitting on a heap of stones at the edge of a field and head in the direction he pointed.

My backpack is lighter. In dirty Genoa, I sell two pairs of Levi's; my tall, red suede boots; a black lace shirt; and a bra to a girl from Chicago who is hitchhiking with her boyfriend. She gives me twenty dollars, and the rising worry about money, which I have been trying to ignore, eases. I have lost weight in just three weeks and think about food as I walk.

Now that I have reached the warmer Mediterranean coast, I see lots of kids traveling together. Like me, they carry heavy backpacks and stick out their thumbs for a ride. They look happy and well-fed, and each night, they sleep in youth hostels they have chosen from their *Europe on Five Dollars a Day* guide. They congregate—little international communities—in cafés and clubs and parks in the centers of the quaint southern towns, finding a common language and sharing tales of their adventures. I avoid them, feeling detached from their youth and the ease with which they travel through the world.

The hole in me grows. I am becoming more and more isolated and recognize that I am walking my way into perfect disconnection. I think of my baby, a boy, every single day now. I make up stories: My baby is a boy named Anthony, with black, black hair. My baby is a boy lying on his back under a maple tree, watching clouds—just like these above me—spin by on an easterly wind. Like me, he has blond curls and crooked fingers. He is shaped like this hole in me. I think of my mother. I think of my father. Under the weight of my backpack, I walk away from home.

The cobbled sidewalks in Florence have been worn down in the middle by centuries of people walking to the market or to work and back home, people who have carried burdens on their backs and in their string bags and in their hearts. The ancient stone steps of the Palazzo Medici and Pitti Palace are worn so deeply they seem to sag in the middle, as if the weight of all those lives has made its mark forever. I am at peace here, trudging down the center of the sidewalks.

I learn to steal oranges and bread and dates from indoor markets, leaving my backpack outside by the door so I can make a fast run with my day's food. At night, I comb my hair and present myself as an American college girl at the doors of *albergos.* Skeptical women in black dresses and stout shoes size me up, but each night, someone agrees to take me in. In rapid-fire English, I refuse to leave my passport with them, arguing that I am going to meet friends later and will need my identification on the city streets. I cannot understand their answers, but if I get away with it, I find myself in a clean room with stiff white sheets on a high bed and windows looking over a quiet side street.

I request that the hot-water burner in my room be turned on, an extra cost. While the widow turns the gas valve and lights the match below the heater, I smile my gratitude. The woman doesn't smile back at me. Left alone, I put the lamp on and ease into the long tub. I soak clean in the deep, steaming water, easing some of my aloneness in its embrace. I climb out then wash my clothes in the tub and lay them across the chugging radiator for the night. In the morning, the woman brusquely brings me a tray of hard-crusted toast and sweet butter and strawberry jam in a little white pot. Later, of course, I lift my backpack onto my shoulders and quietly take the stairs past her rooms. Clean, my hunger appeased and troubled with guilt, I enter the day in Florence. The beautiful old city wakes slowly while I watch, the red-tiled roofs catching the coming sun as it rises over the Arno River.

I make my way toward the rising sun. I no longer care about India. I have no destination. Most days, I speak briefly to one or two people, but I am worlds away. The road is leading in. The walking is a drug.

I cross mountains and find myself again on a sea. Rimini. Ravenna. Ferrara. Venice in the springtime—a liquid, pink city. I am a reluctant but accomplished thief in these cities, stealing food and a bath and sleep. I sell a red dress I like very much and black tights and four T-shirts. I put the fifteen dollars in my pocket. I study a French girl's map and see that I am headed away from tourist cities, from food and beds, a roof. Worry nags at me. I linger in Venice, sitting in San Marco Square or on the boulevard looking across to the Lido. Men on the freight boats in the canals call to me with white smiles. Sometimes I smile back, and a man throws fruit and small parcels of nuts or olives to me. I wave my thanks. I am thin and wonder if they see, yet, the hollowed-out look I met in Alex.

My child turns six on Memorial Day as I walk out of Venice. I will not try to hitch a ride today. I feel my son with me, a light, and I want to be alone with him.

It has been several months since I have had a real conversation with anyone. I am not at all lonely. I choose this way of being in the world. I know I would scare people at home. But I have nothing to say to anyone. I have not been in touch with my family since I left to meet Steve in Amsterdam, and their voices are finally silent in my head. My backpack is lighter. I hum Bach's Partita no. 2 and head through Trieste to the next place that waits for me.

Beograd: I am up to my old tricks—thieving food, a bed. I hoard the thirty-six dollars in my pocket. Summer has come to Yugoslavia. I like this enormous country very much. Tito watches me from posters and framed photos in every building and home. The Danube makes its lazy way past the city, to mysterious places far away. I get rested and ease my constant hunger. My jeans hang from my hips. My legs are strong. I ask a soldier, "Which way is Greece?" and follow his finger. There are fewer and fewer hitchhiking kids as I move from farm town to farm town. Boys drive oxen with goad sticks, stopping to stare open-mouthed as I walk past. I sneak into barns and sheds at night, pulling my old sleeping bag snug against my neck because of the rats and mice I hear in the hay and chaff. The nights are still cold, and my Army-surplus bag offers no warmth at all. I curl my legs tight to my chest, trying to get warm enough to slip into a tired sleep. I have learned the arc of the sun: each morning, before the roosters call the day to a start, I slip out into the dewy, gray light, orienting myself, continuing on my way.

Athens is beautiful—crisp green and white in the brilliant summer sun. it is crawling with travelers, and after weeks in the quiet countryside of Yugoslavia, I feel thrown back into a forgotten world. People speak to me in English and French, and I understand what they want of me—momentary connection, shared experiences. I pretend I don't understand and back away without smiling.

I sell my boots to a shoe vendor on a dead-end street and buy a used pair of sandals from him, giving me an extra seven dollars. I sell my red sweater and all my socks and a yellow jersey. I have twenty-one dollars left. I sit for long afternoons in the little parks lined with orange trees, considering what will happen when I can't raise more money. Going home is not an option I consider.

I have lived inside my brain for months now. The walking is an underlying rhythm for my thoughts, like an *obbligato,* persistent and reassuring. I have accomplished the disconnection, and my wanderings are entirely solitary, free of any voices from the past. Grief is my companion. As the child grows bigger, the hole carved in me grows, too. Silent, solitary, moving—step by step, I measure the distance between me and the woman I thought I was going to grow up to be.

Three times I try to cross the Bosporus and enter Istanbul. Gathering speed in Athens, I sweep up the coast of Greece, through Larisa and Lamia, up through Thessaloniki, through Alexandroupolis, walking, catching rides, and each time, I balk at the border, unable to broach Turkey, I am hungry. I have less than ten dollars left. Each time, at the door to Asia, facing the dark mystery of Turkey, I stumble at the threshold, afraid.

Asia lies behind a curtain, masculine and remote and secretive, having absolutely nothing to do with me. In northern Greece, as Europe gives way to Asia, dark men sit outside their shops, smoking hookahs and drinking tea from small glasses. They stare as I walk past. I feel naked, lost. There are no women anywhere. Small, dusty-legged boys run in packs beside me, screaming their excitement as they jump to touch my sun-bleached hair. I am all white, a floating apparition; their dark hands and shrill voices chase me in the village streets. Nasal prayers blare from minarets, and the sun sears the land.

I slide back down the coast to Athens, confused and worried because, even here, there is not enough room to move. I feel trapped. Remembering the freehand maps we drew in seventh grade, I know the world opens and extends beyond the Bosporus, and I want to be lost in its expanse. Again,

I roar up the coast. I walk fast. Sometimes rich men in Mercedes pick me up. They feed me at restaurants hidden in the hills and smile at me, baffled and aroused. Again and again, I approach the shadowy world that sprawls beyond Europe.

Finally, too tired to turn around, I slip into Istanbul at night and let a kind, young student lead me to the cellar where he rents a room with four others. I do not go out for three days, paralyzed with fear. And then one morning, sliding to recklessness again, I leave the dark hideaway. Muezzins chant their minor-key call to prayer from the minarets of the mosques. I gather my things and enter the old bazaar. It is dark and dreamy and heavy; wool rugs and pungent spices and dates and plastic dolls tumble from doorways into the alleys. I spend a dollar on a length of dark cloth and a needle, and, sitting in a wavering pool of light within the gloom, I sew a shapeless shift, long and loose. I sell my last blue jeans and my bra and my sandals and, finally, my pack. I save my belt, which I pull tight around my rolled sleeping bag.

I have heard I can get $300 for my passport. I make my way slowly through the labyrinth of shops and paths, watching for men who might return my gaze and invite a deal. I wander slowly in the maze, making eye contact with the dark men who embody danger.

Everywhere, men slide next to me, touch my arm insistently and whisper, "Hashish? Hashish?" "No money," I say, emboldened, and then, "Passport? Passport?" The men move away quickly. I know I have scared them.

I am lost. The bazaar is an ancient city of stone tunnels, roofed with great vaulting domes. It is dark and very noisy. Children run past, barefoot and dark-eyed. They pull back against the scarred walls when they see me, so different from the brazen village boys. I walk slowly, watching the men. "Hashish?" "No. Passport?" Finally, a man stares back at me and signals for me to follow. A small man with a sharp nose and scuffed shoes, he leads me through the maze for five minutes, without once glancing back at me. He stops at a stall selling spices from big wooden barrels; the bright orange and green and yellow and red and brown spices fill the alley with a rich, heavy smell, mysterious and seductive. The man speaks to a younger man sitting high behind the barrels. That man stares at me coolly. I make myself stare back. He nods then says something to the older man, who turns to me and says in English, "Twenty-five dollars."

"No," I say. I am shocked. I know that what I am doing is a serious crime, it has to be worth it. "No, $300."

Both men return my look of shock. They shake hands with each other, and the younger man motions me away. I hesitate, but he yells something at me, and I turn away. I am shaken. My plan seems naive and unworkable. Later, I spend four dollars on a large, peaty chunk of hashish; I sew it into the hem of my shift to sell when I need money.

I need food. A fat man watching me from his stall with serious eyes calls me to him. He doesn't smile as he puts me in a chair and lays a tin plate in front of me. He hacks the head off the lamb roasting on his brazier and places it on the plate. I spend an hour picking and sucking every sweet bit from the skull. The man shakes his head when I offer him money. I wander through the bazaar, watching the end of each tunnel for the light outside, the path out. Then I head south with seventeen dollars.

Beyond the city, across the Dardanelles, I am free in that vast far-off space I remember from my childhood maps. This is where I want to be. Nothing here is like home. The disconnection is complete. I sleep alone under the trees at night. It rains some nights, and I am cold and wet. I share dark sheds with small animals—rats, I think—and I sneak out before dawn when men come to do their chores. The land is spare and mimics my stripped life. Voices—shepherds as alone as I am—call across the hills. Goat bells answer. The call to prayer. Wind. Everything has slipped. I am not me anymore.

It is midsummer. I have been walking since January. In southern Turkey, it is warm and very dry. I am always thirsty. My bare feet are strong and calloused. The land is beautiful, rolling and arid and silent. This is an enormous place. I am lost in it.

For several days, I have been following a dusty track that winds south. I don't know how far away the coast is and can't remember how it fits on the planet. I think the Middle East comes after Turkey, and I head that way. I have forgotten about India, the hitchhiker's mecca. I am wandering. The track has been getting smaller and smaller, and now I know I am on an animal trail or maybe a shepherd's path. It winds up and over the dry, brown hills. I have not seen a house or shepherd's hut for two days. Sometimes I hear the heavy tonk of goat bells on the distant hills. I am not lonely. I hear my steps muffled in the stone-dust and the pulse of blood in my ears. I hum a fragment from Bach, the same bit over and over. I am hungry.

Night comes quickly here. In the near dark, I feel the clinking of pottery under my feet: I am walking on tiny mosaic tiles. Fragments, brilliant blue and yellow even in this erasing light, stretch for hundreds of feet in the sparse grass. I know nothing. I know no history. When did Homer live? The Trojan War—could that have been here? Cretans, Minoans, Phoenicians—did they lay these bits of clay? I have no sense of what belongs where, or when. I am old, an old woman walking across time in the dust. Other women have walked here. Other women, I know, have been alone. I feel a momentary jolt of connection, of steadying order.

A small, stone bunding, round and low, rises in the dark. I feel my way to a door. I have to step down three feet to the floor, where more tiles crackle each time I step. It is damp and smells green inside. I feel for the roof—it is a low dome, and tiles clap to the floor when I touch them. There is a raised platform in the middle, an oblong, covered in tiles. I listen but hear no rats. Pleased with my find for the night, I spread my sleeping bag on the platform and wrap myself up as well as I can against the coming cold.

I wake abruptly, knowing suddenly that this is an ancient tomb. I am a trespasser. I am in over my head. The old, deep shame creeps back to me. Glued to the altar all night, I stare straight into the pitch-black dome. At dawn, I crawl up into the faint light, the air, the patterns of lives etched for millennia in the soil. On my hands and knees, I study the mosaic design, searching for clues, a map for how a life gets lived, how it all can be contained, how the boundaries can hold against the inexpressible and unnamed. How I can hold against the past. People called to God in this place, a god who was, I think, furious and harsh. I am not ready. I may never be ready. I gather my sleeping bag and walk toward the rising sun.

Night is coming. I am somewhere in southern Lebanon, on the coast, in a place I can't name. I need to find somewhere to sleep before it is dark. On a narrow beach, I discover a cement-block house still standing, its roof and one wall blasted away. Its whitewash gleams in the dusk, and it is oddly tidy. The shattered glass, the splinters of wood, the furniture and clothes and dishes that must have been left behind when the Israeli mortar shells flew through the night—everything has been scrubbed clean by the winds and shifting sand. Eddies in its corners have left tiny dunes. I push them flat with a sweep of my arm and drop my sleeping bag. It is all I carry now, this bag rolled and bound with my belt; my passport, my pocketknife and matches are tucked into the foot. I shake out the bag, dirty and musty, and lay it neatly in the corner of the ruins. I slide my passport back inside and lay the matches on top. I keep the knife in my hand. In the deep dusk, I wander the beach, gathering driftwood. The little fire whooshes up, and I am home.

I have not eaten today and have no food for tonight. The bats are out as always, their syncopated bursts felt but not seen. The Mediterranean Sea is not dramatic. It pulses in and out softly in the dark. Sparks snap and rise. Although it is August, the nights are chilly, and I am cold. I am always cold at night, my body too thin now to generate enough heat. My bag is lumpy with wadded cotton batting and only serves to keep the bats from touching my skin. I am almost content. I am free from most things. Recklessness has become a drug, and I am walking stoned. I have not had a conversation with anyone for several months; I live in my head, all eyes and ears, a receptor with nothing to return. I have no heart anymore and cannot be afraid.

I hear men shouting suddenly. They come nearer. I can hear their pant legs swishing up the beach and the clatter of what I instantly know are weapons. I wait in the dark, hoping they will march past me, past my small fire, past this already ruined house. They stop in the gaping hole that was a wall. There are six of them: soldiers in camouflage with automatic weapons drawn. I stay seated, wrapped in my flimsy bag. They are very young, some with no hair at all on their cheeks. One of them, short and thick, is older, my age, maybe twenty-one or twenty-two. He shouts at me. I cannot tell if they are Israeli or Lebanese. Maybe I have walked out of Lebanon and into Israel along the shore. I don't know where I am or what the soldiers are protecting, but I know I am in trouble.

"Passport?" the stocky one demands. I know enough not to hand it to them. It will bring them quick cash, and I will never see it again. My answer is long, as if there is a logic to my presence on their beach, as if there has been no War of '67, as if I know what I'm doing here. He shouts at me. I don't know if it is Hebrew or Arabic. "Passport!" I hear in English.

Suddenly, one of the boys jostles another, points at me with his elbow and says something. I know what it must be. They all laugh, excited and a little embarrassed. I flare to life after all these months, and I am afraid. I do not dare to stand up. My dress is thin, and I have no underwear.

My fire has died to a glow. They shove each other and giggle and jostle as if they are drunk, but they are not. They are soldiers, a team, and no one knows I am here. They sit in a semicircle around me, their rifles across their laps, their smooth, olive hands and cheeks luminescent in the night. They are quiet for minutes at a time, watching me. Then they burst into joking laughter. I sit silent, tense, surprised that I suddenly care so much what happens to me. The bats flick down onto our legs and heads and shoulders. The stars are out, the Milky Way stretching across two seas to my other life. I am sitting on my passport, my little knife gripped in my hand. I stare back at these boys, these boys with guns, and I am puffed like a frightened bird to make myself seem brave.

I sit, stiff and cold. Suddenly, all the walking away from my past—from my home; from the baby, just born and alone, that I abandoned in a hospital; from my mother, cold, her love evaporated; from my father, his love withdrawn; from the child I was myself—all the walking has taken me nowhere. Here I am, alone and scared. I remember the days after my baby was born. My young breasts, still a girl's, were large and tight and hard, swollen with milk. My shirt was soaked. I stood over the bathroom sink, crying, pressing the milk from my breasts. I could hear my lost baby cry for me from someplace far away, as if my own cry echoed back to me. My milk flowed and flowed, sticky and hot, down the drain of the sink.

I clutch my arms tight to my breasts and face the soldiers who surround me. The night goes on slowly, hour by wary hour. The tides are small here, and the creep of the sea is no measure of time. Occasionally, the stocky leader shouts at me, asking for my passport. "American?" he asks. "Yes. American," I say, emphatically. "Passport!" he demands, again and again. I shrug my shoulders, gesturing no, as if these are my lines in the play we are all rehearsing. Not one of us moves. The constellations reel around the polestar, and we sit through the deep night. In the quiet minutes, one or another lifts his rifle, clacking and clipping metal against metal as he opens and closes the breach. The sound bangs against the bombed-out walls and echoes back to us. They laugh.

At the first seep of light, the leader suddenly rises. The other boys jump to their feet, brushing sand from their laps. They all look frayed with sleeplessness. The leader stands upright and nods to me. They all turn without speaking and move back down the beach in a slow, drifting line. I shake my bag out, place my passport and matches and knife in the foot, and strap my belt around it. Images rise: my mother's face turned from me; the white and metal hospital where I left my baby; my swollen breasts; my milk slipping slowly, in thick lines, down the sink. The sand in the bombed-out house is scuffed in a half-circle around me. Suddenly, I don't know if these boys spent this long night threatening me or protecting me.

I don't know where I am. My fear settles again as I walk. I head north, pretty sure I'm in Lebanon.

It is my birthday. I want ritual. This place in Lebanon is called Jbeil, "the beautiful place." I wash slowly in the Mediterranean Sea at dawn, dipping my head back into the cool, still water, an anointment. I wash my dress and sit for the rest of the day on a long, smooth ledge that falls away into the water. I have been feeling the silence acutely, the absolute lack of attachment. It frightens me because I know I have slipped into the deepest current and may not come back. But I like the narcotic of walking and will not stop. I know the roads to Damascus and Latakia and Tyre. The walking claims ground as mine, and I am as much at home here as I have been anywhere since I was sixteen.

Between me and my mother, me and my father, me and my castaway child, beyond this quiet sea, is the dark and raging Atlantic. The sun on the Mediterranean stuns the mind. I am blank. I am here in this beautiful place. I am twenty-three. I am alone. I have nothing.

It is late summer—dry, brown, peaceful in the hills. I wander from Syria to Jordan to Lebanon to Syria. I am among Palestinian refugees. Soldiers with machine guns lie behind sandbag bunkers on every corner in every country. The low, flat roofs are sandbagged, and soldiers train their rifles on the dusty streets below. I know that Israel invaded Palestine in 1949. I know that Israel occupied Jordan's West Bank and Syria's Golan Heights in the War of '67; armies of American kids joined the kibbutz movement to help Jews come home. I don't know anything else, except that the Palestinian refugees suffer. They live in vast tent cities along every highway and in crowded warrens of shacks in every town. Everyone, Arab and Jew, has lost someone; some have lost everyone. They try to tell me their stories and weep. My own grief feels smaller here.

I walk, with no plan, through Baalbek and Masyaf and Saïda and Sabkha and back through Masyaf. In every place, men and women greet me with hands extended. They smile, drawing me in as if I belong to them. I have no idea who they think I am. They share food with me: flat bread and warm, tangy yogurt from the bowls on their door stones. It always means they leave their own meals hungry. A woman beating a rug in her yard calls to me as I walk by her house. She looks sad and tired, like all the people here. She holds up her hand: Wait. I sit against the low cement wall surrounding her dusty yard. In ten minutes, she comes to me with two eggs—fried warm and runny and lifesaving—and flatbread to sop them up. She stands, smiling, while I eat, her black skirt and thin, black shoes powdered with dust, her hens wandering near us, pecking in the dirt.

Several teeth ache. Sometimes in the city I steal packets of aspirin from vendors. When I can't sleep, I lay one against the gum. It burns the tissue, but I sleep.

I sell my blood to the Red Cross whenever I am in a city. I get three dollars, enough for a visa to cross back into Syria or Lebanon or Jordan. I try to hide the bruise from the last time. Sometimes they scold me and send me away; sometimes they need the blood badly and reach for the less-bruised arm. I feel vestiges of a familiar shame, broad and deep, with these American and European workers. They ask me if my family knows where I am. I always say yes. They ask, "What are you doing here?" But I have no answer for them and leave quickly with my three dollars.

Abrahim offers me hot bread from the doorway of his shop. He speaks some English and tells me he is getting married. He brings me home to his mother in As Sarafand, the refugee camp south of Beirut. She chatters at me in Arabic while she and four other women crowd around the pitfire to cook for the feast. There is joy here. I have forgotten this kind of happiness, happiness that looks forward. I stay in this tiny plywood and tin house for three days, basking in the large, soft peace of family. I sleep with Abrahim's sisters on mats on the floor; his father snores, and his mother murmurs to him in the night until he stops. I leave on the morning of the wedding. Abrahim's mother wraps a black-and-white *kafiyeh* around my shoulders as I leave. I feel a new stab of dread as I walk away, unsure in which direction to head.

I am stopped at the border. I never know which country I am leaving and which I am entering. I cross these boundaries as they appear before me. I have no plan.

It is still light. A French businessman has picked me up on the road and has driven with me, in silence, for the past several hours. He knows where he is going. At the tiny border station, he is motioned through, but I am held by the two soldiers in the guardhouse. The driver looks very concerned; his fear is contagious, and I try to get back into his car. Rifles come up, and the guards shout at him to drive on. He leans across the front seat, closes the door and drives away, looking back at me in his mirror as if he is memorizing my face.

The guards speak to me in Arabic and motion me to sit on a small bench inside the hut. It is late summer and very hot in their shack. I think I am entering Syria near Al-Qusayr. A few cars pull through; then, after dusk falls, there are no more. The soldiers come inside and close the door. A bare bulb hangs in the gloom. The men sit in chairs facing me, our knees almost touching. They still have my passport. I want to sleep. I am hungry and suddenly feel too tired to face them. It is absolutely quiet outside, and I can't see lights anywhere in the no-man's-land of the border.

They talk, pointing the ends of their rifles at me and clicking their tongues. They burst into laughter. I sit, hugging my sleeping bag to my chest. Finally, one of the men gets up and goes outside. The one left with me taunts me and stares silently and taunts again. When the first man returns an hour later, he has a young civilian with him, a buddy. They are agitated and make jokes for each other. Sometimes the civilian touches my face or arm, or pulls my hair tight in his fist, and they all laugh, their teeth white and shiny in the hard light. One makes me stand sometimes, and the two others speak in low, rough voices behind me. The clock over the door ticks the seconds and the minutes. It is two-thirty in the dark of the night.

A car pulls up to the gate, and the soldiers jump up as if they have been caught at something. I stand quickly and demand my passport. The guard hesitates then hands it to me, smiling ingratiatingly, and lets me push past him out the door. Without asking, I climb into the front seat of the car. People here know trouble, and the driver, a middle-aged Arab in a white *jalaba* and red *kafiyeh,* never says a word. They pass him through, and we drive on into Syria.

The air has changed. It is October, and the nights are very cold. I have no jacket, no sweater, no shoes. I squat by my little fire, the *kafiyeh* wrapped around my head and neck. I am always hungry. I have slept on this rocky beach in Syria for two weeks. The first few days, just before dusk, a very old man walked the length of the beach with his sheep; he murmured to them as they rustled, grazing among the debris of seaweed and trash. He didn't look at me.

Then one night, he came across the beach toward me, his sheep following. He was very thin, and everything about him was dark—his frayed wool jacket and old shoes and dirty cap and lined face. He smiled at me; he had two teeth, both on top. He spoke softly to me in the same vowelly voice he used to herd his animals. Kneeling by my small fire, he took a leather sack from his belt. He used the dented little pot inside to milk one of the ewes, the milk hissing again and again against the tin. She stood for him without moving. His voice hushed in the falling light; he put the pot on the fire. The milk quickly boiled. He jerked it off the fire and dumped a brown clump of sugar into the creamy foam, stirring it with a stick. Sitting back on his heels, he waited while the milk cooled then gave it to me, smiling and nodding and talking. He watched me drink it down, delicious and sustaining. I came to life. He nodded and smiled and smiled.

Every night now, he stops and warms ewe's milk and sugar for me, talking to me softly like my father did when I was a child. His old hands are creased and knobby. I don't want him to leave, and I drink the milk slowly, holding him to me. I am nourished and feel a father's care. All day, I wait for him, feeling how mute I am, how distant I have become from anything I once knew.

One night, I try to tell him I have a child. I hold up six fingers and mime a belly, large and round. I point to the West, across the sea. I very much want him to understand. He finally makes a loud, kind noise of understanding, laughing knowingly, smiling and nodding. But I know he cannot imagine what I am talking about. That night, I feel very alone under the black sky.

I leave the beach the next night. I say goodbye to him after I have drunk the milk he offers. He smiles and nods at me and turns several times to wave goodbye as he makes his way with his sheep, their bells tonking their hollow, peaceful course along the shore.

It is always almost night, the time when I must find a place to lay down my sleeping bag, a place to attach myself for a few hours. The decision feels enormously important every night. When I am tired, the unspoken thoughts that ride under the rhythms of my walking begin to seep out and over an edge I cannot protect. At this haunting hour, I feel like a stray animal, desperate for warmth of any kind. Each night, I watch the countryside go gray then black. I keep walking. Voices I know—my mother's, my father's, mine, the cry of a child—press at my back.

I move in the dark, alone. I search for lights on the arid hillsides, in the steep valleys. I float toward them with an intensity of longing; my outsideness feels contemptible, a failure of great magnitude, which hits each day at this time. There are voices coming from the lights, from behind secure walls—fires and food and entangled lives. The oncoming night leads me to them; I want, for a little while, to weave myself into their web. I do not want to sleep out in the open again, cold and apart, the dry wind swirling the stars out of place. I do not want to be alone. I creep toward the lights. Some nights, I sleep in the dirty sheds with chickens and goats. Some nights, I lie against the low cement walls, close enough to hear the voices, hushed or shrill. Most nights, there are no lights anywhere, no secure walls, and I lay my bag down where I am and curl against the cold.

I walk. It is November. I have been moving for eleven months. In a dusty field, twenty women stoop, preparing the rocky soil for the fall planting. Many of them have babies tied with bright cloths to their backs. Small children stand listlessly by their mothers in the sun. I am walking on a track from nowhere that skirts the field. Heads come up and watch me, but they continue their work. The children stare, slowly turning to follow me with their eyes as I pass. The dust rises. The barren hills lift behind us onto the high plain. Suddenly, at a signal I cannot see, the women stand and call their children out of the field for their midday meal, moving together toward me on the path.

I am struck with shyness. I cannot remember how I got here, what it is I am looking for. I don't know if I have found it, if it can be found. I am outside the world, drifting. I don't think I am lost, but I cannot explain where I am. I want so much all of a sudden, but I cannot name what it is. I am empty and very tired. I don't know where to walk next. I don't want these women—with their babies and their gray, dusty feet and hands and careful eyes—to wonder what brought me here. Things gone rise up in a flood. Suddenly, I am scared of myself and of how far I have drifted.

The women do not speak to me. They lift the baskets they have left by the road and sit to eat their meals on the little ridge of hard dirt beside the field. I walk along in front of the women and children, feeling exposed. We eye each other; the children lean against their mothers. Goats bleat far off in the hills.

Suddenly, a woman smiles up at me and wags her hand: Stop. She is wearing a 1950s short-sleeved sweater, bright red. She swings her dark-eyed baby onto her lap from her back and opens her bag. She lifts her sweater over her swollen breast, her skin the same soft dusk as the soil around her. Holding a dented tin cup under her breast, she presses milk—creamy white, hissing again and again—into the tin. She smiles against the brilliant sun as she hands it to me. I hesitate then take the cup, sitting down beside her in the dirt. She lifts her child to the same breast. The other women nod and smile while I sip the milk. It is hot and thick and sweet. For a few minutes, I am bound to this mother and her baby, to these women and their children. I remember what it is to belong, to be loved. I imagine my child loved somewhere.

For a few moments, I am suspended within this circle. But I do not belong here, and when the cup is empty, I slowly get up. Nodding again and again, I wave to the woman in the red sweater. A different hunger steals into me. Memories of my old life—when I was a girl in a family, a girl with dreams of the life coming to me—flash white and clear as I start to walk away. I want to go home, home to my adult life, with its losses carved forever in my path, with its possibilities, like unformed clouds, calling me forward. I head back the way I came, against the current, orienting myself north and west, toward the Atlantic. The sun is warm. Behind me, I can hear the women and children talking and laughing as they eat and rest. Their voices rise in soft, floating prayers as I walk.

79

BRIAN BROOME

The last bus to the East Hills leaves Wilkinsburg Station at exactly 12:28 a.m. on weeknights, and I am always the last one on it by the time it reaches Park Hill Drive, where I live. The street is midnight-dark apart from the headlights of the bus. The ramshackle homes are set a bit back from the road, behind overhanging trees. Anywhere else, this street would be charming. But poor makes everything ugly.

The irritated bus driver and I sit in silence under the flickering fluorescent lights, which blanch everything an odd shade of greenish blue. I am coming off a late shift at work and the both of us, the driver and I, are impatient to be back in our normally-lit homes. We can just about taste the freedom. But tonight, our quiet time together is interrupted by a rumbling in the distance. A shouting that grows progressively louder as the bus shuffles slowly up narrow Park Hill Drive. And when the rumbling reaches its peak, we are set upon by a horde of drunken children, unruly and shrieking, who have come out of seemingly nowhere. They shout and bang at the sides of the bus with open hands, fists, bottles, and all their energy. They are trying to rock my coach off its wheels and overturn it with me and my terrified white coachman inside. He leans on the horn and, as is frequently the case with such miscreants, this show of weakness serves only to incite them further, fueling their attack. Bottles are thrown. Some shatter against the windows.

I hold fast to the seat in front of me and wonder where their parents are, as if they could do anything to stop the onslaught. Their failure to properly raise their children is the reason I'm caught in the tide of this ocean of bloodthirsty, cackling hooligans bent on the wreaking of havoc. I can only assume my death is imminent. We are at their mercy. The driver, frantic, fumbles with the radio, which crackles and sputters with truncated, static-ridden words as he tries to explain what's happening to some incredulous and disembodied voice at the other end. And then, as quickly as it began, it is over. The banging subsides, and the melee disappears into the darkness. The excitement can't have lasted for more than a minute or so, but it felt like an eternity, and the bus quietly ambles up the road to the stop outside my home, where it heaves a sigh of relief and spits me out under a flickering streetlamp. It speeds away noisily, and I stand there until its engine fades, leaving me to the sound of crickets.

The 79. Your tour bus for the East Hills neighborhood of Pittsburgh, Pennsylvania. It's a bus that exists only to ferry people to the busway that links our little village to the rest of the city. A loop bus that encircles the projects like a noose.

If you look at the area on a map, the loop resembles the Eye of Horus, an ancient Egyptian symbol I once saw in a book about witchcraft. It symbolizes protection, royal power, and good health, and in the East Hills, this is the cruelest of all ironies. I live at the corner of the eye, the very caruncle of the Eye of Horus, but protection and good health are in rare supply here.

Sin, however, is abundant. You can walk around this neighborhood and pick mortal sins off every branch of the overhanging trees. The 79 makes seven stops. I've counted them.

Sloth

THROUGH SLOTH THE ROOF SINKS IN AND THROUGH INDOLENCE, THE HOUSE LEAKS.

–Ecclesiastes 10:18

Someone is ringing my doorbell at 8:00 a.m. on a Sunday, and before I even fully open my eyes I know who it is. He will keep ringing until I get out of bed to answer, so it's best just to get it over with. My vision is blurry, and my body is heavy with all the sleep I didn't get. I throw on an old bathrobe and lumber heavy-footed down the stairs, holding on to the railing for dear life. I close one eye to look into the peephole. There's his face, distorted in the tiny fun house-mirror glass, which makes his bug-eyes bulge all the more comically. They are run through with blood-red spiderwebs. He is *sorry* again. I can feel his shame even before I open the door and when I do, a frigid blast of stale, sick, sweet liquor smell almost knocks me over.

I am so sorry, sir.

I know these are the words he'll lead with. My next-door neighbor has never called me anything but *sir* even though he is easily a decade older than I am. His eyes are leaking, with either the cold or the sting of being cripplingly hungover. Wrapped in dirty clothes and as thin as a chicken bone, he is *sorry*. Riddled with contrition. But he doesn't remember fully what happened last night. Only the flashing of police lights in the wee hours and that men in blue uniforms came to his house. As we stand there, both shivering in the winter chill, I take the opportunity to refresh his memory of the previous evening. Because I remember.

I spent most of my evening on my knees in my bed, banging on the wall that separates our bedrooms. The walls around here are like rice paper, and whatever your neighbor does on his side may as well be done right in front of you. But even if the walls were made of Kryptonite, I would still hear my neighbor's insanity clear as gunshots. Like me, he is a drunk, although a far less responsible one. I work for a living, but he cannot be bothered to take up such intrusions. The bottle requires all his time and energy. I take this opportunity not to invite him in as I have been stupid enough to do in the past. I allow him to shiver on my doorstep while I pull my dirty bathrobe tighter around my neck and recount every detail of his previous evening's antics. The same antics he's performed almost every night since I've been unfortunate enough to move to this place. He braces for my verbal assault. He bows his head and winces; bows his head, unable to meet my seething gaze. I am furious with lack of sleep and righteousness. He and I have been here so many times before.

Last night, you began your screaming through the walls at ghosts, and as you stand there in clothes that you've been wearing for a week, I need to, once again, fill in your memory while you cover your face and feign regret. You are just like every other no-good, do-nothing drunk in this neighborhood, and underneath it all, I can tell that you are perfectly healthy. Able-bodied.

I tell him proudly that I was the one who called the police, and he whimpers with shame. He creaks out another *I'm so sorry, sir.*

The fact of the matter is that no one visits you and you have no family because you cannot be bothered to get your act together. Your life is one long, comfortable nap on the couch, watching your life fall to pieces around you. I have seen you, day in and day out, sitting and staring into space in the driver's seat of that stationary junk heap you call a car, getting drunk, and then I have to deal with the fallout. And yes: I called the police. They came again to laugh at you openly, just like the last time I called the police on you due to the constant noise just on the other side of my wall. But this was the first time they've had to scoop you up from outside in the snow. This is a new milestone for you. A whole new low.

He still has not met my eyes. When he finally opens his mouth to speak again, I am foolishly waiting to hear something new come from his lips. He just stammers and, in a voice brittle as kindling, stutters out another *I'm so sorry, sir.* His sick-sweet breath cuts through the cold. I can tell he's already thinking about how his precious liquor will smooth over the rough edges of my harsh words.

Last night, I watched him fight an invisible assassin in the snow, a ghost that apparently didn't fight fair. I sat at the window and watched him fight it alone under the lazy overhead light of the courtyard. I watched for a long time. A crazy man in the middle of the night, wrapped up in the kind of silence available to the world only in the wee hours after a snowfall. His ghost must have moved quickly. He never seemed to be able to land a punch. His kicks didn't connect, and his slaps went wildly airborne. Flailing. The ice and snow didn't help, putting him on his back frequently, and his shouts were muffled by the snowdrifts and the pane of my window. His apparition didn't fight fair because it knew no one could see it except him and me at the window with my forehead on the cold glass, doing nothing. We were the only two people to bear witness to its existence, and I was afraid of the kind of contact that would be required to make the pain stop for this man. I was afraid to throw open the window and call to him. And then my fear turned to resentment and my resentment turned to anger and then I made the call, waiting at the window until the courtyard was bathed in red and blue lights.

I am not ashamed of calling the police in this neighborhood even though no one else will. I don't know why they won't. The people around here know that I'm the one who calls, and I don't care. That's what they're for, the police. My neighbor drinks himself to the point of dementia and thinks the world owes him something. This is who he screams at every night through the walls. This is who he is fighting. He is fighting the world, and the world doesn't fight fair. The world will always win if you don't keep your wits about you. I plan never again to be as pathetic as he is. I was once. But never again. I work for a living.

He continues standing at my door like a cautionary tale. He tells me through foul liquor breath that he'll never do it again, and vomit hitches in my throat. I know this is a lie. He turns to walk slowly through the snow, not to his apartment but to his hideous purple paperweight of a car. His oasis. I tell him he might want to consider getting a damn job. He gets inside the car, where he'll sit all day in the cold, trying to change reality by looking at it through the bottom of a bottle. I have work in a few hours. I need some sleep. I won't get it. In the East Hills of Pittsburgh, there is truly no rest for the weary.

Gluttony

FOR THE DRUNKARD AND THE GLUTTON WILL COME TO POVERTY, AND SLUMBER WILL CLOTHE THEM WITH RAGS.

–Proverbs 23:21

I used to be my neighbor. I was exactly like him. If you let me take a drink, you'd almost immediately regret it. I can guarantee it. When I imbibed, it was an all-day affair and into the night until my body couldn't take any more. I wouldn't stop until someone pried the bottle from my hands and then locked me up. I loved alcohol and would have bathed in it given half a chance. There was a time when I would have bypassed the circuitous route of the mouth if I could have and injected it directly into my bloodstream to perform its magical workings with even more expeditious mercy. In my fantasies, every vending machine was stocked with delicious brown liquors and little plastic baggies full of powdered goodies, and there would be one on every street corner. In short, I am an addict. I am the poor, innocent, blameless victim of an extended adolescence and an arrested development. I have drunk and drugged so much so as not to remember my own name on some nights, and then I would wake up in agonizing pain and do it all over again the next day and the next. I am a glutton for punishment. But, firstly and more importantly, I am a glutton for intoxicants of all kinds. This is why I live in the East Hills. I live here as punishment.

Life on the outside is expensive, and the East Hills falls perfectly within my price range. Cheap. I am here because I have drunk my opportunities in life. I have drunk away a good job. I have drugged away my vacations; I have snorted my future. I have filled myself to bursting with pharmaceutical delusion, and my punishment for having all that fun is to live here surrounded on all sides by sin. I have sacrificed the privilege of living in the nicer neighborhoods in the city. I live where I can afford, and I will tough it out until I make better things happen for myself. I am not a garden-variety Negro. I don't belong here. I am not like my neighbors, content to live off scraps. I have just temporarily lost my way.

I am clean now and seeing things clearly. I am almost four years clean, and I've learned my lesson. The element who live here continue to flounder inside their own endlessly repeated mistakes, convinced they are society's victims. This is why they don't talk to me. They ignore me because they know not just that I am unafraid to call the police, but also that I am not one of them. I refuse to be an injured Negro. I have made no friends here and try to keep a low profile. I have tried many times to talk to these people and am met with only blank stares every time. Shunned because I am ill-equipped to talk about doing time in jail the way that most people talk about going to the grocery store. It's not my fault they continue to snub me. The problem with being a glutton and recognizing it as I do is that you know that there is always a price to pay in the end. Dues. For me, the East Hills is dues, and once I've paid my debt, I'll stand on tiptoe and wait for the wind to lift me off this hill.

Pride

PRIDE GOETH BEFORE DESTRUCTION AND A HAUGHTY SPIRIT BEFORE A FALL.

–Proverbs 16:18

I stand at my corner every day waiting for the 79 as it ferries people between low-paying jobs and court dates and the grocery store. The projects are the pupil of the Eye of Horus, and whoever built them made sure to make them colorful this time. The units are painted purple and blue and red and, to me, the end result looks like a dysfunctional Candy Land sitting atop a hill. The 79 circles it all day.

My shoe has a hole in it. It's raining today and I have no umbrella, and now my sock is dampening from a puddle I stumbled into. I look up in minor annoyance at the sound of a too-loud engine and notice that the woman who always parks her car right in front of my bus stop is wearing red today. Her car shines silver like new sixpence. It positively gleams. I don't know what kind of car it is, but it doesn't belong here. It should belong to a celebrity or a doctor or a lawyer—the kind of person I was told I could be if only I had applied myself. The woman stops by to visit my other, younger neighbor a few times a week. Today, the vehicle smells of coconut air freshener and some expensive, flower-based perfume that wafts out when she opens the car door. She emerges from the vehicle, haughty and well-dressed, and the rhythmic thump from rap music that was muffled before booms at top volume from her extravagant carriage. She is in a red dress and high heels. I smile big at her and wave, but no return smile is offered. Instead, she fixes me with elevator eyes that start at the top floor of my nappy hair and end at my now waterlogged basement of a shoe with a sock growing soggier and slimier by the second. She moves past me, wordless and lofty, flipping newly done box braids and throwing an expensive shawl over her shoulder in a grandiose motion, and rushes through the rain to my neighbor's house. I am in no position to be acknowledged. She and my neighbor greet one another jubilantly, and they proceed with some sort of hushed business inside his home before she emerges a few moments later and struts past me. Then she climbs back behind the wheel of her brilliant blingwagon and speeds off to park its majesty in the ramshackle driveway of her ramshackle apartment, just a few blocks up the street. She lives here too. I will never cease to be amazed by the great pains people who live in this ghetto will take to try to make it look like they don't live in this ghetto. The number of dilapidated huts around here with brand-new cars sitting in front of them is confounding, and what people from this neighborhood can spend on clothes and shoes alone could most likely settle the national debt with change left over.

Pride is complicated. And money can buy many things. But here it mostly buys impracticality. Intricate hairdos whose upkeep makes it impossible to pay electric bills on time, for example, and ridiculously expensive bottles of liquor from the conveniently located liquor store. The kind of liquor the rappers drink, though presumably the rappers also have money for groceries. The bill of goods on sale is that you are what you drive and wear and drink, but I, with my soaking-wet sock and rain-dripping forehead, am not buying. I won't fall prey to the stereotype that society has laid out for me and be trapped here in a state of perpetual adolescence. It's a modest life that is the key to success, and I won't forget that. Being bested every day by your own pride will keep you struggling. One must learn to adjust to one's circumstances, and you'll get nowhere by trying to show off at the club every weekend. I should tell the woman this, but I won't. I bite my tongue. She has made her decision, and who am I to judge anybody? I know what my priorities are, and pride comes only after you've accomplished something. So I narrow my eyes and assure myself that the Lady in Red's fancy car will be taken from her one day owing to her irresponsibility. Repossessed. Someday, I imagine, I will see her on the 79, laid low, and I'll just politely nod in such a way so that she knows that I know. With no words from me, she will know that I've recognized her fall from ersatz grace and that she should have taken a lesson from me. She'll remember this day when I stood steeping in my own shoe and she barely acknowledged my existence. She will be unable to meet my eyes. It is my humility that will one day lift me out of this place. Slow and steady will win the race, I just know it. I go out of my way to be friendly to the people around here, but they'll have none of it. Too proud to talk to the outsider because he looks poor. Poor is the way you *should* look when you are. Humble. There is no place for pride in the East Hills.

Envy

I HAVE SEEN THE FOOL TAKING ROOT, BUT SUDDENLY I CURSED HIS DWELLING.

–Job 5:3

Community Crime Update: 10/4/2015 Burglary/Assault 2400 Block of Bracey Drive, 7:30 a.m.

A 36-year-old female victim reported that a known female suspect of East Pittsburgh broke into her house by forcing open the front door. The suspect stole a frozen chicken, then pulled a knife and began swinging it at the victim like a woman possessed. Officers arrived on the scene and detained the suspect, whom they found shouting obscenities in front of the residence. The frozen chicken was located roosting in the suspect's purse. The suspect told officers that she and the victim were both romantically involved with the same man. While officers were attempting to get the full story from this ostensibly grown woman, a male, also of East Hills, emerged from the residence and tried to interfere with the arrest. The male shoved one officer and then took a swing at another. Witnessing this, a third officer deployed his Taser, shocking the shit out of the male actor and immediately stopping his assault of the officers. The male was then taken into custody. Both suspects were taken to the Allegheny County Jail. The female was charged with burglary and simple assault while the male was charged with obstructing the administration of law and aggravated assault. When queried, neighbors chalked this incident up to just another instance of supposedly grown women jealous of each other over the attentions of a no-account man. Many people in the neighborhood remain confused, however, as to why a person would express envy toward a romantic rival by breaking into her house and stealing a frozen chicken at 7:30 in the morning. All have dismissed the event as just the latest in a series of ghetto dramas that have made the neighborhood look foolish on the local news. One local resident, standing at the bus stop with a hole in his shoe and suffering from obvious sleep deprivation, who wished to remain anonymous, rolled his eyes at the news of yet another domestic disturbance in the area, saying, "It happens every day because these people have nothing better to do." At the time of this printing, the whereabouts of the frozen chicken are unknown.

Lust

THEY HAVE BECOME CALLOUS AND HAVE GIVEN THEMSELVES UP TO SENSUALITY, GREEDY TO PRACTICE EVERY KIND OF IMPURITY.

—Ephesians 4:19

The 79 is an enormous baby stroller. Never in all my days have I seen so many little babies slung over the hips of young girls. Some have two, three, or even four babies in tow, each one smaller than the next, like Russian nesting dolls. Often, the mother is on the phone in an argument with some unseen boyfather. Variations on the word *fuck* are her favorite way to communicate. The children listen and drink in every obscene word. Her beautiful baby girls with beads in their hair, each one unique as a Tiffany lamp.

The young mother sitting across from me has children crawling all over her. She cannot be more than seventeen, and although the children are vying for her attention, she refuses to put down her cell phone. Her ability to ignore them is remarkable. Today, she is using social media like the teenager she is. Giggling at Facebook and sending messages because no one can just skip adolescence. You have to go through it even if, through your own misdeeds, you find yourself being a parent. Meanwhile, the children, left to their own devices, run around the moving bus, screaming. Not even the sound in my headphones can drown them out. She looks up only occasionally to curse at them, admonishing them for behavior that she will never properly correct. She is weary of them. They bounce around the speeding bus like gumballs free to come back bloody, but she cannot be bothered. When I catch her eye, I take the opportunity to shoot her a scornful look, which she shoots right back. Some may say that I should mind my own business, but I believe in addressing problems at the source. She continues to stare at her phone.

The news that sex can cause children has not reached the East Hills; the housing projects near my home are positively swarming with them. It's certainly not my place to judge anyone, but they run around loose and hang out on the streets until after dark to get up to all manner of lasciviousness. The boys talk dirty and in harsh words about things they could hardly know about. I blame the rap music. Sex. That adult feeling in the hands of children. They have all the working parts and none of the knowledge, and the knowledge won't become clear to them until it's too late. I would never comment on how anyone raises their children, but I see their futures bold as the sunrise. I see the cycle, and if I were their parents, I would impose a strict curfew. I would introduce a comprehensive sexual education program.

For their own good. Unbridled lust can never lead to anything positive, and that's an irrefutable fact.

The girl on the bus is joined by a friend, who also has children in tow. They talk about boys, using dirty language. They talk about nonsense, as girls do. One of their children plops himself down in the seat right next to me. He is sticky with sugar, and I smile down at him. His mother, the one with the cell phone, calls him back to her angrily and shoots me yet another dirty look. I don't know why. Maybe she knows that I know that her pattern of sex and children will continue. She will find out the ways of the world as she gets older. Her children will steal her youth and her opportunities. And money? That is something that will never come, though it will be slightly less elusive than escape. But this is her life and she can live it the way she wants to. It doesn't affect me in the slightest, so I don't care.

They pull the cord and exit the bus in a flurry of confusion. Strollers erected and toys gathered. Baby bottles and diaper bags. Children flying in all directions, holding up the rest of us, who actually have somewhere to be. They continue talking and move slowly as they gather their many belongings. They will make me late for work. They are never in a hurry. They finally exit, off to God knows where.

Greed

BUT THOSE WHO DESIRE TO BE RICH FALL INTO TEMPTATION, INTO A SNARE, INTO MANY SENSELESS AND HARMFUL DESIRES THAT PLUNGE PEOPLE INTO RUIN AND DESTRUCTION.

–*Timothy 6:9*

I am standing beneath the bones of industry. Heavy equipment roars and jackhammers all around me, and workmen in fluorescent yellow vests and hard hats shout instructions at each other as they erect beams and walls. The cement-colored sky is littered with progress, and I'm standing underneath it all, noticing for the first time that everything around here is changing. The low-rent bodega is gone, where I bought my cigarettes from the Indian people, where you could buy illegal loosies when your money was low. The nuisance bar up the street is gone, and the complexions of the people all around me have started to dramatically change. Just above my head, just outside my field of vision, they are working on East Liberty, the neighborhood down the street from the East Hills. The club that used to play hip-hop music is gone, and the whole block has been spruced up with gourmet pizza shops. Artisanal cocktail bars are sprouting up, seemingly from nothing. The projects that were once here have been torn down and replaced by a shiny red-and-white Target, and there are white people taking a spin class in the building that used to house the Arabic bodega. I am there soaking it all in as if it all suddenly appeared by magic when a woman approaches and stands beside me.

She says, as if she and I were in the middle of a conversation, *You know they gonna move us all outta here, right?*

East Liberty is changing faster than anyone can keep up. It's changing, slow but steady, exactly like Lawrenceville did before it, and the people who live in my neighborhood have definitely noticed.

They gonna move us outta here as soon as they need the space, the woman continues to no one in particular. *Far enough out so they can't see us.*

I stand there with this elderly woman I've never met before, and we watch the transformation happening right before our eyes. I don't live here, but I don't tell her that. She's looking up at the construction of a newer, shinier place and making frantic plans. I can see her mind working. She's wondering where she's going to go when all is said and done, and although I don't want to believe her, I know she's right. She is the kind of old, diminutive Black lady who is always right. She has seen this kind of "neighborhood rejuvenation" a thousand times before. I pretend not to know what she's talking about and we both stare up silent at the harbingers of her imminent displacement while newly transplanted white people go about their business all around us. She and I stand close enough to be lovers as her scarf flaps in the wind, and after I've steeped in enough of her reality, I turn on my heel and walk away, leaving her standing there looking up and wondering what on earth she's going to do. I wish I had said something reassuring. I want to tell her that deep down, I don't know what I'm going to do either. I want the two of us to commiserate together, standing there, looking up at all this progress. But instead, I comfort myself by deciding that I will never be her. I tell myself that she should have planned better. Then she would have options. She would have the kind of options that I will have. Options that are soon to present themselves to me. Soon.

But I can't ignore the fact that her fear has uncovered my own. As I walk back to the busway, to the beginning of the 79 route, I can't shake the knowledge that no one can prosper without taking something, and no one can prosper lavishly without taking lavishly. The word on the street in East Hills is that *the white people are coming.* People talk about it on the 79, and I've seen it with my own eyes. I've seen the white men in casual slacks and dress shirts, surveying the neighborhood and measuring things. It's just a matter of time. It's never done in a forceful way. It's always very subtle and always under the guise of progress. But those who live in the neighborhood know that we're on borrowed time. There are many things that capitalism produces, and noble behavior on either end of the rich/poor spectrum is not one of them. But we admonish only the poor.

I admonish only the poor.

The white people will come and uproot the neighborhood because they want the space, and I will ignore that in favor of looking down my nose at the people who live around me. I am desperately trying to create some fictional line of demarcation to separate myself from my neighbors, when I know that I *am* them in the eyes of the people who will come to take whatever they want from us. I have been confused, but my neighbors haven't. They are not fooled by my air of superiority. It is remarkable what the powers that be can delude you into thinking without your permission and what they can trick you into ignoring. And they have fooled me into ignoring the obvious. That I bring home and disseminate every judgment that white people want me to make against the people with whom I have the most in common.

Greed is why the East Hills exists the way it does and why we always end up on some hack writer's "Worst Pittsburgh Neighborhoods" list. Poverty and racism can leave you feeling like less. They skew the priorities and, on some days, make you so angry that you become confused as to where to aim that anger. Late at night, when everything appears to be quiet underneath the flickering streetlamps, there is an angry hum over the East Hills neighborhood. A tension. You can feel it, and you never know when it's going to erupt.

We all know why we're here. I've heard my neighbors talk about it sometimes. It's because of greed. It is the greed of those who have decided they need more space, more gourmet coffee, more spin classes. The greed of those whose toilets we scrub and whose security we guard for a pittance and the promise of a better tomorrow that never seems to come. Someone has to do it, and it may as well be us. But the relationship between the haves and have-nots in America is anything but symbiotic. Often, the quiet around here is split wide open by the sound of gunshots. The anger around these parts is electric and alive, and it has to go somewhere. So we aim it at each other. And we rarely ever miss.

The stories of noble, robust, and hardworking poor people are cherry-picked to make the rest of us feel worthless under a system in which it is almost impossible to succeed, and perhaps I have ignored this system in favor of the easier task of judging those around me. I have left this old woman to her hand-wringing, only to begin my own. I reach the busway, where the 79 is waiting to take me back home. It is lit up and idling angrily. Puffing smoke as if it's annoyed that I am late.

Wrath

REFRAIN FROM ANGER AND TURN FROM WRATH; DO NOT FRET—IT LEADS ONLY TO EVIL. FOR EVIL MEN WILL BE CUT OFF, BUT THOSE WHO HOPE IN THE LORD WILL INHERIT THE LAND.

–Psalm 37:8–9

The couch in my apartment is too close to the window. I don't want to be sitting here one day and catch a stray bullet while I'm watching something I might be ashamed of on television. It happens. I giggle to myself as I'm moving it, thinking that the police would find me, bullet to the brain, mouth frozen open in a laugh, as reruns of *The Mary Tyler Moore Show* crank out canned laughter from my television set. I move the couch because it makes good sense to move the couch. I move the couch because wrath roams this neighborhood freely. It's less visible in the daytime, but it's still here. The murders in this neighborhood are no secret. When liquor and anger start to flow, so does blood down the sidewalk. I try not to watch the local news. I don't really need to, anyway, because I can hear it all on the 79. And I move the couch, giggling at the knowledge that Mary Richards and the whole of the WJM-TV news team would never have to move their couches for such a reason. The next day, I stub my toe on the couch as I'm rushing to catch the bus.

The women sitting behind me didn't know the woman who was murdered, but they knew *of* her. They are speaking about the murder casually and not in the hushed tones that one might expect propriety would dictate for a discussion of such matters. They knew he was no good, the man who killed her. He is only twenty years old and she was twenty-eight. She should have known better, they say. I put my headphones on and pretend not to listen, but I am listening intently to their assessment of the situation. They wonder aloud what her children are going to do. She had six of them, they say, and she should have been more focused on them than she was on a twenty-year-old man. They sound like me. And as they speak of the dead in less than respectful terms, my whole body becomes heavy with the weight of it all. Six children left motherless. She was alive and she was loved and I have more than likely looked down upon this woman in passing on this very bus. I have probably watched her struggling with baby carriage, baby bottles, and diaper bags and haughtily decided that it was her poor decisions that landed her here. I turn to look out the window. My reflection in the glass is ugly, so I look down.

The women behind me gossip on. He shot her, they say. They were arguing over money for diapers, something so ridiculous that they are in disbelief, and now I'm thinking of her children and I wonder what I'm going to do besides sit here on the 79 bus judging people every day. How I'm going to cure the disease within myself that makes me so harsh and critical toward my own people. Where did I learn this? I have no answer other than that I will move the couch. Conditioned like a Pavlovian dog, I will move it every time I see red and blue lights. I will wait for the news crews to leave every time someone is killed in the East Hills, and then I will emerge from my apartment like a sultan to cast judgment. It will be my full-time job, as murder and violence are ever present around this Eye of Horus with its hum of anger.

The women behind me shift their babies from knee to knee as they gossip on, but I am no longer listening. Their voices have indistinguishably joined the rattle of the engine of the bus to create a cacophony inside my head as we roll through yesterday's crime scene.

People from other neighborhoods look to us up here and believe that we somehow deserve to be here. Our bad decisions are what led us to this place. But if everyone made the right decisions all the time, there would be no one for everyone else to look down on, and it is in this way that America works. We live here so that others can convince themselves that the worst of human instincts reside here and here only. They can convince themselves that *something like that* would never happen where they live. They can convince themselves that there has never been a drunk in dire need of mental health care in their neighborhood. They can convince themselves that, in their neighborhood, a lovers' quarrel has never led to ridiculous behavior and that people in their part of town never spend beyond their means in order to impress. Their young daughters are virginal and chaste while ours are irresponsible whores. They wonder aloud why our society can't cast this play in hell and get angels for actors. They feature us on your local news before the blood on the sidewalk even dries. The last stop of the 79 is always Wrath.

There was a time, long before my arrival here, when the building down the street, the one with the enormous pockmarked parking lot, was a shopping center. Now it houses a single church where people go to worship a God who doesn't ever seem to show himself. He's never going to come for them. The only ones who are coming are the police.

Sometimes, I wake up in the early morning and find myself missing my neighbor. One night, the red and blue lights came, and I was confused because I hadn't called the police on him. I heard a lot of men talking outside and then they drove away in an ambulance and everything next door went silent. New people moved in and told me that he died. I guess he finally got out.

But it is at this time of the morning that I know that I won't sleep any longer. So I go outside and walk up to the enormous parking lot where they say a glorious shopping center used to stand. I go there so early that the sun is barely up and the neighborhood is silent as the grave and cannot dictate to me who I am. I stand here knowing full well who I am and I'm not fooling anyone. I am not special. I am a part of this neighborhood every bit as much as those I enjoy judging so much. I stare out at the empty church parking lot with the sun coming up all around me, and I try to imagine what it must have been like a long time ago, bustling with activity and commerce. I can't really picture it. I don't know what I'm going to do. Sometimes, I sit and watch my neighbors out the window and wonder what on earth they could be smiling about. I wonder how the young mothers have the stamina to raise children around here. I wonder how any happiness can exist here at all, and then I remember how flawed my thinking is. I want to talk to them. I don't deserve to talk to them.

I will be sitting on my hands and moving away from the window on cue until they come to take the East Hills. And they will come to take it when they need more room. This, I believe, is certain. I don't believe we'll band together to stop it. I'm as guilty of inaction as anyone else up here and when they come to take it away, I will move just like everyone else. To where, I don't know. And now, as I stand here feeling the sun's first morning warmth on my back, I can hear the 79 beginning its first circle of the morning.

The World Without Us: A Meditation

CAROLYN FORCHÉ

Yesterday, everything changed, lightheartedly—unthinkingly—I went to the clinic to have "additional films taken," and after three hours, walked into the sunlight with the image of two black marbles floating in the snow and fog of what had been an ultrasound image of my right breast. *Do you see them?* Dr. Johns asked, helpfully providing tiny computer arrows to guide me to the pronounced blackness of the "densities," as he called them, and then he said, *I don't know what they are.* Dr. Johns ordered more films and told me he would share all the films and images with Dr. Ott and telephone me in the morning with Dr. Ott's recommendations.

After a fitful night, I woke without remembering this news and then remembered it. When Dr. Johns phoned, he told me they recommended ultrasound guided-needle biopsies, and he told me to call my own doctor, get the order and then make an appointment with Jessica at the clinic. I talked to my doctor, who took notes and reassured me that these biopsies are often negative, and then I spoke with Jessica, who arranged my procedure for the morning of July 28, which was then only days away.

As I cannot write anything else, I will write about how I feel, hour by hour.

Israel is bombing Lebanon again—the beautiful city, Beirut: the airport, the port, all avenues of escape. City of our courtship. These images of rubble cannot but bring me back to winter, twenty-two years ago, in the earliest months of what would become a long marriage. Our wedding rings were made by a jeweler in Beirut, who worked through nights of shellfire from the Christian east and brought the rings to my husband in a velvet box just days after I evacuated with the Sixth Fleet. His jewelry shop had been destroyed, as had most of our quarter, and to come to our darkened hotel, he had to walk streets slick with the shattered glass of shop windows. Never mind, he said, we are all alive, and you are getting married.

America is unbearably, stiflingly hot at this moment. All states are in deep red on the weather maps. Here, it is 38 degrees Celsius or about 100 degrees Fahrenheit. The dogs won't go out. I won't go out. It is a droning heat, as if the trees are crying out and the grass hissing.

Unpacking our library, which has been packed up since our house was flooded three years ago, I notice certain titles: Simone de Beauvoir's *A Very Easy Death* and Jacques Derrida's *The Gift of Death.* I consider taking them up to my bedside table but instead shelve them. I have been unpacking and reshelving for months, a few volumes at a time. I thought our life was beginning again and that all I had to do was put things in place. Things. When, on a winter night, water gushed into the house from a broken main, much was destroyed, and we were stunned into ruin, but now we are back, and the carpets that were left to stiffen in the snow are again spread on our floors. I have only to return everything to where it was—or so I had imagined. *The Gift of Death* will not come upstairs, but I am not surprised that it is among the titles lifted out of the box I open this morning. It has always been so for me: strange correspondences between my thoughts and the outer world. The world has always sent messages, whether from God or an intelligent universe, whether self-issued or bequeathed, and I was ignorant only of how many messages I had missed.

Nothing has changed since yesterday, except the fear that I am running out of time. This alphabetization of my book collection—why?—this careful unpacking and the delight at finding certain things again: a letter on blue foolscap from Graham Greene that I thought might have swirled into the debris that night, but, no, I'm holding it in my hands and reading as if I am someone else reading the papers of a dead poet.

And just now, the clouds above the darkened poplars opened to a late light.

I feel terror, pending loss, isolation and also a strange elation, a floating sense of the present moment, a weightlessness as if I have entered a state of mind leading all the way out of the world. On a clear day, cloudless, to the low hum of beetle and cricket, I tell myself to make a list of everything I remember. The details of my life from the earliest year.

This morning, I think to write a poem titled "The Dove Keeper," arising from the memory of the old man in Beirut who had a dove cote on his rooftop and whose doves alighted on his head and along his outstretched arms; in an earlier poem titled "Curfew," I wrote that he was "cloaked in doves." As he released his flock for me, he tossed his head back and laughed into the rising of their wings, an applause of light before the shooting began again in the streets—*tut tut tut tut tut* answered by *tut tut tut tut tut,* as other old men folded up their backgammon tables and market sellers ran behind their carts of tumbling lemons and dates. Then there was only dust, gunfire, glass in an emptied street and, later, utter darkness, with only candles here and there, guttering in the stairwells.

The darkness into which we sail at death, I am thinking, as I open John Berger's correspondence with John Christie, *I Send You This Cadmium Red,* to a letter written by Berger: "We have no word for this darkness. It is not night and it is not ignorance. Maybe from time to time we all cross this darkness, seeing everything, so much everything that we can distinguish nothing. Maybe it is the interior from which everything came."

These cannot be crickets because it is not night.

The flowers that tiger swallowtails feed upon are in bloom again in the garden, but there are not yet any tiger swallowtails. That is how I remember my last conversations with J, my childhood friend, before he went mad again for a time and again sought refuge in monasteries—first, with the Trappists and, then, the Benedictines. As I talked on the telephone with him several summers ago, I watched, through my study window, the butterflies he and I used to catch in the Michigan fields as they descended to feed on those flowers, and I saw him again, too, running through the fields with his white net held above the chicory and Queen Anne's lace.

This is shock: a floating, oddly disembodied mindfulness, dread without respite, but experienced at a remove.

Write everything, I tell myself. Hour by waking hour. This is my first such clarity.

I spend some of the morning in the study, unpacking, and find, among other things, a photograph of myself amid the ruins of Beirut in 1984 and a list of the items in my friend Ashley's "musée hypothétique," along with a narrative of the museum's history, and I think I might write a poem for him entitled "A Hypothetical Museum" which will include objects from his collection: sand from the Sahara, a bottle of Gauloise smoke, a glove used in renovating the Louvre, a Roman sword dug from an English garden, a shovel from Verdun, the Great War. How much world he has assembled! How much time would I need to write this poem for him? Enough.

This morning, I found two black silk Chinese jackets in a trunk, among rags that should have long ago been discarded, and I took them to the Mongolian women, who examined them very carefully, as if they were seeing before them the ghost jackets of another epoch.

An afternoon of sudden downpours from a sky by turns pearl and pumice. I found a sweater I bought in former Yugoslavia in 1978, summer. I washed it and was hoping it would dry on the rail outside and it almost did, but now it is soaking from the rain. I talked to Jane, who phoned in having heard the news, and it took some time to convince her that I am calm and that I am not trapped in the darkest thoughts. I also talked to other friends—dear sisters, these women who circle me in my hour of gravest uncertainty and fill me with gratitude.

The sweater will smell of rain and sunlight. I think it is from Zlatibor, and I find myself wondering what happened there during the recent war years. I'm sure that Vasko is no longer alive, among the many people I have known who went before me in death.

In my thoughts, I'm heading into the open sea.

A cloudless day. So we have the dove keeper poem to be written and, also, the "musée hypothétique," but they must bewritten by a hand guided by a mind that cannot alight. Like the birds over the fires of Beirut. Unpacking the library is a labor of unpacking a life: the scattered interests in philosophy, religion, poetry, literature, languages and the history of languages, art, photography, ideas, ecology, cosmology and, particularly, books about crimes against humanity. There are many books among them that I have not yet read, that I may have no time to read, and there is also all that I have not written, and the little time left, even if it is measured in years. We are asleep, we are dreaming, we are flickering between two darknesses.

The shed door was open, so I went out to close it, thinking also to turn on the sprinkler for the lawn, and as I approached the shed, I heard a creaking above me, as if a door were opening, and a long-dead branch fell almost upon me and I watched it fall, as if slowly, and then I moved it toward the fence.

There is the first tiger swallowtail, flying above the fan of water.

There are two days of waiting left, then another week of waiting. I am submerged in quiet fear, a giddy courage that is a form of daring, a peculiarly futureless dread. In two days' time, the testing will be over, and then something else will happen that I cannot foresee, that I have yet to experience, but I know that it will be as unfamiliar as what I am feeling now and that what I am learning cannot be learned any other way, nor can it be described or lessened or lifted or altered to any degree, nor is there escape except fleetingly and only through distraction, which is not true forgetfulness, and always the "feeling" returns as strongly, and if this is fifty years ago, then I am a monarch butterfly not yet dead, but nevertheless pinned through the thorax to a poster board, futilely opening and closing its wings.

The feelings wash over and through me. They must be endured then let go. I try to let them come and go without interfering. I try on scarves in the mirror. I pull my hair back to study the shape of my skull. I will get to see my head for the first time without hair.

SOME MONTHS LATER:

Dear M,

Forgive me for not writing sooner, but the hours have been taken up with all manner of medical procedures as, alas, my veins proved insufficient to the task of conducting chemotherapy throughout my system, so I have had a little titanium pillbox sort of object implanted in my chest, and conveniently, it can remain there up to 10 years, if I should wish, and is used to make withdrawals and deposits. A bloodstream teller-window. It is covered by my own skin (conveniently) and appears as a lump (currently a red and sore lump) on my chest near the shoulder. As it happens, I am to lose my hair on Sept. 27 precisely, so I am having it all cut off on the 25th, deliberately and so as not to endure the sight of hair in the basin. My first chemotherapy will be Tuesday, and then every three weeks for a total of four treatments. Near Thanksgiving, I will most gratefully begin daily radiation, and by Christmas, perhaps I will have "ground cover" on my bald head and a tree in the living room with nothing beneath it but medical bills tied up in ribbons and, as I used to receive in my childhood, a Christmas navel orange. (I remember Sean telling me that this–the thought of his mother excited to receive an orange–was sad. And I assured him that it wasn't sad at all, it was delightful, and the trick was to get the orange cold in the fridge without a sibling making off with it.)

I have been thinking about the lake house, and we must think about naming it before it becomes by default The Lake House. But your idea to extend the porch to the second story is delightful, I think, and will very economically enhance the house. As the view is so very fine, perhaps this addition could be many-windowed, almost a glass porch, like the glass church on the raft in "The Illuminations." I miss you and remember often driving along the long and mysterious body of water that was the Hudson River. ... Much love and slightly panicked,

Carolyn

FROM INSOMNIA:

Writing to keep awake, to find my way back with words, to follow phrases back into a lived life, to remember something by way of syllables, to "music" the meaning, stitch the soul to its making, it's impossible not to feel that this poetry by which I have lived is an accident, as it also seems my life has been: the significant events—all coincidence and happenstance, near misses. Only my son was chosen, deliberately, was seen and beheld and welcomed. The rest, all the rest, seemed to happen of its own accord, and only in hindsight may it be assembled into a meaningful whole: this led to that, that led to the next this. In our sojourn on Earth, we are presented a curriculum for the education of a human soul, comprised of lessons that seem mysteriously to repeat themselves as if not properly learned the first time, or as if they were lessons failed, but this curriculum moves in a spiral rather than a circle, never returning quite to the same instruction, and the fortunate few experience, I think, epiphanies in their late years, so that even failure is embraced and welcomed. It is as Samuel Beckett wrote: "No matter. Try again. Fail again. Fail better." The final realization might be that we ourselves wrote this curriculum within the depths of our being.

Along my particular path, I have been taught a little of the experience of "near death": in a car blown across an icy road on a mountain pass, caught by a grove of trees; several times under shellfire and sniper fire in countries at war; and in El Salvador, in the time of the death squads, when "near death" bestowed its lesson as I escaped the fate of the others three times in a month.

In these encounters, death was outside, glimpsed fleetingly, harrowingly. There was no time to learn the lesson of death, only the lesson of heightened terror. This time, death appeared from within, so invisibly that it could be perceived only through radio imaging and magnetic resonance, and could be held back only through surgery, radiation, and chemical therapy. The beginning of death could be cut out, excised, and the surrounding territory bombarded and poisoned, and still it would not abandon me ever—as has always been true for all of us, but I didn't know this. I didn't live my life with this realization constantly before me, teaching me to be in awe of every drawn breath. But is it possible to live without ever forgetting death? Could we endure such turbulent radiance? Isn't it necessary to forget so as to get on with remembering the past and planning the future? Death holds us in the present, a moment that spirals outward, a moment revered and treasured beyond comprehension: the last moment, the moment before we go out. In this moment, it is possible to love having lived, to hold one's life sacred and to be filled with gratitude for the gift bestowed at the explosion of our conception. If the "I" were immortal, the self continuous, unthreatened, in this body or another, from time immemorial to infinity, without interruption, if this "I" could remain conscious forever, without limit, in the prison of selfhood—what? There would be "time" for everything and everyone, for all permutations of experience, and thus all urgency would be removed, all longing and wonder, all disappointment and, with it, expectation, leaving us suspended not in an eternal present but an eternal nothingness, without the immense spiritual satisfaction of having schooled a soul.

The quest for immortality has always mystified me, whether pursued through cyborg research or medical advancement; it seems that, as with other supposed "good ideas," the consequences of success, however tenuous, have not been well-imagined nor entirely thought-out. The prospect of immortality, for me, is as horrifying as certain heavens: endless and unrelieved, whether forever singing in the spheres near an old, bearded God or dwelling in one of the heavenly mansions promised by the Christ. The scientifically bestowed immortal life would keep us here, no longer making room for others, no longer allowing the world to be refreshed and re-envisioned, the soil to be replenished with our remains, and our works to be beheld independent of us and for their inherent value.

There is another immortality, however, that has always been available to humankind, and it is this immortality that I hope to achieve: the possibility of living on in the hearts of others, of having touched lives that will touch other lives, of having made something, a poem or garden, that will somehow be read and visited beyond one's death. The twenty-one-gram soul may depart the body, and the energy within it also—so palpable that it is impossible to mistake a corpse for a sleeping human—and this almost weightless force may be, as with all energy, indestructible, and so we might in some measure survive death.

I hope to remember this—the lesson of "near death," terrifyingly luminous—if and when I leave the tunnel of illness.

MORE MONTHS LATER:

I'm no longer bald. Just as I was becoming accustomed to the woman in the mirror, so pale she shone in the dark, those nights of frequent waking, startling myself at every glimpse, my ghost-self cupping her hands to her face or coming closer so she could see that, no, there were no eyebrows or eyelashes, not a single fine hair anywhere. Without hair, my eyes seemed strangely large, and they were filled with fuller measures of light, grief, terror, and solemnity. *Come back,* I pled with myself. And more than once, I stood before myself in the glass and whispered, *Who are you? Tell me who you are. Who have you ever been?*

I have been going through my things, bearing in mind that nothing should be kept that someone else wouldn't want, that I must prepare everything "just in case," I tell myself, that I must clean and sort and clear away the debris of my life. No two of anything. No duplicates. A friend thinks I should pack up the books having to do with the century's horrors because she wants to fill my room "with peace and light." *You're finished with that,* she said. *It's time for something else.* For something else, room must be made. Emptiness must be created.

AND A LITTLE LATER:

Now the sun comes through the fir branches, and in the window's reflection, the fire I have made is burning in midair above the field, and dew whitens the field, or silvers it, and I'm here in utter silence except for the sound of the flames. Somehow, it seems to me, all of this has been arranged. This is my heaven. I am alone here, yes, and I have always feared being alone, especially in houses, especially at night, but in recent years, I seem to have overcome that. I'm not afraid. And, of course, we go alone in the end, by ourselves, our souls go into the light that is death, and our bodies go into the darkness of the grave or the ash of a cremation. So it is as if I've been brought here, to a cottage on an island in Puget Sound, so that I might experience the heaven I imagined in childhood. My heart is full, as it was then, with love and gratitude for everyone in my life, for all who made me possible, for the light over the Sound, for the owl in the firs, the egrets standing in the thin lagoon. The moment of the present is still radiant, still precious, and this is why I think it's possible that I have come near the end of my life and, perhaps, with luck, veered off again into living.

So this is what I have to say about immortality: we live as radiant beings between two realms of darkness. We die so that the world may go on without us, so as to enable us to give ourselves back.

HEDGEBROOK, DECEMBER 2009

WITH THANKS TO DR. JOHNS.

The Heart

JERALD WALKER

For a decade, my brother struggled to save his marriage, but late one winter night, he accepted that it was over, right after his wife almost cut off his thumb. It dangled from a strip of flesh while his wife, still holding the butcher knife, flailed around in a spasm of remorse. My brother moved to console her, insisting that everything would be OK, displaying the kind of humanity perhaps common only in people who believe they can wed heroin addicts and have things turn out well.

She was, needless to say, high at the time. He, for his part, had had a great deal to drink, but he wasn't drunk, alcohol for him having become, over the better part of his thirty-eight years, more of a stabilizer than an intoxicant. His refrigerator was always full of malt liquor, forty-ounce bottles stacked neatly on the bottom shelf like an arsenal of small torpedoes. There was a lone bottle chilling in the freezer; he had been about to remove it when his wife tore into the kitchen, grabbed a knife from the drawer and accused him of being unfaithful. She frequently displayed this sort of wild paranoia, though it is true that, earlier in the day, he had flirted with one of the moms at a birthday party he had attended with his two daughters and son. His daughters were six and seven; his son, five. Now, having been awakened by their mother's shouting, they stood huddled together at the top of the stairs, quietly watching as she retrieved a plastic baggie from one of the drawers and proceeded to fill it with ice from the freezer, a remarkably astute response, all things considered. She even had the presence of mind to remove the bottle of beer lest it be forgotten and explode, as others had before. She offered it to my brother. He declined, on account of being busy holding his thumb together. She placed the bag of ice against the wound and began wrapping it in place with a dish towel. Seeing them standing so close together, with my brother's back pressed against the stove, a stranger entering the room might have mistaken this scene for something other than what it was—at least until after the thumb was wrapped, when my brother reached for the phone to call 911. "My wife," he said when the operator answered, "fucked me up."

The operator requested more specifics. He explained what had happened. Her voice heavy with boredom, as if my brother's predicament was a common one or simply low-ranking on the crisis scale, the operator told him to keep his hand elevated until the EMTs arrived. When she advised him to keep the thumb cold, my brother felt a surge of appreciation for his wife, for the way she had moved to preserve his finger, which was an example of how caring she could be. Deep down inside, she was a good person; he'd never doubted this. On the surface, unfortunately, was a troubled soul, which—despite his love for her—simply would not, and maybe could not, be soothed.

This realization was long in the making, having been delayed by periods of sobriety when she was soft-spoken and kind. He had met her during one of those periods. They were both studying for their GEDs, trying to reroute lives gone off track, because she didn't *have* to be on welfare forever, and he didn't *have* to be a hospital orderly always. So there they were, taking a class at the local community college, where she sat at the desk to his left, her body petite and fidgety, her skin the color of coffee beans, making it difficult to see, in her arms and legs, the tracks that he'd later tell her didn't matter. It was his unconditional acceptance of her that lengthened her abstinence longer than it had gone before, a full six months, so that when her relapse finally arrived, boring down on him like a massive hurricane, he'd already taken shelter in the area of the heart where reason does not venture. It was while there, no doubt, that he'd decided to marry her.

Our family struggled to make sense of this decision. Sometimes, when we spoke of it in his absence, we offered the kind of pop analyses one would find on a daytime talk show, using phrases like "low self-esteem" and "nurturing complex," and then, exhausted by the futility of this exercise, I'd simply hope for her to overdose and die. It was an awful thing to do, and I regret it now, but she seemed to have a death wish; I merely wanted it to be fulfilled without also including my brother. Every day, I feared receiving the phone call that would tell me their bodies had been found in bed, both temples containing a single bullet in the manner of murders involving illegal debts unpaid. Because while it had reached the point where he was giving her money to get high, he could never give her enough, so she was driven to find it by other means. Often, this required dealing with the kind of people who would hold you hostage, forcing you to perform sex acts with men clutching twenty-dollar bills until the account was settled—this happened to her more than once. It happened, too, that thugs showed up at their house looking for her; threatening messages were left on their phone. So, yes, I wanted her to die. Instead, she gave life. Three children in three years, each one born premature and each one, like her, addicted and pleading for help.

One of them made a plea now. It was their son, whose own thumb was crammed in his mouth, making it difficult to understand him when he begged his mother not to hurt his father.

His parents pulled apart.

"What are you doing up?" his father asked. "Go back to bed. All of you, scat."

"But we heard yelling." That was the six-year-old.

The seven-year-old added, "And we saw Daddy's finger! It's bleeding!"

"Go back to bed, damn it," shouted their mother, "before I make *y'all's* fingers bleed!"

Regardless of the effectiveness of the threat (the children did flee to their rooms without another word), my brother felt it was uncalled for. But there was no point in his saying so, because she was gone, replaced again by the addict who had thrust a knife toward his belly. It was the addict who yelled, *None of this would have happened if you had not been messing around with some hussy! And: You think I don't know what the hell you been doing all day? And also: You lucky only your* thumb *is on ice, motherfucker!* It was the addict who scampered from the kitchen into the living room, from the living room into the dining room, from the dining room back into the kitchen, over and over, like a panther in a cage. But it was the woman he loved who came back, crying now, professing her sorrow, cursing her life, wishing she'd never been born and then wrapping her arms around his waist and tilting up her head to snuggle her runny nose against his neck, and for an instant—but only for an instant, because this thought was interrupted by the blare of approaching sirens—he believed he could still make their marriage work.

Outside, the street swirled in festive lights, celebrating its end.

My Night with Ellen Hutchinson

BUD SHAW

Most of them took place at night—the battles we sometimes lost but always survived. It's not that we wanted to be up all night or that we could breathe easier once the sun came up and the outcome seemed inevitable; we simply had no control over when the phone rang. We went without sleep, oblivious to everything, living in a world where we knew it was morning when the hospital cafeteria was serving eggs. Time reset again and again whenever a phone rang in the night.

That's what brought Ellen Hutchinson and me together on a winter's night in 1983. The phone rang at different times in different places but for the same reason. It pulled us from our beds and sent us into the night, both afraid and expectant.

I'd been training in Pittsburgh for nearly two years by then. My car had caught fire that summer, and the divorce had taken whatever cash I might have had, but if I was careful, I could make it on my bike from the apartment on Marchand Street to the hospital in less than twenty minutes even in winter. At work, I stored my bike in the morgue because I knew a girl who worked there and it was safe.

The night I went to meet Ellen Hutchinson was a Sunday. I remember the day because of the smell in the air as I turned off O'Hara and pedaled up DeSoto. It was a pungent mix of the odors from an electrical short circuit and the coal smoke from my grandmother's stove. It was inescapable, even in the filtered air of the operating rooms. I most associated that smell with

Pittsburgh winters, when a featureless gray blanket blotted the sky and grew impenetrable through the night. It became more evocative of where I was than the sounds of sirens coming up Fifth Avenue or the image of ambulances parked outside the ER.

I asked about it my first week in town. We were just getting started on a transplant surgery that would take us nearly two days to complete. Chester was the scrub tech that Sunday night. I found him in the operating room, laying out the instruments on a large table.

"What's that smell, Chester?"

He stopped stacking instrument trays and looked at me with his head cocked. "Smell?" he asked.

"Yeah. It's in the air at night on weekends," I said. "Take a deep breath. You can even smell it in here."

"Oh, that." He opened a packet of sterile gloves and laid them on the table. "That's the coke furnaces, Doc," he said. "You're in the Steel City now."

Someone said they cleaned the furnaces on Sunday.

"But not till night," Chester claimed. "Not till after the Steelers game when everyone's too drunk to care."

Now, on another Sunday night, I rode down glassy black streets through coke furnace smog and parked my bike in the morgue. I was supposed to give Mrs. Ellen Hutchinson a new liver. That's what I told her husband. He signed the piece of paper that said he understood all the other things that could happen, but I think we both figured it was just a formality.

"Legal stuff," he probably told his neighbors back in Aliquippa when they asked him about it later, after he'd buried Ellen and given away her shoes and hats.

I'd seen people die during surgery over the years, but I was never in charge then. Someone else was—someone older and more experienced, someone whose position or title or credentials (if not always his presence) gave me asylum and an alibi.

Eventually, I worked them out, the deaths in the operating room. Most of the time, I looked for something about the patient: maybe if he'd taken better care of himself, stopped smoking or drinking so much; or if she'd come in earlier, before things got bad; or if he wasn't so old. Sometimes I told myself I was the only one who could have saved the patient, and if I couldn't do it, well, then ... that one was harder to pull off; it fell apart the moment I considered the possibility that someone else, someone smarter or more experienced or just better than I, maybe even someone I knew, would have done what I should have done. Then I wouldn't have ended up with blood on my hands and soaking through to my underwear.

I have to keep in mind that no one else was available when Ellen Hutchinson's time came. The real surgeons were out of town at a meeting, off to Venice or Kyoto or Boca Raton or wherever they all went that time. I was still just a fellow in training. I had to get special permission, emergency operating privileges, to do Ellen's transplant.

The truth is I knew what I was doing. I'd operated alone more than enough to know everything would be fine, which is what I told Mr. Hutchinson when I went to see him and Ellen in the holding area before the surgery.

"How old are you?" he asked.

I told him I was thirty-two years old.

"Is Dr. Starzl here yet?"

Dr. Thomas E. Starzl was the acknowledged father of liver transplantation, and in less than two years after his arrival, Pittsburgh had become the center of the transplant world.

I told him Dr. Starzl was out of town. "He travels a lot," I said.

"We came here for Dr. Starzl," he said.

I explained that Dr. Starzl had trained me. Ellen was lying on her back, looking up at the ceiling while I probed her abdomen with my hand. Her liver was huge and hard and came down almost to her hip. Mr. Hutchinson leaned over so his wife could see his face.

"I've been doing most of the transplants," I said.

Mr. Hutchinson wouldn't look at me.

"For three, four months now." I didn't mention my missing mentors because I didn't believe it mattered.

Ellen Hutchinson stared at her husband's face without turning her head. Her eyes, yellow-stained, were sunk deep into her skull. Mr. Hutchinson brushed a tuft of frizzled gray hair off her forehead. He was missing a finger on that hand.

Afterward, I found Mr. Hutchinson in the waiting room by himself. He was reading *Ladies' Home Journal.* That's what they had in our waiting room, that and *Good Housekeeping.* Some volunteer—a widow, maybe—brought them from home.

He stood and waited for me to come to him. It was early morning, five or five-thirty, I think. A janitor was wrestling with a floor polisher by the vending machines.

I don't remember exactly what I said. I'm sure that in medical school, they tried to teach us how to tell someone a loved one has died, as if that's the same as telling a man you've killed his wife.

I asked him to sit down, but he didn't. He just waited in silence, and when I told him Ellen was dead, he dropped to the chair and sat there for a moment, then started shaking his head and twisting the magazine into a tighter and tighter roll. I started to sit in the chair beside him, but he rose to his feet again and came toward me.

"You told me she'd be fine," he said, poking me in the sternum with his middle finger. It was his index finger that was missing.

I wanted to tell him what I thought went wrong. We didn't have the A-Team for anesthesia, I'd say. I'd never had confidence in that guy, and when everything started going to hell, he didn't seem to have a clue what to do, and by the time they called for help and our best anesthesia guy showed up ... well, it was too late. I wanted to tell him that we pumped on her chest, off and on, for more than an hour, losing her then getting her back. I wanted to tell him that when Luigi, poor old Luigi, who'd come from Italy to learn from Dr. Starzl, stopped pumping and looked up at me from across the table with his tired gray eyes and asked if it was finished, I pushed him out of the way and did it myself and kept going and going until I finally saw that everyone was standing back, staring at me, and I knew then we weren't getting her back.

Mr. Hutchinson paced back and forth, shaking his head, talking to himself, now and then slapping the magazine against his thigh. The floor polisher was coming closer and closer, and I couldn't make out what he was saying above the noise of it. I took one step toward him, thinking maybe I should touch his arm or something.

"What am I supposed to do?" he yelled at me.

The janitor was having trouble with the polisher. He'd have it bumping serenely along when, all of a sudden, it would skitter across the floor and crash into a chair or the Pepsi machine.

I asked Mr. Hutchinson if I should call someone, maybe someone in his family.

"Family?" he shouted. "Family? You want to know if I have a family?"

He put his head down, and I thought he was going to start pacing again, but then there he was, right in front of me and breathing hard.

"You just killed my family, son." He wasn't shouting anymore. "She was all I had. Now she's gone. Thanks to you." He backed away and stumbled into a chair and sat down. The janitor had left the polisher in the middle of the room. He'd probably gone for help. I really wanted to finish for him. It didn't look that hard.

Mr. Hutchinson sat staring at the magazine open in his lap. I sat facing him. I leaned forward with my elbows across my knees, maybe trying to get him to look up at me but hoping he wouldn't.

"Mr. Hutchinson?"

He rolled up the magazine again and held it across his lap like a nightstick.

"We'll need the name of a funeral home," I said.

He looked up and said something just as the polisher started up again.

"I'm sorry," I said. "I couldn't hear." I pointed over my shoulder toward the noise.

"Sheffield," he said. He opened the magazine and smoothed it with his palm. "The one in Aliquippa, out on Franklin."

I left him in the chair. A different man was running the polisher now. He ran it gracefully, back and forth, in great sweeping arcs, moving toward Mr. Hutchinson's corner of the room.

Ellen Hutchinson's cadaver lay naked and drained on the operating table. They'd taken away the blue surgical drapes and turned off the room lights, but the huge operating lights were still on her, and she looked sculpted from alabaster. I walked over and stood in the same place where I'd spent most of the night. The incision I'd made was shaped like the arms of a Mercedes hood ornament, and it was huge. I'd left the others to close it with big looping sutures. They'd been sloppy, and I regretted trusting them with someone they never knew.

Chester came in and walked to the back of the room and stood staring at the metal table on which they'd piled all the surgery instruments in a stainless-steel basket.

"Fuck," he said and shook his head. He picked up a big right-angle retractor blade with the tips of his fingers then dropped it back into the basket. "Jesus, fuck."

Dried blood caked nearly everything in the basket, and brown streaks ran down the side of the table. Chester looked down at the blood pooled on the floor, black and shiny. He backed up suddenly, picking up his feet like someone who'd stepped in dog shit. He didn't notice Ellen Hutchinson or me.

"Where is everyone?" I asked.

Chester jumped. "Jesus, don't do that!" He shielded his eyes with his hand and squinted through the light. "Oh, it's you."

Chester found some plastic gloves and pulled them on. "Fuck if I know, Doc." He grabbed hold of the instrument table with a hand on each side. "Probably another trauma. They sent me to fetch this shit is all I know."

I watched him push the instruments out the back entrance, and as the door swung shut, I saw a man sitting on the floor behind it. He was asleep with his head lying on his arms across his knees. He still had on his surgical mask, and I wondered if he thought it protected him.

"Luigi?" I whispered over the cadaver and across the room. I walked over to make sure.

"Hey, Luigi." I had to shake him. "What are you doing?"

He looked confused at first. He was an old man, and he'd been up all night with me. He was a famous professor in Milan. He had no business sleeping on the floor.

He smiled at me.

I felt very tired.

I went back to the table. They'd washed the body. They'd also removed all the tubes from her, and I worried about that. They should have left them in for the autopsy. A white plastic sheet and a roll of flat white twine lay on the floor beneath the operating table, along with a folder of papers. The Death Kit. They must have left in a hurry.

Luigi was across the table from me, still with his mask up. I reached over and pulled it down and looked at his mouth and asked him if he knew where to find a gurney. He nodded and left.

I stood beside Ellen Hutchinson's body and thought about all there was to do: tie the hands together across her body with the twine, wrap the body in the white plastic, put it on a gurney, fill out all the forms in the Death Kit, and put a name on why she died. Then cover the gurney with a white sheet and roll it down to the elevator, to the tunnels, to the morgue, and then get on my bike and ride away, because someone is going to need this room to do some regular surgery, the kind where the patient—a poor old woman from Aliquippa, the only family a man had—doesn't die because someone doesn't know what he's doing.

Luigi came back and said he couldn't find a goony.

"Gurney," I said. "We call it a gurney."

Luigi watched me knot the string I'd looped around the hands. He looked exhausted.

"Go home," I said. "I can get this."

Luigi came over and stood beside me. He was maybe 5 feet, 4 inches tall, and his hair was gray, and I thought then he might actually be over seventy, and I was at least a foot taller and half his age. He came closer, and I felt his hand on my shoulder. I clenched my jaw, but tears flooded my eyes, and my legs buckled. I staggered backward, away from Ellen Hutchinson. Luigi tried to hold me up, but we both fell to the floor.

The Hippest Bar on Christmas

CHRIS OFFUTT

Fifteen years ago, I went to a Christmas Eve party that ended early. A couple of guys invited me to the only tavern open in Iowa City, and I joined them. They ordered beer and whiskey while I drank pop, my days of liquor long behind me. I was recently divorced. I'd never been much of a womanizer and now found myself at large and alone during the holidays.

My buddies were sad about sitting in a tavern on Christmas Eve. One left early. The other man hadn't had a haircut in forty years. I knew him from the old days of shooting pool in bars like this dump. There was a fake foil tree, very small, on a shelf behind the bar. One wall had a plastic Santa with a single line of blinking lights that led from his pants to the floor as if he was urinating. The crowd was young. Many had shaved heads and multiple piercings of the face. One guy wore a flannel bathrobe and combat boots. The temperature outside was four degrees, but there wasn't a glove, scarf, or hat in sight. Men and women entered, trying not to show how cold they were. Their ears looked brittle as crackers.

"You know," I said, "this is the hippest bar in town."

"Hell if it is," my friend said. "This bar is proof that the sixties failed."

"What do you mean?"

"It's the worst part of the sixties right here."

"It's still the hip place," I said.

"That's what's wrong with it. Right here, man, back in '69 I saw a guy bust a beer bottle and hold it to a man's throat. Glass everywhere. You know what happened?"

I shook my head.

"The waitress came over. She said, 'Oh, man, there's people in here barefoot.' That's all she said. The guy put the bottle down. And, man, that was the sixties for you. These silly fuckers in here now aren't even close."

He finished his drink and left, suddenly angry in the way of lonely men during holidays. I thought about my own dumb past. I was too young to be a hippie like him. My era was the southern outlaw seventies, when country music was defiant and rural men grew long hair. We were rednecks with dope and eight-track stereos. We didn't know any better, but we were very angry people.

At eighteen I lived in Morehead, Kentucky, and owned a red Maverick that I often slept in. Morehead was a small town, and time was marked by the availability of drugs. There was blue microdot month, crank week, and PCP Sunday. Each weekend someone hosted a party featuring the drug of the week. You found out how much it cost, you got directions, and you took cash. One day the word went out that mushrooms were in town. It was an exotic drug, like Thai stick or peyote, and it hadn't been around before. The party was nine miles out of town. I got blasted on some Colombian and let a dope dealer named Beef drive my car to the party. His girlfriend had wrecked his truck the week before and was locked up the next county over. I felt great. One of the top dealers in town was driving my car to the mushroom party. Arriving with him would make people think I was cool.

Twenty or so people stood outside, shadowy figures with long hair. Music blasted from cheap speakers. Beef drove across the yard and parked beside the porch of the old farmhouse. I tried to be cool, seeing who noticed us without letting anyone know I cared. I flicked a cigarette away. I did it like a movie outlaw before stepping inside a church.

The host was fat and already going bald in his mid-twenties. His name was Joe Bob, but people called him Blow Job unless they wanted his drugs. Women liked him because he was generous and wasn't too menacing. He had the habit of sweating all the time. We found him in the kitchen by a pot on the stove. Several people were crowding around it, trying to breathe the steam. Beef and I looked into a pot full of thin white worms with purple heads. I inhaled the steam dutifully.

Joe Bob ladled out two cups of water for Beef and me. "Here, boys," Joe Bob said. "You all are good people." He used a spoon to rescue several of the worms and gently placed them in our respective cups. They were mushroom stalks.

"Thanks, man," Beef said. He passed Joe Bob a rolled-up baggie of pot. "This is for the crowd."

"Just throw it on the table," Joe Bob said.

He gave us each two more mushrooms. The cup was plastic, shaped like a china teacup, very tippy. I held it at an angle to keep the water from running out of a crack. I drank like Beef, as fast as possible, breathing through my mouth to cool it. I ate two mushrooms and put the other two in my shirt pocket. There followed what was always a strange period, waiting for the drugs to kick in, unsure of the signs, and wondering if they already had. Was I too fucked up to tell, or had I got burned? Apparently the mushrooms had plenty of kick because after a while I realized I was standing on the roof of my car, not sure how long I'd been there. Everyone was looking at me. I couldn't understand why they weren't as interested in the moon as I was. It was gorgeous. Human beings had walked on it. It was red and glowing. I could almost touch it, and I invited people to come up. A couple did. Guys I didn't know. They helped me off the car and pointed out that it was still daylight and seeing the moon was a ways off yet.

Someone built a fire. It was October but warm, and it had somehow gotten dark on me. I went in the woods for firewood and could see perfectly. I dragged back huge felled trees. The logs were so big that people sat on them instead of burning them, which was flattering to me. Anybody could find kindling in the woods, but I brought back furniture. I gave a girl the two extra mushrooms, and we smoked a little pot. Our clothes seemed to open on their own. She had her back against a tree with her pelvis thrust forward. My pants were down. I was inside her and we were laughing and all the animals in the woods were watching us in awe and envy that we could have sex on our hind legs. I held her bottom gently so the bark wouldn't scratch it and tore up the backs of my hands instead. Somebody later asked me if I passed out behind a car and got run over. The way we all lived back then, it was a reasonable question.

We returned to the party. Our arms were around each other, and her face was flushed. She was beautiful. Maybe I'd marry her. She had pot in every pocket, rolled and ready. We chain-smoked dope, but it had no effect on the mushrooms. Dogs were barking. The music went off then came back on. Twice more it happened. I thought it was my ears. I went in the house to see if it was the stereo or me. A guy in his underwear was aiming a pistol at the record player. It was a cheap stereo from Monkey Ward, and I wanted him to shoot it. I'd never seen anyone fire a gun indoors except my father, who once shot a dog from a window. He used a rifle, so it barely counted. Everyone was moving away from the guy in his underwear, yelling for him to put the gun down, while I was rooting for him to shoot. I didn't like the song anyhow. It was one of ZZ Top's worst.

He turned around, and I recognized Robbie, a guy I'd known since first grade. He lived across the creek from me, and we'd walked to school together every day for ten years until he quit. He was the youngest of eight, the only boy. He got off to a bad start, but then again, in the hills of eastern Kentucky, everyone did. Robbie was very drunk, swaying on his feet. He aimed the gun at me. It was the first of three times that I would face a loaded weapon. I didn't know that then. It was still the first time and it was just a little .32 and I didn't figure Robbie would shoot me.

"Chris?" he said. "You doing all right?"

"Yeah," I said. "I'm on mushrooms. What kind of gun is that?"

"Fuck, I don't know. Just a gun." He turned it sideways and held it in better light to read the name on the barrel. I stepped beside him. "Harrington & Richardson," he said.

"H&R's a good brand. Used to have me a nine-shot .22."

"A nine-shot?"

"Yeah. On a .38 frame. It was cool."

"Wish this was a nine-shot."

"Listen, Robbie. You going to shoot that stereo or what?"

"Why, you want to?"

He handed the gun to me. It felt good in my hand. I looked around for my new girlfriend, but she was gone. I didn't want to shoot it unless she was watching. Robbie stood in his underwear and waited.

"I don't know, man," I said. "Let's wait till the party's over. I want to hear some Skynyrd."

"No more fucking ZZ fucking Top," he said. "I hate that shit."

I nodded, put the gun in my pocket, and went outside. My new girlfriend was talking to a cool older guy. He was twenty-six, and I didn't like him. He only drank wine. He'd burnt me on some weed once. I smoked an entire quarter ounce at one sitting and only got paranoid and a headache. I had to get her away from him. I had to find out what her name was. I walked up to them and showed them the gun, which made him nervous. She and I found my car. We got in and listened to the radio and told each other our life stories. We smoked pot for hours. We ran the car battery down and wound up sleeping in the house on the floor.

I woke up with smoke in my face. She had the lit end of a joint in her mouth and was blowing the smoke at me, what we called "a shotgun." It was the second coolest way to come out of sleep. My favorite way was to eat a bunch of speed and take a nap. You woke up like a rocket, twitching everywhere. Still, that morning's shotgun wasn't bad either.

I remembered all this while sitting at the bar in Iowa. I was past forty at the time and had given up drugs altogether. I never really liked them. Pot made me paranoid. Speed left me depressed. Hallucinogens scared me. In later years, I tried cocaine, and while everyone else ran around laughing and flirting, I sat immobile in a corner, appalled by how fast my mind was racing. Drugs didn't have the same effect on me that they did on everyone else. I wish they did. I'd have fit in better.

The bartender announced last call, and I looked around and tried to imagine this place in the sixties, full of bell-bottoms and peace-sign pendants. That era was gone.

But then, so was mine, the ragtag seventies with its terrorism, bad economy, and hijacking of airplanes. Like most people rolling into middle age, I still clung to the music of my era. Though I hated disco then, I listened to it now on occasion. In college, a few buddies and I protested a disco concert. We strode about outside, stoned to the gills, holding signs and placards that said *Rock and Roll will never die.* It's embarrassing to remember. The hippies at least had a war to protest.

Fifteen years passed, during which I remarried and moved to Oxford, Mississippi. Last year, a few days before Christmas, my mother called me. She was anxious and scared in a way I'd never heard before. My father was in the hospital. It was bad, and she asked me to come home. I packed rapidly. Just in case, I included a set of funeral clothes and drove all night. Dad was on oxygen from smoking. He'd been diagnosed with alcoholic cirrhosis. He was dying from the drugs of his era, the fifties, alcohol and nicotine.

At the hospital, I ran into a woman I knew from the old days who was a nurse. She told me Joe Bob had been murdered and Beef had turned narc. I asked about Robbie. She said he was thrown out of the Navy for drug use, went to Florida for ten years and to prison once. The new era of drugs in Appalachia included OxyContin and meth. Robbie had gotten mixed up with both. Now he was in jail again, awaiting trial. I felt bad for him. We were the same age, and I tried to imagine being incarcerated in our home county. The nurse told me he'd be going to the pen for fifteen or twenty years. His health was bad, and he would probably die in prison.

On Christmas morning, I put on my dress clothes and headed for the jail. I polished the front of each boot on the back of the opposite calf. I knew Robbie didn't have a lot of people to visit him and hoped the jailer would be kind since it was Christmas. Inside was a foyer with a locked steel door, a camera mounted on the wall, a speaker, and a push-button for talking. A woman's voice asked if she could help me. I introduced myself, knowing my family name was still good in the county, and said I wanted to visit an inmate. When I told her who, she was silent for a long time then said it wasn't visiting hours or even the right day. I explained that I was in town to see my folks and thought I'd visit my old friend. She apologized twice and said I needed to arrange a visit in advance and come on the proper day. I nodded and thanked her. As I left, she said "Merry Christmas" in a sad and lonely tone.

I drove to the hospital. The nurse's station had a forlorn tree, but I figured it was more than the jail had. Dad lay in his small room, sick from years of abusing alcohol and now on morphine for his pain. Down the street, Robbie occupied an equally small room due to his preference of drugs. I'd outlived my era, so to speak, and would outlive my father and Robbie. I didn't drink or smoke or take drugs. I knew I wouldn't ever again. It felt good knowing that.

In a lucid moment, Dad asked why I was late getting to the hospital. I explained about Robbie, and Dad got mad. He said he'd known forty years ago that Robbie was going to prison, and the wonder of it was it took this long. I didn't say anything. I just nodded and listened, consoled my mother in the waiting room, talked to the doctors, and called my siblings. A week later, my brother arrived to take over. I drove back to Mississippi. I left a winter snowstorm in the hills and arrived to a sunny warm spell.

My father and I are very much alike. He's a writer and a recluse. For the last ten years, he sat in a chair and drank himself nearly to death, his legs so swollen from fluid retention he couldn't walk. Both ears were permanently crooked forward from the oxygen tubes. It was an awful end to a life, and it terrified me. No one should die that way, and I feared it for myself. But I'd remarried and had a good job and had stopped my bad habits. I was happy and healthy. As soon as I got back to Oxford, I went to the hippest bar in town. The Christmas lights were still up. A few red felt stockings hung on the wall. I bought a pack of cigarettes and ordered a shot of whiskey. I don't know why. I knew it was a bad idea and that I'd regret it later. But I also knew that for a little while I wouldn't think about my father or my friend or my past. I didn't want to feel anything. I drank the shot and ordered a double. I carried it outside to a small balcony. I drank and smoked until the bar closed, and I loved every minute of it.

Seep

MIEKE EERKENS

I.

In the beginning, there was only a smell. It was barely perceptible under the scent of California grasses, seaweed, and redwood, but it was there: a faint stink oozing into the atmosphere, which was easily dismissed at the time as a leaky delivery truck or lawnmower. As the smell crept into the sky, the sun was slipping into the horizon. I was in the habit of taking a picture every evening; the refracted pinks and reds were so vivid at Rodeo Beach that I had begun stepping out of my office and using my work camera to capture the sunset every day from the same spot as a personal creative project. That evening's was gorgeous: an expansive sunset that reflected off the coastline curving around from the Golden Gate Bridge. It was a spectacular place to have an office, nestled in a protected national park only steps from the Pacific Ocean.

I was working in communications for The Marine Mammal Center, a rescue, rehabilitation, and research nonprofit organization. That evening, we were holding our annual "State of the Ocean" address, so we all hung around after work to prepare. The Center and hospital are housed at Fort Cronkhite, a World War II military post that now lodges nonprofit organizations in the barracks and bunkers. I was tired that day and mildly annoyed at the thought of having to take pictures for the newsletter of our scientists presenting their research data to our donors. It would be an evening of dry numbers and boring PowerPoints charting the spread of toxic algae and domoic acid poisoning in sea lions and the corresponding spread of chemical fertilizers washing into the Pacific in agricultural runoff, or the rate of whale mortality in relation to nautical speed and sonar activity in commercial shipping lanes. When taking pictures, I always preferred the visceral drama of the hospital: the emotion-triggering images of bloody surgeries, extractions of fishing hooks from flesh, or anesthesia masks covering the snouts of prone animals. Such images penetrated the public's consciousness. Donors responded better when they could see the dramatic human impact on a sea lion with a gunshot through the head or a stomach full of plastic bags and fishing nets. In truth, we had far more patients that were simply starving to death due to commercial overfishing, but skinny sea lions sleeping peacefully in a corner and statistics on paper did not bring the news cameras or donations. So I preferred to take photos of recovering baby sea lions suckling at bottles or harbor seals bobbing adorably in their pools like fat floating kittens, the paint stains on their heads identifying them for the staff and volunteers. That was my job. The researchers looked at parasites and tumors through microscopes in the lab or tracked transmitters embedded in elephant seals, and my job was to make people care enough to write checks to keep that work going. I was good at it.

When I stepped outside to snap the sunset that November evening, I was preoccupied with my stories: healed patients being released back into the ocean, dangerous rescues of disoriented sea lions off airport runways, dead whales the size of buses washing up on beaches and our veterinarians standing atop them with carving knives to perform necropsies. In retrospect, I remember a vague smell, that petroleum smell seeping into the salty air. But like the silver flash of a fish leaping out of the water for a moment before disappearing into the sea again, the observation was gone as quickly as I noted it. I felt no cause for alarm. Earlier that day, I had received a call from a news reporter who asked if we had received any reports of an oil spill in the bay. I called our rescue department, and they confirmed that, indeed, out of mere protocol, the Coast Guard had informed them of a ship that had leaked a bit of oil, but that it was only a couple of hundred gallons at most, barely worth mentioning, and would not have any effect on wildlife at all. I relayed the information to the reporter and immediately dismissed it in the steady flow of the busy day.

As anticipated, the evening dragged as researchers presented their data dutifully. *Click, click, click.* Their slides moved across the screen, the light bathing donors' blank faces as they sipped Chardonnay from plastic cups. One of them had brought a toddler, who distracted us with her chatter in the corner. The audience was thanked for coming, the donors were thanked for their support making the Center's research possible, and after two hours, they shuffled out into the night and drove home while we staff folded chairs and wrapped up food. We were looking forward to getting home.

With a colleague, I walked to my car along the road that fronted the beach. Away from the city lights, the ocean was black, with only the mirrored moonlight wavering in the tide as it moved in and out. The smell had grown much stronger now, an undeniable petroleum smell.

"Whoa. Do you smell that?" I asked my colleague. "I'm wondering if that could have anything to do with that oil spill I got a call about today. Could that be from just a couple hundred gallons all the way on the other side of the bay?"

We stopped and peered out into the unyielding dark across Rodeo Beach, hearing only the waves reaching at the shore repeatedly. But there was nothing to see—just blackness.

Of course, it was not a few hundred gallons of oil. Not even close. It was, in fact, 53,569 gallons of heavy bunker fuel that had poured into the San Francisco Bay from the container ship *Cosco Busan* after its drug-impaired pilot crashed the vessel into the Bay Bridge in dense fog, a fact that had been misreported by the shipping company and, then, by the US Coast Guard. I learned all of this even before I arrived at work the next morning. My boss called me at 7:00 a.m., asking me to come in as soon as possible. As I drove into the Marin Headlands, the national park where The Marine Mammal Center is located, there was a news van behind me on the twisting road, riding my tail. When I arrived at the Rodeo Beach parking lot, there were three other news vans parked there, along with trucks from the National Park

Service, the police department, and the National Oceanic and Atmospheric Administration, as well as a National Response Center big rig with the words NRC Emergency Spill Response splashed across its side. Next to that was a phrase, in enormous red cursive letters: *Always Ready.*

II.

We are never ready. I don't care what they tell me, we are never ready, because what does *ready* really mean in the context of an oil spill? Is *ready* meant to convey a sense of inspiration and comfort? *Ready* means we already believe something is coming; *ready* means we have a plan of response for when we inevitably fuck up again. It implies that this disaster is the cost of doing business, that this very scenario has actually been planned. The inherent cynicism in being always ready, when the thing we claim to be *always ready* for is relentless human destruction, does not comfort me. I hate that those men with the Emergency Spill Response team felt ready and that they believed *ready* was a good thing. They were sitting on bulldozers, feeling pleased with their readiness, chugging around on the beach, plowing up the sticky, tarred sand where only weeks before we had released several sea lions back into the ocean. Dozens of men in yellow hazmat suits and blue rubber gloves were busily funneling the sludgy mess from the bulldozers into thousands of plastic bags piled into a towering monument of human failure on a huge plastic tarp. But I was not ready. My colleagues and I, who found ourselves on the front lines both figuratively and literally—we were never ready. And I don't ever want to be ready.

The Marine Mammal Center is a member of the Oiled Wildlife Care Network and the California Department of Fish and Game's Oil Spill Prevention and Response Program. Because the full impact of the *Cosco Busan* oil spill did not become apparent until the sun broke over the tarnished beaches the next morning, the only trained oiled-wildlife responders ready to be mobilized on site were two of our veterinary and rescue staff members, who had coincidentally completed a course legally required for handling oiled wildlife because of their work with marine mammals in the hospital.

It was sheer chance that the Center happened to be based on a beach that had been infiltrated by the oil, black blobs of which speckled the backlit waves in the morning sun before being deposited on the shore to seep into the sand. Our people were already on-site, and they were the logical first responders. But because our trained oiled-wildlife responders were not prepared to respond to oil spills directly, it took a couple of hours for them to locate the mandatory hazmat suits, find two more rescuers, and drive into San Francisco to pick up the regulation transport boxes, hundreds of blue plastic boxes with ventilation holes cut into the sides.

As we waited for them to return, I stood with my camera, looking at the beach I had photographed the day before. The smell was now overpowering, worming itself straight up my nostrils to twine around my nerves. I developed a dull headache and felt nauseous. I could do nothing but take pictures as I stood with the men in uniform behind the plastic yellow police tape that stretched across the beach in front of the sign: *National Park Service. Area Closed. Do not enter. Hazardous contaminants in water.* Behind me, a crowd was gathering, people from the community who had driven out to see it for themselves. We all stood behind the tape, legally restricted from walking onto the beach.

I know with reasonable certainty that we were not ready for what we saw, none of us. Dotted all the way down the beach were birds. They were in every stage of demise. Some lay on their sides, beaks opening and shutting as they attempted to get air past the thick tarry fuel that clogged their gullets and moved into their lungs, where it would slowly suffocate them. Others desperately tried to clean their oiled feathers in an instinctual attempt to get air-bound or restore their buoyancy, unaware that their efforts would create the same lethal situation as that of their suffocating neighbors. Still others never even had the opportunity to clean their feathers, because their bodies were coated completely in thick tar and crusted with layers of sand as they flailed about in their final moments, blind and deaf. The bulldozers drove around them, scooping sand. The pile of plastic bags grew taller.

There was a solemnity in the crowd that I will never forget, a collective sorrow imbuing us as we watched the scene unfold on the other side of the thin strip of yellow plastic that held us mercilessly to the role of witness. It made people whisper to each other. It made the news crews walk down the beach away from the crowd to conduct their reports. And we waited.

A cormorant washed in with the water during this vigil and began to flail in the surf. It flapped one wing, and the other wing was stuck to its back, so that it spun in frantic circles. We all watched as it struggled, waves washing it back and forth at the tideline. It craned its long neck back to pull at the coated wing, its beak growing darker and stickier with bunker fuel. Minutes passed. And then, quite suddenly, a young woman darted from the crowd, ducked under the yellow tape, and was sprinting toward the water, her thin legs gangly and awkward as she ran in flip-flops across the sand. The men in uniform all ran to the tape but did not dare cross it themselves.

They called to her. "Young lady, come back here!" yelled the park ranger. "You are breaking the law!" yelled the NOAA representative. But she didn't come back. She reached the surf and scooped the flapping bird up, holding it against her chest, and ran back to the crowd. She took the bird to the back of a pickup truck and tried to pour bottled water over it, but the water ran off the oily mess. She sank to the ground, her long legs folded under her, and began sobbing. "Why isn't anyone helping?" she kept asking.

The policeman was standing over her. "Ma'am, what you just did is a felony."

"So arrest me then," she said, clutching the bird to her.

Her long hair stuck to the bird, and her shirt was stained black. Her fingers were caked dark brown.

The NOAA rep joined the officer. "Only people wearing protective gear can handle these animals," he said. "That's an extremely toxic substance on your skin."

III.

When I was a representative of The Marine Mammal Center, it was my job to understand the principles behind laws and to communicate them to the public. I learned my talking points for interviews about the Marine Mammal Protection Act and the illegality of human interaction with wildlife for a host of very valid reasons, most of which are to protect the animals from people. In that moment on the beach, I stayed mute because to advocate breaking federal laws as a spokesperson for a wildlife hospital governed by those laws would have cost me my job.

But I no longer work at the Center. So now I can say that my heart leaped when I saw the young woman duck under the yellow tape and run. And now I can say what I was secretly thinking: "Go, girl. Run!" I believe that some realization had been seeping into all of our hearts with the excruciating passage of time, as we were forcibly separated from a horrifying scene of suffering that we knew, on some level, we had helped cause as human beings. We had to bear witness to the birds thrashing helplessly behind a bureaucratic line drawn in the sand to keep us safe from being tarred, and it made us privileged in a way that felt shameful. My heart leaped when I saw the girl run because she refused the division imposed on us by laws and protocol and yellow tape. She was enacting what my heart was screaming, what I believe we all were feeling but were too cowardly to do. Maybe it was stupid, maybe it endangered her, but it was an act of pure emotion. It was an act of love. And I don't believe that people can understand why the facts matter until their hearts know it, too.

Our rescuers arrived in their hazmat suits, and they trudged down the beach, returning again and again with sealed boxes of live birds as their white suits stained black with oil. The dead birds were piled into cardboard boxes to be counted at the emergency command center established at Fort Mason in San Francisco by the OWCN. I helped to stack the rescue boxes in the vans we normally used to transport rescued seals and sea lions, and watched the boxes bounce like jumping beans as panicked birds flapped inside them. We drove to Ford Mason, where we unloaded the boxes into OWCN trucks. Birds had been arriving there from all around the Bay Area, and the trucks were lined with cages. They were filled to capacity with sad-looking waterfowl, all of them black. But the cardboard boxes with the piles of dead bodies were even more disturbing to me. I asked the volunteer to hold one carcass up for me and stretch its wings to show that the mass of sludge was a bird. I wanted to capture images to make people feel it all, to know the visceral loss the way we had experienced it standing on the edge of the beach, to feel the overpowering need to duck under yellow tape and do something. I opened one of the rescue boxes and snapped a photo of a loon covered in oil, twisting its red eyes up at me. The inside of the box was smeared black where the loon had beaten its wings. We left the boxes with the OWCN. Then we returned to Rodeo Beach to pick up another load of birds.

Our two trained responders were women whom I had seen rescue and treat hundreds of injured and ill animals over the years. I had watched them tube-feed malnourished seals, do necropsies on baby dolphins, euthanize sea lions suffering from seizures, and extract embedded fish nets from infected necks. They always did these things professionally, remaining calm and composed. They were scientific, pragmatic women. But when they delivered the last boxes of oiled birds to the vans, wiping the perspiration beading up on their foreheads, one of them walked away and stood staring at the beach, dazed, and the other doubled over. When she stood, there were tears leaking from her eyes.

My God. I've never seen anything like that," she said. "It's just, it's just everywhere."

Over the days following the spill, I spoke to reporters repeatedly. "As first responders on the scene, The Marine Mammal Center rescued waterfowl off of Rodeo Beach," I said, over and over. "We have no way of knowing how much effect it will ultimately have on marine mammals. Our researchers will likely chart the effects of the oil spill on marine mammals over the years—rises in cancer, mutations, decreases in fish populations they feed on. Much of the oil sank and killed additional wildlife, including an estimated 30 percent of the herring spawn."

"And how bad was the oil there, from your perspective?" one reporter asked me.

I paused before giving her another line. "You know what?" I said. "I'll send you a picture of a bird if you publish it."

For many days after the spill, when I stepped out to take my usual photograph of the sunset, the yellow police tape remained there, and the men continued piling plastic bags on the sand. Then they disappeared from the landscape, and a bright-orange fence was erected to separate the part of the beach that was still unsafe. For several weeks, the fence stretched across my photos until it, too, was gone, and the beach looked exactly the same as it had before—pristine and gold-hued, unblemished by fences and machines. I suppose I could have presented our donors with that restored image of an idyllic beach to still their consciences and preserve their illusions. But people always cared more, and sent more money, when I fostered their distress. So I went back inside my office and laid out the photos of oiled birds and men in hazmat suits for the newsletter, because my job was to make people care. My job was to make *always ready* a distasteful phrase. My job was to inspire us all to break from the bonds of witness. To duck under the yellow tape and seize our moment. To run like hell toward the surf.

Any Given Day

JUDITH KITCHEN

ON ANY GIVEN DAY SOMETHING CLAIMS OUR ATTENTION.

–Haruki Murakami

MONDAY:

May. I've been waiting for this all year, and now the talk of the World Cup is all about injury. Suárez, Costa, even Cristiano Ronaldo—all a bit iffy. Ghana's team doctor—a witch doctor whose name translates into "Devil of Wednesday"—is claiming credit for Ronaldo's problems, says he is "working on" a curse that will keep him from playing. My boys—Messi, Modric, di María, Marcelo—will be scattered over the map to represent the places they call "home." Surely they've been away too long. And yet there is something at the back of the brain, maybe a remembered touch, or smell, a ball rolling down a set of steps, a grandmother stirring soup, something that spells the dream of playing for where you belong.

What are the trappings of home? Do they go back to childhood, or can I look for them outside my front door? Sand: the drift of it through the fingers and the glint of stone or shell, small enough to carry in the pocket, small enough to turn in the palm with a grandson. Sand: where to take off your shoes is to enter another dimension, and to wade out into surf is to realize there is no real division between water and land. Water: spewing from the hose as you race through it on hot August afternoons; New England brooks that rush downhill in patchy light; creeks, we called them in upstate New York, not brooks or streams or, ugh, rivulets. Creeks, with beds of large, lazy rocks, slippery underfoot, precarious footing for the leap to the other side. Rivers, too, but that was a different kind of water—less intimate, less part and parcel of the body's sense of a summer day.

Or snow. Ubiquitous memory of falling flakes, snow softening the ground with its pale white brush. Everything hushed, waiting for Christmas. Even the wind seemed quiet. And the mittened hand reached out, caught a flake, then another, the tongue licked wool, metallic. Snow slipping from branches, sliding in slow motion, small splash as it landed. Snow circling back on itself, revealing its dark absence at the base of trees, its swelling proclamation at the bottom of steps. And cutthroat cold—the kind that can bite at the skin, or the kind that creeps up the back, or the kind you welcome as you rush out the door, freed into that new white world.

Now you live in a place where snow limits itself to the mountain passes. Is this home—this unfamiliar forest with its dense, forbidding trees, this coastal town full of foghorn and fable? Your childhood lost in the way that a soldier's sense of self must be lost as he gazes out at meaningless rock and searches for what is worth fighting for, comes up as empty as the landscape that stretches before him. He cannot dredge up the sound of the ice cream truck, or the chatter at the Little League field, or even the way his son babbled in the crib. He cannot call up his brother's broken bike, or how he helped him fix it. He is lost in a land where memory dissipates. So why is he there, staring into lifeless hills waiting for signs of life to pull him back into what he has learned he must do?

This is not the displacement of the striker called to play thousands of miles from where he learned his tricks with the ball. Nor is it the dislocation of the young programmer bringing his skills from one coast to the other, suddenly confused by the palm trees outside his window. This is psychic disruption, and for that he will need to recall the day he realized—in Mr. Harrison's social studies class—that he belonged to something larger. To an idea he hardly knew how to express.

Let's—at the very least—look at the day—this day—to see what it brings.

TUESDAY:

Early June, and still the rain persists, dripping slowly onto the azaleas, as though they could bleed their colors into the ground. It could as easily be any given day—anonymous, indifferent to schedule or event. You sit by your window, letting chemotherapy work its way through your body, work its way into the organs that tell your brain to shut down.

Enjoy this lethargy, they say, because there's nothing you can do about it.

Well, of course there is. You can decide to say "no." And there are moments when that feels like what you should do. At least you'd have some control. At least you'd be able to think your thoughts in a context: let's drive down by the water and listen to the waves' rhythmic *batucada;* let's stop for pulled pork, or, if your stomach's still bad, at least a Popsicle; let's watch the ferry pull into the dock, unload and reload, then pull away again.

It's a Tuesday. All Tuesdays are elastic. And it is June. Any June. Trace them back through time. My sons are young, preschool, and they are playing in the sandbox. Low murmurs as they sift and pat. I don't remember having this much time to myself in weeks … months … years. They are playing happily and, if I'd known this would happen, I would be doing something for myself. But I didn't know, so I am simply waiting to be needed again. And nearly fifty years later, I still wait, a Tuesday in June, for my life to catch up with me.

Breathe in, then out, walk twenty minutes at the slow speed of 1.2 at the hospital exercise group. Twenty minutes reclaimed from whatever bank of days I have stretching before me. Twenty minutes I didn't know I still had in me. This is the day I imagine will catch me unawares, sometime when I look back, trying to pinpoint the time, the place, the exact day I decided what to do with the time I bought.

This is the Tuesday that Suárez, only one month from a knee operation, plays for his country and then betrays everything. Did I see what I thought I saw? A bite! Did he bite his opponent? OK, bad boy biting bad boy—but still, doesn't that cross some line I'm not able to forgive? I still can't quite believe what I've seen, but there it is on replay, and it might as well be preschoolers in the sandbox, some hidden time when the animal rises up, before the diligent mother does whatever it takes to say, "Never bite, never again." This will make headlines. This will divide friends, and marriages, parents from children, me from my son, and it will bring disgrace. This is news!

Never mind that in Iraq leftover weapons are mowing down people, including ancient Christian sects. Never mind that a soldier is being held in a Mexican prison. Never mind that the IRS has "lost" its emails. Never mind that history sidles in, a bit like rising water seeping under the crack in the doorway, spilling a slow trickle onto the floor. History does not care if it is Tuesday or June, or somewhere far away. History does not care that billions of eyes are fixed on a bite. But there it is: the human being reduced to its origins, the rest of the news given a context we do not want to face, but are faced with, nonetheless.

Nonetheless. On the other hand. All the same. Even so. However. Nevertheless. Never the less. Not if we can help it. What we want is more—more of everything. We want to bite off more than we can chew, then chew it. We want to argue this day over and over: what it has done to our sense of our selves. Who are we beneath the façade? Are we tooth and claw? Fist and knee? What do we alter with the slow drip of civilization?

WEDNESDAY:

I'm free—for a while—without poison or pill. Free to retrieve the sense of infinite living, played out against the broad background. Will I be able to play the part? Or has something changed irrevocably? July. Today is sunshine, leaking its way to the hummingbird feeders, sending back sparks from their cylindrical shafts. Catching itself on telephone wires, thin stripe of glinting yellow against the trees. Or the leaves themselves, cupping the shine and turning it back toward its source—even the pine needles' thin mirrors are splayed like torches. Sky as blue and cloudless as it's supposed to be: all of every July coalesced in one long memory of heat, of endlessness, not quite boredom, but bordering on ennui.

My brother will have a stent inserted in his artery today. Extend the life of the heart. Its rhythmic chipping through the day, ta-*dah,* ta-*dah,* the ventricular emphasis on to-*day.*

The sun beats down, memory of past suns, days spent lying on the float just offshore at Keuka Lake, days spent searching out shade by skirting the walls of Rio. Heat rises from the road in shimmering waves and everything seems translucent—seen through the wavering space between the candle and the flame. The sun flares in the sky. And there is music everywhere, floating on its own high notes.

The yard begins to tarnish. Scraps of weeds, taller than the shrinking grass. Rough at the edges, scrawny. But the hummingbirds keep coming, dive-bombing the feeders, whirr of wings as we replenish. Same for the birdbath that seems, each evening, to contain a spectrum—warbler to robin to wren. Dust on the windowsill, caught in a shaft of sun.

Everything gone to seed. Or going.

We are driving through rural Pennsylvania when the road signs announce that we are somewhere between Desire and Panic. An appropriate approximation of the human condition. We glide past Amish buggies, faces mere glimpses in the darkened interiors. What would it be to know so well who you are that there is nothing to question? To spend day after day in the somber cloth of faith, wheels turning backward (or so is the illusion) as the car speeds past. You might think of this as home—green sound of the fiddle, salt stroke of a future you know you will not inhabit.

Early morning light, layers of yellow and gray, an unfamiliar view from the motel window. There's an artificial breeze as the air conditioner blows the curtains into the room. Outside, we cannot tell what type of day this will be—only that the sun has appeared, at this moment weak and watery.

THURSDAY:

Home to a scattering of fog. But who could forget a world that offers up perfect metaphors? Between Desire and Panic. Panic is easy to define—it's the ring of the phone at some late/early hour, the row of medicines on my nightstand. Desire is more difficult. What do I want, now that wanting seems to be beside the point? Now that everything is the object of desire.

I remember Augusts of old. The days stretched over the horizon, and time settled into one spot, one book to read, one soft throbbing of rain on the roof. Nothing went forward; there was no future. Even the past receded, firmly fixed where it belonged, there on the shore. As though the earth were not winging its way through space. As though each of us were not headed our separate directions. For one brief instant, everything could be held in the hand, or beheld by the eye—intact and exclusively ours.

I remember Augusts, and instantly I am eight or nine, old enough to take off on a bicycle and not return until dinner. Something children today do not do—or not enough of them. The world was ours to learn. We didn't have names—not yet—for the things we saw, but nevertheless we saw them: wintergreen, shale, timothy, oriole, woodchuck. And the bicycle—fat-wheeled Schwinn—with its ticket to distance and speed and the edge of the town, where we could pretend we were standing on moors, looking far as the eye could see at heather and bracken, while above us the curlew called and called. Or eighteen, waiting for the phone to ring, waiting on the front steps for his car to round the corner, his easy laugh. Waiting for life to take us out of sight.

Or out of mind. Be that as it may, La Liga has begun again. Messi scores. "He could teach geometry to Euclid," says the announcer. "A human Stradivarius." And it's true. His quality of tone is just as distinctive. Although, truth be told, tests have showed that even experts cannot tell a Stradivarius from other violins if they are played behind a curtain.

Thursday is such an ordinary day. Why give it stature? And what is a week but a string of such days, run of the mill and unremarkable? The deer in the yard grow steadily bolder. Beyond that, the peal of a foghorn, screech of brakes—sound to tell us someone else is out there, someone whose life is separate from ours. That ordinary days contain the lives that live them.

Where is time taking us, we whose time means everything and nothing? How does the month slink off without warning? We measure now in degrees of Fahrenheit. I remember waiting for Pelé to enter the pitch. I remember anticipating Carnaval: the samba schools spinning and drums in the distance. Between then and now? I've waited for the ordinary things: dinner, delight, an idea. I've waited for the eagle to remind me of the meaning of "one fell swoop."

FRIDAY:

The year is turning. And again we are bystanders. Somewhere sumac flares. Woodsmoke rises. Here, the days are doled out as though they were precious. And they are, they are. It's just that we don't know what to do with them. They extend themselves. They go on and on, orderly in the extreme. One, two, three, four, five, six, seven, one, two, three, four, five, six, seven, *ad infinitum, ad nauseam, ad* something we've yet to discover. They go on and on and we go on with them—no way to pluck one up and say, "This, this is the day that defines me."

Until now, my waiting has always seemed anticipatory. But this is different. I wait for the phone call I don't want to hear. If this were soccer, the doctors would be offside. The ball called back: free kick. But what is the goal, now that we know we don't know? There are no rules. What claims our attention? The ball, with its spherical secrets? The cell, with its secret spheres? I move in interior spaces, sometimes the body, sometimes the mind. I move, but nothing moves with me.

What's a little oxygen? The man delivers it, and suddenly I'm tied to the elements. Hooked to a machine. It pulses. For the life of me I can't tell how it really helps. Friday. Almost evening. And I'm a prisoner: helped by what hinders. Friday. Almost evening. Tomorrow I will need to reevaluate. Tomorrow, which comes as inevitably as September.

Face-to-face with an alternative life, would you take it? Would you follow its surrogate options? What if you were offered the chance to go back, start again, eat right, slow down, keep this cancer at bay? What if you were given days and days, but of a different life? Would you take that chance?

Be honest. What would you do with something that unfamiliar? So far off your beaten track that you might not recognize home?

The morning light comes later and later and soon it will be equinox, and then we will move into days of steady gray rain. The body relies on this knowledge. Future-oriented—that's what we are. And, of course, we mine the past. It's a way to predict. And to understand. And to moderate. Though moderation no longer appeals. I'd like to shake things up a bit, as I have been shaken. I'd like to withhold—and reveal—on my own terms. And I'd like to make a bit of unnecessary noise. Meanwhile, at the very center, something wants answers. What word to put on it? What word could suffice?

Meanwhile. For now. For the time being. In the interim. In the meantime. Mean time. Yes, nasty, cruel, uncaring, callous time. It holds out its hands, but that's about it. The rest is what you can make of it. What's left of it. Not what's gone, but what remains.

Ronaldo scores. A sea of white flags. Like ocean waves in moonlight. Like seagulls swarming at the dump. They whip the air to a frenzy. This waiting moves in another direction—into the long, slow wait we all share—and we are defined by its gravity. How to lift the heart again? How to return to the typewriter, furiously tapping out its feast of words? How to stuff the envelope and lick the stamp and send something out into the real, almost-tangible air? How to find you again. You, whom I cannot bear to give up.

Puff. The sound of inhalation. Forget Saturday. And Sunday. What is a day or two? What is a week, or a month? Or a year, for that matter? Days build up—a wall of bricks—then begin to topple. At which point, memory begins. And memory? Puff. It's there, there in that shadow, that word in a book. Puff. There—see—it shapes the passage with images of places we have never been. Though, puff, somewhere, sometime in childhood, puff, words invoked this instant when, puff, the phone is about to ring. This waiting. This interval of time we now call home. This given day.

I Survived the Blizzard of '79

BETH ANN FENNELLY

We didn't question. Or complain. It wouldn't have occurred to us, and it wouldn't have helped. I was eight. Julie was ten.

We didn't know yet that this blizzard would earn itself a moniker that would be silk-screened on T-shirts. We would own such a shirt, which extended its tenure in our house as a rag for polishing silver.

So I didn't make up the blizzard, though it sounds made up, the grimmest of Grimms, windchill forty below, three feet of snow and snow still falling. You had to shovel your drive daily. Later, a neighbor would tell of coming home after two nights away and having to dig down a foot to reach his own keyhole.

My dad had a snow blower, which spewed sheets of snow out of the side of its mouth. Sheets became mountains, and mountains became walls on either side of our front path, reaching almost to the sky. I could still view sky by tipping my head back, but seeing it was no relief because the sky was snow-white, tearing itself into pieces and hurling them at us.

And then the world began shutting down. The airports, which was bad because Mom was in Toronto, visiting her sister. The schools, which was great for the first day, and good for the second, and then less good and less good yet. Because the roads were impossible; the fridge, emptying. *Does this smell OK to you?* Couldn't watch *Little House* because Channel 5 covered the blizzard all day. A motorist, dead of exposure in a stranded car. A man, dead of a heart attack while shoveling snow; ambulance couldn't reach him.

Coat drive, shelters for the homeless. *Check in on your elderly neighbors, folks. If you can get out, that is.* Amtrak trains abandoned. Hundreds of cars lining the highway, buried by snow, white lumps pierced by antennas. Family of five, killed when their roof collapsed. We were a family of four, but with Mom far away, we were only three. I got out of the bathtub to answer her crackling long-distance call.

Then it was Sunday, so Dad said get ready for Mass. We didn't question. He helped us tug and wriggle into our snowsuits, and we slid our feet into plastic bread bags before yanking on our boots. He pushed open the door into the shrieking tunnel of white. We trudged between the walls of snow to the unplowed road. *Follow me,* Dad said. *Step where I'm stepping; this part will hold our weight.* Except sometimes we couldn't match his stride, or the snow wouldn't hold our weight and Julie's boot or my boot would crunch through crust and we'd plummet to the groin, feeling nothing below but more snow. *On the count of three,* Dad said, and hoisted us out, and we battled on, snow melting into our boots, heads lowered against the wind. When we reached the plowed road, we scrambled down, easier walking. I couldn't tell how far we had to go. It hurt to look up.

At last, the dark church loomed. We climbed the stone steps to the doors. Locked. My father raised his gloved fist and knocked. He must have known, even as he knocked, but still he knocked. There was no sign on the door saying that Mass was canceled. But why should the priests post a sign? Probably they couldn't even get out of the rectory themselves.

Righteo, said my father, slowly turning back the way we had come. *Righteo.* Whatever he felt then—gazing out over the tundra, the alien tundra, all the mailboxes and road signs and newspaper vending machines and parking meters blighted and buried—wasn't something he shared. What he shared was, *Home again, home again, jiggety jig.*

We descended the steps, back into the scouring wind. I knew now that white hurt worse than red. Where was everybody? Elderly couple, found in their basement, dead of hypothermia. Fourteen-year-old boy, poisoned by carbon monoxide as he sat in a running car his dad was trying to dig out from a snow bank. Another shoveler's heart attack. Volunteers with snowmobiles taking doctors to hospitals.

Every part of my body was scalding cold, but one part scalded coldest: my neck, my plump child's neck. The wind was wily, cupping my lowered chin and arrowing along the inch of skin before my parka's zipper. The wind, like a squirrel wielding knives. How much farther? I tried to step where my father was stepping. I tried to use his body as a shield. Family of three or four, frozen dead on the road, hadn't even gone to Mass. It was a sin to skip Mass. If you were a sinner when you died, you went to hell.

Finally, I did it, the thing I'd been contemplating for the last half mile. I shouted at my dad's back, asking for his scarf. I didn't want to ask. I wasn't a child who asked. And I knew he must be cold, too. Yet I asked, and when I did, he turned, already unwrapping his red-and-black striped scarf. He squatted and tied it around my neck, he wound it once, he wound it twice, he wound it three times, he smiled at me, his handsome Black Irish smile, and behind his scarf, which covered my neck all the way to the tip of my nose, I smiled, too. And thought I might make it, after all.

Why are people nervous about becoming parents? Children are so gullible. So stupid. For years, I'd think of this as a happy memory, my father snugging his scarf around my neck.

But eventually I corrected myself. First, I heard my parents' late-night argument, the barb about Dad dragging us to church in a blizzard, over two miles round trip. And in time, I recognized the catholicism of my father's rigidity, the Victorian strictures of our house. And eventually, I realized that if he were going to foot-slog us through a blizzard, he should have damn sure dressed us in scarves.

And so, with each year, with each time my thoughts are blown back to the Blizzard of '79, I unwind that scarf, unwind its loops around my neck. With my self-pity I unwind it; with my self-righteousness I unwind it; even with the care I take dressing my own soft children, I unwind it. The very care I take—*Here are your mittens, kitten; here are your warmest socks*—is a reprimand, and then the scarf is off my neck. Yet still I worry it: I pull out the threads, pluck and pull and release them to the wind, the wind that shall never again find the neck of my father, my handsome father, for he is shielded from it, as he is shielded from me, for he is below the earth and has been for years and cares not for the ways I remember him, or remember remembering him.

Prometheus Unbound

ELIZABETH FORTESCUE

Boston's Symphony Hall is filled to capacity, but on stage, there is only a single chair. There is not even a music stand. It is an odd image—simple, daunting, magnetic. I have never seen anything quite like it. The hall lights flicker; then the house lights dim. Stragglers hurry in to claim their seats. And then, suddenly, we are all on our feet again.

The chair on stage is for Yo-Yo Ma, who will perform three of Bach's six suites for solo cello. Ma comes onto the stage, bows a few times, takes his seat, and starts in on the fourth suite without hesitation. He seems free, on fire. His forehead glistens with sweat. Little drips fall down his temples and land on the fingerboard. His eyes are closed, and there is a smile, almost of discovery, on his face. Without an intermission, he brings the house to life with the fourth, fifth, and then the daunting sixth suite.

Since I was a child, Bach's Suite no. 6 for solo cello has been my very favorite piece of music. It has six parts, each harder than the last. I have been playing cello and piano since I could walk, but I have never even attempted the sixth suite. So much of the suite involves rapid string crossings, double stops, and very high notes—way up on the A string in thumb position. I am just not good enough—yet. "Next year," my teacher reassures me. Ma has recorded these works a few times, tracks I own in their entirety, but this is my first time having the honor to hear him perform in person. I am transfixed.

My husband and I spend a lot of time in Symphony Hall, but he does not share my passion for cello. It takes some convincing to get him to go to the Ma concert with me. By the time we reach the box office, only front-row seats remain—one on stage left, one on stage right. Jon takes the right, and I the left.

I focus on Ma. His posture, where his left knee rests on the left corner of his instrument. Ma's body and his cello undulate with the music, especially in the difficult passages I study how he moves with his instrument, as though it is an extension of his body. I marvel at his mastery of the treble clef and higher positions, especially in the later movements. That face of wonderment.

On this night, as he delivers Bach's sixth suite, I can feel the pulsations of the crowd. The rhythms, almost like heartbeats, move right through me. It is nearly too much.

A month after hearing Yo-Yo Ma play, I collapsed during a run one snowy morning. I had been an avid athlete all my life: Division I varsity college soccer, mountain climbing, skiing, distance running, swimming, more. I was training for my second Boston Marathon, but that aspect of my life ended abruptly.

My cardiovascular system had shorted out. A purely electrical problem: my heart muscle was good and strong, but the nerves were incompetent. I was quickly diagnosed and fitted with a combination pacemaker and implantable cardioverter defibrillator. My life depends on a non-re-chargeable lithium-ion battery implanted in my chest within a hermetically sealed device about the size of a deck of cards. Underneath the activity of the pacemaker, my heart is nothing. No rhythm. Sometimes I feel as if that makes me nothing, too.

My cardiac illness was in the making before the running collapse. In fact, I may have been born with some version of it, but it has gotten worse as I have aged. And it does not just involve my heart; my disease has spread out to my whole body. Over the last few years, a rare brain disorder called dysautonomia has led to the failure of the peripheral vascular nerves that strengthen the blood vessels. The result is failure of the vessels to pump the blood adequately. My grave cardiovascular and neurologic illnesses mean that even the slightest common ailment can cause severe hypotension.

A year after my collapse and ICD surgery, I discovered I was pregnant. It was with some hesitation that Jon and I had decided to try to conceive a baby, but both my cardiologist and our obstetrician gave us their blessings. After checking a pregnancy test early one morning, I returned to the master bed and whispered into my sleeping Jon's ear, "I'm thirty today, and we're pregnant!" He rolled onto his back, eyes still closed, and a wide smile spread across his face. He embraced me tightly and whispered back, "Oh, my. Oh, Elizabeth. This is good." My pregnancy went remarkably smoothly. William was born via induction on his due date. His labor lasted only one hour. After birth, the doctors quickly checked his heart for any abnormalities, and found none. Jon and I felt like we had won the lottery.

Never did I tell anyone that during William's pregnancy I rented a portable Doppler instrument off the internet so I could listen to his heartbeats anytime I wanted to. And I did, often. Unlike my own, William's heart rhythms fluctuated with the vicissitudes of our shared lives—our adrenaline bursts and lulls, our moments of stress and contentment. I have never felt so alive as when pregnant. I treated myself beautifully—for William.

In the spring of 1815, a powerful volcano called Mount Tambora erupted in what is now Indonesia. Its aftermath clouded the atmosphere with ash for a long time, shrouding the South Pacific in a long bout of darkness and changing the weather over much of the world. Historical accounts suggest that this climatic disaster had major psychological consequences on the people of the time. Musicians like Beethoven and Schubert wrote some of their most masterful, soulful works during this time. Many European artists became captivated by the myth of Prometheus, giver of fire. Lord Byron left England shortly after Tambora's blast. He soon met up with the great Romantic poet Percy Shelley and the soon-to-be Mary Shelley—Mary Godwin. They spent some time in Switzerland, still darkened by the aftermath of Mount Tambora's eruption, and while there, they shared scary stories. It was at this time that Mary Shelley, in her young adulthood, created Frankenstein—a "modern Prometheus" who takes electricity and makes from it life.

In James Whale's 1931 movie adaptation, the scientist Frankenstein waits for the worst lightning storm of the season to capture the most powerful electrical charge for his experiment and bring his creature to life. Despite the monster's "abnormal" stolen brain, the scientist is determined. Just as lightning is about to strike, he hoists the monster to the top of a tower. The lightning hits, and it works: the monster moves his right forearm. Life achieved.

I take cello lessons from a substitute cellist for the Boston Pops and Symphony Orchestra, who is also the teacher of Pops conductor Keith Lockhart's son. I cherish my lessons, though my experience of them is so different than before my heart's decline. I can play music as always, but the pulsations of the rhythms escape me, even when listening to music played by others. I miss it.

In his book on the Bach cello suites, Eric Siblin describes the prelude to the sixth suite as "a bolt of lightning—searing, rhapsodic, and electrified with ecstasy." He continues: "It harks back to the first suite with its undulating current, but five suites later is bursting its bounds with pyrotechnical energy. Here Bach is working with a large canvas. The trumpets blare, strings soar, drums roll. The composer pulls off the symphonic effect of a full orchestra with one bow and a handful of strings." Part of the Prelude involves repeating exact notes on different strings in different positions, some open and some in fourth position, giving an electric then a muted sound to the note. It is so gratifying to me—or at least it used to be. I know there used to be more.

In the 1931 film as well as Mel Brooks' later satire, *Young Frankenstein,* the monster becomes enamored with the violin; as a woman plays, the monster swoons. There is something about music that seems to make the monsters forget their violent tendencies and get caught up in the moment. At least for a moment.

Percy Shelley drowned off the coast of Livorno in 1822, in a weather-related boating accident on his ship, *Ariel.* He was a month shy of his thirtieth birthday. At the poet's cremation on the beach where his body was found, Edward Trelawney braved the funeral pyre's flames to remove Percy's heart from his burning chest. He gave it to a friend, Leigh Hunt, who ultimately gave it to Mary. Apparently, she kept her husband's heart for the rest of her life, wrapped in a copy of his "Adonais."

There is something magical about the heart. Throughout history, it has often been considered the soul of the body, the emotional core, the spirit. When mine malfunctioned, I felt as if a deep and meaningful part of me had died.

My Medtronic Evera XT ICD's pacing system is programmed to give me a steady heart rate at baseline and to speed up with activity. My ICD's rate responsiveness acts on an accelerometer, a tiny contraption within the device that senses foot strikes. (This differs from other brands of ICDs, which act, for example, on inotropy—heart contractility.) As I step more, my heart speeds up. My device is finely tuned to give me as much energy as possible, but the accelerometer is rather dumb. I cannot swim. I cannot ski. I cannot do yoga. I cannot walk up inclines. The list goes on from there. Another issue for me is that I am left-handed with a thin chest wall. Since my ICD is located in my left chest, this means that sometimes movements just from using my left side lead me into inappropriate tachycardias. Such is life, currently, and it is eerie.

Ever since my running collapse—sixteen years ago now—I have felt as if I am living on borrowed time. It feels as if there is a beast living within me, controlling the very core of my being, my soul. I hate it—but also cherish it because it gives me the life I have to share with William and others.

William is now fourteen and a soccer star, just like I used to be. He recently ran three miles with his heavy eighth-grader backpack on, just to improve his fitness. What a nut. As William enters adolescence and gains perspective and empathy, he is becoming a wonderfully caring and concerned young man who caters to his mom's needs and rarely pushes me too hard. That's good, because as he is getting stronger, I am getting weaker. Recently, we had our first outdoor soccer workout of the spring. The field was half covered in snow, but this did not deter us. I was in goal, to minimize stress on my heart. My goalie gloves were strapped on tightly to protect my delicate cello hands, and William was practicing shooting drills on me. One shot came in so fast and hard that not only could I not catch or deflect it, but it smacked me square in the face, breaking my glasses.

"Mom, oh, Mom, are you OK?" William yelled, as he sprinted in my direction. "Mom, I'm so sorry! I'm stressed! Are you OK?" I reassured him that I was fine, I patched up my glasses, and the afternoon continued.

The first successful pacemaker recipient was a man named Arne Larsson, who got his first device in 1958, when he was forty-three. He lived to be eighty-six years old, and he died of malignant melanoma. He was an avid sailor. I can picture him on his sailboat, tapping his pacemaker for a faster heart rate, for more energy, as he hoists the mainsail or the jib. He had a total of twenty-six pacemakers throughout his life, and he found a calling campaigning for other patients needing such devices.

I have done the math again and again: a typical ICD lasts only about five years, due to battery depletion. Delivering approximately 120,000 heartbeats per day—a steady eighty beats per minute—takes its toll. I'm on my fourth device. How many pacemakers will this mean for my lifetime? Ten ICDs to make it to seventy? Will I make it to seventy?

I know what it feels like to drown, sort of. Every few months, when my cardiologist measures the function of my ICD, he has to check the lead wires that connect the machine to my heart muscle. My leads are sixteen years old now; eventually, they will need to be replaced, too. "OK, I'm ready," I say to my cardiologist, and I rest my head back on the exam table.

"I'm dropping the atrial lead output now. Let's see when we lose capture," he says.

My heart beats along steadily, until it doesn't. I know exactly when this happens. I sink down into the exam table, my whole body disappearing from the room, going down, down. And then: nothing. The rhythm of my pulse stops, and I quickly cease to be.

I go dead for a few seconds, then my cardiologist restarts my heart, electrically, and I come back to life. He tilts the Medtronic computer screen toward me, backs up the rhythm strip on the monitor, and shows me the event: flat line. No cardiac activity. "I guess we won't be changing your atrial pacing settings!" he says, with that nervous smile he has perfected for this awkward routine.

In Whale's 1931 film, there's a scene where the monster and a young girl throw flowers into a pond. The flowers float; throwing them is a fun game. When they run out of flowers, the monster throws the girl into the pond; she, unfortunately, does not float.

In *Young Frankenstein,* there is also a scene with a girl and flowers. The girl is tossing the flowers, one petal at a time, into a well. The young monster observes her doing this, and when she runs out of flowers, he looks menacingly at her for a moment, but she proves to be the stronger one. She retreats to a seesaw and sits down on one end. She tells the monster to sit down. When he does not, she repeats herself, louder. Finally, the large monster obeys, and his weight catapults the girl through the air, through an open window, and into her bedroom. Her parents, searching frantically for her, enter the bedroom moments later and find her sleeping peacefully in her bed. I want to emulate this girl, her strength and command.

When I was three years old, my mother, older brother, and I fell off the wing of a fiery DC-10 aircraft. The rescue slide had broken, and we fell two stories down, through a giant hole at the top. My brother was dropped by my mother and landed on his feet, but she held on tight to me, chest to chest—heart to heart—as one holds a baby. We landed on our heads on the cement tarmac. We were both terribly injured. My mother hit her head on the jet engine on the way down, fractured her skull, and had seizures for decades. Later, I developed seizures, too. Another electrical storm in me.

My heart and my brain. But I try to remind myself of the famous Beckett line: "I can't go on, I'll go on."

Every Thursday morning at ten, I share the psychotherapy waiting room with an older gentleman and his young assistant. Often, when getting up out of his chair in the waiting room, the man must take a few moments to find his rhythm, to get his steps going. It quickly became clear to me that this man suffers from Parkinson's disease, which killed my grandfather. The man proceeds with his festinating gait and makes his way into his therapist's office. Sometimes, he falls. My medical self wants to run to his aid, but Dr. Sommer, our therapist, says not to. It is a point of pride for him to get up on his own.

The winter when I first met this man, the Wellesley Symphony Orchestra played a children's concert. I was a cellist in the orchestra at the time. Just before intermission, we played an Irish rhapsody. We played through it three times, while many children lined up and came onto the podium one by one. They each got to "conduct" the orchestra themselves for a moment. It is actually quite hard to play an orchestral piece without a real conductor. We had to rely on the principal violinist to set the pace and dynamics. I had to be careful with my bow hand so as not to poke any of the excited children making their way onstage. Halfway through the procession, I noticed my eyes moistening.

By then, my husband and I had parted ways. Owing to my ill health and its consequences, Jon was granted full physical custody of William, but knowing that a growing boy needs his mom, I see him frequently. William has a bedroom in my new firehouse-turned-condominium home and sleeps there sometimes, but usually we have a mere several hours together, and then I hand him back to his father. Seeing all the children at the concert brought back a flood of emotions about times missed with William, times I have been in out-of-state therapy programs or in hospitals, getting intensive psychiatric and cardiac care.

At the end of the performance, we played some new music commissioned specifically for the Wellesley Symphony Orchestra. At the end of the concert, a young man came up to the microphone and told the audience a little about the music. He said, "We have the great honor and privilege of having the composer of these works in our presence tonight."

An older man slowly made his way down the side aisle of the performance hall. As he got closer and came into sharp focus, I realized it was the man from the waiting room. He was struggling, but he made the long walk all the way down to the stage, unaided, and took a bow. By that point, the crowd and the orchestra members were all on their feet, clapping and cheering furiously. Tears streamed down my cheeks.

The next Thursday at ten, I saw the man and his assistant again. After five minutes of trying to get up the courage, I walked over to him, kneeled down to his level, and said, "Hello, I wanted to introduce myself. I'm Elizabeth Fortescue, and I play cello in the Wellesley Symphony. It was such a privilege to play your work and now to meet you." A lovely smile came over the man's face, and he held out his hand to greet me.

For the next several weeks, I missed therapy. I entered a terribly difficult period, in which I found myself struggling violently with my illness, wishing things were different. Here was this composer, limited in his motions and their rhythms by Parkinson's but prodigious on the musical page, turning out beautiful songs. And here I was, playing the music but feeling rhythmless and dead inside. I didn't know which was worse. I took it out on myself and wound up locked in a mental ward for many weeks. Finally, the hospital staff decided I was safe enough to go home, and I resumed my work with my outpatient therapists. But my symphony days were over. Too many missed practices.

On my first Thursday back in the waiting room, the man invited me to call him by his first name and asked his assistant for his briefcase. He pulled out a wrinkled old envelope with no writing on it. I opened it up, and the note inside said: *Dear Elizabeth, May I have the pleasure of having dinner with you at my home?* I blushed, took his hand in mine, and thanked him for the invitation.

Just recently, I received an email. It was from Max Hobart, violinist for the Boston Symphony Orchestra for many years and now the Music Director of the Wellesley Symphony Orchestra. His email said: *Dear Elizabeth, it would be my pleasure to have you back in the Wellesley Symphony. May I save a seat for you? Best wishes, Max.* I don't know how this came about, but I am ecstatic. Our first rehearsal is Wednesday.

But before all of this, as I sit on the edge of my seat, listening to Yo-Yo Ma play the last tones of the sixth Bach suite, I feel a brief moment of sadness. It is Valentine's Day. There is snow everywhere, and it is cold out. I don't know where Jon and I will meet up. He likes to make a quick escape from Symphony Hall, to beat the traffic and the crowds, but I am determined to stay for every standing ovation. To try to pry an encore out of Ma. I still want more.

Ma concludes, and the audience uproar is palpable. Like the others, I am on my feet instantly, cheering, "Bravo!" and clapping furiously. An elegant woman comes on stage and gives Ma a giant bouquet of red roses. He manages to accept them, his multi-million-dollar borrowed Stradivarius cello named the "Davidov" in one hand, his bow in the other, and the roses under one arm. As he bows to the applause and the cries for more playing, a rose comes loose from the bouquet. It falls onto the floor of the stage. Instead of exiting stage left as he appears to be intending to do, Ma picks up the rose and scans the audience. He walks over to the edge of the stage, and he hands the rose—handed the rose—to me.

Rooted

EMILY WORTMAN-WUNDER

A tooth can grow in a heart: I learned this from the internet. It is true that when I investigated further, I found that hearts are one of the last places teratomas grow; these tumors containing scraps of hair, bone, and enamel are far more likely to emerge in the ovaries, for example. But I still wake in the middle of the night certain that this ache in my chest is the deep-dug root of a stubborn tooth, one that has resisted orthodontia and the professional aspirations of the middle-class bourgeoisie, where I otherwise reside. This tooth has kept me simultaneously grounded and stuck to the ground. And as I clunk about my darkened house, looking for a place where I can still my anxiety enough to calm myself for sleep, I keep stumbling, mentally, on this misplaced tooth and its metaphorical implications until, at 4:15 a.m., I am certain that the impending loss of my parents' home in southwestern Ohio will be the thing that finally splits this root in two, flooding my internal organs with a bacterial sea from which I will never recover.

The Ohio that I think about when I think about where I am from crinkles when you take a step. It's a maple root curving across a muddy path, last year's leaves on one side, a delicate hasp of baby hair grass on the other. It's snails in the weeds, chiggers in the lawn, limestone paving stones baking in the sun. It's the rainy day my best friend and I took a shortcut across a soybean field and ended up slogging through mud for an hour and a half, soaking wet and covered in burrs. It's the deep algal stink of the reservoir, crawdads trawling the drying creeks, salamanders under rocks in the forest. It's a country full of venal sins and dull prosperity and creeping desperation: decaying storefronts, vinyl siding, old Victorians rotting in the summer heat. But slip down to the woods, and the air is cool. Pileated woodpeckers screech overhead, and wildflowers as intricate as the workings of a clock emerge in spring.

I grew up in a town of buckled sidewalks, in a yard bounded by alleys, with drunk college kids yelling in the night. After I moved away, my parents bought a place in the country, the dark nights loud with tree frogs. You can sit at the table in the breakfast nook and watch two dozen birds mob the feeder while spooning cereal into your mouth. This house is where I return when I go home.

My parents have begun to talk about *what comes next.* Eighty is on the horizon, and eighty is too old to be running the Bush Hog lawn mower and cutting down trees. Seventy is too old to do this, and my parents are several train stops past seventy. We have responsible adult conversations about selling the house and buying something *more manageable.* We've discussed options—something smaller, more in town? Something smaller, and closer either to my sister or to me? There are advantages and disadvantages to all, and we muddle through them, obliquely. My parents don't really want to leave. I don't really want them to leave. *But it's not possible to go on like this forever.*

So: five acres of second-growth woodland, an intermittent stream, a three-bedroom modernist house, and a two-car freestanding garage may soon be on the market. Meanwhile, a petulant voice at the bottom of my heart cries, *And where does that leave me?*

For a decade after I moved to Colorado, I had a ready answer when people asked, "Do you like it here?"

"I love it," I'd say (of course I love it), "but I miss the rain."

Sometimes I'd say, *But I miss the humidity.* Or *I miss the smells.* All small-ball, water-spider talk for *I miss it so much I want to howl.*

Also: I never, ever want to live there again. That toothed lump in the wall of your heart might be your own inalienable tissue, but its mood is not benevolent.

I belong to Ohio even though:

- I was born in Nebraska;
- I left as soon as I possibly could;
- I live in another state;
- I've never voted in Ohio;
- I've never paid payroll taxes in Ohio;
- I've never held title to anything in Ohio;
- My family has no historical presence there—no moldering gravestones, no broken-down farms, no elderly great aunts stashed in a nursing home;
- I hated so much of it: the hot, itchy summers; the overcast winters; the Kool-Aid lip stains on my classmates; the way people spoke—"chimbly" for *chimney* and "Embley" for *Emily* and "chicken pops" for *chicken pox;* and the way people asked, Is that a GEE-tar? when I was carrying my violin case.

But Ohio still operates as the stone I tap, fretfully, when I ask myself, *Where are you from, anyway?*

The thought of never coming back fills me with grief.

Two and a half decades after moving away, I still feel anxious and hollow if I go too long without visiting. It's not just people I miss; it's the place. The places, actually. My visits home sometimes feel like frantic greatest-hits tours, in which I have two days to touch every key childhood landmark: *here's* the Pine Woods, *here's* the limestone falls, *here's* the house where I grew up, *here's* the stark yellow house where the school bus turned from Main Street onto Sycamore, *here's* the ash tree in my best friend's yard that we used as a swing set, *here's* the field where we played and once, on a foggy night, ran through patches of lamplit mist, yelling to each other that we were unicorns. It's a university town, so it is both well-preserved and constantly undergoing change. Every year, there are fewer fields, fewer weedy road-ends, fewer remnants of the town's dour and unsmiling past. More and more of my greatest-hits tours have stops where I whisper, *This is where there used to be....*

But I don't mind. Getting updates is partly why I come. I have always felt vaguely sorry for classmates whose families moved away and who have no reason to visit anymore. *How awful,* I've thought, *to be cut off from the geography of your past.*

And then there are the friends who stayed. From Colorado, I watch their lives on Facebook; they work in the library, teach in the schools, serve on the school boards, invest in the housing developments that eat away at the surrounding countryside. They've become the grown-ups of this place. As I swipe through pictures of these strange my-age adults superimposed on the icons of my past, I probe at the complex and confusing hurt that thickens in my heart. Is it envy, this gray and fatty thing? Or is it merely homesickness, neglected?

For centuries, it was commonly accepted that the cause of tumors filled with hair and teeth was unclean thoughts, spinsterhood, or both. They were clearly obscene, like something out of Hieronymus Bosch—even clinical drawings of teratomas are startling and grotesque, discolored fleshy bulbs with tangled knots of molars. They are so weird they can make a rational citizen of the twenty-first century start to reconsider Bigfoot, evil spirits, and the Loch Ness monster.

Nevertheless, the eighteenth-century physician Matthew Baillie suspected they had a medical cause. In 1789, he published an investigation in *Philosophical Transactions* as to whether teratomas were malformed pregnancies or something altogether different. He described his dissection of a prepubescent girl, whose body had been brought to his home at Windmill Street. A capsule in one of her ovaries contained hair, teeth, and fatty tissue even though her hymen was intact and her womb "exhibited the ordinary appearances of a child's uterus." In a later work, he combined this evidence with similar growths found in the body of an eighteen-year-old virgin and a castrated male horse to argue that these "productions" had nothing to do with impregnation: "[M]y conjecture is put beyond dispute."

These early accounts—often trotted out in historical reviews of the teratoma phenomenon—are characterized by a vivid sense of place: Baillie mentions Windmill Street because his house there was famous, built by his uncle to showcase his own anatomical work (it had an operating theater). You can imagine the body brought in through the back entry—was she in a bag, like potatoes, or a more dignified shroud? Was she stolen or donated? (Given Baillie's uncertainty about her age, the former is more likely.) Did her mother know she was there?

Later reports are more clinical, excising any mention of place or time, the labs stocked with a numb vocabulary of sameness: windows, lintels, bookshelves, fluorescent lights, ducts hidden behind acoustic ceiling tiles. Even the tumors themselves are shorn of identifying detail. They are specimens, relegated to formalin-filled jars on an anonymous shelf. You're not supposed to notice or care whether that shelf is in London, Boston, Moscow, or Beijing. This is science, after all, and scientists are like teratomas, cut from the surrounding landscape and preserved in laboratories that endlessly repeat across the developed world.

Science has separated us from the cosmos, writes Rebecca Solnit in a book about a photographer, and I nod and nod, underlining furiously. Key developments in the making of the modern world, she writes, have "annihilated time and space." Once tied to the moon and the stars, time harnessed to the telegraph became something "administered by technicians" while the railroads "made it possible to ignore the terrain as encounter and experience: they made place into real estate." *Yes.*

For the most part, we go along with this annihilation. But even as we skim along, googling real estate listings in Normandy and Oslo and Lake Tanganyika, adopting the local cuisine of peasants around the globe, our own inalienable selves latch on, put down roots, and cling like death to a single unique spot on the earth's crust.

Age alone is not the reason my parents might need to sell, and this is the great white-sheeted gorilla we are not talking about: my mother has Stage 4 cancer. She's had several years of good luck with treatment, but the business of life is getting harder. She has pain in her back, a permanent catheter coiled uncomfortably in her lung, and the latest CAT scan shows that the tumor is growing.

My parents' modernist multilevel house is not going to work well with hospice. Their house is small and open, and even the main level has stairs. It may open into the forest and ring all night with the calls of tree frogs, but it is terrible for wheelchairs and hospital beds. When we talk about something *more manageable,* we're talking about this.

It wasn't until the 1960s that the mystery of teratomas was finally cracked. Scientists working at the Jackson Laboratory in Bar Harbor, Maine, followed their hunch that these tumors arose from "primordial germ cells" that had not yet matured into their final, fixed identities. (Did they go for a celebratory walk along the waterfront, order up a lobster boil, toss a shell into the waves? Or were they so focused on the lab that they could have been anywhere?) A bit of pluripotent germ-cell layer gets trapped during the development of an embryo. This little pocket then goes rogue, with the germ cells differentiating and becoming a range of mature tissues—hair, bone, teeth, muscle, thyroid, fat tissue, and even eyes. This pluripotency is why teratomas are able to produce so many different kinds of tissue. Scientists hope that by harnessing these pluripotent cells, we will be able to regrow human tissue. The solving of the teratoma mystery, in other words, led to the birth of stem cell research—the dream that we can remake ourselves from scratch.

I was once pluripotent, or so I thought. I left small-town Ohio for New York City, then reversed course and headed west. I've made my home as an adult in various Colorado towns, learning the birds and flowers, and getting worked up about local politics. My husband is from Colorado, and so, of course, are our children. But I have always been ambivalent: the pinch in my heart, the whisper in my ear, the stubborn tooth that refuses to grow anywhere but Ohio.

I think of myself as part of this place, along with the fireflies and the toads and the Dutchman's breeches, but I no longer have any real claim to it. The slow process of my mother's dying has made this clear. Each phase of her treatment reaches me via email, and though I write and call and visit, it is not the same. I buy plane tickets to rush myself back, to help, to be near, to do what I can, but in the end, I am just another guest.

I was of a place, and I abandoned it. In my house in suburban Denver, I get up, grab a pillow, thump down the hall to try the couch. The clanking chain of loss comes with me. *I should have gone to college in Ohio,* I think, watching the thin, shifting play of our neighbors' porch light on the ceiling. *I should have gone back more often. We should have spent a month there every summer.* And the fireflies! We have never visited when the fireflies are at their peak. The kids have never seen the forest floor alive with toadlets. We've only been there once for migration, and twice for the blaze of autumn.

I put the pillow over my head and try to force sleep.

The rootless pluripotent cell, raging through the dark corridors of the body, brings with it a devouring darkness.

Where are you from? The question was once a proxy for *Who are you?* but the dream of pluripotency has swept all that away. Perhaps I am a bone, or an eye, or a tooth. Perhaps I am nothing.

The cells stranded in the capsule start to build, marooned from sense or meaning. They put together a jaw and teeth separate from any food or stomach; their hair neither protects nor decorates. Their eye, unconnected to an optic nerve, will never see.

But my eyes are connected to optic nerves; my teeth chew real food; my hair grows where it ought to grow. The life I have made in Colorado is my real life. When that tooth is finally ripped from my heart—when my parents leave Ohio, or die, or both—I will not drown.

I push off the couch and pad to the refrigerator to soothe myself with food. I am startled by my reflection in the kitchen window: my hair wild, great baggy gouges beneath my eyes, the spoon in my hand disappearing into the ice cream carton. I look like a thieving ghost.

Where are you from, anyway?

It's time to let that go, I tell my reflection, or my reflection tells me. This is where you are now. Right here.

How to Hang a Mezuzah

RACHEL BEANLAND

I pay for my kids' religious upbringing in monthly installments. Every summer, I fill out a little green card that establishes the figure that will be autodrafted out of our checking account for the next twelve months. There are the synagogue's dues, which are steep, and then the tuition for my three kids to attend religious school on Sunday mornings. A building fee—payable over five years—is leveraged on all members. It gets expensive, so there are price cuts for people under thirty-five and deeper price cuts for people under thirty. I ask the woman who works in the business office if there's any way my husband and I might pretend we're thirty-four for the third year in a row.

Kevin looks at our budget and reminds me that we spend more on religion than we do on our daughters' ballet lessons, our cell phone bills, or our homeowner's insurance. Which would be fine, he says, if either of us believed in God.

Kevin was raised Catholic. The church got whatever his parents felt comfortable putting in the collection plate on Sunday. There were no contracts, no invoices, no autodrafts. Sunday Mass was something to be endured, and Kevin will tell you the priests should have been paying him to be there.

When my parents get engaged—several years before I am born—they take a class, specifically for interfaith couples, at their local synagogue. My father, who was raised Methodist, does all the reading assignments. My mother, who is Jewish, reads the books' jacket copy and skims the introductions. They are married by a rabbi in my grandparents' living room, and my mother becomes the first person in her family to marry outside the faith.

When I am five years old, we move to a little island off the coast of Sardinia, Italy.

There's an American elementary school on the island, but my mother is committed to the idea that I should become fluent in Italian. She marches me up the steep steps of the Istituto San Vincenzo, a local primary school run by nuns. She brings a pocket-sized Italian dictionary, points at me with exaggerated gestures, and tries to tell the head nun, "She's Jewish. Can she attend?" The nun nods her head emphatically and says, "Sì, sì." Neither woman is sure she has been properly understood.

Every afternoon when my mother picks me up from school, she peppers me with questions. She is eager to see evidence of language acquisition, and I am eager to please. She asks what I have learned, and I tell her "the parts of my body."

Weeks pass, and she continues to ask the same questions. "Still learning the parts of my body," I say, as we make our way across the Piazza Umberto.

It goes on. Always, I am learning the parts of my body. Finally, my mother asks me to show her, and I point to my forehead, my chest, my two shoulders. "Nel nome del Padre e del Figlio e dello Spirito Santo, amen," I say, as I make the sign of the cross.

When I am young, it is my father who leads the Passover seder, who hides the afikomen, who tells us the story of how the Jews escaped from Egypt. My mother's job is to check the matzo balls on the stove, make sure they're not falling apart.

Growing up, I envy the people on my mother's side of the family who look outwardly Jewish with their dark eyes and brown, wavy hair. I resemble the women on my father's side of the family with my hazel eyes and thin blond hair that eventually darkens to a medium brown.

On a bus trip in ninth grade, a friend compliments me on my appearance. "You're so pretty. Your nose doesn't even look Jewish."

I say nothing and stare out the bus's tinted window, worried my friend will see that I have begun to cry. My indignation isn't for the Jewish people, who have lived with degradations like hers for millennia. I cry because, at fourteen years old, I wish for a sense of belonging, a nose that might trumpet my place in the long history of the Jewish people.

I am sixteen and on the first real date of my life—a day at the beach with a boy I've had a crush on for the better part of a year. On the drive, the windows of my parents' old station wagon rolled down, the wind in our hair, I feel like I'm in a movie.

I park the car and we walk down to the sand, wander for a while until we find a quiet spot to sit and stare out at the water. "I really like you," the boy says, and in my head, I am trying to figure out how our first kiss will work. Should I inch closer? Crane my neck? Close my eyes? I can barely breathe. *Oh my God I'm about to be kissed.*

Then he says that he's worried our eventual kids will go to hell, and it's like I can hear the record scratching, the movie soundtrack coming to an abrupt halt.

"Hell?" I ask, confused.

"Yeah, you know. Because you're Jewish."

In college, I am required to enroll in two semesters of a foreign language. I don't remember any Italian. I studied Spanish in high school. French could be useful if I decide to major in art history. Latin might help me on the LSAT, in the unlikely event I apply to law school.

I scan the course catalog.

College, I have realized, provides me with an opportunity to make up for the areas of my upbringing that have left me feeling weak, unprepared. I enroll in Modern Hebrew.

When Kevin and I start getting serious, I tell him that raising Jewish kids is nonnegotiable.

He does not try to negotiate.

When I'm twenty-one, I backpack through Europe with my younger sister, Ruthie. On a warm July evening in Florence, we cross the Arno River and make the hike from Piazzale Michelangelo to San Miniato al Monte, an eleventh-century church that sits at the top of a hill. We are there for the panoramic views of the city, so neither of us is particularly disappointed to find that services are underway and we won't be able to explore the church's interior. We've already seen a lot of churches on this trip.

We find a spot to perch on a small wall outside the church, where we can watch the sun sink low over the city. In the distance, the Duomo glows. Mass ends, and little old ladies walk, slowly, down the church's steep steps to waiting cars on the Via delle Porte Sante. I am about to turn to ask Ruthie if she'd like to try to get inside the church, now that the service is over, when the most beautiful sound I've ever heard begins to emanate from the building's interior.

The monks have begun vespers, and the air fills with the sound of thousand-year-old Gregorian chants.

Listening to the recitative melody of their song as it floats over Florence's red roofs and the Tuscan hill country beyond is the closest I've come to having a religious experience. I feel humbled. Tiny. And deeply connected to the people around me. To my sister and the monks and the little old ladies on the stairs. To the people who built the Duomo and to Brunelleschi for thinking up the dome that tops it. I am this one minuscule cog in a giant machine that's been chugging for as long as monks have been praising God with their song. It's an overwhelming feeling, and I wonder if this might be what it feels like to believe.

In 2008, the Pew Forum on Religion & Public Life conducted the US Religious Landscape Survey and found that when Jews marry outside the faith, they overwhelmingly marry Catholics. It's an interesting statistic because Protestants outnumber Catholics in the US by nearly two to one.

Why Catholics? In an interview with the interfaith advocacy organization 18 Doors, sociologist Steven Cohen, formerly a professor at Hebrew Union College, says it has everything to do with geography. Jews and Catholics are both concentrated in the Northeast, and "people tend to marry people they encounter."

I think proximity is only half of it. Both Judaism and Catholicism are rich in liturgy and tradition. Many of us get good at repeating the Amidah or the Apostles' Creed, the Aleinu or the Anima Christi, without asking ourselves what any of it really means.

My mother's brother is an attorney who officiates at the weddings in our family as a side gig.

Everyone loves Woody's weddings. He's got a sense of humor, his homilies are heartfelt, and he gets you in and out of the ceremony in seven minutes flat. Do you take this man? Do you take this woman? Before you realize what's happened, the happy couple is lip-locked and it's on to the reception. There is seldom, if ever, any mention of God.

Kevin and I could—probably should—invite Woody to officiate at our wedding. Instead, we go with a rent-a-rabbi we find on the internet, someone with a good-looking beard, who is willing to marry a Jew and a Catholic in a traditional Jewish ceremony. Kevin and I meet him once before the wedding, in the living room of his suburban DC home, and my parents pay him $700 for his services.

The rabbi leads us through the reading of the ketubah, the blessing of the wine, and the exchange of the rings. There are the seven wedding blessings and the breaking of the glass. Afterward, he encourages Kevin and me to take a short walk, just the two of us, in the spirit of yichud. It's an archaic tradition, a reference to the period of time, directly after the wedding ceremony, when a man and woman would have consummated their marriage. At first, the walk feels awkward, forced. But once we are alone, I begin to appreciate what the rabbi has asked of us. He has asked us to step back, to observe the big and beautiful thing we've done.

We buy a house in South Carolina, and I google "How to hang a mezuzah."

After fertility treatments fail, I arrange a meeting with our rabbi. Judaism recognizes matrilineal descent; people are considered Jewish if their mother is Jewish. It is a religion of bloodlines, and I want someone in authority to tell me that it's 2004 and bloodlines don't matter.

Sitting in the synagogue's reading room, Kevin beside me, I ask the rabbi, "If we adopt, will our children be Jewish?"

"By the standards of Reform Judaism," he tells us, "unequivocally, yes."

I start calling around to local adoption agencies. In South Carolina, most of them are Christian. I call one and it takes the intake coordinator just seconds to ask, "And what church do you and your husband attend?"

"Tree of Life Synagogue," I tell her.

"Oh," she says. I can tell she is weighing her words.

I help her out. "I'm Jewish."

"Oh, well, we only work with Christian families in our domestic programs," she says. "You'd qualify for some of our international programs." It's strange how she manages to make international programs sound like a consolation prize.

I don't know why I push it but I say, "My husband's Catholic. Does that help?"

"Catholic?" she repeats. "Oh, no, we only work with Christians."

After I hang up, I call Kevin at his office.

"Did you know Catholics aren't Christians?"

"Huh?" he says, only half paying attention.

It is news to me.

The baby is a boy, and we name him Gabriel. He is a month old when our Minnesota-based adoption agency sends us his referral, two months old when we fly down to Guatemala City to meet him for the first time, and five months old when I fly back to the United States with him in my arms.

Our pediatrician proclaims him perfect, and when I ask what, if anything, can be done about circumcising an infant who is long past his eighth day of life, she refers me to a Jewish urologist who is willing to allow our rabbi, freshly scrubbed, into the operating theater to act as an honorary mohel.

I wear a pantsuit to the hospital, Kevin a coat and tie. Our outfits feel all wrong, not the sort of thing a baby coming out of anesthesia can cuddle up to. But there will be prayers in pre-op and, when we return home from the hospital, a party in full swing.

At home, the rabbi rests a hand on Gabriel's head and repeats the prayers he said in the operating room. Aunts and grandmothers bustle around, unwrapping extra deli platters, washing abandoned wineglasses, cutting pieces of cake. Gabriel—still woozy—sleeps through all of it.

Months after the bris, we meet our rabbi at the mikvah, which is owned and maintained by a more conservative temple than the one we belong to. It's time to cross our t's and dot our i's, officially converting Gabriel to Judaism.

In the changing rooms, I slip into a bathing suit, then strip Gabriel naked. Kevin stands at the ready with a camera and two towels.

Tentatively, the two of us make our way down the steps and into the small square of chlorinated water, as deep as my chest. Gabriel is slippery and squirms in my arms, and when I dunk his head once, twice, three times, he spins around and looks at me, as if to ask: *What did you do that for?*

When I am twenty-six, I travel to Israel with the Birthright Israel program. The program, which was established in 1999, sends young adults from across the Jewish diaspora to Israel for ten days, all expenses paid. If you identify as Jewish, you qualify to go. No questions asked. The hope is that participants will connect with their faith and, in the process, become advocates for Israel.

I am assigned to a travel group made up of forty young professionals, about my age, and together we crisscross Israel in a generously appointed motorbus. "Go home and have lots of Jewish babies," our tour guide jokes on more than one occasion.

I am already raising a Jewish baby, though when I tell my travel companions about Gabriel, no one can quite believe that I am old enough to be a mother, let alone a mother to a baby I adopted.

The producers of an Israeli documentary about the program are tailing our bus. They reached out before I left for Israel and asked if they could visit me in the United States, meet my family, then document my experiences on the trip. Each time the forty of us file off the bus to see something new, they pull me aside and ask how that something—the Yad Vashem memorial and museum, the military cemetery on Mount Herzl, Ben-Gurion's desert home—makes me feel.

When I arrive home, Kevin and Gabriel meet me at the airport. As soon as Gabriel sees me, he flies into my arms, and I think about how, for all the ancient and holy places I've just seen, this moment might be the best part of the trip.

A few months later, a DVD arrives in the mail, accompanied by a note. I learn that the documentary has aired in Israel and this English-language copy is mine to keep. I pop the disc in the DVD player, and Kevin and I watch as I experience the Western Wall, Masada, the Dead Sea.

In a background segment, the producers share some of the photographs I provided the crew: a still of my grandparents celebrating Passover, one of Kevin and me getting married, another taken soon after we traveled to Guatemala to adopt Gabriel. The voiceover, English in a thick Israeli accent, says that we adopted "a little Catholic baby," and I laugh out loud. "Did you hear that?" I ask Kevin as I pause the DVD, rewind, and hit play again. "They just called Gabriel 'a little Catholic baby.'"

I'm amused—it's a funny way to identify a baby—but also maybe a tiny bit annoyed. Gabriel was never baptized, never took Communion, never said so much as a single rosary. I think of him as Hispanic, always, but Catholic, never.

There's something about the way the phrase is used to define my son that feels intentional, exclusionary. Israel is meant to be a safe haven for the world's Jews, an escape hatch if the shit hits the fan. It's a country for all of us, but now I find myself wondering, is it also for him?

We are in our late twenties, living in Richmond, Virginia, when our synagogue hires a young assistant rabbi named Jesse. He and his husband, Andrew—also a rabbi—buy a house down the street from us. They don't have kids yet, so they come hang out on our front porch in the evenings after Gabriel and his new sister, Clementine, are asleep.

The four of us drink beer and play Cards Against Humanity. The first time I have Jesse and Andrew over for a proper dinner, my mother has to remind me not to serve shrimp. Another time, I make a salad that contains both steak and blue cheese crumbles.

"I'm the worst," I say, when I realize I've just trampled a major dietary law.

"It's why this relationship works," Jesse consoles me. "Ordinarily, it's hard to be friends with congregants. But you guys are barely Jewish."

Kevin's mother, Beverly, used to buy an ornament for each of her three children every year at Christmastime. Most of them are customized with the child's name and the year: a bear in a tutu, marked "Stephanie 1989"; a whale in a stocking cap, "Brian 1990"; a miniature sled with "Kevin 1987" spelled out across the seat.

Kevin's siblings move out, get married, buy houses, and eventually start putting up their own trees. When they do, their ornaments go with them.

For about a decade, Kevin's ornaments fly solo on Beverly's fake fir.

"How come Daddy's the only one with ornaments?" the kids like to ask as they admire the seven-foot-tall Christmas tree in the corner of my in-laws' living room.

"Because I'm Gramma's favorite," Kevin yells from the next room.

One Christmas, the Kevin ornaments aren't on the tree. The kids notice right away, and when they alert my mother-in-law to the problem, she hands Kevin a shoebox.

"What am I gonna do with these, Ma?" he says, lifting the lid off the box.

"Put them on a tree."

We don't have a tree. Have never had a tree. Aren't ever going to have a tree.

"If you want me to enjoy them," Kevin says, "keep hanging them on yours."

When Kevin and I decide to adopt a third child, domestically this time, our social worker tells us to write a letter, introducing our family to prospective birth mothers.

This is new to me. With international adoption, you fill out a mountain of paperwork and your name gets put on a list. Eventually, when your name moves to the top of that list, you receive the referral of a child. It would be possible for our application to be discounted because we didn't stamp the right affidavit in triplicate, but never because I'm Jewish.

In the US, pregnant women read letters and peruse photo books in an attempt to pick the perfect parents for their baby. The letters read like advertising copy, intended to sell a confused sixteen-year-old on the prospective parents' homes, pets, jobs, extended families. *The baby will have its own room! We've got a dachshund! We love going to the beach! I'm a teacher, so I've got my summers off!* No one knows exactly what will appeal, so prospective parents throw everything at the wall and see what sticks.

I don't know where to begin with the letter. But I do know that 83 percent of American Jews—more than any other major religious group—believe abortion should be legal. Jews are also, according to the Pew Research Center, the religious group with the highest household income; 44 percent of Jews in the United States live in households that make more than $100,000 per year. This means that if a Jewish woman wants an abortion, she's likely to be able to afford to get one. What I come to understand is that the women reading our letter aren't likely to be Jewish.

I agonize over the letter, and when it's finished, I decide it might be the most beautiful thing I've ever written. In it, I describe our century-old row house, Kevin's job as a professor (*Education is important in our family!*), our commitment to diversity and to maintaining ties to our kids' birth cultures. I call out the cute park down the street from our house, the ice cream parlor where we take the kids for treats, and the fact that we travel down to Orlando each winter to celebrate Christmas with Kevin's family. What I do not say, anywhere in the letter, is that I'm Jewish and that we're raising Jewish kids.

Kevin is offered a job at a private liberal arts college. Everything about the job is better than the one he's got—except the college's location in a rural Virginia town of seven thousand residents.

After the moving truck has come and gone, we drop by the campus Hillel House. I know they offer programming for the Jewish students at the university, but I've heard they also work hard to engage the larger Jewish community, particularly since there's no synagogue in town. The director ushers us into his office with the kind of familiarity that tells me he knew we were coming.

He talks about the High Holy Days and how Hillel pays for a rabbinical student to travel in from out of town to perform the services. But if we want our three kids to get any kind of regular religious education, we'll have to drive an hour down the road to Charlottesville.

"We've only got fifty-nine Jewish families in town," he says, and I laugh at the exactitude.

"I guess we make sixty."

He shakes his head. "No, no. You're fifty-nine."

On the drive to Charlottesville one morning, nine-year-old Gabriel tells us he hates Sunday school.

Clementine, who is three years younger and lives for contradicting her brother, says she likes it.

He makes his case. "All we ever do is learn religious stuff."

I turn around in the passenger seat and look at both of them. Neither of them would have been raised Jewish if their lives had taken a different turn.

"That's kind of the whole point," I say.

I join a book club. The club's members seem like smart, engaged women who, one way or another, have managed to make small-town life work for them, and I want to know their secrets.

When it's my turn to host, I make guacamole and pour salted almonds into a pretty ceramic bowl. I wash some grapes and unwrap a selection of cheeses. By the time I'm done putting out the spread, I feel embarrassed. It's more food than anyone needs, but I want to make a good impression.

Some women show up with the book. Others admit to not having read it. One arrives with a bridesmaid dress slung over her shoulder. She says she wants to try it on for all of us, so I show her the bathroom down the hall. Do we think she needs to get it hemmed, or can she make it work with a tall pair of heels? Everyone's got an opinion, and a story about an alteration they paid for that was bad or expensive or both.

One woman starts in on a seamstress who charged far too much for far too little. As the story winds down, this woman leans over the salted almonds conspiratorially. "No offense," she says, looking directly at me, "but she really jewed me."

"I *am* offended," I tell her, but saying the words out loud doesn't begin to alleviate my confusion. I can't believe there are people still saying this shit. That she knew I was Jewish and said it anyway. In my house. In 2015.

We move back to Richmond. I survey the new house, soften, tell Kevin he can put up a tree, string lights if he wants. Since it's not my thing, I warn him that I won't lead the charge, buy the tree, drag it home. Any pagan/Christian traditions we introduce into our home have to come from him, born out of his own personal desire to reconnect, if not with his faith, then with the things that mattered to him as a kid.

Kevin barely looks up from whatever he's reading. "I'm good."

"You don't miss the tree? The decorations?"

"I don't want to be taking lights down in January."

It's one of the unsung benefits of being Jewish. Not standing on an exterior ladder, numb-knuckled and hungover, for several hours on the first of the year, the tree an oversized tumbleweed on the curb.

Jesse and Andrew, the rabbis, have moved out of state, but they return to Richmond for a visit with their twin boys in tow. Kevin and I serve a big brunch—no bacon—and the four of us sit around the dining room table, drinking coffee and watching our kids get to know each other. Their family exists because a woman in North Carolina was willing to serve as a surrogate, carrying their beautiful boys to term in the same womb where she once nurtured her own children. Ours exists because three separate women in three separate parts of the world made the decision to place their children for adoption. It's a weird and wonderful fact that neither family would have existed a hundred years ago.

I start to clear the table, and Jesse follows me into the kitchen. Asks how the congregation is doing. "Truthfully," I say, as I open the dishwasher and stack sticky plates, one next to the other, in the bottom rack, "I'm beginning to wonder if I should quit. It's a lot of money."

"Don't give up on it," he says.

I stand up straight, grab a handful of flatware from the sink. Do I dare tell him the truth? He's our drinking buddy, but he's also a man of faith. "Jesse, I don't believe in God."

"Oh, Rachel, that's half the congregation."

In 2012, Gallup polled fifty-one thousand people in fifty-seven countries, asking them: "Irrespective of whether you attend a place of worship or not, would you say you are a religious person, not a religious person, or a convinced atheist?"

Among people who self-identified as members of a religious community, Jews were found to be the least religious. Of Jews, 54 percent said they weren't religious, and 2 percent said they were atheists.

Since Judaism is both a religion and an ethnicity, scholars suggest it is possible to be both ethnically Jewish and religiously atheist.

This sounds pretty good to me. Except I've got three kids who aren't ethnically Jewish. If I don't raise them to be religiously Jewish, then where am I leaving them?

I contact the temple's office and ask if I can change the payment method on file.

"Do you accept credit cards?" I ask.

It has occurred to me that if I'm going to pay all these fees, I should be earning the air miles.

My grandmother dies on the eighth of December, and by the time her five children descend on the assisted-living community where my grandparents lived together, it is Hanukkah.

In an effort to capture some semblance of normalcy, my mother and her siblings light the menorah and say the Hanukkah blessing. *Baruch atah, Adonai Eloheinu, Melech haolam, asher kid'shanu b'mitzvotav v'tsivanu l'hadlik ner shel Hanukkah.*

"You're saying it wrong," says my aunt.

"How do *you* say it?" one of them asks.

They go around the table, reciting the same blessing they all learned as kids. Every single one of them says it differently.

My mother texts me a video. In it, my aunts and uncles are doubled over, laughing at their religiosity, or lack thereof. "You can't even recognize Woody's version," my mother writes.

The video is heartwarming. It's good to see my mother and her siblings together, funny to watch them realize they've all taught these mutated versions of the blessing to their own children, who have in turn passed them on to their partners and kids. It's Judaism reduced to a giant game of telephone.

There are plenty of studies that say it's good for children to be raised with religion. Kids who believe in something display signs of improved mental health, demonstrate stronger self-control, and react more positively to discipline.

There are also lots of studies that say that the abovementioned studies are crap, and that kids raised without religion are more generous and empathetic and a whole lot more likely to be able to distinguish fantasy from reality.

My younger daughter, Florence, calls the Star of David "the Sunday star," and I find I am both tickled by her perception (she does see it on Sundays, after all) and overwhelmed by how much I have gotten wrong. If I had done a better job with this religion stuff, she wouldn't have relegated the symbol to a single day of the week.

It's August and another green card must be returned to the synagogue.

"I'm really thinking about quitting," I admit to Kevin. I believe in Planned Parenthood and the Pancreatic Cancer Action Network and the community-arts center where I work, and I don't give those organizations a fraction of the money I give our temple.

Then several hundred neo-Nazis descend on Charlottesville, and we watch as they shout anti-Semitic slurs, physically attack counterprotesters, run down pedestrians with a car. President Trump offers empty platitudes and ultimately sides with the perpetrators, not the victims.

Alan Zimmerman, the president of the board of Charlottesville's Congregation Beth Israel, where my kids used to attend religious school, writes a blog post for ReformJudaism.org. In it he describes what it felt like to be Jewish in Charlottesville that weekend: "When services ended, my heart broke as I advised congregants that it would be safer to leave the temple through the back entrance rather than through the front, and to please go in groups."

The blog post could have been a journal entry written by any Jew living in prewar Germany. But he reminds us, "This is 2017 in the United States of America."

I read his words and sob. Then I share the post with everyone I know.

Finally, I fill out the little green card, agreeing to make twelve equal payments of $150 per month.

It's December, and I'm in the back of my mother-in-law's Christmas closet. It's a daunting place—a six-foot-deep nook under the stairs, full of shirt boxes and gift bags, carefully refolded and stored in large plastic bins so they can be reused year after year.

I am returning a stack of shirt boxes, folded down at their cardboard corners, to their rightful place when I spot a ceramic menorah—painted in splashy shades of blue—under some abandoned tissue paper.

"Bev," I yell to my mother-in-law, who is at the kitchen sink, "did you buy a menorah?"

"It was on sale," she shouts back. No one loves a sale as much as my mother-in-law.

I touch the thick base, the stubby candleholders. Is her plan to send it home with us?

The water in the kitchen shuts off. "I figured we'd keep it here," she says in a quieter voice, from the doorway of the closet, "save you from having to bring one when Hanukkah falls on Christmas."

Gabriel's bar mitzvah is four months away, and he refuses to practice his Hebrew. Once a week, before his tutoring sessions, I force him to get out his three-ring binder of photocopied prayers and Torah readings, and I stand over him as he moves haltingly through the kiddush, the tallit, the haftarah. Within moments, he's screaming in frustration, or I am, or we both are.

It's hard to watch him struggle with this because there's so little I can do to help. He's learning a series of prayers I don't know, learning to pray to a God I cannot reach. I wanted to raise him with religion, hoped to nurture in him a belief in God. His bar mitzvah marks his entrance into manhood, and I am becoming increasingly aware of the passage of time. All I may be able to do is teach him to ask his own questions, to go in search of his own God.

I receive a letter from the Jewish Community Center, asking if our contact information has changed. It's for a directory, which the JCC publishes and distributes to Richmond's Jewish community—about three thousand people total. There's space on the form to submit new information and a box to check if I'd prefer not to be included.

The directory is both a resource and, if it ever got into the wrong hands, a risk. I picture some lunatic turning it into a hit list, going after the city's Jews in their homes, one by one. The temperature of the nation isn't the same as it was the last time this directory was published. In the wake of Trump's election, hate crimes against Jews in the US have more than doubled.

I consider checking the box. *Please don't include us, thanks very much.* My dad was a Methodist; my kids are multiethnic; my last name is Beanland. I've been told even my nose doesn't look Jewish. If there is anyone who should be able to slip off the rolls, it's me and my family.

But in the end, I can't do it. I leave the box unchecked.

On a Saturday morning in October, a gunman walks into a synagogue in Pittsburgh and opens fire.

Throughout the day, my phone buzzes with news alerts. Eleven people are dead. Six are injured, including several police officers who responded to the scene. The shooting is the deadliest attack ever on a Jewish community in the United States.

That evening, Gabriel is to go to a bar mitzvah at our synagogue, and I wonder how I will manage to let him walk out my front door. My one, precious son.

I wait for word that the bar mitzvah is to be canceled, postponed. Instead, I get an email from our rabbi, addressed to the entire congregation: "The mission of the Jewish people is to be a 'Light unto the Nations,' that is, it is our obligation to act and react in a way that shows the world the morality that we wish for all."

I go through the motions. Tell Gabriel to put on his suit, brush his teeth, wet down his hair. Write a check, scribbling "Mazel Tov!" in the memo line. Hand him a card to sign. Finally, there is nothing left to do except let him go.

I count the hours until it's time to pick him up. Four, three, two, one.

In front of the building, a uniformed police officer waits on the sidewalk, not far from his patrol car. If something were wrong, I tell myself, there would be blue lights. More cars.

"I'm here to pick up my son," I say when I'm in front of the man. "At the bar mitzvah."

He waves me over to the doors, and I stand by as he unlocks them.

"Thank you for being here tonight," I say, when he holds a door open for me. "Especially tonight."

"It's terrible," he says quietly. Then he ushers me into this house of God and locks the door behind me.

On the occasion of a child's bar mitzvah, it's customary for the parents to go to the bimah and say a blessing, called an aliyah, before he reads from the Torah. A few weeks before Gabriel's ceremony, the rabbi hands me a copy of the aliyah, and my eyes widen. It's a lot of Hebrew for Kevin and me to learn.

The blessing sits on the kitchen counter for several days before Kevin and I gather around an ironing board in our living room and pull up a YouTube channel called *Prayer-eoke* on my phone. With the words in front of us and a voice singing the incantations in our ears, we stumble through the blessing. The video is helpful, so we keep playing it, which the kids think is both nightmarish and very funny.

I write a novel that's based on a family story my mother told me. My great-great-aunt Florence was training to swim the English Channel when she drowned off the shoreline of Atlantic City. Her sister Ruth was pregnant and on bedrest after losing a baby the previous year, and the girls' mother made the decision to keep Florence's death a secret until Ruth had delivered a healthy baby.

"Can you even imagine?" my mother always said of her great-grandmother. "Visiting her daughter in that hospital room, and never letting on that Florence was dead?"

The week the novel is to go to auction, my agent schedules calls with editors who are interested in acquiring it. Almost all of them are Jewish. When we talk, they want to know what's fact and what's fiction, so I outline the real story, which took place nearly ninety years ago. There comes a point, on nearly every call, when the editor says, of the story, "It's just so Jewish."

What makes the story a Jewish one, I wonder, as I hang up the phone after each call. Sure, I throw in a few prayers, references to sitting shiva and observing Shabbat. But that's not what they mean. They're referencing the secret my mother's great-grandmother kept. Her inclination to protect the living rather than honor the dead. The edict she issued, in a moment of gut-wrenching agony, which everyone else in the family willingly obeyed.

I didn't set out to write a Jewish story. In fact, I feel barely qualified to write one.

But I'm learning that the stories I know in my bones are Jewish ones.

We attend our daughter Florence's consecration—otherwise known as the beginning of her formal education in Judaism. A dozen five-year-olds wiggle in a pew at the front of the temple, and Florence turns in her seat, trying to spot us among the other parents.

"Your beginning, here, means Judaism will continue," says the rabbi as he calls her up to the bimah.

On the morning of Gabriel's bar mitzvah, I worry about whether our out-of-town family will find parking and whether the caterer will be able to get into the venue, whether the knot on Gabriel's tie is too big and whether my brother will arrive in time for the family photographs we're taking on the temple's front steps. What I do not spend much time considering, until I am staring at my son, who sits on the bimah, beaming, is what will actually happen at the ceremony.

There is a part of the service called the dor l'dor, which, when translated, means "from generation to generation." After the rabbi opens the ark and removes the Torah, he passes it to my mother, who passes it to me. The sacred scrolls are heavier than I anticipate, and Kevin helps me position them, securely, against my shoulder before we pass them to Gabriel. He receives them, his arms open, and I am wholly moved by the significance of what we have just done.

The Shema is the oldest daily prayer in Jewish tradition. It is said at morning and evening services and is considered to be a declaration of faith. It's big and important and also really, really beautiful.

I never learned the Shema as a kid but my own children have been singing it for years. Sometimes, they'll be in the bath or doing their homework, and I'll hear them saying the words under their breath, the melody as soothing as a lullaby.

One day at services, when the congregation begins to sing the prayer, I realize I am singing too. *Sh'ma Yisra'eil Adonai Eloheinu Adonai echad.* I sing the next verse and the one that follows that. I can't tell you what the words mean, or if I believe them. But maybe, I tell myself, it's enough to sing along.

Behold Invisibility

ANNE MCGRATH

IT IS ONLY WITH THE HEART THAT ONE CAN SEE RIGHTLY; WHAT IS ESSENTIAL IS INVISIBLE TO THE EYE.

–Antoine de Saint-Exupéry

Thunderclouds gathered in the late afternoon as I climbed the subway stairs and bumped into Polly, a former Jackie Gleason dancer now living in a shelter I helped run on the Upper West Side. Belting "Unforgettable" with abandon, her raspy, world-weary voice revealed undercurrents of tenderness and longing. Pigeons jerkily pecked the ground at her feet, and steam billowed like something feral and alive behind her, slicing the dark gray sky into rays of light. It felt like Polly had enough goodwill to energize the whole city that night. I stopped to listen. This was the early nineties, before I had a husband or kids. Before I'd had much opportunity to contemplate loss and loneliness.

Singing strangers home seems to me one of the loveliest things you could do.

New York's infrastructure helps shape and define the rhythm of the city. While bridges, subway stations, and revolving doors are visible features, there is also a labyrinth of unnoticed systems—water, sewer, electric, and steam.

Sturdy workhorses, their apparatuses lie in the periphery or underneath the skin of the city, like organs of a body, sustaining life on the island.

The most visible and poetic of these mostly underground networks is steam. With its operatic, rebellious temperament, steam evokes the very hue of the city, the same way its softer, more demure cousin, fog, might define a sea town. Fog and steam clouds are scene stealers. It has to do with the way mindless mist catches slivers of light, swirls, and changes shape. In New York, the steam ascends from manholes as if the underground muses are working around a large, bubbling cauldron, linking us in a collective dream that ties us together across time and death. In the dream we reassure one another that our homes will always be safe and warm.

If not for the steam system, each building in Manhattan would have its own chimney, and the iconic skyline would look very different. District steam, an underground one-hundred-plus-mile grid of pipeline, is the least sexy direct-heating source in NYC. The roughly twenty-three square miles that make up Manhattan have been built on steam since 1881, when the first piping was laid beneath the streets to deliver water vapor to buildings. The original boiler house in lower Manhattan would eventually replace individual coal-burning boilers. Today, the antiquated yet sturdy piping system still distributes up to ten million pounds of steam per hour to heat and cool more than eighteen hundred commercial and residential structures, offsetting the demand for electric power. New York's steam system is the largest in the world; the next nine systems across the country combined do not surpass it. The pipes built under our feet to channel the steam—rushing, soaring, never resting—hold fast under the pressure. We might hear a primordial hum if we were to press our ear to the ground.

I was born in a trailer in North Carolina because my World War II merchant-marine father moved around the country building boiler plants for what was then one of the largest industrial boiler manufacturers, Babcock & Wilcox. The plants my father built generated steam for the facilities that made America an international leader in manufacturing. No one did what our country did back then, manufacturing-wise, and steam was integral to our success. Before steam power, back in the seventeenth century, factories and mills were powered by hand, water, wind, or horse, and most were located near a water source. Once steam power was developed, manufacturing plants could instead be located anywhere, forever changing the way we live and work as cities and towns developed around new manufacturing facilities.

Even today, except in cases of solar panels, wind turbines, or hydro-power, most of the watts of power we consume—to charge phones, power TVs, cool our houses—come from a power plant that generates electricity from old-fashioned steam. It's a mostly safe energy source. Accidents are rare, but that doesn't mean they don't happen.

Polly's hair, gray-blond dyed purple, was teased into a French twist, and her makeup had been applied with the heavy hand of someone who wants to be noticed. Her tired, swollen feet were pressed into thin fabric shoes. She paused once to scream, *I'm still here,* as if her past were slipping away while she moved forward. When she finished her song, I went up to her to say hello as the sun set and people bustled past us. For some, this was their destination, for others, their point of origin. All of us strangers, finding our ways. I ended up staying for nearly an hour. There was no one waiting for me at home, and Polly was never boring.

That night she said to me, "I used to be a starlet. A showstopper. Legs up to here." She pointed to someplace up around her ears. "Now everybody walks right by me like they don't see me." I thought about how uncomfortable, guilty, and complicit we feel when we see someone living on the streets. How we fear that with a slight change of luck we could be them.

In and out of psychiatric hospitals for a large part of her adult life, Polly had lost most of her teeth. She sometimes introduced herself as Doris Day or Elizabeth Taylor, but that night, she was just Polly. While we were talking, she walked over to her knockoff Gucci bag, pulled out two mints, and offered me one with a Liz Taylor-slow-smoking kind of grace.

I moved to NYC from Virginia in the late eighties to study psychology in graduate school. I was in my twenties and able to afford city life by working as a live-in nanny. I saw my neighbors living on the street far more frequently than I did the ones living in my building. I knew the names of the regulars I passed on the stoops, street corners, and benches near my apartment, and they knew mine. I marveled at their resilience and wondered how long I could last facing daunting challenges and harsh indignities, what skills, grit, or street smarts I might discover within myself. I wondered if I could make room for all that grief, loss, fear, and occasional joy.

After I graduated I stopped nannying and took a job with a program that originated in what was then called the Columbia University School of Social Work. The program worked to house homeless people and provide them with services so that they could successfully remain housed. I worked in the basement of a public-housing facility on the Upper West Side of Manhattan, where I arrived many days to find our front door littered with trash and leftover syringes. One morning there was a smashed-up car. I squeezed around the abandoned vehicle and went inside to find one of my coworkers, Margarita, making calls to track down the car's owner. Later that day, I looked up from my desk and laid eyes on something I'd never seen in that basement: a young, healthy, handsome, hip, joking, flirty male, talking to Margarita. I jumped up, and she introduced me to Steve, the owner of the abandoned car and my future husband.

When Steve and I first started dating and he asked how I had chosen my line of work, I said something offhand about how I helped others for the same reason any of us did, to distract myself from my own problems. I think of that now, and it still seems mostly true. It was a surprising choice given my sarcastic, short-tempered, and self-indulgent nature. I was choosy about where I directed my empathy. I had attended graduate school planning to work as a therapist, but quickly realized that I had little patience for privileged people like myself who paid experts to listen to their problems. I was more interested in working with people who were struggling with the kinds of hardships I had only experienced through books and films, people I had a chance to really help. It is a gift, only fully understood in action, to be of service to another person. I told Steve that the lives of homeless people were often sliced in half, marked by the time *before* and *after* they lost the ability to secure the most basic of needs: a place to safely close their eyes.

Steve was a singer-songwriter turned engineer who made his living telling NYC building managers how to efficiently operate their steam systems. His father, a Chilean immigrant, was also an engineer and had influenced his son's choice to embark upon the unusual steam management career path. Our friends call Steve the Steam God. If I made a meme of him I would place a light-infused halo of steam around his head. When he was not yet my husband and I was trying to get on his wavelength, I said to him, "Don't you love the way steam is romantically portrayed in so many pictures of the city, like light transformed into something you might hold, something collecting an intelligence within."

"Steam is actually invisible," Steve said, interestingly but also unromantically. He explained that steam is just water in its gaseous state. This takes a great deal of energy, which is released when it is used as a heating source and condenses back into liquid. That change is the key to the power of steam. He told me that most of what we call steam, the clouds we see billowing up onto the streets, the foggy veil that the yellow cab emerges from in the opening of Martin Scorsese's *Taxi Driver,* is actually condensate—minuscule water droplets, each one a fraction the size of a raindrop. The island of Manhattan has a high water table, and most of this "steam" is caused by underground fresh water that rises when it rains, or as a result of flooding, that hits the steam pipes.

In heating systems like the ones Steve works on, steam always exists as a bi-phase flow, with vapor and liquid fighting for dominance. When liquid is allowed to build, it creates instability, which can cause the pipes to explode—visible to all and destructive to anything in its path.

After hearing about the bi-phase flow and liquid business, I started noticing and connecting more things like that, things on the brink of becoming something else. Everyone in Manhattan seemed to be preparing for the starring role they hoped to play in their own lives. As a social worker,

I saw people build new selves out of whatever indestructible raw material they contained. Their transformations were predicated on loss—of group affiliations, home, family, personal identity, or sense of self.

I worked with many people who were transforming into new versions of themselves, people looking backward and forward at the same time, people who dug inward to discover the self must be created, not found. People whose safety required them to hide when so many of them hoped to be found.

When raw, piercing, private pain is made public, filters and masks finally fall away. But how fierce it is, our need to conceal the parts that don't fit the self we've constructed.

Wallace, one of the homeless men I worked with in the nineties, was not an angry man, but he could be provoked. I'd seen him explode on occasion. He was usually funny and charming, had a certain way of saying my name, *Aye-Ann,* twisting it into two syllables. In some ways he was very visible—six foot seven, skinny as a needle, African American, and usually dressed flamboyantly in women's clothing—but he was also often dismissed, mocked, or told that his body was not made for public places. He claimed a spot sleeping on a steam grate in my Upper West Side neighborhood, and I saw him as often as I saw any of my friends over a five- or six-year period before he fatally overdosed.

One hot afternoon, Wallace had followed me into a bodega, wearing tight electric-blue shorts under a short, gauzy orange dress. The store owner took one look at his bare feet and told Wallace he had to leave.

He did leave, and returned a moment later, clickity-clacking in women's heels that appeared three sizes too small. The store owner told us both to get out. Wallace's humiliation and anger ricocheted around his body, around the bodega. Before I could reach the door, he'd pulled a gun from the waistband of his blue shorts and pointed it squarely at the owner.

We say we are "letting off steam"; we "vent" our feelings. As a menopausal woman, I know about sudden rage. I used to be so pleasing and accommodating. But these days I rarely hold my tongue. I've yelled at strangers who tailgated me, cursed at able-bodied people who didn't give up their subway seats to less able ones, and once punched Donald Trump's face on the TV.

Boundless, steam expands. Without narrow, fixed pipes to direct its flow, it dissipates and is absorbed into the air. Steam guys know that when vapor escapes a pipe and you hear the ominous hiss of it leaking, like deafening static on a TV, you must stop everything and find the leak immediately. A thin jet of scalding hot high-pressure steam cannot be seen by the naked eye. To find it, you need a broom or other long-handled tool to wave around in search of the invisible machete. Because even a thin leak can pack enough pressure to slice your broom, or you, in half.

Time turned hyperreal. The bodega owner went pale and started apologizing, begging for mercy. I grabbed Wallace and pulled him outside. He returned to himself—kooky, kind, spontaneous—and buried the gun in a corner trash can while I tried not to contemplate the implications.

"You got to understand. No one listens to me until I have a gun," he said softly. "Then … everybody listens."

Wallace knew something that I'm just beginning to understand about how power can be exerted over people, how they can be silenced, and how humanity can be erased from an individual, no matter how large or conspicuous he might be. No matter how capable she thinks she still is. It is one thing to be looked at, another to be seen.

In the early nineties, while Steve was testing steam traps, measuring flow, and helping to make commercial buildings like the World Trade Center more energy efficient, I was a social worker reaching out to people living on the streets and inviting them to our shelter. I visited shanty towns in the abandoned train tunnels under Manhattan, where everything smells like wet stone.

There, hidden from view, subterranean dwellers made their camps in the recesses of a narrow dirt-tube with no natural light. The buried passages provided a natural roof, less chance of harassment, and a cocoon of safety. A muting of the constant chorus of noise above, while comforting, also blurred their connection to reality. Like all communities, underground camps have their own rituals and rules. Most of the people living there are introverted and don't welcome strangers. I was visiting an older man who had to vouch for me every time someone questioned what I was doing there.

The rats ran from me but didn't seem to mind the people who lived there, who made their homes from cardboard and newspapers and blankets and coats and roots and dirt and dark matter and music and dollars and drugs and whiskey and bones and wings and swords and cups and wands and protection and resilience and courage and compassion and forgiveness and knives and guns. To be homeless is to use everything you've got.

When I started writing this essay, I visited the steam room in the basement of the Empire State Building. It features a lovely panel of polished brass gauges, a remnant of the original 1931 installation that evokes *Downton Abbey*'s bell system in the servants' quarters. The spotlessly clean open space gleams in fluorescent light, and rows of brightly painted pipes line the ceiling—blue for chilled water, yellow for steam, and red for hot condensate. The pipes contain the infinity that is steam and are as beautiful as any modern art exhibition. The basement steam room is the heart of a building, the pipes its energy-delivering arteries. The system still heats the Empire State Building as it has done since the building first opened in 1931. Something so old and hidden, still meticulously maintained.

Urban planners are keen to phase out fossil-fuel consumption at the building level in favor of renewable electricity. We might have to find new uses for steam.

In a dream I had the other night I am deep underground in the basement of a large commercial building. I'm walking along when I step on a three-quarter-inch pipe, snapping it in two, accidentally triggering a steam leak. Unlike the thin, invisible-machete leak, this is what the engineers would call a *catastrophic system breach.*

Disaster rolls in like a fog, and the basement fills with furiously darting molecules. A thick cloud of vapor reduces visibility, and I find myself lost in a blinding stew of whiteness. A raw display of extreme energy. My ears swell with the deafening thunder of escaping vapor. My heart pounds and my eyes tear; I could just as well close them for all I can see. Trying to find a way out seems futile, but I crawl on the ground. Miraculously, I find things are clear enough down low for me to see the glow of the exit light. Sometimes a change of perspective is all you need to find your way.

Other times, through no fault of your own, you end up in the wrong place at the wrong time.

On July 18, 2007, it rained so heavily in New York City that water flooded the area underground around some of the steam pipes near Grand Central Terminal. By the time the evening rush hour rolled around and people were running to their trains and buses, condensate caused by the flood water exceeded the capacity of the steam traps that had been designed to filter it out. Water on the outside of a pipe caused condensation inside of it, leading to a dangerous condition called water hammer. Steam penetrated the water inside the pipe, collapsed violently, and caused an explosion. The burst pipe resulted in a geyser of hot steam contaminated with mud, flying debris, and asbestos from piping insulation; the force blew a hole roughly thirty-five-feet wide and fifteen feet deep in the street, leaving one woman dead from a heart attack and dozens more injured. People thought it was a terrorist attack. They were screaming and running in all directions, trying to escape the next possible phase of disaster.

Following the explosion, sensors were installed in the steam labyrinth. Today, automated technologies are in place to measure condensation and pressure and to alert emergency personnel to problems before they become critical.

I am now sixty, heading into old age, and realize we're—all of us—always becoming. To be ignored or erased, as we older women so often are, is to experience a kind of death.

To be seen again can be a resurrection, an idea the cosmetic industry is more than happy to cash in on.

The science behind camouflage involves scattering light away from an object so it can't be detected, much as some makeup is designed using light-diffusing technology to mask the signs of aging.

Examining my own transformations—from daughter and girl to woman and mother, and to old lady—I think perhaps every life shift requires a loss that must be mourned. In my twenties and thirties, jobs were easy to come by. Now that my kids have grown and I again have time to devote to meaningful work outside of the house, I find the work world has washed its hands of me. I'm moving on the natural currents these days. I've taken up writing, weaving, and collaging, not with any direction or endgame in mind, but rather because I enjoy these activities—free-flowing, spontaneous, and uncontained. I use recycled materials in both my visual art and my writing, borrowing from those who came before and imagining myself leaving something for those who come after me. I like giving new life to things deemed past their prime.

Polly was staying in our shelter back in the nineties when she told me about a bizarre dream she'd had. In it, a staff of people were working on her hair and makeup, like they had back when she'd been a chorus-line dancer. I said that sounded glamorous, and she agreed that it was. "But," she said, "they weren't preparing me for a show. No. They were prepping me for my funeral!" She seemed to find the dream amusing, so I went along with her, though I found it disconcerting.

She was in her sixties and healthy then. But a few mornings later an aide knocked at my office door and said, in a frantic voice, "Polly is cold. I can't warm her. She won't get up."

I followed the aide up to Polly's room. She looked peaceful, as if she were asleep. But she was gone.

I'd like to tell you that I sang Polly home, the same way she had sung so many tired, cold, let-down and worn-out New Yorkers home. But it was the first time I'd ever touched a dead body, and I was in shock. While the aide stood in the doorway softly crying, she repeated the phrase, "She's so cold, I couldn't warm her." I crouched by Polly's bedside, my hand on her icy forehead. When I think of her now, I hum the "Unforgettable" tune in my head and imagine her young, gorgeous, and dressed in her sequined showgirl getup.

I think about all the people living on the streets, many with special needs, through this pandemic. How frightening the lockdowns, overcrowded shelters, and increased deaths have been for all of us, let alone for those without a safety net. Many were left outside and alone while our nation braced for the spread of COVID and those with resources took shelter. We could ensure that no person in our country had to make their home in a box or go without food, if we had the political will.

Age sneaks up on humans and city infrastructures. It reminds us to look beneath the surface, where there are layers upon layers still undiscovered. *It's only with the heart that one can see rightly.*

Steam is a pure substance: its chemical composition is always H^2O. We're about 60 percent water ourselves, and like steam, we go through different phases. We are sometimes seen, sometimes not. Sometimes beheld, sometimes ignored. We act differently when we are being observed, and for all we know so does steam.

Rolling clouds of steam look light and fluffy when seen from a distance. You can walk right through the mist without considering the larger unseen forces underground carrying the kind of heat and power that can energize whole cities.

Everything Gets Worse

An Antarctica Story

JOHN O'CONNOR

BUT HIS SOUL WAS MAD. BEING ALONE IN THE WILDERNESS, IT HAD LOOKED WITHIN ITSELF, AND, BY HEAVENS! I TELL YOU, IT HAD GONE MAD. I HAD—FOR MY SINS, I SUPPOSE—TO GO THROUGH THE ORDEAL OF LOOKING INTO IT MYSELF.

—Marlow, *Heart of Darkness*

The winter of 1912 was Raymond Priestley's third in Antarctica in five years. A palm reader had once told him that he would die in this year, his twenty-sixth. But Priestley figured that if he were going to die in Antarctica, he'd have already done so. During the 1907-9 *Nimrod* expedition, he had found himself adrift one morning on an ice floe that was surrounded by killer whales. After a harrowing day at sea, he somehow managed to drift back to land. Later, he had become trapped in a blizzard on Mount Erebus for seventy-two hours without food or a tent or a hope in hell of surviving. Scrunched inside his reindeer-skin sleeping bag and being blown slowly downhill, he was in constant danger of plunging off a hundred-foot cliff into Horseshoe Bay. The experience, he later said, steeled him for the trenches of Amiens.

By 1910, when he signed on to Robert Falcon Scott's *Terra Nova* expedition, which was racing the Norwegian explorer Roald Amundsen to the geographic South Pole, Priestley was a hardened Antarctic veteran. A geologist from the Cotswolds with "a hereditary Nonconformist conscience which has frequently given me trouble," as he put it, he had pale, appraising eyes, a spindly Van Dyke, and a hairline that was holding on for dear life. In February 1911, while Scott began his preparations for a dash to the pole, Priestley and five others—the "Northern Party"—went exploring along Antarctica's Victoria Land coast, in the southeastern part of the continent, hard against the Southern Ocean. It was a landscape that had swallowed men and ships for the better part of a century. They passed a winter in a hut at Cape Adare, where the men mostly sat around staring at penguins. After eleven months, the *Terra Nova* returned and eventually deposited them farther south, at Terra Nova Bay, where things took a turn for the worse.

The land was desolate, a heavily crevassed, wind-scrubbed plateau, and beyond that, impassable white-ruffed mountains rising and falling for a thousand miles. Their plan had been to spend some pre-winter weeks poking around until the *Terra Nova* returned again to fetch them. A sound plan, all agreed. And it was. Except for one detail: winter came early that year, and the *Terra Nova* couldn't get through the pack ice. Gazing out to sea for a ship that wasn't coming, the men discovered they were short on nearly everything, even matches. Their boots and wind clothes were rotting from their bodies. Gale-force winds had torn their canvas tents to shreds. The burning question in the back of all their minds was: Now what?

Some of them, being God-fearing men, prayed on it. Then, they chopped a hole out of the ice high up in the foothills where they could keep watch for the *Terra Nova*. Their "warren," as Priestley called it, was nine by twelve feet and five and a half feet high. "Inexpressible Island" was the name that stuck—not a literal island but a figurative one, an island of the mind. Priestley's sketch of it in his wonderful account of the expedition, *Antarctic Adventure,* is inexpressibly stark and horrid: two rows of sleeping bags laid three abreast, with penguin and seal carcasses stacked to one side and bones to the other, and a filthy sack strung up for privacy in the commode. There was barely enough room to stand. The roof was always close to collapsing and burying them alive, and they were almost asphyxiated in their sleep before they thought to add a chimney. There was no warmth to be found anywhere; it was never more than a few degrees below zero inside the cave, and often far colder. The walls were ice, the ceiling was ice, the floor was ice, the furniture, such as it was, was ice. Their sleeping bags, encrusted with ice and blubber, eventually shed their reindeer hair, which found its way into their tea, along with the ice and blubber. Everyone's nose became a barnacled, frostbitten horn. Their skin itched miserably. Soot from their blubber stove caked their faces and hands and painted the walls coal black.

Priestley's most frightful passages, however, concern the endless hunt for palatable, "clean-tasting" food. They ate seal blubber every day, for every meal. Priestley considered stewed seal brains their "best luxury," while Lieutenant Victor Campbell, the party's leader, thought them "simply perfect." Partly digested fish found in the throat and belly of a Weddell seal and fried in blubber was a culinary miracle. Blood left on the ice after butchering penguins was simmered into gravy. For salad, they munched raw kelp.

Diarrhea became their greatest torment. They sometimes got up to shit seven or eight times a night. Simply making it to the toilet in time could be, as it were, a crapshoot. Campbell had his "privates & stern frost bitten changing drawers" after shitting himself in his bag one night. When full winter commenced, a great silence settled over them. The darkness became a double darkness: dark outside and in, as dark as the night sky, with the thinnest light flickering from their stove.

The winter before, fellow *Terra Nova* expeditioners Bill Wilson, Birdie Bowers, and Apsley Cherry-Garrard had nearly died while collecting emperor penguin eggs at a rookery at Cape Crozier. (Wilson was an ornithologist, and at the time it was thought that emperor embryos might reveal evolutionary links between birds and reptiles. The penguins lay their eggs in winter during Antarctica's fiercest weather.) They hauled 850 pounds of supplies on two sledges, and thick snow forced them to work by relay, pulling one sledge at a time, gaining a mile for every three they walked. In eight hours they might cover a mile and a half, while shedding chunks of dead skin from their frostbitten feet. They traveled in total darkness, as temperatures fell to -77°F. At those temperatures your corneas freeze. Cognitive disarray causes speech to become slurred, and judgment and coordination go completely to hell. Despite the cold, the men sweated profusely as they walked. When they stopped, the sweat froze, forming a carapace over their skin. It sometimes took them forty-five minutes to chop into their sleeping bags at night. After they crawled inside, the ice melted, so they slept in puddles. When they finally reached the rookery, a gale carried away their only tent, and they all lay down and waited to freeze to death, only to have the tent miraculously reappear. After collecting five eggs (two of which broke), they stumbled back to Cape Evans, having finished the 140-mile round trip in five weeks. In his memoir, *The Worst Journey in the World,* Cherry-Garrard wondered whether the Northern Party's suffering took a more desperate form:

They ate blubber, cooked with blubber, had blubber lamps. Their clothes and gear were soaked with blubber, and the soot blackened them, their sleeping-bags, cookers, walls and roof, choked their throats and inflamed their eyes. Blubbery clothes are cold, and theirs were soon so torn as to afford little protection against the wind, and so stiff with blubber that they would stand up by themselves, in spite of frequent scrapings with knives and rubbings with penguin skins, and always there were underfoot the great granite boulders which made walking difficult even in daylight and calm weather.

Although they were at risk of starving to death, the Northern Party's real hazards were mental. By this expedition, Priestley had become, he liked to say, something of an authority on polar madness. It was, by and large, a seasonal affliction, brought on by the unsparing cold and darkness of the austral winter and usually waning with the return of the sun. Taken on their own, the darkness and cold were tolerable. Added to a daily menu of filth, barrenness, silence, and solitude, they acquired a quality of redaction, as if one's personality was being gradually rubbed out. "If it does not include depression to the point of suicide it appears to be curable," Priestley wrote. He'd known a few incurables over the years, including his friend Bertram

Armytage from the Nimrod expedition, who shot himself shortly after returning home.

The men of the Northern Party had all heard about the experiences of the British Southern Cross expedition, the first to winter over on the Antarctic mainland, in 1899, at Cape Adare. Led by a cranky Norwegian boozehound named Carsten Borchgrevink, ten men were crammed into a one-room hut while their seventy-five sled dogs laid waste to a colony of Adélie penguins outside, and then to one another. It didn't take long, once the sun vanished, for the men to turn on each other as well. The darkness, it seems, freed them from an obligation to be nice. "A strange spirit of irritation prevails among members," the Tasmanian physicist Louis Bernacchi wrote in his diary. "Scarcely bear [the] sight of one another. Some crusty and others morose, [making the] most unpleasant remarks they can possibly think of to one another." He came to hate Borchgrevink, who stayed constantly drunk. "Wish [to] God I had never joined such a numskull and his expedition. Getting to positively loathe the sight of all." In October, a zoologist named Nicolai Hanson died after a long illness, probably scurvy. Borchgrevink and another man nearly drowned. Like the Northern Party, they all came close to dying from carbon monoxide poisoning in their poorly ventilated quarters. Bernacchi's diary is full of descriptions of the hemmed-in feeling of winter, of the darkness and cold pressing in, of sickly companions and of those he suspected of cheating at cards. "What beasts we all are and how astounding our conceit. One would think that here at the extremity of the globe one would at least be spared these contemptible human passions. But it is quite the contrary for I have never before seen them in such nakedness."

As winter descended at Inexpressible Island, so did the Northern Party's mood. Although none of them had the experience of Antarctica that Priestley did, they must've known what awaited them, how barbarous their suffering would be. With six months to go before they could expect a rescue, their "tempers were so much on edge that conversation was impossible." The threat to their survival, Priestley suspected, would come from within.

I remember, years ago, reading the opening pages of Roland Huntford's *Scott and Amundsen* and feeling awed, haunted, in the grip of something momentous. This was back when I knew squat about Antarctica, when in fact I had only the vaguest sense of a difference between Antarctica and the Arctic (for the life of me I couldn't keep the two straight; one held the North Pole, the other the South, of that I was almost certain, but which held which?). "The poles of the earth had become an obsession of Western man," Huntford wrote, summing up what those dueling maniacs, Scott and Amundsen, were doing in Antarctica in 1912, trudging off into "the lonely wastes" for the dubious honor of being the first to the South (!) Pole, without a single pair of Smartwool socks between them.

It was during a brief crisis, a stretch of self-isolation when I had little interest in anything or anyone, and no desire, really, except to reach the end of what was troubling me. In the absence of any real hardship myself, with no right to complain, I found Scott's tragedy irresistible. "Since the obsession was there," Huntford went on, "it had to be exorcised, and the sooner the better." (Spoiler alert: when Scott arrived at the pole, he found a Norwegian flag snapping in the wind. Amundsen had beaten him by a month. "The worst has happened, or nearly the worst," Scott wrote in his diary. Even worse was yet to come. He and his four companions died on their return journey.)

Ever since, I've been exorcising an obsession of my own. Or perhaps not obsession so much as, say, horrified fascination. For Antarctica, as Fridtjof Nansen wrote, is nothing if not a "realm of death," a place of squandered lives and ravaged minds, of dashed ambition and futile courage—a place, experience also tells us, from which good news rarely transmits. Reading about Antarctica, I'm often reminded of something Paul Bowles, author of *The Sheltering Sky,* said about the message of his fiction: "Everything gets worse." This is notably true of the Heroic Age of Antarctic Exploration, when men like Scott contrived to meet the most appalling ends, hurtling themselves into the void for queen and country, slowly starving to death a million miles from home. Probably you've heard of Scott and Amundsen. But Priestley? The rest of Scott's supporting cast? Their stories have, on the whole, gone unexplored. Most were barely more than teenagers who had led, like Frank Bascombe in Richard Ford's *The Sportswriter,* "the normal applauseless life of us all," until they found themselves caught up in extraordinary circumstances at the bottom of the world. Some escaped with their lives.

At least six early Antarctic explorers committed suicide, either during or after expeditions, and many more went mad. Hjalmar Johansen, a sledge driver for Amundsen, shot himself on the streets of Oslo in 1913. Ten years later, a biologist under Scott, Edward Nelson, killed himself. Another of Scott's biologists, Dennis Lillie, never recovered from a breakdown he suffered after the *Terra Nova* expedition. No fewer than three of Shackleton's *Endurance* crew lost their minds during their open-boat journey to Elephant Island. When the *Deutschland* became trapped in the ice in 1912, its crew split into rival groups, some sleeping with loaded guns. In 1913, the wireless operator for Douglas Mawson's *Aurora* team began to suspect his companions were plotting to murder him; he later claimed he'd been hypnotized by Mawson. He was relieved of his duties and, upon returning home, hospitalized for schizophrenia. Things grew so strained between members of a 1953 French expedition that some would communicate with others only by registered letter. The same year, a thirty-nine-year-old British mechanic, Arthur Farrant, walked out of his hut on Antarctica's Deception Island and shot himself in the head. In 1960, a Soviet scientist reportedly killed a colleague with an ice axe after finding that he was cheating at chess (Russia thereafter banned chess at its Antarctic facilities). A few years later, the doctor at Mawson Station began sending "lunatic incomprehensible" cables home and, after threatening to cut people's heads off, was relieved of his duties. "It can happen so easily," writes Stephen Murray-Smith, who in 1985 found the crew at Casey Station on a knife-edge. "A wrong word here, a suspicion of too much clubbiness among a few there, a decision to go out bivouacking in the old Antarctic way. ... Suddenly authority has crumbled."

Of the many descriptions of polar madness, none surpasses Frederick A. Cook's *Through the First Antarctic Night,* a breathless account of an 1897-99 Belgian expedition that was the first to endure the soul-crushing darkness of Antarctica's winter. It's a spectacular case study of wholesale mental disarray. Cook was a physician aboard the *Belgica,* which became trapped in the Bellingshausen Sea pack ice in 1898. They started with nineteen men, including a twenty-six-year-old first mate, Roald Amundsen, on his first polar journey. Considering how catastrophically unprepared they were, the crew fared reasonably well at first, supplementing their meager tinned rations with seal and penguin meat and dutifully compiling climatological and oceanographic data (data that's still used today to measure ice sheet loss in East Antarctica). The sun, however, was quickly fleeing their world. "Time weighs heavily upon us as the darkness slowly advances," Cook wrote. "The night soaks hourly a little more colour from our blood." In mid-May, the sun vanished for good and the men went instantly to pieces. "The curtain of blackness which has fallen over the outer world of icy desolation has also descended upon the inner world of our souls."

Partly what makes *Through the First Antarctic Night* so remarkable is that Cook mentioned polar madness at all. Until then, as he tells us, madness was typically suppressed in polar narratives. To complain about such things was unheroic, ungentlemanly, and potentially disastrous from a PR point of view (in seeking recruits, polar expeditions tended to undersell the dangers and deprivations). Often led by ex-Navy men, expeditions were run like military campaigns, with unquestioning allegiance and acceptance of one's lot being the rule. I can imagine the advantages of such discipline while man-hauling sledges in the interior, where men's lives hung in the balance. But it infected their private lives and correspondence as well. Among Scott's polar party there's almost no soul-searching to speak of, even after they'd begun to suspect that Scott was in over his head. (Huntford calls Scott a "heroic bungler" unequipped to lead a party of men.) They're discreet to the point of being deceptive, as if they couldn't tell the truth without bringing posthumous shame on themselves. Having lost confidence in their leader, the men nonetheless carried on across the ice, marching toward their deaths, and "being eminently decent, as perhaps only the English can be," Caroline Alexander writes, "they did not complain, but hung on and hoped in dread for the best." To my ear, Scott's dying words—"We took risks, we knew we took them; things have come out against us, and therefore we have no cause for complaint"—have an impudent ring to them, as if five chums had encountered unexpected traffic after gambling on a shortcut to the pub. On this count, Cherry-Garrard's *The Worst Journey in the World,* widely judged to be the greatest polar narrative ever written, is a work of fiction. When he says of his Cape Crozier egg-collecting trip with Wilson and Bowers, "How good the memories of those days are," you have to read between the lines, because what he's also saying is, "It is a nightmare that has haunted me for years."

Cook, at least, was more honest about what Antarctica extracted from you. All eighteen of the *Belgica*'s crew (a young sailor had earlier been washed overboard and lost) eventually developed what he called "polar anaemia." The symptoms, as Cook describes them, read like the onset of zomboid contagion:

We became pale, with a kind of greenish hue; our secretions were more or less suppressed. The stomach and all the organs were sluggish, and refused to work. Most dangerous of all were the cardiac and cerebral symptoms. The heart acted as if it had lost its regulating influence. Its action was feeble, but its beats were not increased until other dangerous symptoms appeared... .

... The blood retreats from the skin, but the larger veins are abnormally full. Piles, hemorrhoids, headache, neuralgia, rheumatism, are the systemic complaint ... .

All seem puffy about the eyes and ankles ... The skin is unusually oily. The hair grows rapidly, and the skin about the nails has a tendency to creep over them, seemingly to protect them from the cold... .

... The men were incapable of concentration, and unable to continue prolonged thought... .

... We have aged ten years in thirty days.

The ship also stank to high heaven. A -22°F day was considered balmy. And there was an abiding fear that they could be crushed by the ice at any moment or by giant icebergs that occasionally plowed right past the *Belgica* without warning (they were very nearly smashed by one), or that the ice would never release them. The captain, Lecointe, fared so poorly that he wrote out his will. Ditto the expedition leader, de Gerlache. Cook helped as best he could, but some were beyond help. On June 5, after languishing for months, a beloved geophysicist, Emile Danco, died of heart failure. Two others went mad. One attempted to walk back to Belgium. After thirteen months, the ice finally released the *Belgica,* and the survivors sailed home. Cook, undaunted, went on to make a stab at the North Pole, which he claimed to have reached in 1909 (a claim that's probably hogwash).

"Polar T3 syndrome," the term today for the illness associated with wintering in Antarctica or the Arctic, encompasses a range of psychosomatic disorders related to sensory deprivation and extreme cold, such as forgetfulness, insomnia, increased anxiety and anger, depression, and cognitive decline. "Winter-over syndrome," as it's also called, is evidenced by a fugue-like "big eye" or "Antarctic stare" and a corresponding feeling of your mind having gone totally blank. It can strike even new arrivals. The scholar Stephen J. Pyne spent the 1985 austral winter at McMurdo Station, the US National Science Foundation hub, and noticed in himself "a general feeling of being unwell, lethargy, disorientation." The station is claustrophobic, insular, and in winter inescapable: "Living there was a process of social reductionism that led to a cultural numbing, a mental hypothermia." It has a year-round population of about 250: Sno-Cat drivers, sous chefs, plumbers, construction workers, dishwashers, bartenders, hairstylists, janitors, air traffic controllers. Together, they endure six sunless months of constant blizzards and subzero temperatures and nights that grow so long they essentially never end, when life acquires the leaden, changeless tenor of a prison colony. Among the harder cases during Pyne's stay were people suffering from "depression, outbursts of hostility, sleep disturbance, social withdrawal, and impaired cognition." The following year, amid a winter of discontent, a cafeteria cook attacked two others with the claw end of a hammer.

"The quintessential Antarctic experience," Pyne writes, "is of something taken away." Namely, your sanity. Despite the material comforts of station life today, compared with the biblical scarcity of Priestley's Northern Party, you're still far from home, as far as it's possible to get short of a space flight, enveloped in the world's most inhospitable abyss. One could very well die of boredom. "Typical are the hazards of boredom arising from a progressive and pervasive lack of sensory stimuli," Pyne writes. The most obvious corollary to boredom is a scrupulous lack of interest in everything and everyone, perhaps the sense that you have ceased to be of interest to others, and also to yourself. Your wisest course of action, it may seem, is to withdraw and become emotionally cold and vacant, like Marshawn Lynch in a postgame interview. "The relentless passivity, silence, emptiness, and deprivation" are immediate and overpowering, Pyne says. The antiseptic uniformity of the ice, its changeless and indistinct appearance—"singularly inert, empty with an awful simplicity"—begins to overtake you. May to October, when night is indistinguishable from day, are the nightmare months.

Which is roughly when, in 1934, Rear Admiral Richard E. Byrd decided to isolate himself at a remote unventilated hut called Bolling Advance Weather Station, 123 miles from his expedition's base at the Bay of Whales. Nobody had ever spent an Antarctic winter alone. It's safe to say that nobody had ever thought of it, as the idea was plainly nuts. Byrd's snowbound hovel, in which he planned to pass six months of darkness, was perched on an ice shelf riddled with crevasses and continuously blasted by Category 5 winds. Nighttime temperatures hovered between -58° and -76°F. Byrd justified his plan by claiming he wanted to do meteorological research. In truth, he harbored Thoreauvian pipe dreams of simplified living, a retreat to monastic solitude that would be, he predicted, "an experiment in harmony." Recapitulating sentiments that go back at least to Ovid's pastorals, Byrd hoped that out there, away from it all, he could finally "let the bodily processes achieve a natural equilibrium."

"The desire to discover essences through deprivation is an ancient one, as old as the fast in the desert," Pyne reminds us. "But the Antarctic desert is a ruthless reducer." For starters, there are no trees, shrubs, grasses, meadows, rivers, lakes, dunes, beaches, wheat fields; no rain or lightning; hardly any animals or fecundity to speak of; for months not even light and dark; none of the stuff we take for granted and which our minds need to create context and contrasts. There is only ice and sky. As a result of "information underload," Pyne says, "sights, sounds, smells, and feels erode away."

Things started off OK for Byrd. Freed from the soft comforts of civilization, he found his senses sharpening, a veil of inner peace descending. "I came to understand what Thoreau meant when he said, 'My body is all sentient,'" he wrote. "There were moments when I felt more alive than at any other time in my life." Before long, however, he started hallucinating and soon lost sixty pounds. It didn't help that he got carbon monoxide poisoning from his stove. After five months, he had to be rescued, at considerable risk to his rescuers, who'd become alarmed when Byrd's telegraph messages all but dried up. His book about the ordeal, *Alone,* reads as if Robinson Crusoe had washed ashore in a Thomas Hardy novel: "The dark side of a man's mind seems to be a sort of antenna tuned to catch gloomy thoughts from all directions," he wrote. "It was as if all the world's vindictiveness were concentrated upon me as upon a personal enemy. I sank to depths of disillusionment which I had not believed possible." Like a slightly more ghastly version of apartment living in New York City. Except whereas you or I might struggle to breathe the suffocating New York air and become maddened by the city's arrhythmic natural void, and by direct and daily contact with our fellow man, Byrd felt the opposite. He struggled to breathe the asphyxiating air of his final enlightenment. Like Tom Hanks in *Cast Away,* he went batty in civilization's absence, by direct and daily contact with his own consciousness. "Solitude, too," as Martin Amis says in his study of the Soviet gulags, "has its penal applications."

It brings to mind John Carpenter's movie *The Thing,* about a bunch of Antarctic scientists, holed up at an isolated post, who are stalked by an alien being that assumes the identity of its victims. Inevitably, the entire crew turns on each other, as nobody knows who's human and who's an alien wraith. Kurt Russell plays a hard-bitten, J&B-swilling chopper pilot named R. J. MacReady, wielding a flamethrower and formidable neck-beard (we're to assume, given the blended Scotch and an absurd cavalry hat, that he's a Vietnam vet accustomed to horrors of a different kind). Fresh off the success of *Halloween,* Carpenter reweaves themes of random vengeance and pained, plaintive heroism onto an icy scrim, with the silence of Antarctica filling the screen like the ominous mist in his 1980 film *The Fog.* It's extraordinarily violent. But the violence is cartoonish, as if Jim Henson had been in charge of special effects. *The Thing* invests Antarctica with malice and intention—it's the ice that has preserved the alien in a natural cryo-freeze, unleashing it eons later on our unwitting men of science—when really it's just a void, without kindness or cruelty, a place where nature gets boiled down to its Rousseauian, primordial elements.

Looking back, I can see that *The Thing*—I recall it being on television one winter break when I was twelve or thirteen and thinking, Carpenter's a world-beating genius! Later I discovered it's based on a novella by John W. Campbell—held for me the animating fear of Antarctica: not so much that you'll be hunted by an amorphous manifestation of evil but rather, in a nutshell, that exposure to visceral, incoherent nature leads to an erasure of the self. MacReady and Co. are clearly somewhere they don't belong, trapped in a landscape that may very well swallow them alive. Isolated and helpless, they come to dread not the monstrous cold or hunger, the gaping crevasses or ice falls, or even boredom, but something else entirely, something or someone that's not one of them but is indistinguishable from them. Because no one can be trusted, because rescue brings the risk of exposing the outside world to the identity-less Thing, MacReady makes the executive decision to burn down the research station and with it the source of life for them all. (In a strange case of life imitating art, a couple of years after *The Thing*'s release, the doctor at Argentina's Brown Station followed MacReady's cue and burned the entire station to the ground, in his case to force an evacuation home.)

To some, of course, erasure is the whole point: to disappear, reinvent oneself, hit the psychic refresh button. A few years ago, when a friend of mine vanished in New York City—I suppose "vanished" is putting it dramatically, but that's how people put it; what I think happened is he just switched off his cell phone for a while—I half expected him to turn up in Antarctica living under an assumed name, driving a forklift, smoking a Dunhill pipe and reading Alan Watts. Part of the allure of New York, to say nothing of Antarctica, is how easily you can disappear; the potential to refresh is omnipresent: shut your eyes, plop a finger on the MTA map, who knows where you'll end up or who you'll become? A Midwood yoga teacher moonlighting as a Mister Softee truck driver in Canarsie? Presto! When my friend resurfaced after a few weeks, without explanation, he was living in Bay Ridge, which back then might as well have been Antarctica. Today it's exactly like every other neighborhood in New York, colonized by hipsters with rescue dogs named Django.

Even if we never intend on reinventing ourselves, few of us would truck with Nietzsche's maxim of *amor fati*—the love of fate—a notion the philosopher struck on late in life, perhaps not coincidentally at the very moment he began cartwheeling between sanity and madness. The path to true happiness, he'd come to believe, lay in an uncritical acceptance of one's life circumstances—the good, the bad, and the ugly—to the point where "one wants nothing to be different, not forward, not backward, not in all eternity." Seeking change and insight, Nietzsche decided, was the express train to Crazytown. Most of us, it's fair to say, believe the opposite of this; we put our faith in growth, in self-actualization, in changing trains at the next platform for the unlived life. We may occasionally even think of ourselves as free agents, unshackled from the petty inconveniences of work, kids, love, mortgages, and library overdue notices. Perhaps a sliver of chromosome from our nomadic past gnaws at the walls of our sedentary ribs? Deep down, we yearn for freedom, long to strike out for undiscovered country. Move aside, Scott and Amundsen, it's the Age of Discovery and Midlife Crisis!

For all but a few of us, though, the fantasy of freedom is just that: a fantasy. Despite our noblest attempts, we're undone by warring desire and dependence, subverted by comforting familiarity, manacled by fear, drowned by inertia, hopelessly cement-shoed in the murky estuaries of daily life. I am, of course, talking about myself. I've spent the past fifteen years in an idle, thumb-twirling stupor, toiling away on the corporate-slave matrix, working without purpose, dreaming passively of a different kind of life. To say I've lacked drive and direction would be an affront to understatement. Mine has been an aimless, undisciplined existence, an ever-widening project of evasion and indecision and self-deception in which I'm forever having a circular conversation with myself: Which path should I choose? Which direction warrants the jettisoning of all others? How do I choose just *one* life knowing I'll be unsatisfied with whichever I choose? Instead of choosing I do the safest thing: nothing. Doing nothing, as I've always done, comes naturally to me. Oh, the time I've wasted! The books I've failed to write! Thankfully the internet came along and suddenly doing nothing while pretending to do the opposite became totally effortless. We've moved into an evolutionary phase of frantic non-doing. In this light, my years of myopic dawdling, of hemming and hawing, of whining and self-editorializing in a bottomless, fatalistic chasm (see, I'm doing it again!) feel almost virtuous. The long and the short of it is, I've always been waiting. For what? For something new and better to come along, sensing all the while that nothing ever will, which is quite possibly what I wanted in the first place: to remain cozily settled among my possessions, mainlining *Game of Thrones* while sailing through my Xanax prescription, nevertheless feeling thwarted by circumstances from pursuing a different path. So I keep on waiting, making little progress in any direction, moving glacially, my life taking shape like Antarctica on a nineteenth-century map: an uncharted, meaningless blank spot.

Anyway, when the *Terra Nova* slipped its moorings in Cardiff, bound for Cape Evans, Raymond Priestley wondered if they were all sailing straight to their deaths. Even so, he was glad to be going. Glad to be going someplace, even to a forsaken place like Antarctica, *especially* to a forsaken place like Antarctica, perhaps the very last forsaken place left on earth and therefore well worth another peek. If he could get Antarctica out of his system, his thinking went, then he could get on with the rest of his life. He didn't give a shit about the pole or being part of some desperate errand for a dwindling empire. Unlike Byrd, Priestley wasn't using Antarctica to access a deeper, spiritual psychic realm. Driven by something more akin to Camus's "longing, yes, to live, to live still more," he simply had an aversion to sleepwalking through life. The continent's indifference to human ambition, its deathly secrets hidden away in crevasses, its promise of hardship and repose, made him feel reckless and bold and alive. Plus there was the added bonus of getting away from stuffy old England and its Dickensian caste system, to find himself in a land, he wrote, "where a man stood or fell by his own merits" as opposed to his birthright. There's something very moving about Priestley, just twenty-six but already a loner and brooder of intense gravity, taking Nietzsche to heart and finding solace in Antarctica, where so many others found pure terror. It was the kind of solace *The Thing*'s MacReady—another loner holed up and brooding away at the ends of the earth—went looking for, before he got sidetracked into stopping a global alien takeover.

I feel for Richard Byrd, that Priestley wannabe, whose dream of perfect solitude in the Antarctic desert turned into a perfect nightmare. Brave and headstrong, he was no longer the man he'd been a few years earlier when he'd made a death-defying flight to the South Pole in a flimsy trimotor plane. Now, suddenly, a darkened room was life-threatening. It's depressing to think about, this sensitive Thoreauvian fleeing the clamor of modernity for the solitude and serenity of Antarctica, imagining he'd be magically transformed, only to discover that the clamor of modernity was precisely what was keeping him sane. Life in the wild, Byrd found, can quickly shed its consolations, accumulating its own peculiar load of drudgery and disaffection. Without others around to share his experience, a crucial part of his identity went missing. It killed him to admit it, but like his snowbound hovel the realization was inescapable: solitude bred a strange kind of self-doubt. Or maybe not strange at all but perfectly natural, since the self isn't an isolated, independent entity that requires no one else in order to exist—I'm baldly plagiarizing William James here—but is directed outward, toward others. Self-recognition is as much external as it is internal, based on the attention paid to us, no matter how fleeting, by our friends and enemies. Without such attention, Stephen Pyne decides, the Antarctic self can easily "succumb to solipsism or a whiteout of personality."

For one reason or other, either because the men forgot to bring them or because they broke in transit, Scott's expedition was curiously short on mirrors. The members of the Northern Party went almost two years without seeing their own reflections. Some of them wrote of the initial pleasures of going mirror-free, unburdened of the compulsion of "checking" themselves, and happily abandoning the habit. As with all things in Antarctica, however, it began to grate. The lack eventually fed a desire. Mirrors serve more than one purpose, after all. Like the narrator of Norman Rush's novel *Mating,* looking into them, we're not just making sure we don't have spinach in our teeth; we're checking to see that things are more or less as they were the last time we checked. We expect to recognize the person looking back at us and feel relief in knowing that person is us. When George Murray Levick grew a beard for the winter, he assumed it was the same color as his hair: a reddish brown. Priestley assured him it was nothing of the sort, but rather "like burnished gold." Mirrors are a kind of compass that return us to ourselves. Without them, we can lose our way.

During their first winter, the Northern Party had some welcome company in the form of several hundred thousand Adélie penguins at Cape Adare. The men grew fond of these curious, companionable animals, and it pained them later when they were forced to butcher them for food. Levick, a meticulous, buttoned-up Edwardian if there ever was one—his personal motto was *festina lente:* hasten slowly—became the first scientist to study the penguins' entire breeding cycle, and he was ill-prepared for the wild bacchanal he encountered. Cape Adare appeared to be a kind of Plato's Retreat for Adélies: males having sex with females and males; males raping females and chicks and, as if that weren't enough, even killing them. Horrified, Levick recorded his observations in Greek so that few would understand the blood orgy he'd witnessed. Prone to anthropomorphizing, he chalked it up to moral decay as a result of too much loafing: "It is interesting indeed to note that, when nature intends them to find employment, these birds, like men degenerate in idleness," he later wrote. (Levick seriously misread Adélies, however, and it took biologists a century to parse everything he'd gotten wrong—viz. all that rape and murder stuff.)

In his Antarctica documentary, *Encounters at the End of the World,* Werner Herzog asks the ecologist David Ainley whether penguins suffer from "insanity or derangement." A lone Adélie has marched away from his colony toward the mountainous interior and, Herzog assures us, certain death, an inexplicable event that sends Herzog into a tailspin. He wonders aloud whether the acute, elemental violence of Antarctica has driven the poor fellow over the edge. (No one captures the music of glum indignation quite like Herzog.) Ainley, who has studied Adélies for almost twenty years, is clearly irked by Herzog's question but remains a good sport for the cameras: "I've never seen a penguin bashing its head against a rock," he monotones. When I called him at his office in San Francisco, Ainley said that Herzog "kept harping on about penguin insanity," having fallen for the same kind of anthropomorphizing that Levick once had. "It's not right to call them insane," Ainley said. Some penguins just lose their ability to tell left from right, as if their internal radar had gotten knocked askew. "The same phenomenon has been shown in migratory birds, where they end up going in the opposite direction that they mean to. The Adélie in the film simply had a loose wire in its neural capacity, an imperfection in its brain."

An imperfection in the brain, then, might be a way to think about how some people process Antarctica, too. It's not only that, as life winnows down to its most abstract and invariant form, insanity awaits us around the bend. It's that a kind of reversal takes place, wherein an inherited trait is seemingly scrapped for its opposite. The process of winnowing coincides with the inability to register what's being winnowed. If Priestley's years in Antarctica had taught him anything, it was that the things we take for granted as being most fixed and solid in ourselves—our inner strength, character, virtue—have a dramatic way of faltering. Crammed into his icy warren at Inexpressible Island, he became mindful of the dread that, as Pascal described, can arise in "the eternal silence of these infinite spaces." Darkness and barrenness begin to exert a gravitational pull, he noted. In fact, darkness and barrenness are pretty much the sum total of experience in Antarctica. To be sure, there's real menace there, insofar as there's anything there at all.

Had there been a Northern Party yearbook, George Percy Abbott was a cinch for most likely to survive. Legend were his courage and cheerfulness, his daunting physical prowess (he was judo champion of the entire Royal Navy), his unfailing decency. A contrary word about his five companions never passed his lips. Nicknamed Tiny, he was big and bony and fearless, with hair the color of gunmetal and a hammered prow of a chin. A Navy man, he came from a tradition and training, the historian Meredith Hooper writes, "that assumed and expected an ability to cope in all circumstances."

Yet he couldn't cope with Inexpressible Island. Priestley dated Abbott's decline to an accident that occurred while he was killing a seal: Abbott's knife slipped, cutting the fingers on his right hand down to the bone and severing ligaments. Levick patched him up, but Abbott was never again able to bend his fingers more than an inch. For "a man whose physical well-being was central to his sense of self and whose career was now at risk," Hooper writes, this was catastrophic. According to Priestley, the physical torments tended to double back on the mental stuff, so that one turned the other inside out, until the whole package got laid open like a chest of drawers. Abbott wasn't alone. Petty officer Frank Browning had recurring night terrors and delusional premonitions. Levick, who'd busied himself with penguin pederasty at Cape Adare, had nothing to distract him at Inexpressible Island and suffered for it. Restless and panicky, he pissed himself at night and told no one. His otherwise ceaseless journaling stopped altogether. In their letters home—which wouldn't be posted until long after the fact—the men made hardly any mention of what was troubling them.

Something else that goes largely unmentioned in early Antarctica literature, refusing to surface again and again, being so resistant to surfacing that it comprises a distinct subgenre of self-censorship, is the total absence of women and, by extension, one presumes, sex (the first woman to set foot on the continent, the Scandinavian explorer Caroline Mikkelsen, arrived in 1935). Edwardian decorum all but forbade mention of sex in official accounts, but it's missing from diaries and letters as well, and even from scholarly histories. These were twentysomething men, most of them, away for three or four years without a woman in sight. It stands to reason that this particular lack might have ratcheted up the (ahem) hardship considerably, and maybe heightened any latent existential angst. While I can kind of imagine spending nine months in an ice cave without Netflix or Grubhub and nothing to eat but seal blubber, under no circumstances can I imagine doing so in an all-encompassing dungeon of testosterone. No wonder they went nuts.

True, maybe some of them didn't care for women and therein lay Antarctica's charm. Perhaps desire merely took on new dimensions. Ranulph Fiennes, who came close to completing the first unassisted crossing of Antarctica in 1993, claimed he never once thought of sex. "Food took the place of sex," he said, "anticipated with salivating eagerness and savoured to the last lick." Priestley and the others were racked with hunger. Their wet dreams, I suppose you could call them, were about food. He says in *Antarctic Adventure* that all six of them had recurring dreams of sumptuous banquets being whisked away at the point of eating, or of arriving at a grocer's shop moments after it had closed. Suffering silently was part of their code, but talking about food got a pass because they had food of a sort, with the promise of a windfall if they ever made it back to Cape Evans. Sexual deprivation was a whole other deal. The reality hit too deeply. Levick might've even feared something like the dismal tide he'd recorded among Adélies at Cape Adare.

To put another spin on it, familiar to anyone who's been in a slow-burn, long-distance relationship, there's no cave deeper and darker than jealousy. Every Northern Party man save Browning had a wife or girlfriend back home. It's best to keep images of betrayal bottled up, lest they become unbearable. In *Scott and Amundsen,* Huntford claims that at the time of Scott's death, his wife, Kathleen, was having an affair with none other than Fridtjof Nansen, the legendary Norwegian explorer and booster of Scott's loathed rival, Amundsen. We can't know for sure, but whether or not it was true, if Scott suspected this, it'd be impossible to imagine a more emphatic and humiliating betrayal, or a more solitary torture, given the absence of a potential revenge fuck within five thousand miles. I have to wonder whether, as Scott lay dying in his tent in 1912 a mere dozen miles from safety, his inability to continue—or as Huntford implies, his *refusal* to continue—wasn't colored by it. Could the hero's death have been, in part, a farewell middle finger to a philandering wife? There's not a hint of it in

Scott's letters. No public shaming ensued. Neither he nor Kathleen would've risked the ignominy of exposure. The case remains, as it were, cold.

Incredibly, for the most part the men of the Northern Party got along all right, bonded by their misery. In such circumstances, according to Byrd, "Everything that one does, or says, or even thinks, is of importance to one's fellows. They are measuring you constantly, some openly, others secretly—there is so little else to do!" An unspoken rule emerged to "avoid controversial subjects as you would the devil," Priestley wrote. Campbell kept strict discipline, docking the men for infractions like being late with the tea, and maintaining traditional divisions between officers and sailors, which everyone took as welcome reminders of their former lives. They also drew a literal line in the ice, and agreed to act as if what was said on one side couldn't be heard on the other. You'd expect the knives to come out, for a nest of vipers to bare their fangs. But things rarely reached a simmer. They dwelled on the positive, took their grief silently. Priestley, in his way, even thrived. "I have dreamt the day away again," he wrote of having lain in his bag all day, day after day, determined to take refuge in his enforced idleness, seemingly inured to the drama going on around him. "I could never have imagined that I could have been so contented, even happy in a circumscribed way with nothing to do but just exist, with insufficient to eat & an utter lack of news about anything & anybody I cared about." Buried in ice at the edge of the known world, sleeping, eating, and shitting in a pit of concentrated darkness, he found himself "content for the most part to lie and dream about past times, and not worry my head about the future." This wasn't some solipsistic rabbit hole. Nor was it God that bore him up (in all of *Antarctic Adventure,* God hardly warrants a mention). Priestley could just … endure. As a hurricane shrieked over the roof of the cave, he scrawled in his journal: "The happiest days of my life." The extreme deprivation served to amplify smaller comforts: "We could get as much pleasure out of an unexpected lump of sugar, or a peaceful day … as the most costly luxury or the most entrancing holiday could give to us now," he wrote. "It has been a most decisive proof that in many cases the luxuries of civilization only fulfil the wants they create." I love this about Priestley. His ability to do absolutely nothing, to remain contentedly stuck for months on end, feels less like laziness than a hopeful vision for humanity, a refutation of the very idea of progress.

But they couldn't very well stay there, not for another winter. Priestley admits they'd all have gone mad. Browning was gravely ill with dysentery, probably from rancid seal meat. Someone else—he isn't named in Levick's diary—lost his head for a day and had to be talked back to his senses. Each of them found their thoughts losing shape and meaning. "The dismal misery of this dull & filthy hole is beginning to work on us a little, & that's a fact," Levick wrote. They hadn't bathed in ten months and were down to their last candle. Although they suspected that as the winter pack ice began to break up the *Terra Nova* might soon try to reach them, or that a rescue party could also be on its way by land, they were tired of waiting. In September, with the first glimpse of the sun, they bolted for Cape Evans, 230 miles south. Now that they were out on the ice, they became aware of how poorly suited they were to deal with it, debilitated as they'd become by idleness and a starvation diet that had reduced them nearly to skeletons. "We were entirely free from fat, and, indeed, were so lean that our legs and arms were corrugated," Priestley wrote. Carrying only a week's worth of chocolate and biscuits, they needed food, real food, desperately. One morning, they managed to kill a seal that turned out to have a golf ball-size cyst in its liver, but they ate the liver anyway, along with the brains. A few days later, they happened upon a depot laid earlier that year by fellow *Terra Nova* crew, including tea, butter, cocoa, sugar, salt, and raisins. The cache very likely saved their lives. Levick sat in his tent gobbling chunks of butter from one hand, the first fat of any kind besides blubber they'd had in ten months. "We have had such a blow out today, as we haven't had for a year," he wrote, "... and tea of the proper strength too, and not just coloured water."

Sledging along the coast over unexplored land, falling into and hauling themselves out of crevasses, suffering painful snow blindness and diarrhea, the men marveled at how thoroughly they were enjoying themselves after their long captivity. It's worth recalling that they had no flashlights or GPS to point the way, no Gore-Tex gloves or moisture-wicking base layers, no dehydrated quinoa bowls or glycogen energy gels. They navigated by sextant, wore frozen blubbery wool and gabardine that later had to be sawed off, and survived by killing seals and penguins as they went. The weather, predictably, was abominable—"every step was like drawing a tooth," Priestley wrote—and with Browning being pulled along in a sledge, the pace was maddeningly slow. By all rights they should've died several times over. But the thrill of saving themselves acquired a particular flavor. It's not much of an exaggeration to say they were ecstatic at the dangers that stood in their way.

They reached Cape Evans after five weeks, swinging open the door to Scott's hut to find no one at home. Sitting in chairs for the first time since Cape Adare, the men soon heard the barking of dogs. Walter William Archer and Frank Debenham walked in, stone-faced. There was a stammering silence, then an explosion of joy. Debenham told them the *Terra Nova* had made several attempts to reach them the previous year, at one point getting frozen in ice for two days, before abandoning the effort, and that an overland party had also given up after forty miles. Scott and his polar team, he told them, were presumed dead, lost on the barrier. But never mind that now. Put your feet up. Have a bloody drink.

In another five weeks, safely aboard the *Terra Nova,* Abbott finally cracked. He'd kept it together through two awful winters, but now all at once a seam opened and he started raving about this thing or that. No one recorded the details. Priestley says only that Inexpressible Island "left its mark on all of us." But we know what it must've looked like: too exhausted to sleep, or with his sleep beset by nightmares, Abbott likely grew sullen, disoriented, and withdrew from the others; perhaps there was an outburst, an undertone of dementia. Abbott's was a special case, of course, his period of darkness and danger being greater than any other man's save that of his five companions, and amounting to unimaginable stress. After a hospital stay in Southampton, he was forced out of the Navy on account of his injured hand, as he'd long feared. Slowly, over months, he regained himself, but in a way he never recovered. He died of pneumonia, of all things, at age forty-three. Today, Mount Abbott, a thirty-three-hundred-foot-tall granite dorsal fin that backs up to Inexpressible Island and dips into the sea, is being cored by scientists studying glacial erosion. The story there isn't a sunny one. The entire West Antarctic ice sheet may eventually collapse, adding sixteen feet to global sea levels. Cape Adare's Adélie colony, which has thrived there for millennia, is expected to vanish before the end of the century, owing to rising seas. It might be said that Antarctica—with its calving glaciers, fast-warming Southern Ocean, and mass penguin deaths—is where humanity is hurtling itself into the void, where we're contriving to meet our collective, appalling end.

It'd probably be of little consolation to Abbott to know that not far from where he sliced open his hand a century ago, there sits an Italian research station whose year-round crew is served by thermal generators that heat their quarters, a seawater filtration system that makes drinking water instantly, and nitrogen-helium liquefier refrigerators that round out a well-appointed kitchen. There's a landing strip, harbor, helipad, isotope laboratory, and administrative buildings linked by power, sewage, and state-of-the-art surveillance. It looks remarkably like a self-storage facility: deliberately nondescript, repulsively utilitarian. From on high, the roof resembles a blood-red lattice scattered over ash. At twilight the mountains beyond are like bodies thrown into black space.

DIANE ACKERMAN

Attention Please, This Island Earth

Diane Ackerman is the author of two dozen works of poetry and nonfiction, including the *New York Times* bestsellers *The Zookeeper's Wife*, *A Natural History of the Senses*, *The Human Age*, and the Pulitzer Prize finalist *One Hundred Names for Love*. She has received the Stephen Hawking Medal for Communicating Science, the PEN Henry David Thoreau Award for Nature Writing, and a Guggenheim Fellowship. In Issue 3 of *Creative Nonfiction*, she spoke of her work writing prose and poetry and added, "I suppose if I have a philosophy on this it's that if you set out to nourish your own curiosity and your own intellectual yearnings and use yourself as an object of investigation, then, without meaning to, you will probably be touching the lives of a lot of people."

RACHEL BEANLAND

How to Hang a Mezuzah

Rachel Beanland writes essays and fiction, and she is the author of two novels: *The House Is on Fire* and *Florence Adler Swims Forever*. *The House Is on Fire* was named one of the best books of 2023 by NPR and *The New Yorker*. Beanland's debut, *Florence Adler Swims Forever*, was selected as a book club pick by Barnes & Noble, a featured debut by Amazon, an Indie Next pick by the ABA, and one of the best books of 2020 by *USA Today*. It was also named a *New York Times* Editors' Choice and was recognized with the 2020 National Jewish Book Award for Debut Fiction.

JANE BERNSTEIN

Taking Care

Jane Bernstein, a novelist, essayist, and screenwriter, contributed seven essays to *Creative Nonfiction*, beginning with "Taking Care" in Issue 3—helping to beat the drum for the genre long before the literary and academic communities accepted it. Her 1988 memoir, *Loving Rachel*, preceded the memoir revolution in the mid-1990s, and it helped to create a path for other writers with personal stories to tell despite the risks of what early critics dismissed as "navel-gazing."

VALERIE BOYD

In Search of Alice Walker, or Alice Doesn't Live Here Anymore

Valerie Boyd (1963-2022) wrote the critically acclaimed biography *Wrapped in Rainbows: The Life of Zora Neale Hurston* and was the editor of *Gathering Blossoms Under Fire: The Journals of Alice Walker* and *Bigger Than Bravery: Black Writers on the Year That Changed the World.*

BRIAN BROOME

79

Brian Broome's debut memoir, *Punch Me Up to the Gods*, was a *New York Times* Editor's Pick and the winner of the 2021 Kirkus Prize for Nonfiction. He is a contributing columnist for *The Washington Post.* His essay "The Red Caboose" appeared in Issue 60 of *Creative Nonfiction.*

A.D. COLEMAN

Sea Changes: Traveling the Staten Island Ferry

A.D. Coleman is publisher and executive director of a digital magazine, The Nearby Cafe, where he publishes the blog Photocritic International. Formerly a columnist for the *Village Voice*, *The New York Times*, and the *New York Observer*, Coleman has published eight books and thousands of essays on photography and related subjects.

TOI DERRICOTTE

Beginning Dialogues

Toi Derricotte is the author of six collections of poetry, most recently, *I: New & Selected Poems*, which was a 2019 National Book Awards finalist. She is the recipient of the Academy of American Poets' 2021 Wallace Stevens Award, given to recognize outstanding artistic achievement in the art of poetry. The Poetry Society of America awarded her the 2020 Frost Medal for distinguished lifetime achievement. With Cornelius Eady, she co-founded the Cave Canem Foundation to remedy the underrepresentation and isolation of African-American poets in the literary landscape. She contributed three essays to *Creative Nonfiction*; "Beds," which appeared in Issue 39, was selected for *The Best American Essays 2011.*

BRIAN DOYLE

Two on Two

Brian Doyle (1957-2017) was the author of more than two dozen books and the longtime editor of *Portland*, the University of Portland's alumni magazine. In Issue 9 of *Creative Nonfiction*, he shared some advice for aspiring writers: "Get to the point. Cut to the chase. Tell a tale. All things are stories; romance, work, education, religion, and stories are how we most commonly and easily eat information, eat the world; so the storyteller has enormous power and pop if the story is naked. The best tales are direct and unadorned." He contributed five of his own tales to the magazine.

MIEKE EERKENS

Seep

Mieke Eerkens is a Dutch-American writer who grew up between the foothills of California and the canals of the Netherlands. Her work has appeared in publications such as The Atlantic and The Sun, among others. Her book *All Ships Follow Me: A Family Memoir of War Across Three Continents*, was published in 2019.

BETH ANN FENNELLY

I Survived the Blizzard of '79

Beth Ann Fennelly was Poet Laureate of Mississippi from 2016 to 2021. She has received a Fulbright to Brazil and grants from the NEA, the United States Artists, and the Academy of American Poets. Fennelly has published three books of poetry, a novel, and the memoirs *Great with Child* and *Heating & Cooling: 52 Micro-Memoirs*; and a novel she co-wrote with her husband, Tom Franklin, *The Tilted World*. In Issue 64 of *Creative Nonfiction* she offered this description of micro-memoirs like the one that appears in this collection: "Get in and get out as quickly as possible: that's the first rule I made for myself. Create the world in a bright flash. Easy on the exposition.... Although some of my favorite writers—such as Maggie Nelson, Anne Carson, and Claudia Rankine—are doing interesting work with the fragment, I didn't want my micro-memoirs to be read as fragments. I wanted them to stand alone, each a small thing but a complete thing."

CAROLYN FORCHÉ

The World Without Us: A Meditation

Carolyn Forché is a poet, translator, editor, and activist. She is the author of five books of poetry, including *In the Lateness of the World*, a finalist for the Pulitzer Prize, and *Blue Hour*, a finalist for the National Book Critics Circle Award. She also edited the anthology *Against Forgetting: Twentieth-Century Poetry of Witness*. She has been awarded fellowships from, among others, the National Endowment for the Arts, the Guggenheim Foundation, and the Lannan Foundation.

ELIZABETH FORTESCUE

Prometheus Unbound

Elizabeth Fortescue has degrees from Harvard in English Literature, Medicine, and Public Health. She left a Harvard Medical School appointment in pediatric cardiology in 2010 for health and family reasons and focused on writing creative nonfiction, using her medical background in her work.

MEREDITH HALL

Without a Map

Meredith Hall's memoir *Without a Map*, a *New York Times* bestseller, was named a best book of the year by *Kirkus Reviews* and *Book Sense*, and was a 2007 *Elle* Reader's Pick. She is also the author of a novel, *Beneficence*. Hall contributed two other essays to *Creative Nonfiction*: "Killing Chickens," which appeared in Issue 18, and "Shunned" in Issue 20. In the latter issue she described writing as realizing that "there are moments in my life, not large events so much as very distinct moments, that tug at my memory and tug at my desire to put all the pieces of the puzzle together and understand. But, mostly, as a writer they catch my attention. I know they're big moments; I know they're moments that are waiting to be exploded into a larger understanding, and I can't do that in my head so I end up doing it on paper. But I'm very aware that they hold some potential for a discovery beyond the moment itself."

MARY PAUMIER JONES

Meander

Mary Paumier Jones's interest in nonfiction began in 1991, when she enrolled in an essay class taught by the novelist, poet, and critic Judith Kitchen. "The class really opened my eyes to the fact that nonfiction writing didn't have to be journalistic," she said, "that I could bring a lot of the same things I was learning in fiction to nonfiction." Working with Kitchen, Jones helped to pioneer the subgenre of flash nonfiction with two anthologies, *In Short* and *In Brief*, that highlighted the possibilities of short pieces that capture a moment in time with dramatic impact.

JUDITH KITCHEN

Any Given Day

Judith Kitchen (1941-2014) was the author of five collections of essays, including *The Circus Train*, and the novel *The House on Eccles Road*. She also edited several anthologies, including *In Short* and *In Brief*. Her awards included an NEA fellowship in poetry and two Pushcart Prizes in nonfiction. In the second issue of *Creative Nonfiction* she predicted the staying power of the genre: "There's been an influx of memoir by relatively ordinary people—by people whose lives are not necessarily of interest, but the writing of the lives is of interest. In five years, no one will be asking the question about the genre's name because it will have defined itself more. In ten years, the reading public will be as receptive to creative nonfiction as it is now to a strict, straight nonfiction book."

STEVEN KURUTZ

Fruitland

Steven Kurutz is a features reporter for *The New York Times* and the author of *Like a Rolling Stone: The Strange Life of a Tribute Band* and *American Flannel: How a Band of Entrepreneurs Are Bringing the Art and Business of Making Clothes Back Home*. He wrote "Fruitland" for the first edition of *True Story*, *Creative Nonfiction's* pocket-sized series of thirty-five longform narratives. He originally wrote about Joe and Donnie Emerson for *The Times*, where he covers style and culture, but wanted to say more about their lives and music. That longer exploration was adapted into the 2023 feature film *Dreamin' Wild*, starring Casey Affleck, Zooey Deschanel, and Walton Goggins.

GORDON LISH

Self-Interview

The Guardian said of Gordon Lish, "Not since Maxwell Perkins has an editor been so famous—or notorious—as a sculptor of other people's prose." Lish worked as the fiction editor of *Esquire* and as a senior editor at Alfred A. Knopf for eighteen years; he also founded and edited the literary magazine *The Quarterly*. As an editor, he has worked with writers including Raymond Carver, DonDeLillo, and Joy Williams. He is a prolific author of fiction and the winner of a Guggenheim Fellowship and the O. Henry Prize.

PHILLIP LOPATE

The Story of My Father

Phillip Lopate, a frequent contributor to *Creative Nonfiction*, is widely considered a master of the essay. He is the author of *To Show and To Tell: The Craft of Literary Nonfiction* and the editor of *The Art of the Personal Essay*. Lopate is also a poet and novelist, a film and literary critic, and he has written five collections of essays—a form that, as he wrote in Issue 39, "feasts on doubt, self-doubt, contradiction, and paradox."

ANNE MCGRATH

Behold Invisibility

Anne McGrath is a writer and visual artist. Her work has been noted twice in *Best American Essays*, and her work has appeared in *Fourth Genre*, *River Teeth*, *Ruminate*, and others. She is the recipient of fellowships from Vermont College of Fine Arts and the Virginia Center for the Creative Arts.

JOHN MCPHEE

The Conching Rooms

John McPhee's interview with Michael Pearson, which appeared in the inaugural issue of *Creative Nonfiction*, provided early credibility to a then-unacknowledged genre and to a little magazine at its very beginning. In 2002, when McPhee began an all-sophomore writing course at Princeton, he named it for the magazine: Creative Nonfiction. McPhee began contributing to *The New Yorker* in 1963 and has written more than a hundred pieces for the magazine. He has also published more than thirty books, including *Annals of the Former World*, which won the 1999 Pulitzer Prize for general nonfiction.

JOHN O'CONNOR

Everything Gets Worse: An Antarctica Story

John O'Connor is the author of *The Secret History of Bigfoot: Field Notes on a North American Monster*. His story "Badlands: Portrait of a Competitive Eater" appeared in Issue 32 of *Creative Nonfiction*. His writing has also appeared in *Open City*, *Post Road*, *Quarterly West*, *The New York Times*, *GQ*, *Saveur*, *Men's Journal*, and the *Financial Times*.

CHRIS OFFUTT

The Hippest Bar on Christmas

Chris Offutt is the author of four novels, two short-story collections, and three memoirs: *The Same River Twice*, *No Heroes*, and *My Father, the Pornographer*. He has written screenplays for *Weeds*, *True Blood*, and *Treme*, and has received fellowships from the Lannan and Guggenheim foundations.

ADRIENNE RICH

How Does a Poet Put Bread on the Table?

Adrienne Rich (1929-2012) won the National Book Award for Poetry in 1974 for *Diving into the Wreck: Poems 1971-1972*. For Rich and many other poets and fiction writers, *Creative Nonfiction* encouraged and offered space to writers who wanted to expand their work into another genre. By the time of her death, Rich had written two dozen volumes of poetry and several prose works. Her other honors included the National Book Critics Circle Award and a fellowship from the MacArthur Foundation.

RUTHANN ROBSON

Notes on My Dying

Ruthann Robson is a professor of law and University Distinguished Professor at CIty University of New York School of Law, where she has taught since 1990. She writes legal scholarship and theory, fiction, poetry, and creative nonfiction. She contributed two essays to *Creative Nonfiction*—the one in this volume and "Notes from a Difficult Case" in Issue 21.

RICHARD RODRIGUEZ

The Brown Study

Richard Rodriguez is most widely known for his autobiographical trilogy on class, ethnicity, and race: *Hunger of Memory: The Education of Richard Rodriguez; Days of Obligation: An Argument with My Mexican Father*; and *Brown: The Last Discovery of America*. He is also the author of *Darling: A Spiritual Autobiography*. Rodriguez worked as an essayist for nearly twenty years on PBS NewsHour and has written documentaries for British and American television. He published two other pieces in *Creative Nonfiction*: "Proofs," in a special issue about "Surviving Crisis," and "The Loss of Five Minutes" in Issue 38. In that last essay he spoke of his time at PBS and the power of the essay by celebrating Virginia Woolf's 1942 classic "The Death of the Moth": "I do not equate a five-minute television essay with a master's essay, but that—the impulse, I mean, to sound a personal voice in the midst of the world's tumult—that is what an essay can do."

SUSAN FROMBERG SCHAEFFER

Memories Like Splintered Glass

Susan Fromberg Schaeffer (1940-2011) was the author of fourteen novels. She also published six volumes of poetry; her collection *The Granite Lady* was a finalist for a 1975 National Book Award. She received a Guggenheim Fellowship and won the O. Henry Award for short fiction three times.

BUD SHAW

My Night with Ellen Hutchinson

Byers "Bud" Shaw is the author of *Last Night in the OR: A Transplant Surgeon's Odyssey*. He received his degree in medicine from Case Western Reserve University. He completed general surgery training in Utah and a transplant surgery fellowship in Pittsburgh under the direction of Thomas Starzl, the father of liver transplantation. Shaw moved to Omaha in 1985 to start the solid organ transplant program at the University of Nebraska Medical Center. Starting in 1997, he served twelve years as chairman of UNMC's Department of Surgery. In 2011, Susan Orlean chose "My Night with Ellen Hutchinson" as the winner of a contest sponsored by *Creative Nonfiction* and the Salt Institute for Documentary Studies, for the best essay related to the theme of "The Night." The essay also received special mention among the 2013 Pushcart Prize entries.

CHARLES SIMIC

The Necessity of Poetry

Charles Simic (1938-2023) was awarded the Pulitzer Prize in Poetry in 1990 for his collection *The World Doesn't End* and was the fifteenth Poet Laureate of the United States. In "The Necessity of Poetry," which was selected for the 1995 edition of *The Best American Essays*, Simic's Uncle Boris makes a cameo appearance. He was captured even more vividly in Simic's essay "Dinner at Uncle Boris's" in *Creative Nonfiction's* Issue 24—which was chosen for the 1997 edition of *The Best American Essays*.

LOUIS SIMPSON

The Stone Collector

Louis Simpson was born in Jamaica in 1923 and came to the United States at seventeen. A contemporary of confessional poets like Robert Lowell, John Berryman, and Sylvia Plath, his collection *At the End of the Open Road* won the Pulitzer Prize in 1964. His essay in *Creative Nonfiction* showcased flash nonfiction long before the form became popular; it also featured a working man outside the literary world—the kind of story that *CNF* valued and encouraged. Simpson died in 2012.

JERALD WALKER

The Heart

Jerald Walker is the author of *How to Make a Slave and Other Essays*, a nonfiction finalist for the National Book Award and winner of the 2020 Massachusetts Book Award in Nonfiction. He is also the author of *Street Shadows: A Memoir of Race, Rebellion, and Redemption*, which received the 2011 PEN New England/L.L. Winship Award for Nonfiction, and *The World in Flames: A Black Boyhood in a White Supremacist Doomsday Cult*. He has received fellowships from the Guggenheim Foundation, the National Endowment for the Arts, and the James A. Michener Foundation. "I wanted to write an essay," he said of the piece in this collection, "that explored my affection for my brother, my resentment for his wife, and the anxiety caused me by both emotions. So I definitely brought a strong subjectivity to the piece.... Objective narration has its place, for instance, with some types of reportage. But with the personal essay, honesty and fairness are important, not objectivity."

JOHN EDGAR WIDEMAN

Looking At Emmett Till

John Edgar Wideman is a novelist, short story writer, memoirist, and essayist. His books include *Brothers and Keepers*, *Fatheralong*, and *Hoop Roots*. His novels *Sent for You Yesterday* and *Philadelphia Fire* each won the PEN/Faulkner Award, making him the first writer to receive the prize twice. He has twice been a finalist for the National Book Critics Circle Award and the National Book Award. He is a MacArthur Fellow and a recipient of the Lannan Literary Award for Lifetime Achievement, as well as the 2019 PEN/Malamud Award for Excellence in the Short Story. He also contributed another essay, "At the Penitentiary," to *Creative Nonfiction*.

EMILY WORTMAN-WUNDER

Rooted

Emily Wortman-Wunder's book of short stories, *Not a Thing to Comfort You*, won the 2019 Iowa Book Award and the Colorado Book Award. Her writing has appeared in *Guernica*, the *Kenyon Review*, *High Country News*, and elsewhere.

EDITORS

LEE GUTKIND

has been called the "godfather behind creative nonfiction" by *Vanity Fair*. He founded *Creative Nonfiction* magazine in 1994 and is the editor or author of more than thirty books, including, most recently, *The Fine Art of Literary First-Fighting: How a Bunch of Rabble-Rousers, Outsiders and Ne'er-do-wells Concocted Creative Nonfiction*. He lives in Pittsburgh, Pennsylvania."

LESLIE RUBINKOWSKI

is the director of the MFA in Nonfiction program at Goucher College and the author of *Impersonating Elvis*. A journalist and essayist, her work has appeared in a number of publications, including *Harper's*, *River Teeth*, and *Creative Nonfiction*. She has also taught journalism and creative nonfiction at the University of Pittsburgh, directed the newswriting program at West Virginia University's journalism school, and has been a guest lecturer at The Poynter Institute and the Chautauqua Institution, among many other places. Her current book project is a hybrid: part memoir, part history of Pittsburgh.

How exciting it would be to spend five minutes with John Bunyan every day for one year—perhaps in his home or before his hearth, in his prison cell or before his pulpit—to hear his testimony of salvation, to sit under his preaching, and to listen to him muse upon such glorious doctrines as justification, imputation, the fear of God, and the free offer of the gospel. That opportunity is now possible in this Christ-centered, gospel-saturated, and experiential collection of John Bunyan's personal and theological reflections. May the Lord richly bless your year with the persecuted tinker, brilliant allegorist, and fiery preacher of Bedford!

Joel R. Beeke
Chancellor and Professor of Homiletics & Systematic Theology
Puritan Reformed Theological Seminary
Grand Rapids, Michigan

John Bunyan knew by experience the richness and freeness of God's love and grace. And, as a result, his corpus is powerfully drenched with heartfelt, biblical Christianity. It is a privilege to be able to recommend this new selection of daily readings from Bunyan's grace-filled works. May the Puritan preacher speak afresh in our days through these expertly-chosen excerpts and encourage the readers of this devotional to live lives that honour Christ as Bunyan so powerfully did in his day.

Michael A. G. Azad Haykin
Professor of Church History
The Southern Baptist Theological Seminary
Louisville, Kentucky

"No sin against God can be little because it is against the great God of heaven and earth; but if the sinner can find out a little god, it may be easy to find out little sins." Thousands of such pertinent quotables penetrate this book. Soul-health and mind-delight combine as advantages that consistently accrue to the reader of John Bunyan. Bunyan was a tinker, Roger Duke is a "pipe-fitter." They are brothers not only in their useful trades but in their desire for knowledge of the holy. This 365-day journey through the works of Bunyan will nourish the spirit and give a good grasp of the sanctified literary treasury that constitute the Bunyan corpus of literary production. Dr. Duke has brought forth from Bunyan an excellent treat to look forward to every day.

Tom Nettles
Senior Professor of Historical Theology
The Southern Baptist Theological Seminary
Louisville, Kentucky

When it comes to doctrinal clarity, theological vigor, and applicational warmth, there may be no greater Puritan writer than John Bunyan. His was a heart full of love for the Lord, His Word, and His people, and to read his writings is to encounter the Balm of Gilead that cleanses, renews, and strengthens the weary heart. Dr. Duke has done a great service by compiling these daily readings from Bunyan, and I warmly commend it to all.

Jacob Tanner
Pastor, Christ Keystone Church, Middleburg, Pennsylvania
Author, *The Tinker's Progress: The Life and Times of John Bunyan*

John Bunyan Daily Readings

Edited by
Roger D. Duke

CHRISTIAN HERITAGE

Unless otherwise indicated, Scripture quotations within the reading itself are from the King James Version (KJV).

Softback ISBN: 978-1-5271-1172-1
Ebook ISBN: 978-1-5271-1212-4

Published in 2024
in the
Christian Heritage Imprint
by
Christian Focus Publications,
Geanies House, Fearn, Tain, Ross-shire,
IV20 1TW, Scotland, UK
www.christianfocus.com

Cover design by Daniel van Straaten

Printed in India by Imprint Press

Dedicated to

Katie Melinda Young Duke

In Our 50th Year of Marriage
(50th Anniversary October 5th, 2024)

Her Family of Origin Called Her "Linda"
Her Grandchildren Call Her "Kay Kay"
I Call Her "Kate"

The Scripture declares:
"Her children have arisen up and call her blessed:
her husband also, and I praise her."
Proverbs 31:28 (KJV, personalized).

"She has done me good and not evil all the days of her life."
Proverbs 31:12 (KJV, personalized).

Since Then,
She Has Been:
My Wife
My Lover
The Mother of My Children
My Best Friend
My Confidant
My Encourager
My Business Partner
My Fellow Laborer in the Lord's Vineyard.
The Doctor and Nurse of My Family
The Primary Caretaker of Our Special Needs Adult Son Dale
The Glue That Binds Our Little Tribe Together

I cannot fathom what my life would have been without her!